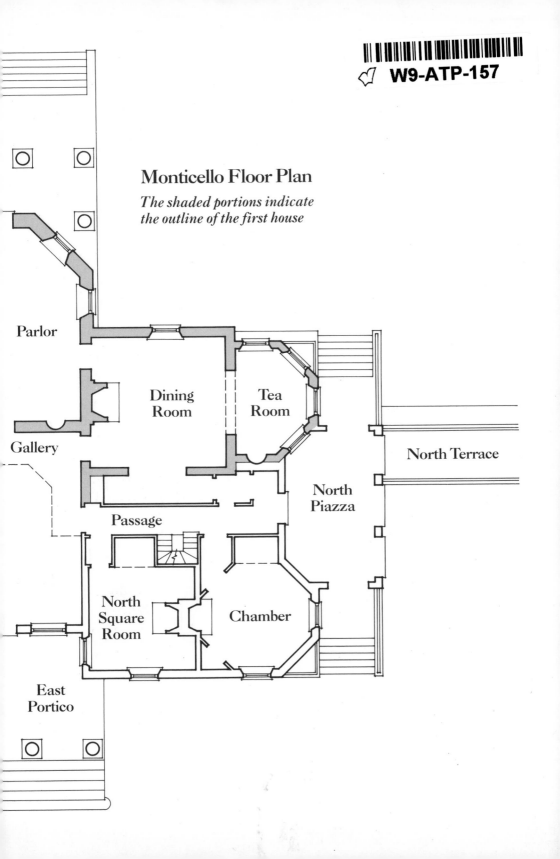

Monticello Floor Plan

*The shaded portions indicate
the outline of the first house*

Parlor

Dining
Room

Tea
Room

Gallery

North Terrace

North
Piazza

Passage

North
Square
Room

Chamber

East
Portico

JEFFERSON AND MONTICELLO

ALSO BY JACK MCLAUGHLIN

The Housebuilding Experience

JACK McLAUGHLIN

JEFFERSON
AND
MONTICELLO

*The Biography of
a Builder*

HENRY HOLT AND COMPANY   NEW YORK

Published by Henry Holt and Company, Inc.,
115 West 18th Street, New York, New York 10011.
Published in Canada by Fitzhenry & Whiteside Limited,
195 Allstate Parkway, Markham, Ontario L3R 4T8.

Library of Congress Cataloging-in-Publication Data
McLaughlin, Jack,
Jefferson and Monticello.
Includes index.
1. Jefferson, Thomas, 1743–1826—Career in
architecture. 2. Jefferson, Thomas, 1743–1826—
Family. 3. Monticello (Va.). 4. Presidents—United
States—Biography. I. Title.
E332.2.M43   1988   973.4'6'0924   87-23664
ISBN 0-8050-0482-3

Henry Holt books are available at special discounts
for bulk purchases for sales promotions, premiums,
fund-raising, or educational use. Special editions
or book excerpts can also be created to specification.

For details contact:

Special Sales Director
Henry Holt and Company, Inc.
115 West 18th Street
New York, New York 10011

Grateful acknowledgment is made
to Alfred A. Knopf, Inc., for permission
to quote from "Anecdote of the Jar," from
The Collected Poems of Wallace Stevens, by Wallace Stevens,
copyright © 1954 by Wallace Stevens;
and to W. W. Norton and Company for permission to reprint from
Anton Chekhov's Plays, A Norton Critical Edition, translated and edited
by Eugene K. Bristow, copyright © 1977 by W. W. Norton
and Company, Inc.

A continuation of this copyright page will be found on pages 459–61.

Designed by Kate Nichols
Printed in the United States of America
3   5   7   9   10   8   6   4   2

Contents

Contents

Foreword

THIS IS NOT the usual kind of Thomas Jefferson biography; his revolutionary activities, political life, and public career as governor of Virginia, secretary of state, Vice President, and President are only glanced at obliquely. To use an old-fashioned term, it is a domestic life. It attempts to capture a personal and private Jefferson, to detail his relationships with his extended family and friends. The prism through which I view this life is the most creative artifact of an exceptionally creative man—Monticello—the house he "put up and pulled down" for most of his adult years.

In our century, Jefferson has acquired a deserved reputation as one of America's foremost architects. Monticello and the University of Virginia are his two masterworks of architectural design. It is not primarily as an architect that this biography examines Jefferson, however, but as a builder. My premise is simple: those who construct their own shelter replicate themselves, at their deepest and most significant level, in their houses. They *are* what they build. By following the building process, therefore, one should be able to dig beneath externals and reveal unaccommodated man, the thing itself. In Jefferson's case, this is made possible beyond the scale of any other house or builder of the period by the extraordinary number of documents he left behind. He was an obsessive recorder and saver, and virtually everything he wrote, drew, or sketched having to do with Monticello is still extant in his published and unpublished papers.

I have drawn upon all of these to tell about Jefferson's love affair with a house and the remarkably difficult time he had consummating it. But he ultimately did, and left for us a detailed portrait of himself in timber, brick, plaster, and paint. I have attempted to bring to life this house-as-portrait: as it was born more than two hundred years ago in the imagination of an ambitious young Virginia law student, as it took shape on the mountaintop of a brilliant revolutionary, was redefined by a sophisticated American minister to France, was enlarged, remodeled, and rebuilt by the nation's third President, and came close to ruin with the death of its patriarch-sage.

Thomas Jefferson was undeniably unique, one of the most brilliant and complex individuals in the nation's history, but those who have ever fallen in love with a house, or who have been even mildly infatuated with one, will find in the scaffolding of his story the shapes of an all too familiar identity.

JEFFERSON AND MONTICELLO

1

"A Very Long Time Maturing His Projects"

SUMMER RAINS had made the roads between Orange and Albemarle counties even more gouged and treacherous than usual. Two carriages had left the Virginia plantation of the Madisons, James and Dolley, at 10:30 in the morning, early enough on a mid-September day in 1802 to make the twenty-eight-mile journey to the home of President Jefferson before nightfall. So slow and tortuous had been the carriage ride, however, that it was now close to dark. From the nearby Blue Ridge Mountains, silhouetted by the almost constant flashes of lightning, came the distant rumbles of an approaching thunderstorm. As the horses slipped and strained on the ascending and mud-rutted road, the carriages pulled to a halt. James Madison, the nation's secretary of state, short, slight, dressed almost entirely in black, emerged from the lead carriage and talked with his driver. Madison then informed the passengers that it was too hazardous to continue. They were less than a mile from their destination, however, so they could safely walk to the Jefferson home through a path in the woods. If they hurried, they could get there before the storm broke.

In the two carriages were Dolley Madison, her younger sister Anna Payne, Dr. and Mrs. William Thornton, and Mrs. Thornton's mother, Mrs. Anna Brodeau. Dr. Thornton worked under Madison as director of the newly created Patent Office, and the two men were close friends as well as colleagues. The women quickly decided that the steep climb to the top of the small mountain where the house stood was too difficult for Mrs. Brodeau and that she would stay with the carriages; the servants would carefully walk the horses the rest of the way. After giving instructions to the drivers, the five travelers filed at a quick pace into the forest, a clap of thunder announcing the storm at their heels.

The French-born Mrs. Thornton had accompanied her husband to Washington, leaving the cosmopolitan city of Philadelphia for the new capital, little more than a bustling, rapidly growing village at this time. The Thorntons lived in a town house next to the Madisons, and the two wives were intimate friends. Women like Anna Maria Thornton and Dolley Madison, married to talented men of power and influence, quickly made themselves indispensable to the social life of the nation's capital. They were to define and shape the rules of social etiquette suitable for a democracy at such important governmental rituals as the formal dinner, diplomatic reception, private luncheon, public entertainment, and the "at home." They were among the first to assume a title that was to become rich with ambiguity—the Washington Hostess.

Anna Maria Thornton was short and slight—she had weighed only 106 pounds, fully dressed, two years earlier when "we all went to the scales near the President's house [later to become the White House] to be weighed." In Gilbert Stuart's portrait, painted in 1804, she is shown with large brown eyes and a delicate complexion, her hair fashionably tied up. She wears a low-cut empire gown calculated to accentuate her modest bustline. Organ pipes in the background and a score in her hand allude to her musical talents—she was an accomplished organist and pianist.

She and her husband had just concluded a pleasant two-week visit at Montpelier, the Madison house. Like many eighteenth-century men and women, she kept a daily diary, and in it she had recorded the pleasures of her visit. During the week she was to remain at the Jefferson plantation (the entire party was stranded for several days by the almost daily rains), she would note with the eye of a well-traveled tourist and amateur artist her impression of President Thomas Jefferson's unfinished home, Monticello.

The party quickly crossed the third "roundabout"—one of four roads that girdle the mountain upon which the house rests. The first roundabout is only a half mile in circumference directly around the house; the other increasingly longer ones circle the mountain at progressively lower elevations. All are interconnected by a series of short roads or paths. By the time the party reached the top of the mountain, Mrs. Thornton could see the house illuminated eerily by lightning; "the exercise of ascending the hill and the warmth of the evening [had] fatigued us much." Nevertheless, they had reached shelter, "about a quarter of an hour before it began to rain violently."

Mrs. Thornton had been told that Mr. Jefferson's house, like the Madisons', was still in the process of remodeling; indeed, she knew he had been building it, on and off, for many years. But she was unprepared for what she found when, finally reaching the entrance, she was admitted by a servant. Winded, tired, and feeling ill from a harrowing trip, she no doubt thought she would at last step into the furnished comfort, indeed the luxury and ease, of the house of the nation's chief executive—a man of courtly polish and acknowledged taste. She was, however, sorely disappointed. The stately columns and portico that would one day embellish the front of the house were not yet completed, and the large entrance hall was a cavern of raw brick, with boards covering window openings. It was lit by a single lantern, which dimly revealed a ceiling of rough beams and a floor of dangerously unnailed planks thrown loosely over floor joists.

"Tho' I had been prepared to see an unfinished house," she later recorded in her diary, "still I could not help being much struck with the uncommon appearance . . . which the general gloom . . . contributed much to increase." The party was led across wobbly planks "into a large room with a small bow [room] separated by an arch, where the company were seated at tea. No light being in the large part of the room, part of the family being seated there, the appearance was irregular and unpleasant." Visitors entering the dining and tea rooms of Monticello today would no doubt be surprised by Mrs. Thornton's description, because both rooms are bright and cheerful, particularly the octagonal tea room, with its arc of windows. Both rooms were nearly completed, approximately as they now appear, but it was a stormy evening, candles had not yet been lit, and the lady was very tired.

Mrs. Thornton might also have been struck by the large company of family and friends having tea—about fifteen—but likely not, for Mr. Jefferson was known for his hospitality, and it was not unusual for travelers to drop in for a day or two at the great plantations of Virginia. Accommodations on the road were poor or nonexistent, and travelers often proceeded from house to house, stopping with family, friends, or mere acquaintances. The visitors were no doubt offered a late dinner; Jefferson had written Thornton to "be here half after three, our dinner hour," but the travelers had left much too late to have arrived by then.

The man who greeted the Thorntons and Madisons would have resembled the figure in the portrait by Rembrandt Peale, painted three years later in 1805. Although it is a "public" portrait, designed to depict its subject as a dignified statesman, an Augustan paterfamilias, it also reveals some of Jefferson's known personal traits. The most striking feature of the portrait is the eyes, which gaze forthrightly at the viewer with a crystalline intelligence. Any attempt to penetrate beyond them to the inner man is reduced to conjecture, for the eyes are reflections rather than portals. The nose is patrician, the mouth firmly set, the facial muscles in perfect tune beneath the skin. His hair has by now turned from red to a sandy grey and is worn collar length. It falls in loose curls around his ears and neck, softening the tight line of his jaw.

Augustus Foster, secretary of the British legation in Washington at this time, described Jefferson in terms quite different from the Peale portrait: "He was a tall man, with a very red freckled face and gray neglected hair, his manners goodnatured, frank, and rather friendly, though he had somewhat of a cynical expression." Jefferson did not meet strangers easily; he was reserved and distant, often described as cold. His body language was telling: a characteristic pose when standing was with his arms crossed in front of him. Once assured of acceptance, however, he became more open, with a remarkable power to charm and disarm, even those who had come prepared to dislike him. With friends like the Thorntons, he was warm and affable. He was most open with his family, particularly his grandchildren, with whom he liked to frolic and play.

After introductions—the Thorntons and Madisons knew most of those present—Mrs. Thornton asked to be shown to her bedroom, for by now she was "exhausted and quite unwell." The Thorntons were given one of the second-floor bedrooms on the east, or entrance, side of the house, and as they were shown to their room by a servant, Mrs. Thornton observed a singular anomaly, one that confounds everyone who has ever visited Monticello. "We had to mount a little ladder of a staircase, about two feet wide, and very steep," she noted critically.

The staircases of Monticello, which Mrs. Thornton described perfectly, are perhaps the most serious design flaw in the building. Visitors to the mansion today are not permitted to view the second and third floors, largely because the stairs are a clear danger to life and limb. No building code in America would permit such staircases to be constructed, yet Jefferson, one of the most gifted architects the nation has produced, designed and built them. There are two of these staircases, on the north and south wings of the house, and each climbs from the basement to the third floor. They are built into stairwells a scant six feet square, so small that the stair treads are only twenty-four inches wide and the risers dangerously high. Because the staircases turn twice on each floor, the stairway is virtually spiral, with hazardous, narrow, wedge-shaped steps. The stairs are located in the interior of the house and, although Jefferson built small skylights in the roof above them, they are not illuminated by natural light from windows, which means they were often mounted candle in hand. Ascending this staircase with her floor-length dress pulled up to avoid tripping, Mrs. Thornton must have wondered how the house servants ever managed to climb from floor to floor, their arms full, without breaking their necks.

The staircases would prove to be even more of an enigma to Mrs. Thornton when she learned next day how almost every other part of the house was painstakingly designed for convenience and domestic efficiency. When the President later showed her his drawings of the house, he might have explained, as he did to others, that his staircase design was patterned after those of the fashionable new residences of

Paris. During his stay in Paris as minister plenipotentiary to France, from 1784 to 1789, Jefferson made it a point to study continental architecture at every opportunity. Although he admired much of what he saw in France, he was particularly taken by a new style of architecture that abandoned multistoried houses in favor of single-story, horizontal dwellings. The logic was compelling when applied to a nation like America: in a country where real estate was cheap and plentiful, why build expensive three- and four-story buildings, which were originally designed for costly high-density urban land? A single-story house, or a two-story house that gives the appearance of being one-story, eliminates grand staircases "which are expensive, and occupy a space which would make a good room in every story." The theory may have been flawless, but Jefferson designed not a single-story dwelling, but one with four stories, if the basement, with its important functional rooms, is included. The four levels of the house were divided roughly into the utilitarian basement level, with its storage areas, warming kitchen, and servant's rooms; the main floor, which included Jefferson's bedroom-library suite, the dining and entertainment rooms, plus several bedrooms; and the second and third levels, which were, except for the dome room, entirely given over to bedrooms. Because the stairways were used mainly by guests, children, and servants, it could be argued that there was no practical need for more spacious stairways; the stairs Jefferson built were adequate enough for temporary visitors, youngsters, and slaves. This assumes, however, that in an eighteenth-century house the stairway was merely functional.

In the baronial halls and palaces of Europe, a staircase was much more than an inefficient elevator, a way of lifting a body from one floor to another. A staircase was part of an elaborate ritual of rank. At social functions, where class and status were publicly displayed, the staircase was an important prop. One received guests at the top of a staircase, resplendent and regal, gesturing welcome from olympian heights to those who climbed to be greeted. Conversely, grand entrances were made by descending a staircase, while those below, their faces turned upward, admired and paid homage. Those subservient to power climbed to pay obeisance; those in power received guests from elevated heights and descended to adoration. These ritualistic ceremonies of caste and privilege required a suitable theatrical setting; therefore the grand staircase—spacious, ornate, designed with elegance and grace, preferably of marble—became the central fixture around which the entrance halls of the mansions and palaces of Europe were constructed. Such staircases were opulent symbols of the life, blood, and spirit of aristocracy.

One could easily predict what Thomas Jefferson, the author of the Declaration of Independence, with its ringing salutation to the princes of Europe, "all men are created equal"—one could anticipate what his notions about grand staircases would be. In contrast to the palatial staircase, the simple stairway produces domestic democracy; it reduces climbing or descending to a utilitarian nuisance, and demands that meetings of those who are equal before the law be conducted on an egalitarian surface, level ground.

While working for more than fifty years on his home—building, altering, remodeling, putting up and tearing down—Jefferson created, as all owner-builders do, a dwelling that mirrored himself. Monticello is the man, and the house is a living testimony to the truth, "I am what I build." It is not unusual, therefore, that the man who has been called one of the most complex and enigmatic personalities this nation has ever produced should build into his home some equally puzzling components. To reduce the staircase from a representation of power to a functional architectural space is one thing, but to further constrict it to a dark, cramped passageway suggests that it was perhaps more deeply symbolic of its owner's difficulties with free access and disclosure.

The Thorntons would not, of course, have preoccupied themselves with such speculations, because they lived in a pre-Freudian age where terms such as "retentive personality" were subsumed under two broad psychological states—sanity and madness. In between were vagaries such as "eccentricity" and "whimsicality." In fact, Mrs. Thornton's conclusion about the house, stairs, and bedroom was, "everything has a whimsical and droll appearance." The window in her bedroom appeared strange to her because it was virtually at floor level and was only about four feet square. Instead of opening on a sash, it pivoted on a center pin, somewhat like a modern awning window. She was not to learn until next day that the windows were planned to deceive the eye of one who viewed the house from outside. Jefferson had designed the first- and second-story windows as a single unit to give the house the appearance of being one story. The tiny window Mrs. Thornton thought "droll" seemed from outside the house to be the upper sash of a single large window in a high-ceilinged room. This was one of the ingenious ideas Jefferson incorporated into his house plan from the building styles he had observed in France.

One final "whimsicality" that Mrs. Thornton pondered, not only upon seeing her bedroom, but perhaps during the night, was the fact that the beds were "fixed up in recesses in the walls." She referred to the alcove beds, which are a feature of nearly every bedroom in the house. Jefferson also borrowed the idea for alcove beds from his observations of French architecture. The alcoves are designed into the rooms in roughly the same way clothes closets fit into modern bedrooms; indeed the alcove is approximately the same size as the average clothes closet, a little over six feet in length. (Eighteenth-century houses rarely had built-in clothes closets; like many continental homes today, a piece of furniture—a clothes press or armoire—was used to store clothing.)

The alcove bed was an exercise in design efficiency on Jefferson's part. In most small bedrooms, a double bed is an intruder, its head against a wall, its body thrust into the center of the room, consuming much of the usable space. The alcove bed, tucked into a wall, allows the rest of the bedroom space to be used as a small, unobstructed sitting room. A single person sleeping in an alcove is enclosed on three sides in a womblike cocoon, somewhat like a modern Pullman compartment, an experience that can be either comforting or claustrophobic, depending on the individual. A married couple, however, faces certain problems with an alcove bed. Mrs. Thornton did not record for posterity whether she slept on the inside or the outside of the alcove, but the inside person must climb, crawl, or roll over the outside sleeper in order to get in and out of bed. For newlyweds, this would no doubt be more of an opportunity than an inconvenience, but for couples like the Thorntons, who had been married for twelve years, the alcove bed was more likely to be a recurring nocturnal annoyance. The only alcove bed in the house that was designed to eliminate this problem was that of the master of Monticello. His alcove was located between two rooms so that he could theoretically get in or out of bed on either side. He soon discovered, however, that his open alcove was drafty and afforded no privacy, so he closed one side, first with glass sashes, and later with paper-covered screens.

Next morning, a bell rang at seven o'clock to rouse the guests and allow them time to dress for breakfast at eight. Jefferson would have been awake and at work in his private bedroom-study-library suite long before this. Late in his life he commented that the sun had not caught him in bed for fifty years. (The last time he apparently slept past dawn was during his ten-year marriage.) His habit was to wake at dawn, read, and then work on his huge correspondence—he often wrote as many as a dozen or more letters daily. He would meet the rest of the household at breakfast.

Mealtime shifted with the seasons at Monticello; in the summertime, when days were long and weather hot, breakfast was normally at eight and dinner at five. During the short days of winter, breakfast was at nine and dinner at three-thirty or four, so that meals were always eaten by natural light. (That September, dinner had obviously been shifted to the winter schedule, "half after three," as Jefferson wrote Thornton.) Tea and coffee were served two hours after dinner.

The Thorntons would expect to dine well, for the President had the reputation of serving a fine table; however, breakfast, although ample by today's standards, was not the "Virginia breakfast" served at some of the great plantation houses. A guest of Jefferson's in later years, Margaret Bayard Smith, wife of the editor of the *National Intelligencer* and one of the foundation stones of Washington society for a generation, expressed some disappointment that breakfast consisted only of "tea, coffee, excellent muffins, hot wheat and corn bread, cold ham, and butter." At Montpelier, where Mrs. Smith, like the Thorntons, also visited, Dolley Madison served "a most excellent Virginian breakfast—tea, coffee, hot wheat bread, light cakes, a pone or corn loaf—cold ham, nice hashes, chickens, etc." Jefferson characteristically ate a moderate breakfast of tea or coffee, hot bread, and occasionally some cold ham. At the President's House in Washington, he at times had what his French chef, Etienne Lemaire, whose English was minimal, referred to in his recipe as "pannequaiques." Lemaire's pancakes were made with egg yolks, cream, and flour, and with whipped egg whites in place of baking soda. The light griddle cakes were coated with sugar and stacked into a small torte. The stack was then cut into wedges like a cake and served. This recipe later became a favorite at Monticello.

The Thorntons joined some twenty others, family and guests, at the breakfast table, including William Short, "lately from France," Mrs. Thornton noted. Short had been Jefferson's secretary in Paris. Also present were Jefferson's two daughters and their husbands (Martha and Thomas Mann Randolph, and Maria and John Wayles Eppes) and several of Martha's five children. After breakfast the Thorntons, like all guests at Monticello, were on their own until dinner time. Jefferson had a daytime schedule he adhered to rather rigidly, forcing guests, as is still the tradition in the country houses of England, to amuse themselves. He did take time after breakfast, however, to show the Thorntons the house and to go over with them his drawings for those parts that were not yet completed.

William Thornton would be particularly interested in the President's architectural drawings, for Thornton was himself an amateur architect; he had recently won the competition for a plan for the nation's Capitol building in Washington. The Capitol, as it stands today, after undergoing numerous deletions, additions, and alterations, after being burned by the British and rebuilt, after consuming the creative powers of numerous architects and engineers, still contains a hard core of Thornton's original prize-winning plan. Thornton was a man Jefferson could understand and admire, for the two men shared a broad cultural education, inventive minds, and the kind of intellectual curiosity which motivated so many of the nation's founders.

Thornton studied medicine in Scotland and took his M.D. degree, but never practiced. He was an indefatigable inventor. He had been associated with John Fitch in the development of paddle steamboats some years before Fulton's historic steamboats, but his was not a commercial success. In 1814, he wrote Jefferson that for several months he had been employing a craftsman "making a musical instrument that I invented abt. 12 or 14 yrs ago." It will be the size of a large chamber organ, he explained, with 68 strings, and "Keys in the manner of a piano Forte." The instrument, he promised, would give all the tones of the "violin, violincello—bass—double bass etc." It uses neither catgut nor horsehair for its strings, Thornton wrote, but an artificial material that is "far superior." It "produces notes which equal the above Instruments." He never told Jefferson whether his ingenious musical instrument was ever finished, or whether it worked. A year later he sent a drawing for what Jefferson termed "a beautiful hydraulic machine," to be used for raising water from the cisterns at Monticello. He also gave Jefferson detailed instructions on how to waterproof his cisterns, and included a drawing for a "Filtering Machine" he invented for purifying water or cider.

He was a talented writer and painter as well. He copied a Gilbert Stuart portrait of Jefferson and "placed it in the Congressional Library in my superb gilt Frame, that when the members view the works by which the inside of your head was so well stored [a reference to the library Jefferson had sold to Congress] they might also have a good Idea of the outside of the Head." Thornton was also a successful farmer and horticulturist and the foremost breeder and racer of fine horses in Washington. The term "genius" was frequently applied to him because of his many talents, but if he was a genius, he was certainly not of the reclusive kind. He was the friend and confidant of George Washington, Benjamin Franklin, David Rittenhouse, Thomas Jefferson, and James Madison, and he and his wife Anna Maria rode the Washington social carousel for nearly three decades.

Gilbert Stuart's portrait of him shows something of his intensity and intelligence. He was described by a contemporary as "a scholar and a gentleman—full of talent and eccentricity—a Quaker by profession, a painter, a poet, and a horse-racer—well acquainted with the mechanic arts. He was a man of infinite humour—humane and generous, yet fond of field sports—his company was complete antidote to dullness." Jefferson obviously found Thornton and his wife amiable company, for not only did he invite them to his home in Virginia, but he entertained them at dinner on a number of occasions at the President's House in Washington and dined at their home. In explaining to William Thornton his architectural drawings for Monticello, Jefferson would have been assured of a knowledgeable, sympathetic listener.

Although both men were amateur architects, they were amateurs in the eighteenth-century sense of the term. Indeed, the word had only recently entered into the language; it was lifted from the French and quickly underwent a sea change from its original Latin derivation, *amare*, to love. Its initial meaning was "one who loves or is fond of," but by the turn of the century, an amateur was described in the newly published *Cyclopedia; or, Universal Dictionary of Arts, Sciences, and Literature* as a "foreign term introduced and now passing current amongst us, to denote a person understanding, and loving or practicing the polite arts of painting, sculpture, or architecture, without any regard to pecuniary advantage." Thornton and Jefferson were amateurs only insofar as they did not earn a living by designing buildings; although self-taught, their expertise was professional. Besides the Capitol building, Thornton designed a number of ambitious structures, including the Octagon in Washington, now an historic house owned by the American Institute of Architects Foundation. He also acted as general contractor for some buildings, including the Madison town house, which adjoined the Thorntons' on F Street, two blocks east of the President's House. Unlike most eighteenth-century architects, whose work was limited to the drafting table, Thornton and Jefferson were "hands-on" designers who did not share the gentleman's traditional disdain for the "mechanic arts," defined as those occupations "wherein the hand and body are more concerned than the mind." Both men were raised in traditions that, even before the egalitarianism born of the Revolution, had no aristocratic contempt for handwork. Thornton was a Quaker, and the Society of Friends took as an article of faith the dignity of physical labor. Some of the leading members of the Philadelphia gentry were Quaker silversmiths, carpenters, and cabinetmakers. Jefferson was a Virginia planter, and members of his class, as a matter of survival, were involved in every detail of plantation economy. They supervised coopers, blacksmiths, and sawyers, and like farmers everywhere, at harvest time they were in the fields. The notion that trade or physical work was tainted would have been absurd to most of them. One of Jefferson's favorite stories about his father, Peter Jefferson, a man of prodigious strength, was that he once directed three husky slaves to pull down an old outbuilding with a rope. After they had repeatedly tried and failed, Jefferson's father "bade them stand aside, seized the rope and dragged down the structure in an instant." It is difficult to believe that the man who repeated this story could be contemptuous of physical work.

In constructing their own homes, Thornton and Jefferson were much closer to modern owner-builders than to architects. They took into their own hands the autonomy of creating shelter for themselves and their families. Because Jefferson was a planter and slaveowner, a member of the Old Dominion landed gentry, it might be thought that he had little in common with those men and women two hundred years later who also design and build their own houses. But this is not the case. The difficulties he faced in planning and executing the construction of his house are a paradigm of what every owner-builder overcomes in building a home. Allowing for the differences of two centuries of cultural change, Jefferson experienced all of the successes and failures, the triumphs and mistakes, the rewards and frustrations of twentieth-century house builders. One of his spiritual sons was to write some fifty years later, "It avails not, time nor place—distance avails not, / I am with you, men and women of a generation or ever so many generations hence." Like those of Walt Whitman, Jefferson's experiences have leaped the ages. His white-domed mansion, with its classical porticoes echoing the grandeur that was Rome, belies the mundane stuff of which it was made. Its brick walls, burnished with the patina of as many years as have yellowed the Declaration of Independence, were molded of mud from the mountain on which it stands. Its finely wrought architraves are from trees felled nearby. Its designer and maker, like his descendants across the centuries, was troubled by finances, could not find skilled labor, had to search for special building materials, and was frustrated to the very edge of his well-tempered emotional restraints by the creeping pace, the snail-crawl progress, the endless delays, the foreverness of it all.

But to say that Thomas Jefferson was simply among the first of millions of Americans who designed and built their own homes, or that Monticello is a typical, if somewhat large, example of domestic architecture, is to deny the palpable genius of the man. He was larger than life in most things he did—America's outstanding example of a Renaissance man in an age that produced more than its share. As in virtually everything he attempted, Jefferson's lifelong involvement in rendering into reality the house of his creative imagination was heroic in scale. Most owner-builders take inordinate lengths of time to complete their projects; Jefferson took fifty-four years. Many owner-builders construct dwellings larger than necessary; Jefferson, a widower, built a thirty-five-room mansion. Owner-builders invariably extemporize as they build, adding to and modifying their original design as the house grows. Jefferson built one house, tore much of it down, doubled its size, and continued to alter, remodel, improve, and add to it for decades. It is a wonder that the house was ever finally completed; many thought it never would be. One of those was probably William Thornton.

Anna Maria and William Thornton apparently had a very good marriage. Although there were no children, they shared artistic interests, enjoyed reading and entertaining, and took mutual pleasure in the farm they owned outside of Washington. In a fit of depression, she did once confess to her diary that "this little journal is rather an account of my husband's transactions than mine. . . . There is so little variety in our life that I have nothing worth recording." But the diary then continues with the rounds of visits, teas, dinners, and shopping trips that consumed her days. At times she became impatient with her social obligations. After a tea at her house, for example, where she was forced to play the piano with a nagging headache, she concluded that "tea drinking is very stupid." On another occasion, she sat uncomfortably through a student musical and left with the opinion that "it was intolerably stupid." Then there was the time she and Thornton went with Dolley Madison "to hear a madman preach." They walked out after ten minutes.

Thornton was apparently not at home as much as she would have liked—his many interests pulled him away on business trips constantly—but she and her husband seemed to share a full and varied life together. Her comments in her diary about Monticello, therefore, undoubtedly reflect not only her own, but the opinions of her architect husband as well.

After examining the floor plans with her husband and Jefferson and taking a daylight tour of the house and grounds, Mrs. Thornton thought that the inside of the house would be "handsome and convenient" when it was finished. "The President intends completing it next summer," she wrote. It was not completed the next summer, in spite of Jefferson's best intentions, nor the summer after that, nor the one after that. It was seven years later, in 1809, that the interior of the house was completed in roughly the state it appears today, but the porticoes on the exterior were not finished until 1823. Mrs. Thornton (and probably her husband), after being told how long Jefferson had been working on the house, came to this conclusion: "Mr. J. has been 27 years engaged in improving the plans, but he has pulled down and built up again so often, that nothing is completed, nor do I think ever will be. A great deal of money has been expended, both above and below grounds, but not so as to appear to the best advantage." To take this much time on a house, and still have it in the condition that Mrs. Thornton described, would appear to confirm her conclusion that the President was "a very long time maturing his projects." Moreover, the house had been so long exposed to the weather, unpainted, that even those parts of it that had been finished were badly deteriorating. After walking around the exterior of the house and observing the condition of the wood trim, door jambs, and window sashes, Mrs. Thornton observed, "he has altered his plan so frequently, pulled down and built, that in many parts . . . it looks like a house going to decay from the length of time it has been created."

The same conclusion was reached by another Thornton. The British chargé d'affaires Edward Thornton, who was also one of Jefferson's guests during Mr. and Mrs. Thornton's visit (but was no relation to them), commented critically that the house was in a "state of commencement and decay," and added that only in Virginia did people inhabit an unfinished house "till it is falling around their ears." Obviously, this was not the way it was done in England. Even Jefferson himself had admitted earlier, in 1796, when he first began rebuilding Monticello, that "during a war of 8 years and my subsequent absence of 10 years [my house had] gone into almost total decay. I am now engaged in repairing, altering & finishing it."

In his campaign to complete the house, his first priority was to alter rather than repair it. He might have first repaired the deteriorated woodwork in those parts of the house that remained from the older, original building. Those were the rooms on the western—the domed—side of the house, the face that is turned toward the mountains. This was also the weather side, the portion of the structure that took the brunt of cold fronts that swept over the mountaintops during winter months, and thunderstorms that punctuated the summer. It was no wonder the woodwork, unpainted and unrepaired for some twenty years or more, was ravaged by neglect.

Instead of repairing this first, and thereby giving at least part of the house a respectable appearance, Jefferson chose to proceed with his plan for enlarging the house to more than double its original size. His reasons would be readily understood by anyone who has ever built a house. The repair work required finished carpentry, but the additions called for a great amount of masonry work—the cellars and walls had to be built—and rough carpentry for framing floors and roofs. Workmen had to be hired and used the same way they are today: teams of specialists were assembled to work on each house system sequentially. Masons were followed by carpenters, who in turn were followed by plasterers, joiners, and finally painters. Hiring workers out of sequence for a repair job is expensive, and in Jefferson's Virginia, where there was a shortage of skilled tradesmen, it was often impossible. To paint deteriorated woodwork, for example, would have meant bringing a painter to Monticello, arranging for his housing and board, and then letting him go, only to rehire him again when newly completed work was ready. Instead, he chose the only rational alternative, to postpone repairs on badly weathered woodwork until the new construction had reached a parallel state of completion, and then to complete the repairs.

Mrs. Thornton's belief that Jefferson never would finish his house was not an unreasonable assumption. If, after twenty-seven years of building (the figure was obviously the estimate Jefferson gave her, based on the number of years he actually was in residence at Monticello and doing some kind of building), the house was still in its present condition of simultaneous incompleteness and disrepair, there were not enough years left in the life of a nearly sixty-year-old man ever to finish. But Jefferson proved her wrong: during his presidency, he made slow but steady progress, for the first time regularly returning to Monticello from Washington twice a year every year. Moreover, he acquired, for the first time, some excellent, dependable craftsmen who could be trusted to work on their own initiative. And he lived to be eighty-three.

*Jefferson at sixty-two, at the start of his second term as President.
Portrait by Rembrandt Peale.*

Anna Maria Thornton and her husband, William, by Gilbert Stuart, 1804.

One of a number of sets of chessmen
Jefferson owned.

One of Jefferson's polygraphs, the device he used
to make copies of his correspondence.

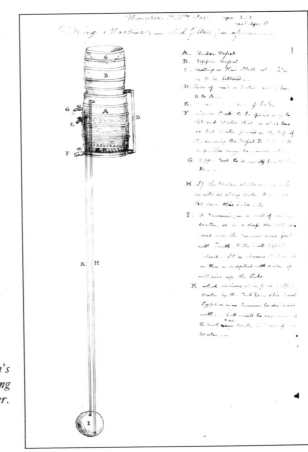

William Thornton's
"Filtering Machine" for filtering
cider or water.

Anna Maria Thornton was an avid reader, but like many literate women of her generation, she was largely self-taught. Her commonplace book contains careful lists of those books she owned, those she had read, and those she desired to read. Her taste in reading was impressively varied—history, drama, biography, geography, poetry, and some fiction. She read and wrote French, and was particularly fond of French drama. She had been looking forward to browsing in Jefferson's library, which she had heard was "one of the best private libraries on the continent." But she learned what every guest at Monticello quickly discovered, that no one but Jefferson had access to his private quarters. Although there were three inside doors to this suite, they were all kept locked, and only the door from the entrance hall to his bedroom-library was used by Jefferson. To get to the library, guests had to be personally escorted by their host.

Mrs. Thornton wrote in her diary that on the first day of her visit she found the library suite "constantly locked, and I have been disappointed much by not being able to get in today." On the following day, however, Jefferson invited her, and no doubt her husband, into the library. He probably also showed the Thorntons his adjoining bedroom. Mrs. Thornton would have observed that the room was two stories high, illuminated by a skylight. The bed was located in an alcove between the bedroom and the adjoining study; over the alcove was a small room with three oval windows, something like a ship's portholes. This was Jefferson's clothes closet, which was reached by a small ladder at the head of the bed. Typically, Jefferson designed this closet with an eye to the future. Structurally, it would allow him to build another room above the bedroom if he ever wanted to in the future. Like most rooms in the house, this too was being worked on.

Walking through the doorway at the foot of the bed-alcove, the Thorntons would have entered the study—he called it the cabinet—one of the half-octagon rooms on the southwest corner of the house. This room, its opposite semi-octagon room on the southeast corner, and the "south square room"—an adjoining bedroom that had been converted into a book room—were Jefferson's library-study suite. The first thing that Mrs. Thornton would have noticed was that there were more books, all neatly shelved, than she had ever seen in a private home in her life.

This library, which numbered some six thousand volumes, was the second of what was to be a total of three collections Jefferson compiled for himself during his lifetime. When the British burned the Library of Congress in the sack of Washington in 1814, Jefferson sold his library, the one Anna Maria now admired, and this became the nucleus of the new Library of Congress collection. After selling his books, for the bargain price of $23,950, Jefferson immediately began a new, much more specialized collection, one that numbered more than a thousand volumes at his death.

His first library, books he had inherited from his father and those he had purchased throughout his college years and during his early days as a lawyer, were destroyed when Shadwell, his ancestral home, burned in 1770. He immediately began purchasing books at a frantic pace to build his second and greatest library. Thirteen years later, he catalogued it; in 1783, he had 2,640 volumes, an average purchase of 200 books a year. This was in an era when a good private library of a Virginia planter numbered no more than a few hundred volumes. Jefferson more than doubled his library during the five years he spent in Europe. When he offered his collection to the Library of Congress, he wrote to Samuel Harrison Smith and described how he had haunted the bookstores of Paris during his stay in France:

> While residing in Paris, I devoted every afternoon I was disengaged, for a summer or two in examining all the principal bookstores, turning over every book with my own hand, and putting by everything which related to America, and indeed whatever was rare and valuable in every science. Besides this, I had standing orders during the whole time I was in Europe, on its principal book-marts, particularly Amsterdam, Frankfort, Madrid, and London, for such works relating to America as could not be found in Paris.

The volumes that Mrs. Thornton gazed upon that morning, as she ran her eyes over the shelves of books, floor to ceiling, covering every available bit of wall space in the suite, were the result of a massive, self-indulgent gorging by one of the most omnivorous book collectors the nation had yet produced.

It is not surprising that Thomas Jefferson was a collector of books because from his earliest youth he was a collector of knowledge, and books were its repository. He was what we would now term a compulsive personality; he retained, either physically or in his Memorandum Books, virtually everything that passed through his hands during his entire life. The Memorandum Books record, over a period of nearly sixty years, a daily note of every cent he spent or acquired, as well as jottings about the trivial events that most people allow to fall through the grates of memory into oblivion. Yet, what seems to observers of these daily records to be meaningless quotidian trivia, often conceals a long-term methodology. There is a record, for example, of his counting the number of garden peas that make a pint—2,500. One puzzles over the kind of personality that would engage in and record this kind of event. But he was as ardent a gardener as he was a reader, and this record allowed him to determine the exact number of rows of peas that a pint of seed would produce. And peas were his favorite vegetable. While in Washington he recorded, over a period of eight years, the days of the month of the earliest and latest appearance of some thirty-seven varieties of fruit and vegetables at the Washington vegetable market. One asks, what earthly reason could have motivated him to seek this information? The response is that the data enabled him to compare the agricultural climate of Washington with that of other parts of the country, particularly with Monticello, where he kept parallel accounts of the harvest dates of a long list of garden products.

But this explanation is still not satisfactory; the information he gleaned from this experiment does not justify the amount of energy expended over an incredibly long period of time. Assembling data of this sort had to be an end in itself for Jefferson, just as his collection of books was more than a convenient library of knowledge. Collecting odd pieces of data and fitting these meaningless bits into a rational system was a way of structuring and ordering his personal universe. He was a man who demanded of his life the same symmetry he found in the Newtonian universe he believed in so explicitly. This could not simply be because he was a product of the European Enlightenment and its worship of reason—Franklin swam in these same intellectual currents, yet he lacked Jefferson's compulsive need for order. It was, perhaps, because of an offset, a dissociation at the very core of his personality, which had to be balanced with the weights of systems.

Even his library had been fashioned by Jefferson into a self-contained cosmos, a Monticellean microsystem. Most eighteenth-century private libraries were arranged by size—folios, quartos, octavos, and duodecimos were gathered together on shelves of a suitable dimension. If any attempt at all was made to classify books, it was done by such broad categories as literature, history, politics, or natural philosophy. Indeed, it was done the way most home libraries are arranged today. Jefferson, on the other hand, devised an extended system of classification based on the Baconian structure of knowledge. This system, divided into forty-four subject categories, was the formula adopted and used by the Library of Congress for a hundred years after Jefferson sold his books—arranged according to his classification system—to the federal government.

Because books were such an important part of his intellectual life—"I cannot live without books," he once wrote—he gave a great deal of thought to their physical storage. His foremost need was to be able to locate any single book instantly; his classification system accomplished this. But there were other practical matters to be dealt with. Bookshelves had to be built and fitted into rooms that were poorly designed for a library. The ideal room for a library is a simple rectangle with no windows or doors, allowing all four walls to be shelved floor to ceiling. Jefferson's library-study suite included a pair of semi-octagons with doors, windows, an alcove bed, and a fireplace consuming valuable space. The remaining wall space was odd-sized, with no wall longer than 6½ feet. The length of the cases could not be standardized, but had to be custom-constructed to fit each wall space. This suite might have accommodated the library Jefferson owned when he designed it, but his appetite for books rapidly outstripped the amount of space he had to store them in, and his library, when Mrs. Thornton entered it, was badly cramped. Every inch of available wall space was covered with bookshelves.

The construction of these bookcases was utilitarian; they were built of pine in the Monticello cabinet shop under the supervision of John Hemings, one of the most talented of Jefferson's artisan slaves. The cases themselves were cleverly designed to utilize space most efficiently. Each case, approximately nine feet high, was a series of individual book boxes stacked atop each other. The bottom of the case was designed to hold folios, the largest of Jefferson's books; it was thirteen inches deep and consisted of two boxes. The second tier of three boxes was designed for quartos; they were approximately seven inches deep. The top three boxes were less than six inches deep, and held the smallest volumes. Even with Jefferson's rather complex system of classification, he still arranged books, within each category of the system, according to size in order to conserve precious space. Jefferson owned several bookcases of fine wood, including a "mahogany book case with glass doors," and two walnut cases. As his library rapidly grew, however, he abandoned any attempt at shelving his books in pieces of fine furniture. He chose instead to shelve his book collection as it expanded, adding small inexpensive cases that could be moved and handled easily as they were needed. Moreover, when his collection was finally sold to the Library of Congress (he had always planned to bequeath it to some public institution, for he felt it was improper for a single individual to hoard so valuable an intellectual property), he was not left with rooms filled with empty, fixed bookshelves. The books were moved to Washington packed in the cases upon which they rested in Jefferson's rooms, their classification system intact. Lids were simply nailed over the fronts of the cases, making them into sturdy packing boxes. Because the cases were inexpensive pine, they were expendable as furniture, and with their removal, the library rooms could be readily put to new use.

After Anna Maria Thornton had made herself comfortable in one of the library chairs, Jefferson brought to her several volumes of architectural engravings of the antiquities of Greece and Rome. For most owners of them, these expensive works were the equivalent of the modern coffee-table book. In an age before the invention of the camera, etched or engraved prints, with their exquisitely wrought fine line, could approximate a black-and-white photograph in detail and modeling. During most of the eighteenth century, amateur archaeologists had fanned out from England, France, and Germany to the far reaches of Attica and the Roman empire to measure and record in drawings the fabled ruins of the past. The books they produced took cultivated Europeans by storm; never before had the architectural and sculptural grandeurs of antiquity, so loved and admired in the abstract, been made readily available for after-dinner perusal in handsome folio form by ladies and gentlemen of taste. For Jefferson, however, they were more than handsome books to page through and admire. Because the architecture of Rome was the model for his own construction plans, these books, along with the works of Palladio and the English Palladians, were scriptural texts for what was beautiful and right. And he no doubt studied them with the same care that he had exercised as a young law student in mastering his Blackstone and Coke.

One of the folios that impressed Mrs. Thornton, for she mentioned it that night in her diary, was Robert Wood's *The Ruins of Balbec*, which contained a number of fine prints of the remains of the Roman city of Heliopolis at Baalbek in present-day Lebanon. Because she was French, Jefferson may also have shown her his copy of Antoine Desgodets's *Édifices Antiques de Rome*, which he had purchased during his stay in France. This work, with its measured drawings of such Roman monuments as the Pantheon, the Temple of Vesta, the Arch of Titus, the Arch of Constantine, and the Colosseum, was used by Jefferson as a pattern book for the architraves of a number of Monticello's rooms. And he may have taken down from the shelf his copy of Charles-Louis Clérisseau's *Antiquités de la France*, a book he purchased from Clérisseau himself. This work illustrated the Maison Carrée at Nîmes, still one of the best preserved of all Roman buildings. So infatuated was Jefferson by this temple when he visited it in 1787 during a tour of southern France, that he used it as the model for the Virginia state capitol. It was in part because of Clérisseau's book that Jefferson chose him as a collaborator on the design of the capitol at Richmond.

Mrs. Thornton spent the rest of the day reading in the Monticello library until it was time for her to dress for dinner. She could be expected to arrive at the dining table stylishly attired; even while traveling she wore the latest fashions. On one of her later trips to Virginia, she confessed in her diary how she embarrassed herself at a ferry crossing: "Stepping into the boat," she wrote ". . . I fell flat into it in consequence of my petticoat being too fashionably narrow." Apparently incidents such as this prompted her to change her mind about her travel wardrobe. A year later, she wrote a reminder to herself that she had been in the habit of taking "too many clothes," and added acerbically, "at least for the part of the world we have been in." She included several items of summary wisdom gleaned from years of travel in rural America, advice that is as timeless as it is universally unheeded: "In going on a journey take as little baggage as possible." Among indispensable items are "a pair of sheets and pillow cases, lavender water, biscuits in the carriage, as the stages are very far apart," and for undressing in rooms where there was little privacy—a frequent inconvenience on the road in eighteenth-century America—"take a long wrapper from head to feet." As gifts, "take little books to give to *smart* children," but as for herself and her husband, she concluded that they traveled with "too many books." She also decided that chessmen were unnecessary.

Apparently, Mrs. Thornton was not as much a lover of chess as was her husband. Chess was played frequently at their home in Washington, and it was played at Monticello throughout her stay. Jefferson did not believe in gambling, although he had done a little in his youth, and he did not permit cards—the universal gambling game in Virginia—to be played at Monticello. Chess, on the other hand, is a game of skill that appeals both to the intellect and to the architectonic imagination; it was one of his favorite amusements. Chess had become enormously popular among the intelligentsia in France and England during the eighteenth century—Diderot, Voltaire, and Rousseau were passionate players, and the coffee houses of London resounded with cries of "Check!" Jefferson had been in France during the final years of the great French chessmaster François Philidor, who astounded his countrymen by playing—it was the first time it had ever been done— as many as three games simultaneously while blindfolded. (In December 1801, Jefferson requested his son-in-law Thomas Mann Randolph to send him "Philidor on chess which you will find in the book room.") Jefferson no doubt played chess often in the salons of Paris while he was minister plenipotentiary to France, and he played in Washington during his presidency. In his old age he told a visitor to Monticello, "I played with Dr. Franklin at chess, and was equal to him at the game." He purchased two chess sets in France, one a "light neat pattern" for his friend Francis Eppes, the other for himself, although he already had three sets at home. Several of these sets have survived; two can be seen at Monticello.

In spite of bad weather, Mrs. Thornton, no doubt with her husband and several other of the visitors, got out of the house the next day, Wednesday, for a stroll over the first roundabout. "Took a walk of half a mile which has been made around the Hill, this through the trees," she wrote that night. "Below there is another of two miles." This may have been the day she also took paper and paint to the lawn on the west side of the house and started a watercolor of Monticello, one of the few records of the appearance of the house at this time. She attempted to paint not what she saw, but what the house would look like when finished. Since the north pavilion was not yet built, and the porticoes and steps were incomplete, she must have consulted Jefferson's plans. (She inadvertently drew five columns instead of six on the portico; only four temporary supports were in place.)

What Mrs. Thornton would have observed on her walk was a plantation designed unlike any she had ever before seen. The appearance of an eighteenth-century house from the outside is deceptive; it seems little different from its twentieth-century counterpart. In fact, there are many contemporary homes, built in the Georgian style, that could pass for James River plantation dwellings on the exterior. Inside, however, there are worlds of differences. The utility core of a modern house is entirely missing from eighteenth-century dwellings; there is no kitchen, no pantry, no bathrooms, no laundry room, no storage rooms, no servants' quarters. All of these utility spaces are invariably set apart from the main structure, in separate buildings known as dependencies or offices.

The rooms inside the main dwelling are those for sleeping, dining, entertainment, and leisure. The reasons for the separation under different roofs of the two functions, the living and the utilitarian, had to do with considerations that were both practical and aesthetic. The main reason for having cooking facilities under a separate roof was because of the very real danger of fire. Cooking in an open fireplace presented a constant hazard because a fire had to be maintained and tended during the entire year, virtually night and day. This sustained, intense heat caused the hearth and chimney masonry to deteriorate rapidly. Chimney flue fires, as well as those caused by carelessness—slaves had the reputation of showing inadequate respect for fire—accounted for the frequent loss of kitchen buildings in colonial America. If the kitchen was located in the main house, all would be gone instead of only one outbuilding. For this reason, the kitchen building was usually separated as far from the main dwelling as was consistent with keeping food warm as it was carried from kitchen to dining table in all kinds of weather.

Aesthetic considerations were equally important. In an age with no refrigeration, where sanitary conditions were often primitive, when all foodstuffs had to be processed on the premises, the sounds and particularly the smells of food preparation as well as of laundry, horses, and waste disposal, were ubiquitous. An absence of offensive odors was one of the marks of civilized living, and if disagreeable smells could not be entirely removed, they were masked by generous applications of perfume and toilet water—by both men and women. (This explains Mrs. Thornton's reminder to herself never to travel without lavender water.) Getting the noise and stench out of the house was usually accomplished by constructing a series of outbuildings clustered around the central dwelling, each building usually satisfying a single function—kitchen, laundry, stable, carriage house, storerooms, ice-house, pantry, smokehouse, and privy. Slave quarters were usually located farthest from the house. The result was a series of architecturally nondescript buildings scattered in the vicinity of the main residence, their chief distinction often being their randomness.

When Anna Maria Thornton took her walk around the first round-about, she was able to observe how Thomas Jefferson had solved the aesthetic problems associated with dependencies. Extending from the main house on each side were two L-shaped wings that, combined with the central residence, formed a U facing the western mountains. Anchoring each end of the U would be two small buildings or pavilions; between them, in balanced wings on each side of the house, most of the dependencies were to be located. Not only did this ingenious arrangement of outbuildings create an ordered architectural symmetry, the kind favored by Jefferson's architectural mentor, Palladio, but the contour of the mountaintop made it possible to construct all of the dependencies partially underground so that they could not be seen— or heard or smelled—from the main house.

Of course, like virtually everything else at Monticello, the dependencies were not yet completed, although work was in progress on them, and the south wing was close to being finished. The south pavilion, a twenty-foot-square, single-room brick building at the end of the south wing, had been the first structure completed at Monticello. This was where Jefferson and his bride, Martha Wayles Skelton, lived when they first arrived at their new home in 1772. Then, as in 1802, the mountaintop was a construction site. In 1801, a year before the Thorntons' visit, Jefferson had begun construction of the dependencies connecting the south pavilion with the mansion, and this series of joined rooms, which included the kitchen, smokehouse, dairy, and slave quarters, had just recently been completed to the intersection of the L. The short section connecting the dependencies to the house, an all-weather, covered passage, was still incomplete.

Mrs. Thornton would have been particularly impressed with the new kitchen. She enjoyed entertaining and cooking; her commonplace book includes a number of her favorite recipes, including potato pudding, vegetable soup, crabs and lobster, pot au feu, marrow pastries, custards, and pound cake. The kitchen in her Washington town house, however, was located in the basement. It was not only dark and damp, but it "inundated" several times a year after heavy rains. One time, four men had to be hired to bail water out. The new Monticello kitchen was spacious, well-lit, and because it faced south, would be sunny during the cold winter months. Most important, however, for those who had to carry food as well as those who ate it, the kitchen was much closer to the main house than when it was located under the south pavilion.

The north-wing dependencies were still under construction; work was currently being done on an icehouse. The north pavilion, the outbuilding matching the one on the south, would not be started for a number of years.

Mrs. Thornton's walk also took her past Mulberry Row, a plantation street on the south side of the first roundabout. In 1771, shortly after he began building at Monticello, Jefferson had planted the mulberry trees that gave the street its name. As everywhere else on the mountaintop, Mulberry Row was also in the process of transformation. Before the south dependencies were completed, Mulberry Row had been not only the manufacturing and shop center of the plantation, but also the living quarters for the house slaves, those who worked in and around the mansion. With the completion of the southeast wing, these slaves moved into new, improved quarters. These rooms were of brick, well lighted, and certainly much more comfortable in poor weather than the log cabins the house servants had been living in on Mulberry Row. Some of the now-empty log houses, utility buildings, and privies would later be dismantled.

There were a number of other outbuildings along Mulberry Row, including several that played a crucial part in the operation of a plantation as large as Jefferson's. The stable, for instance, was as important to an early American dwelling as a garage is to a modern one. This was particularly true among Virginia gentry, who not only rode horses and had them pull their coaches and carriages, but also bred them, traded them, bought and sold them, gambled on them, and talked about them incessantly. Virginians were no doubt as boring on the subject of breeding and racing horses as modern sports car enthusiasts are on the subject of fast machinery. Jefferson was as much an admirer of horseflesh as any other Virginia aristocrat. Throughout his life, his stables contained some of the finest-blooded horses in his part of the country.

The other buildings along Mulberry Row housed the important industrial activities of the plantation. Jefferson went into the business of manufacturing and selling nails in 1794 and continued at it, on and off, for most of his life. The nail manufacturing was attached to the blacksmith shop in a single wooden building, but the two were now being separated, the smith shop to be relocated to a new position on the roundabout. As Mrs. Thornton and her party of strollers passed Mulberry Row, they may have looked in on the nailery and exchanged pleasantries with some of the workers there, nearly all slave boys between the ages of ten and sixteen. Jefferson employed male children in his nailshop before they were old enough to do field work or be trained for a trade.

When the party of strollers returned to the house, the Thorntons made preparations to leave next day, Mrs. Thornton being anxious to continue her journey. A violent storm, however, prevented departure. "Rained all the day—chilly and damp," she wrote. She spent the day reading a French opera. "Miss Randolph," the sister of Jefferson's son-in-law, "and the gentlemen play[ed] at chess almost all day and evening." The next morning, the weather cleared enough for the party to leave on the trip that was to take them back to Washington. On

The Natural Bridge, by Frederick Edwin Church.

the way, they visited several of the scenic attractions in the area, Weyer's and Madison caves and the Natural Bridge. The Thorntons no doubt learned much about the Natural Bridge from Jefferson before their departure. He was one of its most enthusiastic admirers, so much so that some years back he had purchased it.

This was not the last time that Anna Maria Thornton would visit Monticello; she returned again four years later in 1806 and found "the house and grounds amazingly improved since we were here before. It is now quite a handsome place." Her impressions of her week-long stay in 1802 had been vivid ones, heightened no doubt by the fact that she was the guest of the President of the United States. After her return to Washington, she gathered together her diary entries and, in a flawless calligraphic hand, copied the following entry into her commonplace book, one of the most candid contemporary descriptions of Jefferson's mountaintop estate to come down to us:

Monticello

The seat of Thomas Jefferson (president of the United States) is situated in Albemarle County in Virginia. The House, placed on the summit of a conical Mountain, on an elliptical level, formed by art, commands a very grand, uncommon and extensive view. The small town of Charlottesville, and a little winding river called the Ravenna [Rivanna], with a view of the Blue ridge & even more distant mountains, form a beautiful scene on the north side of the house. On the West there is [a] high mountain covered with wood, and on the other sides a varied appearance of mountains and distant country. The house is of brick, but in an unfinished state, tho' commenced 27 years ago; the ground plan is a good one, & the elevation may look very well if ever completed, but Mr. Jefferson has so frequently changed his plan, & pulled down & rebuilt so often that it has generally more the appearance of a house going to decay from the length of time it has been erected, than an unfinished building. A great deal of money must have been expended both above & below ground, but not so as to appear to the best advantage. The grounds are very little improved, except the level on the top of the mountain, & two walks, one of ½ mile, the other of two miles encircling the mountain. The whole is in a state of rude nature. There is something rather grand & awful, than agreeable or convenient in the whole place, a situation you would rather look at now & then than inhabit. AMT 1802.

2

All Warm in the
Bosom of the House

THOMAS JEFFERSON was in his twenty-fifth year when he began leveling the top of a small mountain with the intention of building one of the handsomest houses in his part of Virginia. The mountain was the legacy of his father, land that Peter Jefferson had amassed during a lifetime of real estate acquisition. When he died in 1757, the elder Jefferson owned approximately 7,500 acres, mostly in Albemarle, a county that leaned against the Blue Ridge mountains to the west and bordered the James River on the south. The Jefferson lands lay for the most part around the Rivanna River, a tributary that flowed southeast, past Charlottesville, and emptied into the James.

The rivers of Virginia were the commercial arteries that joined the interior counties of the Piedmont to the Tidewater, the Chesapeake, and the world. As Anna Maria Thornton's trek from Washington to Monticello had demonstrated, land travel by wagon, carriage, or horseback was hazardous, painful, and slow; during bad weather, it was often impossible. The great rivers of Virginia, on the other hand— the Potomac, Rappahannock, York, and James—allowed the colony's chief commercial product, tobacco, to be transported with relative ease from inland to the shipping ports of the Chesapeake. It was along these rivers that the early plantations had been carved from primeval forests, and it was at the river's edge that the great manor houses of Virginia were raised. Building next to the river was an obvious choice: the river was not only a roadway for commerce and supply, it also provided convenience for visiting neighboring plantations by small boat. There was an ample water supply readily at hand, and by clearing the land from house to river, a magnificent vista of lawn, garden, and water could be had.

In spite of all these advantages young Jefferson ignored the banks of the Rivanna River as the site for his house and chose instead the top of a nearby 867-foot mountain. In doing so, he defied conventional wisdom to the point where many of his friends and neighbors must have thought him mad. By building on top of a mountain, he not only forfeited the economic benefits and practical conveniences of a riverside location, but took on a formidable set of obstacles as well. He had to construct roads to the building site through dense, virgin forests; materials had to be hauled for considerable distances up steep inclines over poor roadbeds; and there was little water atop the mountain. Clearly then, there was only one overriding consideration that prevailed against common sense in his choice of a building location, and that was the view. As Anna Maria Thornton's description testifies, and as any modern visitor on a clear day can verify, the view is spectacular. As a young man, Jefferson frequently climbed to the top of his mountain to enjoy that view. During the five years he studied law in Williamsburg he usually spent the summer months at his ancestral home, Shadwell, located at the foot of his "little mountain." (He was learning Italian at the time he named it Monticello.) He would study from daybreak until late afternoon, at which time he would take a gallop on horseback, and then hike to the top of his mountain to contemplate the vista, and perhaps his future plans for building a house there.

Throughout his life Jefferson had a deep and abiding love of the Virginia land and its beauties, particularly for what eighteenth-century intellectuals were fond of characterizing as "the sublime." As a counterweight to the rationality of a neoclassical age, a number of writers, including Boileau in France and Edmund Burke in England, seized upon the idea that we can be transported to moments of ecstasy by the emotions of terror, horror, and fear. These emotions are experienced most profoundly by violent manifestations of nature—tempests, raging seas, cataracts, forest fires, untamed rivers, and craggy mountains. In the eighteenth century, for example, the Alps were discovered as objects of sublime beauty rather than mere natural obstacles. Indeed, heights of every kind were admired for their vertiginous euphorias and as lofty balconies where one could view the drama enacted upon nature's stage. In later life Jefferson was to write rapturously about the performance:

> And our own dear Monticello, where has nature spread so rich a mantle under the eye? mountains, forests, rocks, rivers. With what majesty do we ride above the storms! How sublime to look down into the workhouse of nature, to see her clouds, hail, snow, rain, thunder, all fabricated at our feet! And the glorious Sun, when rising as if out of distant water, just gliding the tops of the mountains, and giving life to all nature!

And in describing the Natural Bridge, in his *Notes on the State of Virginia*, Jefferson joined dozens of other writers of his age in affixing to a lofty natural phenomenon an ineffable spasm of feeling: "It is impossible for the emotions arising from the sublime, to be felt beyond what they are here; so beautiful an arch, so elevated, so light: and springing as it were up to heaven, the rapture of the spectator is really indescribable." If these aesthetic notions derived from the literature of the sublime were not motivation enough, he also had the authority of his architectural mentor Palladio, who urged building "upon an eminence" in "elevated and agreeable places."

By deciding to build upon a mountaintop instead of at the riverside young Jefferson made an aesthetic decision over a practical one. In this first significant choice in his building program he established a pattern that was to prevail throughout a lifetime of construction. Visitors today are captivated by the practical conveniences of Monticello: the dumbwaiter, the indoor privy, the double doors that swing in unison, the cannonball clock and its ladder, the revolving table in his bedroom, the all-weather passageways from house to dependencies. These are the domestic practicalities that were in conflict with abstract aesthetic decisions in a continuing struggle throughout Jefferson's architectural career. His design style was to choose what was often an impractical but aesthetically satisfying architectural motif, and then modify it to make the space as comfortable and livable as possible. One example where a modification could not be made was in one of the outstanding architectural features of the mansion, its dome. The dome consumed a large amount of Jefferson's financial resources and creative energies. By all practical considerations it should never have been designed into the building. It was reputedly intended to be a billiard room with its own set of stairs leading from the entrance hall, but the stairway was never built. The dome room could only be reached by a narrow staircase and a dark hallway. Because of its poor accessibility on the third floor, the dome room, or "sky room" as it was sometimes called, was used as a children's playroom, as a spare bedroom, and finally as an elegant, expensive attic storeroom. Building it was an aesthetic decision, which overrode the practical fact that the room was useless as lived-in space. So it was in deciding to build upon the top of a mountain. The site was sublime, and there he would pitch his tent, come hail or no water.

Although there were no architects in the modern sense of the word—those who professionally designed buildings—in colonial Virginia, the more substantial plantation homes were constructed by professionals. It was usually a master bricklayer or carpenter who took on the functions of what today would be a building contractor. Designs were either copied from existing houses or selected from pattern books and modified to the specifications of the owner. The master carpenter or bricklayer would then hire and supervise other carpenters, sawyers, joiners, bricklayers, masons, plasterers, and painters. Slaves usually provided the common labor, although many were also skilled artisans. Most of the Virginia plantation houses were built this way, as were the homes and public buildings of Williamsburg, the political center of colonial Virginia. Thomas Jefferson, on the other hand, from his earliest decision to build a house, made a commitment to design and supervise construction of it himself. Only once, in a moment of panic when he was getting married and the house was woefully behind schedule, did he send out a frantic appeal for help.

His decision to become his own architect and general contractor was not surprising, given what we know of this unusual young man. From his earliest years he was bookish and intellectually precocious. Family tradition has it that by the age of five he had read all the books in his father's small library. As a young boy he was taught by tutors, but at the age of nine he was sent to be boarded at the Latin school of a Scotch clergyman, William Douglas; at fourteen, the year of his father's death, he attended the log schoolhouse of the Reverend James Maury, no more than a dozen miles from Shadwell. Jefferson's opinion of Douglas was that he knew little Latin and less Greek, but to Maury he attributed the solid foundations of a classical education. After two years with Maury, young Jefferson could read Latin and Greek and he did so with pleasure the rest of his life. His intimate knowledge of the classics encouraged an interest in architecture, because in reading the Latin authors at an early, impressionable age, he absorbed the literary authority of the monuments of Rome. In later life he was to comment that he valued the classical education his father gave him above his patrimony in land and slaves. At the end of his sixteenth year he entered William and Mary College at Williamsburg, second only to Harvard as the oldest institution of higher education in the country. It was founded in 1693, but by 1760 the college held no more than a hundred students, and its faculty numbered only seven. During the first of his two years at the college Jefferson was taught exclusively by William Small, one of the men most influential in shaping his intellect. Small, who was only ten years older than Jefferson, taught natural philosophy at the college—that would be science today—but because of a shake-up of the staff during Jefferson's first year, he taught the young scholar everything—physics, metaphysics, mathematics, rhetoric, logic, ethics, and belles lettres. In particular, Small instilled in him a love of mathematics, a discipline that was to be indispensable in the geometry-based neoclassical architecture he designed. In later years, in his *Autobiography*, Jefferson wrote of Small:

> It was my great good fortune, and what probably fixed the destinies of my life, that Dr. William Small of Scotland was then Professor of Mathematics, a man profound in the most useful branches of science, with a happy talent of communication, correct and gentlemanly manners, and an enlarged

and liberal mind. He most happily for me, became soon attached to me, and made me his daily companion when not engaged in the school; and from his conversation I got my first views of the expansion of science, and of the system of things in which we are placed.

Jefferson was to speak of Small as one who was like a father to him, and no doubt the young Scotsman, who came into Jefferson's life after the death of his father, served as a surrogate parent. But Small was only in his late twenties during Jefferson's undergraduate years and he was unmarried and alone, so the friendship was probably closer to one between male peers rather than a strictly student-instructor relationship. Small was one of those brilliant products of the Scottish Enlightenment whose interests spanned all of the arts and sciences, and it is not improbable that it was through him that Jefferson was introduced to architecture as a fine art.

William Short, who for many years was Jefferson's secretary and a lifelong friend, wrote that he often heard Jefferson say that his first acquaintance with architecture came from a book he acquired from an old cabinetmaker in Williamsburg during his student days at William and Mary. This book might possibly have been an edition of Palladio's *Four Books of Architecture*, or perhaps Robert Morris's *Select Architecture*, both of which Jefferson read early in his life. (An edition of Palladio, Ware's English translation, was offered for sale in Williamsburg by the *Virginia Gazette* as early as 1751, when Jefferson was only eight years old.) The book was at any rate lost in the fire of February 1, 1770, that destroyed Shadwell. The fire was a personal tragedy, because the law papers, correspondence, records, accounts, and books of a man whose writings and books were the nucleus of his existence, vanished in smoke. It was an equal loss for Jefferson scholarship, for it destroyed nearly all the records of the formative years of his life, the crucial period that saw the growth and development of an extraordinarily complex personality. How his interests in architecture, in building, in constructing his own house, were formed can only be conjectured from the fragments of evidence that survived the Shadwell fire and from the later recollections of a man who was notoriously reluctant to reveal anything about his personal life.

During his boyhood, the example of his father must have influenced him powerfully. In 1753, when Jefferson was ten years old, his father commenced work on the house and outbuildings at the Shadwell plantation seat. Peter Jefferson's account books show that a great deal of construction was going on in 1753–54, including work on a mill and on various small houses and outbuildings. A roofing bill of £15 was paid for "covering a house." The elder Jefferson hired a professional builder, one John Biswell, and two slaves, Jupiter and Samson, were hired from their owner to work on his house. There is no way to determine how much of the work was directed by Jefferson's father, but he was a professional surveyor and he would have at least laid out the foundations square and true, a task traditionally performed by a surveyor in colonial America. Whether the new construction was an addition to an original smaller house or a completely new building cannot be determined from what remains at the site today. Certainly, there was an earlier house there—Thomas Jefferson was born in it— and it is quite likely that it formed the nucleus for the larger dwelling. A small cellar and foundations of an adjoining outbuilding have been found, but the fire, rebuilding in 1800, farming and plowing on the site, and subsequent construction at the plantation in the late nineteenth century have obscured the archaeological record. What Peter Jefferson built at Shadwell was probably a conventional Virginia farmhouse of the period.

These houses were patterned after rural English dwellings of the seventeenth and eighteenth centuries. Typically, a Virginia farmhouse was a gabled, story-and-a-half wooden house with a chimney-fireplace on each end and a central passage, front to back, dividing two rooms on the ground floor. The passageway, or hall as it was called, provided much-needed cross ventilation during the hot Virginia summers. The two lower rooms were usually a "parlor" for dining and entertaining, and a bedroom. The "chambers" on the second floor had dormer windows and sloping ceilings with poor headroom; these rooms were invariably bedrooms. An average house of this type might be 36 by 18 feet, a total floor space on both levels of about 1,300 square feet.

By modern standards this is not much space, particularly for what was usually a large colonial family. At the time Peter Jefferson was constructing the Shadwell house, he and his wife Jane had six children—two others had died as infants—and a year later, in 1755, twins were born. Accommodating a family this size in a typical Virginia farmhouse would require stuffing children into every nook and cranny, so the elder Jefferson, who was a substantial landholder at this time, no doubt built an expanded version of the Virginia farmhouse. It could be enlarged two ways: extending it lengthwise by adding a room past one of the end chimneys, or by adding a shed, running the length of the building, at the rear. If both additions were made, the result would be very much like the John Blair House, one of the oldest of the restored buildings in Colonial Williamsburg. Such a house would have between 2,500 and 3,000 square feet on both floors. There is some indication that outbuildings may have formed a balanced pair of U-shaped wings, not unlike those that Peter Jefferson's son was to design on a much grander scale atop a nearby mountain. While not spacious, a house of this dimension would allow the Jefferson family a modicum of comfort. Kitchen and privy were, of course, outbuildings, and slaves did all of the menial household work. Because young Tom Jefferson was the only son at the time Shadwell was built—he had two older sisters and three younger ones—he may have claimed an upstairs bedroom as his own when he was home between school terms. Still, there could not have been a great deal of privacy in such a house, which perhaps explains Jefferson's long rides and walks as a youth, and the bedroom-library suite he built at Monticello as his private sanctuary.

Jefferson was ten when the work started on an enlarged Shadwell, so he lived through an extended building project during which the family was forced to crowd into whatever outbuildings were available on the plantation. A boy his age would have found the construction activity exciting and educational. Those who choose to build their own homes invariably learn about construction details by observing other houses being built, and Jefferson had this experience at an early age.

In spite of what may have been fond childhood memories of family life during the construction of Shadwell, Jefferson was never very pleased with the kind of architecture it represented. In later years, in his *Notes on the State of Virginia*, he wrote that the houses of Virginia "are very rarely constructed of stone or brick; much the greatest proportion being of scantling and boards, plaistered with lime. It is impossible to devise things more ugly, uncomfortable, and happily more perishable." Shadwell was just such a house, and his comment on the ugliness and discomfort of traditional wood frame houses must certainly have reflected his experience of living in his ancestral home. There is something of an irony in his wry remark about wood frame houses being "happily perishable." Shadwell proved to be unhappily so, for when the house went up in flames while he and his mother were away visiting neighbors, he lost those things that he prized most. When the time came to design a house of his own, it was of brick, and it has not perished after well over two hundred years.

Because a building was made of brick was no guarantee that Jefferson would admire it, however. Of the public buildings in Williamsburg, he termed the College of William and Mary and the Hospital "rude, mis-shapen piles, which, but that they have roofs, would be taken for brick-kilns." One brick house in Williamsburg that he could not help but admire was the home of George Wythe, and it no doubt influenced him in a number of ways. After two years as an undergraduate at William and Mary, Jefferson, at the age of nineteen, began reading law under the tutelage of George Wythe (pronounced "With"), one of the most distinguished members of the bar of the General Court of Virginia. Because there was still no formal legal education in the colonies, this was the approved way of studying law. Wythe was a friend of Small and this friendship undoubtedly influenced Jefferson's choice of Wythe as a mentor. Wythe was also one of the most respected jurists in the colony; he was to become the nation's first law professor, and was a signer of the Declaration of Independence. According to Jefferson, he was also the best classical scholar in the colony. His letters to Jefferson in later life, printed in a large childlike hand, show a laconic wit derived from his deeply ingrained classicism. Jefferson's five-year association with him as a law student occurred at the time when he was working on plans to build atop his mountain. Wythe most certainly reinforced Jefferson's belief that the models for a pure architecture had been cast in concrete by the Romans, and formulated mathematically—with the finality of a papal bull—by the sixteenth-century master, Andrea Palladio. And during the many hours Jefferson spent in George Wythe's house, as a student and as a friend, his eye could not have failed to appreciate its fine proportions. Even though the house, built for Wythe at about 1755, is in the Georgian style that Jefferson was later to condemn, he could hardly fail to notice its elegant simplicity, the modular symmetry of its design, and the fine craftsmanship of its brickwork and carpentry.

More important perhaps than Wythe's house as an influence on Jefferson was its architect and builder, Wythe's father-in-law, Richard Taliaferro. Taliaferro (the name was pronounced, and sometimes spelled, "Toliver") is one of those elusive figures in colonial history whose name brushes against a number of prominent men and places, but whose identity is reduced to a handful of opaque records. The few biographical facts known about him are that he owned a plantation at Pohatan, a few miles from Williamsburg, where he built a substantial brick house for himself, which was torched during the Civil War. He served as sheriff and justice of the peace for James City County, so he was a respected member of the Virginia gentry. At about the same time he was building the town house in Williamsburg for his son-in-law George Wythe, he was involved in doing repairs on the Governor's House in Williamsburg. In a tantalizing comment, Thomas Lee, president of the Governor's Council, wrote to the Board of Trade in London in 1749 that a cost estimate for repairs on the Governor's House, or Palace as it was known, had been received from "our most Skillful Architect." The epithet, which from context undoubtedly referred to Taliaferro, suggested that by mid-century he had established a considerable reputation as an architect-builder. On stylistic evidence alone, several historians have assigned to Taliaferro credit for designing and building a number of the grandest houses in the colony, including William Byrd II's Westover and Carter's Grove, two of Virginia's most splendid Georgian mansions. Because Taliaferro was a part of the Small, Wythe, Jefferson circle, the young law student would have had the opportunity to discuss architecture with one of the colony's leading architect-builders. It may even be that Taliaferro shared his architectural library with Jefferson at the time he was designing the house that would grace the summit of his mountain.

One other man was important in establishing Jefferson's artistic and architectural tastes. The royal governor of the Virginia colony, Francis Fauquier, was an unlikely person to befriend Jefferson, just finishing his studies at William and Mary and beginning to read law, but this is exactly what happened. With William Small, George Wythe, and Fauquier, Jefferson became the fourth at frequent dinners at the Governor's Palace. These were cultural seminars for young Jefferson, for not only was he included in conversation with several of the best minds in the colony, but in Fauquier he found a social role model, one of those bright products of an enlightened English aristocracy: a classically educated man of cultivated gentility and a genuine scientific curiosity. Fauquier entered upon the colonial scene in 1758 like a blazing comet, "the ornament and delight of Virginia." He was, wrote John Burk, an early Virginia historian, "everything that could have been wished for by Virginia under a royal government. Generous, liberal, elegant in taste, refinement and erudition." He was a Fellow of the Royal Society, and during his tenure sent back reports to London on scientific phenomena in the colony. He also loved to listen to and perform music; he held weekly concerts at the palace, at which Jefferson, an accomplished amateur violinist, was invited to play. Fauquier was a man who craved society and who heartily enjoyed the privileges of his office. When the courts were not in session at Williamsburg, he traveled among the mansions of the Virginia plantation gentry as if conducting a royal progress. He was apparently incapable of dining alone, so when his family returned to England, he frequently called upon Small, Wythe, and Jefferson as dinner companions. In later years, Jefferson was to liken these dinner parties to something like Greek colloquia. At them, he "heard more good sense, more rational and philosophical conversation, than in all my life besides."

One of Fauquier's pleasures, which Jefferson did not approve of or acquire, was an obsession with gambling. Legend had it that during a single night at cards he lost his inherited lands and fortune. He brought to a Virginia plantation aristocracy already addicted to gaming a penchant for reckless, big-stakes card playing, a passion he indulged in at every opportunity. Although Jefferson, in his youth, gambled a bit and lost trifling sums at it, he was temperamentally incapable of taking the risks that gaming demands. During the Revolution, he would risk his very life on a political gamble, but this involved a philosophical and moral commitment to a deeply felt belief. Gambling for large sums threatened one's economic stability, and a man who accounted for every cent he made or spent during his entire life was not going to take monetary risks simply for the thrill of it.

Jefferson's admission to Fauquier's inner circle of friends raises a question: Why did the urbane royal governor welcome to his company a young man raised on a distant, backwoods plantation on the edge of the frontier, who had never seen a town before coming to Williamsburg? It is true that Jefferson had the social credentials: although his father had been one of those opportunistic land speculators who had lately carved a plantation from the western regions of Virginia and was therefore not from one of the established families in the colony, his mother was a Randolph whose family ties were the Tidewater dynasties associated with that illustrious name. Jefferson's schoolmates and friends were the scions of some of the great plantation owners of the colony, John Page, Dabney Carr, John Walker, William Fleming, and Thomas Nelson. All would distinguish themselves in later life. But it was not his family connections alone that brought him invitations to the governor's table; it was his intellectual precocity. In his early twenties, he was probably the most widely read young man of his generation in the colony.

From the time he began reading law until he started his career as a lawyer at the age of twenty-three, he read and studied as much as fifteen hours a day, a self-discipline that some of his friends found incomprehensible. He had started this regimen of intense study while he was still a student at William and Mary. During his college years he would rise at dawn and study at times until two next morning. His only exercise during this period of concentrated reading was a mile-long run at twilight. John Page, one of his closest college friends, recorded that Jefferson was able to "tear himself away from his dearest friends" to return to his studies. Jefferson himself reported in later life that during his years of preparation for the law he was a "hard student," and this was confirmed by a course of study for the law he prepared at this time for a friend, one that undoubtedly paralleled his own reading. It shows a staggering list of prescribed studies not only in law but also in languages, mathematics, science, history, politics, and literature.

It would not have been Jefferson's reading in law that impressed Governor Fauquier, but his wide knowledge of science and the arts. A list of books Jefferson proposed a few years later for a "private library," based in all likelihood on his own replacement library for the one lost in the Shadwell fire, shows a close acquaintance with the major novelists, dramatists, poets, philosophers, and literary critics of his age. He was, then, a young gentleman who could hold his own at the Governor's Palace by reason of a serious interest in the life of the mind, as evidenced by what he was to call later his "canine appetite for reading." If Fauquier impressed Jefferson as a model English gentleman of education and taste, the royal governor must have been equally impressed with so much erudition in one so young.

But Fauquier may also have encouraged Jefferson's interest in architecture in a more direct way. In London, before coming to the colonies, Fauquier rented a house in a fashionable section of town, now Argyll Street near Oxford Circus, from none other than James Gibbs, one of England's most illustrious architects. Like Fauquier, Gibbs was a member of the Royal Society, and in the close-knit circles of the privileged classes of London, the two men were quite likely social acquaintances. Gibbs had designed some of the most impressive buildings in England in the Wren style. His masterpiece, St. Martin-in-the-Fields Church, remains one of London's architectural landmarks, its monumental Corinthian portico and soaring baroque steeple overlooking Trafalgar Square. His reputation was increased throughout England and the colonies by two publications, *A Book of Architecture*, a pattern book of his most popular buildings, and *Rules for Drawing the Several Parts of Architecture*, a textbook to be used for designing the orders correctly. *A Book of Architecture* was the most popular style book of the eighteenth century, and Jefferson had a copy of it, quite possibly purchased at the urging of Fauquier. He also owned Gibbs's *Rules* and used it to set the proportions for the earliest drawings of the porticoes at Monticello.

Because of the paucity of records from this period of his life, one can only infer from admittedly thin slices of evidence the part played by Small, Wythe, Taliaferro, and Fauquier in Jefferson's architectural education. All no doubt influenced him to some degree, perhaps Taliaferro and Fauquier more directly. His urge to build was not entirely a product of his architectural education, however; there were other forces at work, more psychological than rational, and the roots of these are also elusive and conjectural. Again the Shadwell fire is to blame for the absence of historical fact, but in later life he also destroyed some of his correspondence in a conscious effort to preserve his privacy.

[45]

One significant observation does emerge from the scant records, how-ever—his relationship with his mother was not a loving one.

Virtually nothing is known of her as a personality; after her death, Jefferson apparently burned every piece of correspondence with her. Unlike his father, about whom Jefferson wrote with admiration, his mother is never mentioned in an emotional context in the few surviving references to her. Jefferson's relationship with her is established not by what he did or was as a son, but by what he didn't do, and what he wasn't. Perhaps the most telling comment on his feelings toward her is contained in the letter to John Page recounting the Shadwell fire. Although Jane Randolph Jefferson, a widow, lost her house, all of her possessions, and was left homeless in the winter with five dependent daughters and a teenage son, there is not a line about her or about his five sisters and younger brother. Was anyone injured? Was anything saved? How were they managing with all their possessions gone? Where were they living? Not a word. His only care is the loss of his own books and papers, and how he is going to conduct his court cases without the notes that went up in flames. The letter reveals several things about Jefferson and the age he lived in. At this point in his life, his world was circumscribed by his own concerns; there is seemingly a hard, unattractive glaze of selfishness on this polished young man. This callousness about the misfortunes of his family is directed primarily, however, at his mother. He was, throughout his adult life, generous and affectionate toward his brother and sisters, but merely dutiful toward his mother. Where his mother was con-cerned, there appeared to be deep conflicts, the details of which can never be known, but which were expressed mostly in silence. The only place she is mentioned in a public document is in his *Autobiog-raphy*, started at the age of sixty-six and abandoned, seemingly when he reached a point where he would have had to reveal something of his inner life. There, his mention is coupled with a sarcastic reference to her English background. Jane Randolph Jefferson, he wrote, "was the daughter of Isham Randolph, one of the seven sons of that name and family settled in Dungeness, in Goochland. They trace their pedigree far back in England and Scotland, to which let every one ascribe the faith and merit he chooses." Even when one discounts Jefferson's anti-British bias, the comment seems gratuitously cold toward his mother.

The reference to "they" (it was, after all, his own pedigree as well) distances Jefferson from her, in spite of the fact that he lived with her at Shadwell on and off until he was twenty-seven. This coolness is perhaps nowhere clearer than in his passing reference to her death in 1776, a letter he wrote to her brother William Randolph, then living in England: "The death of my mother you have probably not heard of. This happened on the last day of March after an illness of not more than an hour. We supposed it to have been apoplectic." As in the case of the letter to Page, there is no expression of emotion or loss associated with his mother; the news of her death is passed on to her brother as an obligatory duty.

The cause of his difficulties with his mother can only be guessed at. One source of antagonism was certainly the terms of Peter Jefferson's will, whereby Jane Jefferson remained, during her lifetime, the mistress of Shadwell. As long as Jefferson lived with her, he was under her control. He was a guest in her house and not the master of his own. In the paternalistic society Jefferson lived in, women were essentially breeders and housekeepers; economic and social power belonged to men. Jane Jefferson had given birth to ten children in fifteen years, and had run the plantation when her husband was away on his frequent surveying expeditions. After she became a widow, she continued to raise her children and, with the help of overseers, to manage Shadwell. She was anything but a passive, retiring adornment to a plantation squire's household. She must have been a formidable woman and a difficult one for her eldest son to live with. He was forced to straddle the male world of Williamsburg, with its privileged caste of genteel intellectuals, and the matriarchy at Shadwell. At Williamsburg, women were the objects of flirtation and courtship; men conducted the affairs of state, engaged in business, and played at male games. Shadwell was a woman's domain ruled by his mother and five sisters. The contrast must have been made abundantly clear to him each time he changed his residence from Shadwell to Williamsburg to Shadwell.

There is an important new piece of evidence of this antipathy toward his mother. A recent redating of his Literary Commonplace Book, a journal into which he copied passages from his reading, has forced scholars to reinterpret a series of bitterly antifeminine quotations

Jefferson recorded from a variety of literary sources. From Milton's *Paradise Lost*, for example, he copied:

> O! why did God,
> Creator wise! that Peopl'd highest Heav'n
> With spirits masculine, create at last
> This Novelty on Earth, this fair Defect
> Of Nature? And not fill the world at once
> With Men, as Angels, without feminine?

And from Milton's *Samson Agonistes* he transcribed:

> Once joined, the contrary she proves, a Thorn
> Intestine, far within defensive arms
> A cleaving Mischief, in his play to Virtue
> Adverse & turbulent, or by her Charms
> Draws him away enslav'd
> With Dotage, & his sense deprav'd
> To Folly & shameful Deeds which Ruin ends.

Some of the most aggressive passages were from Thomas Otway's *Orphan*:

> I'd leave the World for him that hates a Woman,
> Woman the Fountain of all human Frailty!
> What mighty ills have not been done by Woman?
> Who was't betray'd the Capitol? A Woman.
> Who lost Marc Anthony the World? A Woman.
> Who was the Cause of a long ten years War,
> And laid at last old Troy in ashes? Woman.
> Destructive, damnable, deceitful Woman!

> Wed her!
> No! were she all Desire could wish, as fair
> As would the vainest of her sex be thought,
> With Wealth beyond what woman's pride could waste,
> She should not cheat me of my Freedom. Marry!

When I am old & weary of the World,
I may grow desperate,
And take a Wife to mortify withal.

                                    . . . Your sex
Was never in the Right; Y'are always false,
Or silly; ev'n your Dresses are not more
Fantastic than your Appetites . . .

"O Zeus," he copied in Greek from Euripides, "why hast thou established women, a curse deceiving men in the light of the sun?" And, "Mortals should beget children from some other source and there should be no womanhood; thus there would be no ill for men." From Virgil: "Woman is always a changing and inconstant thing."

This misogynistic collection has been seen by Jefferson's biographers as a reaction to his being rejected by Rebecca Burwell, whom he had courted and hoped to marry; his hurt and humiliation came pouring out into his Commonplace Book. Recently, however, one Jefferson scholar, after closely analyzing Jefferson's handwriting in these passages, has argued persuasively that they were written years before Rebecca rejected Jefferson in 1764. Some of the quotations may have been copied as early as the 1750s when, after the death of his father, he began living under the rule of his mother. "The strain of misogyny in the Literary Commonplace Book," this scholar concludes, "must be put down to another cause" than Jefferson's unsuccessful courtship of Rebecca Burwell. The one who is the most likely target of his woman-baiting is the mother whose authority he was forced to live under until he reached the age of twenty-one. That his antifeminine literary collection is really antimatriarchal is supported by the many passages he copied having to do with rebellion to, and anger at, authority, and the difficulty of attaining women's love. He took from Milton's *Paradise Lost* the lines:

                                    Thus it shal befal
Him who to Worth in Women overtrusting
Lets her Will rule, restraint she will not brook . . .

And from Shakespeare's *Julius Caesar:*

[49]

Do not presume too much upon my Love;
I may do that I shall be sorry for.

From Nicholas Rowe's *Tamerlane*:

Yet ere thou rashly urge my Rage too far,
I warn thee take Heed; I am a Man,
And have the Frailties common to Man's Nature;
The fiery seeds of Wrath are in my Temper,
And may be blown up to so fierce a Blaze,
As Wisdom cannot rule.

From Mallet's *Euridice*:

. . . I have try'd
Each shape, each Art of varied Love to win her;
Alternate Prayers, & Threats, the soothing Skill
Of Passionate Sincerity. The Fire
Of Rapturous Vows, but all these Arts were vain.

From Milton's *Samson Agonistes*:

It is not Virtue, Wisdom, Valour, Wit,
Strength, Comeliness of shape, or amplest Merit
That Woman's Love can win or long inherit;
But what it is, hard is to say. . . .

Therefore God's universal Law
Gave to Man despotic power
Over his Female in due awe,
Nor from that Right to part an Hour . . .

No single one of these passages can be said to offer more than a hint at rebellion to the authority of his mother, but taken together, and placed alongside the antifeminine excerpts, the outline of a fundamental conflict emerges. Peter Jefferson died at the beginning of Jefferson's adolescence, an age when boys struggle with issues of independence-dependence, separation from parental control, and the assertion of their maleness. In the paternalistic world of eighteenth-century Virginia, these developmental struggles could be excruciatingly painful; how much more so for one such as Jefferson, who was again placed in the power of a mother to whom his ties of dependency had been severed years before. Once he reached the age of his majority, these developmental anxieties were, at least in part, resolved and the antifeminine, angry, frustrated, and rebellious passages in his Commonplace Book disappear. Significantly, he became twenty-one in 1764, the year of his rejection by Rebecca Burwell. This year may have been unhappy in love, but it marked his legal independence from his mother.

Jefferson's decision to build a place of his own seemed to be motivated by a conscious desire to escape from the rule of his mother and the crush of too much family in too little space. It was to be a hermitage—in fact, he called it the Hermitage before changing the name to Monticello—a place where he could retire to his studies and enjoy the intellectual companionship of a few choice friends. It was to be, in short, everything Shadwell was not—spacious, elegant, private, artistic, and *his*.

At the unconscious level, the house of his imagination was to satisfy his needs for both inner space and outer space. Its exterior face, the one exposed to the society of his intellectual peers, was a Palladian mask: abstract ideas of order rendered in ancient post and lintel forms. It was a counterpart to the face he himself showed to the world. Its inner space, however, was to be something quite personal—maternal even. By his artifice, he could create, perhaps, a womblike place of warmth, comfort, and love. Palladio was not to be abandoned in this space; on the contrary, it was to be as pure in its Palladianism as was the exterior, but through the architect's skill the public impersonality of the traditional Palladian palace or villa could be transformed to the intimate domesticity of hearth and home.

This urge to break away from the Shadwell bonds came very early. In 1763, when he was only twenty and beginning to read law with George Wythe, Jefferson had toyed with the idea of building a house. In a letter to his friend John Page, he wrote that "to prevent the inconveniency of moving my lodgings for the future, I think to build. . . . No castle though I assure you, only a small house which shall contain a room for myself and another for you." Whether he intended to build a house in Williamsburg, where Page was staying and where Jefferson was reading law with George Wythe, or at the Monticello site is unclear, but the comment does indicate that the young man had already decided to build a house five years before he actually started clearing the land on his mountain. The fact that he was shortly to come into his inheritance at the age of twenty-one may have had something to do with these plans. Nothing came of them at the time, but during those years when he was studying law he was thinking about designs for a house on his mountain and putting them down on paper.

The design he ultimately settled on was by no means an original one; it was richly derivative of the works he had been reading, particularly one of the architectural pattern books, Robert Morris's *Select Architecture*. The house consisted of a central two-story block of rooms with wings on each side, a design typical of small country retreats for aristocratic gentlemen. What gave the design its architectural distinction and made it one of the most stylishly advanced buildings in the South were its classical porticoes on the east and west front, each an exercise in academic Palladianism.

It is sometimes difficult for a generation living in the space age, with its vision fixed steadily on the future, to understand the eighteenth-century intellectual's obsession with the past. All ideas about progress were tempered by the belief that in the distant past, the golden ages of Greece and Rome, giants had discovered the great truths of nature and had fixed them to the grid of the universe. Our notion that scientific law is an ongoing evolutionary process, where new hypotheses overturn old theories, only to be overthrown by a later generation, would be nonsense to Enlightenment philosophers. In the previous century, Newton had unlocked the secrets of the universe and had discovered a vast, exquisitely ordered permanent mechanistic system, which operated from microcosm to macrocosm by immutable law. Newton's new physics, however, did not cancel the wisdom of the ancients in matters of aesthetics. They had intuitively discovered the laws of order in the arts and had left perfect paradigms in the literature, sculpture, and architecture of Greece and Rome. (In music, the sounds had been lost but the Pythagorean principles survived.)

Aristotle had codified the laws of drama in his *Poetics*, Polyclitus did as much for sculpture in his *Canon*, and Vitruvius had formulated the laws of architecture in his *De Architectura*. That these laws had been arrived at inductively, by studying the works of poetry, sculpture, and architecture of their generations, did not seriously concern those who rediscovered them, first in the Renaissance and later during the Enlightenment. So complete and unchallengeable was the authority of the ancients that to deny them was to forfeit one's credentials as a serious artist or critic.

Whether Vitruvius, who lived during the reign of Augustus, was a genius or a mediocrity was inconsequential, for his book was the only one to survive from antiquity; therefore his authority was absolute. It was Vitruvius who handed down to posterity the classical orders, a repertory of pedestal, column, architrave, frieze, and cornice derived from Greek and Roman temple architecture. He defined in detail three of the orders: from simple to more ornate, the Doric, Ionic, and Corinthian, and mentioned, briefly, a fourth more primitive order, the Tuscan. Renaissance theorists added a fifth, the Composite, a combination of Ionic and Corinthian.

The rediscovery of Vitruvius's work by the Renaissance humanists led to the canonization of the orders into architectural law, as if the marble columns had been carried down from Mt. Sinai by Moses. The religious metaphor is not inappropriate, for each order was associated by Vitruvius with a derivative place and was appropriate to a particular God. Vitruvius had also related the harmony of the various parts of an order to the proportions of the human body. This became a permanent part of the iconography of the Renaissance through the depiction of a drawing of Vitruvian man, his arms and legs extended to form the perfect geometrical forms, the circle and square. (The figure was drawn by many artists, but it is Leonardo's version that has been reproduced to the point where it is now a cliché.) During the Renaissance, the relationship between column type and the human figure took on an almost mystical Neoplatonic significance: because the human body was created by God, the orders too were divinely ordained. Gender was also given to the orders: Tuscan and Doric were ruggedly masculine, Corinthian chastely virginal. A church dedicated to a male saint would be appropriately Doric, while a chapel in honor of the Virgin Mary should be Corinthian.

It was not the quasireligious overtones of the Vitruvian dogma that attracted eighteenth-century intellectuals such as Jefferson to classical architecture, however; it was the rational, mathematically perfect ratios of the orders, the relationship of part to whole that gave to Roman buildings the purity of Newtonian law. No one expressed this purity with more elegance and authority than Andreas Palladio in his *I Quattri Libri del' Architettura*, the work that was to become the biblical text of neoclassical architecture. Indeed, Jefferson used that term years later in referring to it: "Palladio is the Bible," he told a friend, and added that he should get a copy of the master's treatise "and stick close to it."

In his *Quattri Libri*, first published in Venice in 1570, Palladio defines the orders, gives technical details on construction, then presents examples of town houses, villas, public works, and measured drawings of some of the monuments of antiquity. All parts of a building must be in perfect balance with the rest, and this harmony of proportion must conform to the choice of order used. The grammar of the orders is as prescriptive as the syntax of language. The basic unit is the module, the diameter of the column; each of the orders has a different diameter and a different ratio of diameter to length. Doric is thick and relatively squat, Corinthian thin and slender. The distance between the columns, the intercolumniation, is also fixed by rule, as are the decorative motifs associated with each column type. To a modern architect, this would seem positively shackling, but to an eighteenth-century mind like Jefferson's, it was as liberating as the sonnet form was to Shakespeare or the fugue to Bach. The rules were indeed inflexible, as were Newton's laws, and as are the structural rules of English grammar, but the fenced boundaries gave to the architect an aesthetic and a moral norm: if a building was designed according to the rules, it was not only beautiful, it was right. As long as an architect designed by the rules, he did not have to worry about matters of propriety or taste; it was a liberation from concerns about excess or vulgarity. This did not mean that one could slavishly imitate the Palladian rules in a mechanical way. A successful building combined the vocabulary of the architect's spatial design with the syntax of the orders; the designer's goal was to press his creativity against the fixed form.

Palladio's *Four Books* had influenced English architecture for more than two centuries, particularly through the work of Inigo Jones and Christopher Wren. In the early seventeenth century, Jones adapted Palladio's Italianate designs to the English climate and taste; his Banqueting Hall at Whitehall Palace is a monument of early English Palladianism. Christopher Wren, who rebuilt London after the great fire of 1666 and designed St. Paul's, was responsible for a more modest style of Palladian country estate that was eminently exportable to the colonies. Numerous Wren-influenced builders were to develop a country house that was compact, private, and livable. The style of Wren and his disciples became unfashionable in England in the eighteenth century under the powerful influence of Lord Burlington. Rediscovering Palladio in the original, Burlington built for himself one of the most Palladian buildings in England, Chiswick House, patterned after the master's Villa Rotunda at Vicenza. This kind of monumental architecture was unsuited to the colonies, however; planters had neither the inherited fortunes nor the skilled labor and technology to build on such a scale.

It was the Wren-inspired Palladianism of the English country house that found its way to Virginia, mainly through three Williamsburg buildings, William and Mary College, the capitol, and the Governor's House. Indeed, tradition has it that Wren designed the college and the Governor's House, although modern scholars question both attributions. At any rate, these two-story brick buildings in the Wren tradition, with a central hall and four rooms on the ground floor—known as a double-pile—became models for a number of Virginia mansions and established what was to become known as the Georgian style in Virginia. It was an architectural style well suited for the Virginia climate: it had high ceilings and two walls of windows in every room for ventilation in the summer, and its brick construction and massive fireplaces made it a tight, warm house in winter. Although its exterior lacked the Palladian portico—the columns and pediment that are the distinguishing trait of Palladianism—the interiors of eighteenth-century Georgian mansions were often graced with Doric or Ionic pilasters, architraves, and decorative motifs.

This was the simple, straightforward English country house plan that Jefferson rejected in favor of textbook Palladianism. It was not the monumental style of Lord Burlington's circle to which he turned, however, but to the modest Palladian villas of the pattern books. With a copy of a style book in one hand and Palladio's *Four Books* in the other, he was ready to design his house. If this seems inordinately academic, it is because Jefferson, in spite of his associations with Fauquier, Small, and Wythe, was still quite provincial. Until 1766, when he was twenty-three and took a three-month trip to Annapolis,. Philadelphia, and New York to do some sightseeing, but mainly to be inoculated against smallpox, he had not traveled beyond the Virginia colony. Virtually all of his knowledge of Palladian architecture came from the engraved plates of books. The two literary sources of his designs were mainly Palladio and Robert Morris. From Morris's *Select Architecture* he found a plate that fit the scale and style of house he had been searching for. Morris's work was the ideal pattern book for someone like Jefferson, a young bachelor who wanted to build a residence that was stylish, yet affordable. Morris's plates showed a variety of small houses and outbuildings, each with an elevation and a floor plan. The fifty plates in the book were accompanied by brief descriptions of what each building was designed for and the approximate cost of constructing it. One can almost imagine the young law student paging through *Select Architecture* and returning to plate 3 to ponder its possibilities. It was a center block of two stories with symmetrical one-story wings; on each side of the wings was a courtyard to which was attached a dependency. "It was proposed for a single Gentleman," Morris wrote, and added, "to execute this Building in a workmanlike Manner it will amount to the Sum of 680 £." Jefferson made a tracing of the plan, eliminating the dependencies—he had other plans for these—and inked in some dimensions. He made the wings of the two-story house 17 by 17 feet and the center block 24 by 28, a total of 2,500 square feet, an average-size house by today's standards, but much larger when one considers that kitchen, laundry, privy, and utility spaces were relegated to outbuildings; the floor space was all living space. A house this size would allow a master bedroom in one wing, a dining room in the other, and an entrance hall and large parlor or entertainment room in the center. Upstairs, there was room for a library and two bedrooms. Although Morris's plate shows no architectural orders, there was no question that Jefferson intended to have them. On the tracing he penciled in four circles to indicate free-standing columns for a classical portico.

No doubt, Morris's cost estimate seemed rather steep to Jefferson, for it was nearly a third more than what a house this size would cost if built by a professional in Virginia. The Robert Carter house in Williamsburg, a two-story mansard-roofed building of 3,500 square feet, for example, had sold in 1761 for £650, including the lot. More-over, Jefferson would have calculated that by designing and building the house himself, using materials from his plantations and his own slave labor, the house could probably be raised for a small fraction of Morris's estimate.

His tracing of the Morris plate was only the start of an evolving series of designs that would culminate in a finished plan for the Mon-ticello residence. His surviving drawings show that during this period he executed a number of studies, exploring the possibilities of a large rectangular building, as well as the center block and wing design. In one, he had an arched loggia in place of one of the porticoes; in another, there were four porticoes indicated, one on each side of the building, somewhat like Palladio's Villa Rotunda, the most famous of the mas-ter's country villas. He also made renderings of dependencies and outbuildings, some of which appeared in the final house plan; others were architectural études, five-finger exercises in house design.

These detailed architectural drawings were in themselves re-markable for Jefferson's time. Very few houses in Virginia were con-structed from finished drawings such as Jefferson's. Although some builders drew finished plans and elevations—particularly the master carpenters of Philadelphia, the finest craftsmen in America—most worked from no more than perfunctory sketches. When one builds in the vernacular tradition, no plan is really necessary; each new house, with minor modifications, is constructed like the last one. This is still true today. Any professional carpenter can build a conventional stud-frame house with no more plans than the room dimensions and the placement of doors and windows. Most colonial builders worked in much the same way, relying on pattern books or the sketch of another house for the basic floor plan, and executing the construction according to the ways of the hand that dated back to the Middle Ages.

Jefferson apparently learned to do architectural drawings at an early age. His father was not only a surveyor, but he had drawn, with Joshua Fry, a map of Virginia that won considerable recognition for him. His son was understandably proud of Peter Jefferson's achievement, so much so that years later he appended a copy of the map to his *Notes on the State of Virginia.* Jefferson inherited his father's drawing instruments, and also the surveyor's concern for precision and accuracy. His early architectural drawings are executed entirely in ink, a medium that allows no errors and requires thorough planning before touching pen to paper. It was only much later in his career as an amateur architect that he switched to pencil, a freer and more creative medium.

These early drawings and the voluminous notes that accompany them reveal much about the Jefferson personality. They are of a kind with his other known character traits: self-discipline, his insistence on personal privacy, his need to save and account for everything—money, books, records, facts. Even his choice of the law as a profession was a measure of his desire for an ordered social and political universe made permanent by rationally ordained statutes. He became a revolutionary in part because of what he perceived to be the crown's breach of the integrity of the English legal system. This was not simply a political or ethical decision on his part; in taxing the colonies without representation, Parliament denied the validity of his very personality, of everything that he was. His architectural drawings are symbolic of his kind of compulsive personality. Lines are executed mechanically, with rule and compass, to precise scale. Measurements are carried out to four or five decimal places, an absurdity in the building trades where carpenters and bricklayers are often lucky if they can keep to the inch rather than the ten-thousandth of an inch. For Jefferson, these measurements were not simply practical means to an end, instructions to an artisan; they were mathematical absolutes that recorded universal verities.

When Jefferson made freehand drawings, as he sometimes did, they were terrible. He seemed incapable of drawing a straight line, or of joining two lines together. It was as if he consciously made a distinction between mechanically accurate drawings, which were ink-and-paper maps of Palladian law, and mere sketches that were only the dance of ideas around these laws. A freehand sketch could never be precise and accurate, so it had no business looking accurate; that could only lead to confusion and error. No doubt he could have drawn a better freehand elevation or plan if he had wanted to learn—he was certainly capable of learning just about everything else—but such a drawing would have been at odds with the very ethics of architecture, the rightness and wrongness of it.

The house design he finally settled on had a double portico—one order on top of another—on the east front, and most likely an identical portico facing the west. He drew a detailed elevation of the eastern double portico, and this is the only surviving indication of what the original version of Monticello looked like from the exterior. This two-story portico, a Doric order on the ground floor topped by an Ionic order on the second story, was the most striking architectural feature of the plan. In deciding on a double portico, he chose a design that was both expensive and difficult to build. Columns in particular were costly because they required the kind of skilled labor that was scarce in the colony. The double portico had eight columns, four of them fluted Ionic columns with carved volutes on the capital. They presented a real problem in cost and skill, which is why they were never completed. As a rule, Jefferson almost always considered expense and the difficulty of execution in his construction equation. However, he often designed what he desired, and trusted that he could produce the money and skilled labor to build it.

The double portico was vintage Palladio; in fact, it was one of his favorite architectural motifs. In his *Four Books*, there are nine houses or villas with superimposed porticoes. One of them, plate 36 of the Ware translation, is a similar, if grander, version of the one Jefferson designed. The house for which this plan was drawn, the Villa Cornaro, still stands in the small town of Piombino Dese, Italy.

Jefferson had an example of a double portico much closer at hand, however. The capitol building in Williamsburg was one of the more impressive pieces of architecture in the colony. The version of the capitol that now stands at Colonial Williamsburg, an H-shaped brick building with rounded turrets, was built in 1704 and lasted until 1747, when it was gutted by fire. It was rebuilt in 1753, and this was the version that Jefferson knew. (This burned down in 1832; Colonial

Williamsburg reconstructed the original version in 1934.) The second capitol building had a double portico, which Jefferson described in *Notes on the State of Virginia*:

> The Capitol is a light and airy structure, with a portico in front of two orders, the lower of which being Doric, is tolerably just in proportions and ornaments, save only that the intercolonnations are too large. The upper is Ionic, much too small for that on which it is mounted, its ornaments not proper to the order, nor proportioned within themselves. It is crowned with a pediment, which is too high for its span. Yet, on the whole, it is the most pleasing piece of architecture we have.

Only recently has a small painting of the second capitol building been found, and it matches perfectly Jefferson's description of it. The faults Jefferson noted are apparent even to the untrained eye.

Jefferson's admiration for the capitol building, in spite of its less than perfect Palladianism, helps explain his choice of the double portico for his home at Monticello. The capitol was the building he grew up with during his formative years at Williamsburg; it was the only example of anything like classical architecture he knew. At Williamsburg, he would have seen it daily. When he discovered the *Four Books* and compared the capitol's flawed double portico with those of Palladio, he may well have determined that he could do it much better. And he did. The orders he designed for Monticello are painstaking examples of Palladian orthodoxy.

Two unusual features of the house design, the semi-octagon rooms at the ends of both wings, and an octagon bay facing the west portico, were not on the original plan. They were added after the basement walls were already up. There is no record of why he changed his mind and added the octagons, but it is typical of the way he worked during a lifetime of construction, and is consistent with the way all owner-builders think. As long as the control of house construction is in the hands of the owner, changes are always possible. Building is a fluid, evolving process, each addition to the house presenting new possibilities and new ideas. No amateur builder can ever fully imagine what a floor plan on paper will look like and feel like as enclosed space until it is realized in brick and wood. Jefferson was no exception. When he was able to stroll through the enclosed walls of his basement and perceive what the parlor, bedroom, and dining room would feel like a floor above, he obviously decided that his house was too small. The octagons on each wing added two new rooms and the octagon bay in the parlor enlarged that room by twenty percent.

His choice of octagons for this additional space established a pattern that he was to repeat throughout his career as an amateur architect; it was to become one of his favorite design motifs. Years later, he designed and built at his plantation at Poplar Forest an octagon-shaped house as a retreat from a Monticello that had become more of a hotel than a house. The octagon rooms were an original idea when Jefferson designed them into his house; there were none in the houses or buildings he knew in Virginia. Rather than Palladio, his inspiration was Morris's *Select Architecture*, which has numerous octagon designs. In his *Four Books*, Palladio uses the circle and square, the perfect forms of antiquity, for his buildings. His authority was the small Roman circular temple, such as the Temple of Vesta. The circle or elliptical forms may be fine for monumental architecture, but they are a nightmare for domestic house design, which is why Morris largely abandoned them in favor of the octagon. Curved surfaces are difficult to build (timbers and bricks have ninety-degree edges) and rectangular windows and doors in a curved surface take a great deal of skill to execute.

The octagon, on the other hand, squares the circle. Its virtue is that it gives the illusion of a circular space while retaining flat surfaces for the carpenter and bricklayer. And furniture naturally fits better against a straight wall. Each of the eight walls (or five where a semi-octagon is used, as it was at Monticello) allows a single window or door, the whole permitting a maximum penetration of light and air. In this respect, the octagon shape is a very modern architectural design, and its use by Jefferson places him among the earliest of those architects who assaulted the barriers between inside and outside. This was particularly desirable on Jefferson's mountaintop because of the splendid views. In his octagonal bedroom, he could sleep among the stars and rise with the sun on his brow.

The light and air did not come without a price, however. The octagon bow rooms had no fireplaces and therefore were icy in the winter, particularly the one facing north. Years later, when he remodeled the house to its present plan, a stove was added to the bow room, and a double glass door was placed between it and the dining room. The octagon on the south side would, of course, be bathed in sunshine in the winter, and this was the reason that Jefferson placed his bedroom here. He later found, however, that the glass walls of his bedroom octagon gave him no privacy, so he took pains to modify them with blinds.

There is one further observation about Jefferson's infatuation with the octagon. If the house one builds is indeed an attempt to recapture maternal love and protection, then the design of the house should in some way symbolize this need. "Life begins well," writes Gaston Bachelard, the modern Aristotle of architectural space; "it begins enclosed, protected, all warm in the bosom of the house." When Jefferson added the semi-octagons to his house, changing its geometry from angles to angled curves, he may at some very deep level have seen in this new form the suggestion of the house as bosom—"enclosed, protected, all warm." When he remodeled the house, he not only retained his semi-octagons, he doubled them at each wing and added that most obvious mammillary architectural form, the dome, making his house upon a mountain rich in maternal echoes. Erik Erikson saw these echoes as a "deep nostalgia" and asked whether this nostalgia was for that "mysterious mother" Jefferson concealed from us by destroying her correspondence. In rebuilding Monticello into "his own maternal shrine," Erikson wrote, Jefferson "crowned the building with an octagonal dome, thus adding an equally dominant maternal element to the strong facade."

In designing the dependencies, Jefferson once again drew upon Palladio's authority. A number of the designs for villas in Palladio's *Four Books* contain L-shaped wings of connected utility buildings (offices) extending on each side of the main structure. At first, Jefferson flirted with a grandiose plan for throwing a complete rectangle of outbuildings around the mountaintop. Then common sense asserted itself and he redrew his plan to a more modest Palladian double L-shaped configuration. Extending from the wings of the house, forming an L on each side, would be a row of rooms containing all the necessary dependencies for a Virginia plantation seat. Each L would be anchored at the end by a pavilion, a square, one-room brick building with a gabled roof. What was ingenious about this plan, and where it departed from the Palladian model, was that the double string of dependencies would be partially below ground. From the house, all one would see would be a wooden deck, or terrace as Jefferson called it, built over the roofs of the dependencies. This deck would join the house to the above-ground pavilions at the end of the L, and present an unobstructed view from the house. He also planned to add decorative aboveground temples or "outchambers" at the ninety-degree turns of the two L's, and toyed with various architectural styles for them over the years, but they were never built.

Placing the dependencies below grade was, of course, made possible by the downward slope of the mountaintop. Selecting this difficult location had certainly given Jefferson a number of problems to deal with, but in this one respect it was an opportunity, and he took advantage of it by cleverly adapting his plan to the site. The basement of the house would be level with the dependencies, but only one wall of each of the offices would butt up against the mountain; the opposite wall would have above-ground doors and windows open to light and ventilation. Outside of the string of offices would be a roofed corridor allowing a dry passage from any of the dependencies to the main house. Although Jefferson juggled the placement of the various service rooms within the string of dependencies during his long years of construction, the basic plan he drew in his twenties when he first started to build is the one that remains today. This was not to be true of the main house; it would be partially dismantled and rebuilt to twice its original size.

A study of the architectural drawings for Monticello shows a rapid mastery of the neoclassical architectural idiom by a young man who was a quick study in everything he did. When he turned his hand to architecture, he did it with the same degree of concentration and thoroughness that he showed in his law profession and later in politics. His method when he set about learning anything was to research the subject completely, first by a bibliographic search through his rapidly growing library, and then through conversations with whatever experts he could find, and finally by direct observation. Although he had a phenomenal memory, he did not rely on it; he took copious notes. His architectural drawings, whether quick sketches or finished plans, are accompanied by written notes on construction details and measurements.

When he began drawing designs for his house, his ideas were completely derivative; he turned to authorities readily at hand in books available in the colonies—Palladio, Morris, and Gibbs. As he gained confidence, he explored variations on the themes of these three authorities, always keeping close to Palladian orthodoxy, however. We in the twentieth century seek flights of creative originality from our artists, but in the eighteenth century, originality was not a virtue when it passed the narrow boundaries of the "rules." In what was to become one of the catch phrases of the age, Alexander Pope admonished that true originality "was nature to advantage dressed, / What oft was thought but ne'er so well expressed." "Nature" was the universal laws of Newton and the ancients and one did not tamper with those, but seen through the artist's veil, they took on a new luminescence.

Jefferson's plan for his house on a mountaintop fit this definition perfectly. There was nothing really new about his design; it was a composite of ideas drawn from common sources. But it was conceived with high intelligence and a complete mastery of the theory that supported it. For its day and its place, it had elegance and style, exactly what one would expect from the Thomas Jefferson we have come to know.

3

"Today My Workmen Assemble"

DURING THOMAS JEFFERSON'S first term as President, on the recommendation of a friend in Philadelphia, he hired a blacksmith to work at Monticello. On his way to the Jefferson plantation from Philadelphia, the smith, William Stewart, passed through Richmond and presented himself to one of Jefferson's agents for an advance on his salary. He did not make a favorable first impression. "I advanced him $40 on his showing me a letter from you," wrote the agent, Jefferson's cousin, George Jefferson. He then went on to admonish the President that he must have hired Stewart "on very slight acquaintance" because "he was with me twice a day (once in the morning) and was either much intoxicated, or is actually a madman. I do not know in what capacity he is going to Monticello, although I asked him; for he gave me such incoherent answers that I could not understand him." He then advised the President to be "on your guard" if Stewart was to be in charge of anyone or anything.

Five months later, Stewart appeared before George Jefferson again in Richmond. This time he wanted and received $105—"which I was obliged to let him have or I supposed suffer him to go to jail." The President wrote back that he approved of getting Stewart out of whatever scrape he was in by advancing him the money and added, "he is the best workman in America, but the most eccentric one."

When Stewart first arrived at Monticello, Jefferson built a special shop for him on Mulberry Row, and when he was not drunk, the smith was a productive worker. He was, however, a constant source of difficulty for Jefferson. He was apparently living with a slave woman, and her owner sued Stewart "for the hire of the woman." Jefferson promised to supply his bail money, but this was one more instance of the kind of public airing of private plantation affairs that Jefferson tried to avoid. He kept Stewart at Monticello for six years, and during that time the smith produced much of the fine metalwork seen today in the mansion. His behavior became increasingly unmanageable, however, and he was finally fired. Edmund Bacon, the Monticello overseer at that time, commented that, because of Stewart's drunken "sprees," Jefferson would have fired him earlier, but he wanted the blacksmith to teach some of the Monticello slaves his skills.

Those who have watched a blacksmith at work may feel that the skills are minimal—a strong pair of arms and shoulders for swinging a twelve-pound hammer and an ability to take the intense heat of the forge. It is true that the hammer and anvil are the smith's main tools, but crafting a wide variety of iron or steel products from bars of iron rod requires a mastery of fire and metal, a practical knowledge of metallurgy, and the artist's eye that separates any fine craftsman from his journeyman colleagues. Stewart was such a smith, but like many working-class men of his times, he was also an alcoholic.

Sobriety was much desired in craftsmen in colonial America, but apparently not often obtained. In advertisements for workmen, and in recommendations written for them, the word "sober" is invariably listed as a desirable characteristic. Jefferson, a man of temperate habits himself, was opposed to having any of his workmen drink. In attempting to hire a mason to work on rebuilding Monticello in 1796, he declared that he would provide a house and food, in addition to wages, "but give no liquor. This is an absolute article, as I never saw work go on well if the workman had liquor. It is therefore a point which I never give up." Never proved to be too absolute a term, however; when he needed a first-rate workman, he was willing to bend on the prohibition of liquor. Two years after making this statement, he hired James Dinsmore, a superb carpenter from Philadelphia who stayed with him for ten years and was responsible for much of the woodwork seen in the interior of the mansion today. Jefferson regularly provided Dinsmore and an overseer-craftsman, Richard Richardson, with a half pint of whiskey a day, obviously convinced that it did not impair their work.

Jefferson's prohibition on liquor was prompted by his experience with two workmen, a blacksmith, William (Billy) Orr, and a carpenter, David (Davy) Watson, both deserters from the British army whom Jefferson hired in 1781. Watson had written to Jefferson that he would be "much obleadged" if Jefferson would hire him, for he was "full of want," without "Any Spair Clothing to Change my Self." Jefferson did oblige, hiring him at three thousand pounds of tobacco a year or its equivalent in paper money. Orr was hired at £3 a month. Orr and Watson began work at Monticello, immediately became close drinking companions, and went off on a series of monumental binges. One of Jefferson's slaves, Isaac, who left a memoir of his life at Monticello, recalled: "Davy Watson and Billy . . . both workmen, both smoked pipes, and both drinkers. Drank whiskey; git drunk and sing; take a week at a time drinkin' and singin'." In the course of three months, Watson and Orr consumed nearly eighteen gallons of whiskey. Jefferson reported his laconic disapproval in his Memorandum Book: "Feb. 5 Orr has lost 4. days work"; "Feb. 23 he has lost 5. days work"; "March 13 Orr has been absent 4. days." Given the drinking record of Watson and Orr, Jefferson's desire for sobriety in his workmen was understandable.

Jefferson nonetheless did provide liquor from time to time to his slave laborers. Field workers were given whiskey in cold weather, or for sickness, and also during harvests, when everyone on the plantation worked around the clock. Each worker received about four ounces of whiskey a day at harvest during the workday. A cart followed the harvesters from field to field periodically doling out liquor. As a rule, however, Jefferson believed that supplying slaves with drink was "an injurious and demoralizing practice" because "they do more for a day or two but less afterwards."

Jefferson's experience with the blacksmith William Stewart typifies the difficulties of acquiring and keeping labor at a Virginia plantation. If a workman was highly skilled, as Stewart was, he could command the best wages and working conditions—including a good house and food for himself and his family. Even drunkenness, or "madness," might be overlooked as long as he did his work. A talented blacksmith was essential to every working plantation and a necessary adjunct to Jefferson's building plans, for a smith not only shod horses, repaired wagons, coaches, and carriages, and made hoops for barrels, the traditional tasks associated with the craft, but he manufactured anything made of metal. Repairing tools, for example, was one of the necessary tasks of a smith in colonial America. There were no hardware stores to replace broken tools; they were usually manufactured in England and were specially ordered from there. In America, the blacksmith repaired these tools, often repeatedly, until they literally wore out. Sometimes he made them. The smith could also manufacture that most important building material—nails. Jefferson's nailery was in the same building as the blacksmith shop, and Stewart was placed in charge of it.

John Anderson, one of the most prosperous blacksmiths in Williamsburg—Jefferson was one of his customers—left an account book that gives some indication of the range of the smith's work. Among Anderson's jobs were making and repairing locks, keys, and latches; making chains and an anchor; and working on kitchen utensils of all sorts: pot hooks and racks, kitchen tongs, repairing kettles and pots. He made a pair of curtain rods, a clapper for a cow bell, a new lock for a pistol, "a Truss for Negro boy Matt," and "leg irons for the Lunatic Hospital." (The latter item is a powerful comment on the treatment of mental illness in the eighteenth century.)

Because it was so difficult to hire skilled craftsmen in Virginia, Jefferson hit upon the idea of inducing a blacksmith to work on the plantation by going into a business partnership with him. In 1774, at a time when he was attempting to push work on his house to completion, Jefferson went into business with a master blacksmith, Francis Bishop. The shop was established at Shadwell rather than on the mountaintop, no doubt to make it more accessible to others in the vicinity. Shadwell was next to the Three Notch'd Road, which connected the Jefferson lands with other plantations in the area. Jefferson supplied all of the venture capital for the business: he built a house for Bishop, provided him with 400 pounds of pork and enough corn for himself, bought tools and iron rod, and apprenticed one of his slaves, Barnaby, to learn the trade. Jefferson's own blacksmith work would be charged like any other job and he and Bishop would split the profits. His Memorandum Book for 1778 shows that there was not a great deal of profit to split, mainly because most of the work done at the shop was Jefferson's. Perhaps because there was so little outside business for the shop, it was moved in the early 1790s to Mulberry Row on the mountaintop. Jefferson's program of having his slaves learn the blacksmith trade as apprentices, first to Bishop and then to Stewart, was so effective, however, that for the rest of his life, various slaves did much of the blacksmith work on his plantations.

In starting work on his house, Jefferson's immediate needs were for skilled stonemasons, brickmakers, and bricklayers to build the cellars and walls of the dwelling. There was never any question that his house would be constructed of brick rather than stone, the material used for the great Palladian mansions of England and the continent. Most of the stone that was used in Virginia houses—for mantles, chimney pieces, or the ornaments of the classical orders—was imported, already carved, from England, mainly because there was no suitable stone to be quarried in Virginia. For this same reason, there were few stonemasons in the Southern colonies, and those that were available were not trained to do the decorative cutting demanded of Palladian architecture. Nevertheless, Jefferson did manage to find a mason and enough stone to make columns for his east portico, the only stone columns on the building. The mason was William Rice, an indentured servant. Late in 1775, Jefferson purchased the remaining portion of Rice's indenture, and when his contract was completed in 1778, he was hired by Jefferson as a free worker. In February 1778, he made an agreement with Rice "that he shall make 3 stone columns, to find himself provisions, and assist in quarrying." The capitals, bases, and one of the Doric columns had already been completed by Rice during the term of his indenture. Rice would have the use of "my two stone cutters"—probably slaves—and would be paid £10 per column, a considerable sum. He apparently cut the stone for the four columns of the east portico. Columns were made as they had been from the age of Pericles, by cutting a series of stone drums, each about three feet high, and fitting them together, a task that took considerable skill.

In spite of the fact that there was little stone to build with, stone was clearly perceived by colonials to be the most prestigious building material: the great palaces, churches, and public buildings of the mother country were mostly all built of stone. An attempt was made in a number of houses to create the illusion of a stone façade by "rustication"—plastering and painting wood, blowing sand on the wet paint, and incising it to create artificial stone blocks. George Washington produced this effect at Mt. Vernon, and Jefferson, in his remodeling of Monticello, rusticated part of the east front.

Because Jefferson was using brick for the house, his need for stone was limited to the Palladian orders and other decorative work and to door sills and steps. The basement of the house would be rubble-laid fieldstone, what Jefferson called "unhewed" stone. In his locality it was gneiss, and was abundant around Monticello. Any journeyman mason could lay this up. The reason for stone in the foundation and cellars was because stone, where it was readily available, was much cheaper than brick. Jefferson made a comparison in his Farm Book between brick and unhewed stone construction and found stone to be nearly half the cost of brick. It was common practice to construct all underground foundations of stone and then to switch to brick at the ground level. Stonemasons for even this kind of basic work were rare, however; Jefferson was to comment to the Duke de la Rochefoucauld-Liancourt of France, who visited Monticello in 1795, that "there were not four stone masons in the whole county of Albemarle." This was when Jefferson was enlarging the mansion to twice its size and therefore needed masons to build more stone foundations and cellars. He obviously had canvassed the entire county and knew exactly how many masons were available. He was driven to impatience and frustration when he finally hired a stonemason who then failed to show up at the last moment, an eventuality that happened all too frequently, as it still does today. The failure of workmen to arrive on the job as promised is an affliction that has crippled the best-laid plans of house builders from time immemorial—and Jefferson was no exception.

Brickmakers and bricklayers were much more available, because brick was the building material of choice for a Virginia plantation seat.

There was some prejudice against brick houses by those who thought they were always damp and therefore unhealthy. In his *Notes on the State of Virginia*, Jefferson wrote that the fear of contracting disease from living in a brick house prevented the improvement of housing in America. He then went on to show, in a formal scientific proof, that the moisture that sometimes appears in the rooms of brick buildings does not enter from the outside through the porous brick, but in condensation that forms on the inside. Only on rare occasions when storms battered the northeastern walls of brick houses for days did moisture enter a house. As for the condensation, "a little fire kindled in the room, whenever the air is damp, prevents the precipitation on the walls." Far from being unhealthy, he wrote, brick houses are warmer in winter and cooler in the summer than wooden ones. He clinched the argument by noting that the inhabitants of Europe, who live mostly in brick or stone houses, are "surely as healthy as those of Virginia."

Jefferson's bias against houses of wood was not for health reasons, but because he thought they lacked durability. The loss of Shadwell no doubt helped form this opinion, but the Virginia climate also had something to do with it. In 1784, when Jefferson published his observations about American housing in *Notes on the State of Virginia*, he had already seen the ravages of termites and dry rot on his own unfinished house. When he tore down part of Monticello at the start of his remodeling program in 1796, this was confirmed by the discovery of many rotten structural timbers. As Anna Maria Thornton was to observe six years later, the exterior woodwork was also in a deplorable condition. Jefferson was convinced that the life of a wooden house was no more than fifty years, and therefore every half century the nation became a housing "tabula rasa, whereon we have to set out anew," rebuilding the country's supply of houses. If brick or stone is used, on the other hand, "every new edifice is an actual and permanent acquisition to the state, adding to its value as well as to its ornament."

Jefferson misjudged the staying power of wooden houses that were well-built, moisture-free, and periodically repaired. The number of seventeenth- and eighteenth-century wooden houses still standing in America is a tribute to the fact that maintenance, as much as the building materials, determines the life of a house. Even Monticello, in spite of its solid brick walls, came close to destruction in the nineteenth century when it was allowed to deteriorate for lack of care.

The bricks for Jefferson's house were molded from clay dug at the building site, creating a bond between the house and the earth it rested on, a tie found in few twentieth-century dwellings. This was not unique to Monticello; most brick houses in colonial Virginia were built of bricks manufactured of clay at the building location. Because of this, each house took on the hue and texture of its particular brand of soil. The houses of Williamsburg, for example, are of a salmon coloring lighter than Monticello, a result of the difference in soils between Tidewater and Piedmont. Jefferson's bricks are a darker red, and some are overfired and overporous. The flaws are those of the brickmaker, a profession that was more an art than a science in the eighteenth century.

Brick is the product of earth and fire; its technology is simple, yet powerful, and goes back to the shadows of prehistory. In brickmaking, fire transforms a rectangular piece of dried mud into one of the cheapest, yet most durable, building materials known to humankind. In the eighteenth century, the medium for this transformation was the brick kiln, not an object like a pottery kiln, which is an oven for firing pots, but merely a stack of bricks. How they were stacked defined the kiln. Constructing the kiln and controlling the fire in it determined the quality of the bricks.

The brickmaking on Jefferson's mountain would have progressed in a standardized series of labor-intensive steps that had been perfected over the centuries. The bricks first had to be molded from a mixture of earth and water. In large, permanent brickmaking operations, a mill could be constructed for mixing the mud, but where there was ample labor, the same work could be done with hoes in a shallow pit dug for this purpose. Because Jefferson had been excavating atop his mountain in order to level it and to dig his cellars, much of the topsoil had already been removed, revealing the sandy clay needed for brickmaking. There would have been plenty of earth available for making bricks; what was not readily at hand was water. Jefferson had not yet dug his well when he first started making bricks, so water had to be hauled from springs farther down the mountain. For this reason, a well atop the mountain became a high priority. At one point, he calculated whether it was more efficient to make bricks where the water was and carry the bricks to the building site, or to haul water up the mountain to where the earth was. His decision was to make his bricks at the building site. In his Garden Book on July 27, 1769, he noted that it took six hogsheads of water to make 2,000 bricks. Eleven days earlier he had hired a professional brickmaker, George Dudley, to make his first batch of bricks. Jefferson's personal labor force was still relatively small, so Dudley would have provided the labor—slaves, of course—and if a later brickmaking crew was an indication of the amount of labor needed, Dudley would have used a team of at least two men and three boys.

The bricks were made of stiff mud that had been well mixed, either by hoeing, or by "treading"—using a mule or ox to circle the clay pit repeatedly. A lump of this mud was pressed into the brick mold, a topless and bottomless box partitioned into four brick shapes and dusted with sand so the mud would not stick. Excess mud was struck from the top with a stick, and the mold was carried to a drying area where the mud bricks were demolded. As soon as the bricks were dry enough to be handled they were turned on edge and placed in low stacks to dry further. Carrying and stacking bricks was boys' work, although it was not light—wet bricks weighed eight pounds each, and they were made by the thousands. Weather was crucial during this step because the bricks had to be sun-dried for five days, and even with wooden planks laid atop them for protection, extremely wet weather could be ruinous. An efficient team of brickmakers could produce about two thousand bricks a day.

The next step, building the kiln, or "clamp," as it was called, was where the brickmaker practiced his art. Bricks were stacked in intermeshed layers, each brick separated from those around it by a half-inch or more of air space to allow heat to surround it. The kiln could be eight to ten feet high, so that it resembled a small house. Through the center of the stack of interwoven bricks, at ground level, was the "eye" of the kiln, a corbel-arched tunnel about two feet high that ran the length of the kiln. In this tunnel were built the fires that heated the entire stack of bricks. The size of a kiln was measured by the number of eyes it had; brickmakers figured roughly three thousand bricks per eye. (In 1778, John Brewer burned "90,000 workeable bricks" for Jefferson in a kiln of thirty-six eyes, estimated "to contain 103,000 bricks which is 2861 to the eye.")

Before the kiln was fired, the bricks on the sides and part of the top were plastered with mud to hold in the heat. When the eyes were set ablaze with hardwood logs (soft pine did not produce enough heat for well-fired bricks) black smoke and steam billowed from the top of the kiln for a full day as moisture and impurities were burnt off. The brickmaker had to feed the fires in the kiln's eyes for five days at the rate of roughly a cord of wood a day; during this time, the temperature at the interior of the kiln reached 2,000 degrees, and the top of the kiln glowed a brilliant red as the clay was metamorphosed into brick. Jefferson must have watched his first kiln with considerable pride as it glowed in the summer night on his mountain, perhaps reminding him of his reading of Aeschylus when news of the fall of Troy was signaled to Greece by great bonfires lit from mountain peak to mountain peak.

On the fifth day, the top of the kiln slumped a bit as the heat rose to 2,500 degrees, and this was a sign to the brickmaker that the firing was complete. The eyes of the kiln were then sealed up and it was allowed to sit for two weeks before it was cool enough for workmen to start taking it apart. Bricks made by this process were usually the standard British size, 2¼ by 4¼ by 8¾ inches. (This compares with the standard brick today: 2½ by 3⅝ by 7⅝ inches.) Numerous variations of the British standard existed in the colonies, however. Because of uneven firing, differences in size were common in a single kiln of bricks. Jefferson showed an uncharacteristic indecision over the size of brick to make. While calculating the number of bricks he would need for the house, he decided on bricks 3 by 4 by 9 inches. Even while making this decision, however, he noted that the bricks at Rosewell, the ancestral home of his friend John Page and the largest brick plantation house in the colony, were somewhat smaller at "2½, 4, 8½." The size that he finally settled on was 2¾ by 3¾ by 8 inches, a dimension that did not produce a modular wall. By not allowing for the standard half-inch mortar joint between bricks (his brick length should have been 7¾ inches) he produced walls of odd-sized thickness. The walls of the octagonal bow rooms on both wings, for example,

Rip-sawing timbers (from the Encyclopé-*die). In practice, the lower sawyer was often in a pit, hence the name pit saw.*

Illustration (from the Encyclopédie*) for making crown glass.*

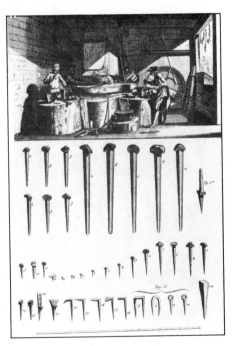

Jefferson's nailery and the nails he made were much like these in the Encyclopédie.

A brick kiln with three "eyes" at Colonial Williamsburg.
Monticello's bricks were fired in kilns such as this.

"Rustication" on the east front of
Monticello. Stucco over wood is in-
cised and painted to resemble stone.

were 12½ inches, and those in the center block 22½ inches thick. This meant that carpenters working on door and window frames and paneling had to deal with fractional measurements at every turn, and these had a way of multiplying as the work progressed.

The firing not only produced variations in size; it also produced differences in hardness. Those on the outside, called "samel" brick, were invariably underfired and had to be discarded or used as "nogging"—filling that went inside walls and between floors. Only about half of the bricks from the kiln were well-fired and perfectly hardened. Those at the very center of the kiln, directly above and around the eyes, were heated so intensely that the sides were glazed. These were used for a stylish kind of Flemish bond brickwork where the glazed "header," a brick laid end outward, alternated with unglazed "stretchers," the long side showing, to produce a checkerboard effect. (In Williamsburg, kilns fired with oak logs gave the gray-green glaze seen on the Flemish bond of some of the restored buildings at Colonial Williamsburg.)

Once the brick kiln was dismantled, and the bricks sorted and stacked—the hardest "stock" bricks to be used on the exterior of the walls, and the softer "place" bricks embedded within the walls—the brickmaker's work was done. This did not mean that kilns disappeared from the building site, however; limestone also had to be burned. Burning it was possibly one of the worst construction jobs in colonial America, as evidenced by the saying, "My mouth is as dry as a lime-burner's wig." Mortar for laying bricks was made much the same as it had been in ancient Rome, by combining burned limestone with coarse sand. The more thoroughly the two were mixed, the better the mortar. Both at Rome and in colonial Virginia, the mixing was done by slaves. The limestone was burned in a brick kiln that remained in place for as long as mortar was needed. In his *Notes on the State of Virginia,* Jefferson described a vein of limestone that ran through his part of the Piedmont, but aside from this source, limestone deposits were scarce in western Virginia. He owned a plantation called Limestone, but to assure a readily accessible source that could be easily quarried, he bought a four-acre limestone quarry and used it for his building projects. Oystershells were a suitable substitute for quarried limestone, and these were abundantly available in the Tidewater. The buildings of Williamsburg and the surrounding plantation mansions were all constructed with lime mortar made of burned oystershells.

The amounts of lime needed at Monticello were considerable. For the mortar used in most brickwork, it was mixed with even amounts of sand; for bricks on the exterior of the house, two parts lime were mixed with one part sand. Jefferson reported in his Memorandum Book on September 11, 1771, that Old Sharpe—the workman from whom he purchased his limestone quarry—"says a bushel of Limestone will weigh 114 lb and if well burnt will make 2 bushels of slacked lime." (In practice, Jefferson realized only 1½ bushels of lime from a bushel of limestone.) He also noted that "Stephen Willis says it takes 15 bushels of lime to lay 1,000 bricks." (This proved to be an accurate estimate for the brickwork at Monticello.) Willis was a master bricklayer who laid many of the bricks in the house and who also supervised construction at times. The two notations show that Jefferson, still a novice at building, learned about house construction not only from books, but by being a good listener. Unlike some bookish men of his age who were contemptuous of the practical lore of working men, he listened and observed closely, and made notes in his pocket Memorandum Book. His grandson, Thomas Jefferson Randolph, recorded that Jefferson's "powers of conversation were great, yet he always turned to subjects most familiar to those with whom he conversed, whether laborer, mechanic, or other; and if they displayed sound judgment and a knowledge of the subject, entered the information they gave, under appropriate heads, for reference."

This was equally true of his interest in gardening and farming. He kept a Garden Book and a Farm Book in which he periodically entered not only records and observations about the planting cycles at Monticello ("peas of Mar. 5 just appearing"), and accurate rolls of his slaves, but also bits of information gleaned from talks with neighbors ("Nich. Lewis thinks 40 f. square of watermelons will supply a family that is not very large"). He queried anyone, regardless of class origin or economic status, who had information to offer him. During his stay in France, he took a trip south from Paris to learn as much about the country as possible. To the Marquis de Lafayette he wrote: "I am never satiated with rambling through the fields and farms, examining the culture and cultivators with a degree of curiosity which makes some take me to be a fool, and others to be much wiser than I am." He advised Lafayette to do the same, to

> ferret the people out of their hovels, as I have done, look into their kettles, eat their bread, loll on their beds under pretense of resting yourself, but in fact to find if they are soft. You will feel a sublime pleasure in the course of this investigation, and a sublimer one hereafter, when you shall be able to apply your knowledge to the softening of their beds, or the throwing a morsel of meat into their kettle of vegetables.

This was one philosophe to another: knowledge that was only of theoretical or abstract interest was of trivial value. The French Enlightenment was fired by the kind of factual knowledge that inspired Diderot and d'Alembert's *Encyclopédie*, knowledge that would make the world a better, happier place to live in, with softer beds, and meat in the soup pot. Jefferson was fully committed to this belief.

Egalitarianism would, of course, be expected from the author of the Declaration of Independence, but Jefferson had never placed social restrictions on his curiosity. He followed where it led him, to palace or hovel. In seeking out information he needed to build his house, the wisdom of a bricklayer, based on years of practice, was knowledge inferior to none. His comment that "those who labour in the earth are the chosen people of God" is a famous one, illustrating his deeply felt agrarianism. But he had an equal respect for laborers whose lives were spent mastering and practicing a useful trade. Late in life, passing the house of a neighbor, Jesse Lewis, an old blacksmith who still worked at his forge even though he was now a man of means, Jefferson noted, "It is such men as that who constitute the wealth of a nation, not millionaires."

In choosing to build his house of brick, Jefferson selected a versatile building material. Brick differs from stone in that it is uniformly modular and does not have to be altered in any way before it is laid up in a wall. Because of its small size, brick is structurally flexible, equally comfortable in a curved surface as in a straight one. Twentieth-century architect Louis Kahn, who has worked extensively with brick in his designs, observed that it is important for an architect to "honor the materials that he works with," and that brick loses its character if it is given an inferior job to do. In a whimsical dialogue with a brick, he asks, "What do you want, brick?" and the brick replies, "I like an arch." An arch does real work in a wall; it shifts weight from its head to its sides and safely distributes it to the earth, allowing an opening for light or access. Jefferson used arches in the exterior and interior walls of Monticello. They allowed wide, graceful portals at the entrance, from the east portico to the hall, and in the piazzas at the terminations of the wings of the house. Interior doorways were arched in brick, "to prevent door and window frames from too great pressure," then framed with wood to display the Palladian orders.

Brick also likes a heavy wall. Most brick houses built today have veneer walls, four-inch-thick screens of stretchers concealing a wood frame structure. The brick is an ornament supporting nothing; the wooden stud walls hold up the roof. Such walls do exactly what stone rustication did in the eighteenth century: they give the illusion that a house is built of a more prestigious material than mere wood.

Monticello's brick walls were not for show; they were massive and supported equally robust wood timbers used for floor joists, rafters, and other structural members. During restoration of the house in the 1950s, the wooden floors were pulled up to reveal more than one hundred tons of nogging—brick, mud, and straw packed between the floor joists as fireproofing, ratproofing, and insulation. The brick walls of Monticello had been quietly carrying this incredible dead load for 150 years, a tribute to Jefferson's design and his brickmakers' and bricklayers' skills. The standard in the eighteenth century was the "brick-and-a-half wall"—a little over a foot thick. The walls of Monticello were more than two feet thick in places, much stronger than was required for even the kind of weight that Jefferson heaped on his masonry, but like most owner-builders, he had a tendency to overbuild. When in doubt, use more materials. (At one point, he wondered whether his walls should be another half brick thick.) He used twice as much lime in his mortar as was necessary; as a result the east front walls of the house were so well constructed that when he had to demolish them during his remodeling campaign in the 1790s, his workmen could scarcely pull them down. Jefferson observed with some

Monticello's rough-textured, porous, irregular bricks. The walls are laid in Flemish bond.

frustration that new bricks could have been made as fast as the old ones were dismantled.

The strength of a brick wall is derived not only from the quality of its mortar, but also from its bonding, the way headers and stretchers are alternatively interlocked. There were two basic kinds of bonding used in colonial houses, English and Flemish. English bond is the easier for a bricklayer to lay, and is stronger. It consists of a course of stretchers alternating with a course of headers. (A variation of English bond, American bond, has five or six courses of stretchers to one course of headers.) Flemish bond alternates a header with a stretcher in each course. It is more difficult to lay because greater attention must be given to the placement of each brick in relationship to every other one around it, but its pattern is a more interesting one. Colonial houses usually have English bond up to the water table; this is the place in a wall, about two feet above ground, where its thickness is reduced the width of a brick, producing a setback in the wall. (It is a basic engineering principle that foundation walls are always thicker than upper walls in order to distribute the weight of the building over a greater area of earth.) Above the water table, English bond changed to Flemish bond; this is the combination that Jefferson used at Monticello. Whichever bond was chosen, the mortar joints were usually struck with an incised line, made by running a jointing tool along a straight edge. This gave a regularity to the wall that the rough, hand-made brick lacked.

The art of the bricklayer has not changed appreciably in a millennium. An eighteenth-century bricklayer laying up Jefferson's walls at Monticello would feel quite at home working on a twentieth-century wall. The rhythmic, fluid motions with which a brickmason applies mortar to a brick, inserts the brick in place, and strikes the excess mortar from the joint are as timeless as housebuilding itself. The brick is perfectly sized to fit the hand; the trowel, a tool that has evolved to an optimal shape for applying mortar to a brick, is manipulated as deftly as a fiddler's bow. Baked earth and tool dance in the bricklayer's hands in an unvarying repetition, and walls rise.

An apprentice bricklayer can acquire these movements; a journeyman has perfected them; but a master bricklayer must be something of a mathematician as well. Estimating the numbers of bricks in a wall, compensating for openings such as doors and windows, calculating different wall thicknesses, and figuring arches, chimneys, and fireplaces, involves close measurement and accurate calculation. In an age where many craftsmen were only semiliterate, the kind of functional mathematics required for estimating and executing a brick building of ambitious size must have strained the capabilities of some bricklayers. For those who could read, however, there were a number of handbooks with mathematical tables and geometric drawings to aid bricklayers and carpenters in translating raw materials into finished houses. Some of the most popular were a series of books by Batty Langley and William Halfpenny, two English builders. Each published nearly twenty books, many with euphonious Latinate titles, such as Halfpenny's *Mellificium Mensionis: or the Marrow of Measuring.* Every master workman would own several handbooks of this kind.

Handbooks were hardly necessary for Jefferson's bricklayers, however. He loved mathematics and enjoyed doing the kind of number crunching that we, in the age of the pocket calculator, would find maddening. He kept a building notebook in which he recorded all sorts of calculations, including mathematical conversion tables and solutions to practical problems in geometry. Working for a man with Jefferson's demands for accuracy must have taxed the patience of his artisans. An architect who planned his building details to five decimal places or more (one measurement in inches was "1.8991666 &c.") could not have been pleased with anything less than perfection. He was apparently in the habit of checking his workmen's labors closely. He disliked hiring anyone to work at a piece rate, convinced that workmen were then interested only in turning out quantity rather than quality. He preferred to hire them by the day or month because, as he once declared, "I wish to have great pains taken" with the work. In a drawing of the floor plan of the house, Jefferson recorded measurements he made after his bricklayers had laid up the walls to the water table. The width of one of the wings of the house was measured at 21 feet, 9²/₁₀ inches, but in a footnote added to the measurement, he wrote "in measuring, this time out but 21 f. 6 I." The end wall, in going up, had quietly drifted inward by more than three inches, making a mockery of his five-decimal-point accuracy.

Brickmasons were not only bricklayers in colonial Virginia; they were usually brickmakers and plasterers as well. Where labor is extremely scarce, there is often an erosion of job specialization. Every owner of a farm was by necessity a jack of all trades, able to do some blacksmithing, rough carpentry, and perhaps some masonry work. Small farmers often hired themselves out as part-time laborers. Many of the workers whose names appeared briefly in Jefferson's Memorandum Books were local farmers who were handy at a number of useful plantation or construction jobs.

Even professional craftsmen branched out into other kinds of work because there was a demand for jobs that could not be filled by specialists. A Williamsburg bricklayer, Humphrey Harwood, left a detailed account book for the years 1776–1794 showing a lucrative business in repair work. (The capital had been moved from Williamsburg to Richmond and there was little new construction being done.) Kitchen fireplaces were used for cooking as well as heating; they were therefore in constant use, and had to be repaired frequently. Harwood "mended" hearths, kitchen chimneys, and ovens. He also repaired wells and remodeled brick-walled rooms by adding windows or doors, or by replastering and whitewashing walls.

David Minitree, a brickmason of an earlier generation, was a builder as well as a brickmaker and bricklayer. He did the brickwork on one of the handsomest and most famous of the James River plantation houses, Carter's Grove. This was the home of Carter Burwell, a grandson of Robert "King" Carter, Virginia's most affluent land baron. So pleased was Burwell with Minitree's work at its completion in 1752, that he paid him a bonus of £25 as "a present." Minitree also

[83]

glazed the windows of the house, a total of 540 panes of glass. Little is known of the personal lives of any of the craftsmen of the colonial period (working class people are not letter writers), but in Minitree's case a notice appeared in the *Virginia Gazette* in 1762 that might have been clipped from the classified section of any newspaper in America today:

> Whereas my Wife *Elizabeth* has eloped from me, without any reasonable Cause, I do therefore forewarn all Persons from crediting her on my Account, as I will not pay any Debts she may contract.
>
> David Minitree

Though Monticello was a brick house, the greater part of the labor that went into it was by woodworkers—sawyers and carpenters. Only the cellars, foundations, walls, and chimneys were masonry; virtually everything else was wood: floors, roof, porticoes, windows, stairs, and most of the decorative interior work—paneling, trim, and molding. Measured by Jefferson's slow building pace, the brick walls went up rapidly; however, Jefferson had various carpenters working on the house for decades.

Much of the wood in the house came from Jefferson's lands. A good portion of the more than 10,000 acres he owned was forested, and he guarded this resource carefully. He commented during his presidency that he had repeatedly declined offers to purchase timber from his land because "without that resource I could not have built as I have done."

Transforming felled trees into lumber was the work of the sawyer, one of the most labor-intensive of all the colonial building trades. There were sawmills in Virginia in the colonial period, although not as many as in the Northern colonies, where the streams were faster, but hand sawing was cheaper with slave labor. An important part of Jefferson's building equation was the availability of wood and the slave labor to saw it into usable building materials. This did not mean that he was spared hiring professional sawyers; he did, but as in brick-making, the sweat labor was supplied by blacks.

Hand sawing trees into lumber was done at a pit saw, by a two-man team handling a large, frame-mounted saw. One man, the pitman, worked his end of the saw standing in a four-foot-deep trench, the pit that gives the technique its name. The log to be sawed rested on a low scaffolding of supporting cross timbers directly above the pit. The second sawyer stood on the log and handled his end of the saw. There was not a great deal of skill involved in what one contemporary observer called "the stupid slavish work of sawing." Once a flat surface was sawed into the edge of a log, board widths were measured on it with a chalk line and the arduous work of rip-sawing the length of a tree commenced. The junior member of the team was the pitman, the one who took the endless shower of sawdust. The sawyer on top followed the chalk line and periodically placed wedges into the cut to prevent the saw from jamming. With a piece of technology as primitive as this, Jefferson, like thousands of colonial builders before him, produced much of the timber and plank that went into his house.

The need for lumber was so great at Monticello that Jefferson set up on Mulberry Row a permanent saw pit "where a considerable quantity of timber" was kept. Next to it was a wooden building for drying and storing cut lumber; it was also "used at times as a carpenter's shop." There was also on Mulberry Row a fifty-seven-by-eighteen-foot joiner's shop, a large, well-made building with stone foundations, fireplace, and chimney, and wooden walls. It was here that much of the fine woodwork and furniture for Monticello was crafted.

In the eighteenth century, a distinction was made between the crafts of carpentry and joinery. Carpenters engaged in house construction; joiners worked on a smaller scale on furniture, paneling, and decorative details. In the language of a popular handbook, "Joynery is an Art . . . whereby several Pieces of Wood are so fitted and joined together by straight Lines, Miters or any Bevel, that they shall seem one entire piece." The distinction was complicated by the fact that there were also housejoiners who cut the mortise and tenon joints and assembled the timber framing for house construction. Both of these trades traced their history to the medieval guilds of Europe, the carpenters being the oldest. In England, joiners were incorporated in 1571, during the reign of Elizabeth I.

The division between the two trades had already broken down

in England by the eighteenth century; in the colonies, most wood-workers advertised themselves as "carpenter and joiner." When a distinction was made between the two skills, it was usually to identify the fine craftsmanship expected from the joiner, whose art consisted of concealing his art. The joints should never show. The bastion of carpentry in America was Philadelphia, where the Carpenters' Company, a guild of master craftsmen, controlled the profession by setting prices and standards. The Carpenters' Company was never more than a minority of those practicing the carpenter's trade in Philadelphia, but its influence was far greater than its numbers. Like the plantation aristocracy of Virginia, which controlled that colony through an inter-locking dynasty of friendships and intermarriage, the Carpenters' Company of Philadelphia was a tightly meshed professional caste with considerable authority over all building in the city. The medieval guild tradition of sons following their father's trade, intermarriage among the families of tradesmen, and an apprenticeship system that de-manded loyalty to the craft combined to create a prosperous class of artisans with social status and political power. Moreover, members of the Carpenters' Company were invariably master builders who acted as general contractors and therefore exercised control over all of the other building trades in the city.

When Jefferson went to Philadelphia for the Second Continental Congress, he had an extended opportunity to compare for himself the building craftsmanship of Philadelphia with that of Virginia. He be-came convinced that Philadelphia artisans were the finest in America. He was not the only Southerner who admired Philadelphia's craftsmen. By the Revolutionary period, Philadelphia was an exporter of crafts-men, sending a steady stream of ambitious journeymen southward to Baltimore, Annapolis, and Charleston, intent on setting up their own shops. Jefferson succeeded in luring several of these skillful Phila-delphia-trained workers to his mountaintop. The madman blacksmith William Stewart may have been a questionable acquisition, but James Dinsmore, the housejoiner and carpenter Jefferson brought from the Quaker city in 1798, was a prize catch. Dinsmore was in large part instrumental in the completion of Monticello to Jefferson's satisfaction. "A more faithful, sober, discrete, honest and respectable man I have never known," Jefferson said of him in writing a letter of recommendation. During his presidency, Jefferson hired another Philadelphia housejoiner, John Neilson, and he stayed at Monticello for four years. Jefferson called Dinsmore and Neilson "house joiners of the first order. They have done the whole of that work at my house, to which I can affirm there is nothing superior in the U.S."

While the bricklayer's craft has not changed appreciably in two hundred years, this is not so for the carpenter. An eighteenth-century carpenter or joiner was closer to what today would be a wood carver, a craftsman who worked exclusively with hand tools. Most of the work that Jefferson's carpenters did at Monticello would now be manufactured in a factory and assembled at the building site. Window units, doors, stair railings and steps, molding, paneling, even the Palladian orders, are turned out by machine. In London, it is possible to duplicate a seventeenth-, eighteenth-, or nineteenth-century pub by ordering factory-produced paneling, complete with detailed carvings, in the style of the period. Indeed, many an "eighteenth-century" pub is no older than the liquor on its shelves.

A colonial carpenter started with a rough board; with simple, relatively primitive hand tools, he was able to shape this board into the intricately turned contours of a Palladian order. The parts of the order were all named—ovolo, cavetto, abacus, astragal—and the compound curves of each part were detailed in carpenter's handbooks. Much of the shaping that went into this decorative woodwork was done with the hand plane, the most commonly used tool of the eighteenth-century joiner and carpenter. A journeyman might own two dozen different planes; a master would use many more. The inventory of the estate of master carpenter Edmund Dickeson of York County, Virginia, filed in 1778, showed that he owned "81 planes of different sorts." These were of three basic kinds. The jack plane, with a slightly curved blade, was used for rough planing. The "trying" or "truing" plane—two to three feet long—was the workhorse tool, used to make a board perfectly flat and smooth. Molding planes with contoured cutting blades produced the coves, beads, rabbets, rounds, and other decorative work found on fine molding and paneling. Much of the interior woodwork at Monticello was fashioned with hand planes of these three types.

Also commonly used were the adze, a long-handled tool with a curved chisel blade for hewing timbers or cutting rough curved surfaces; the auger, and brace-and-bit, for drilling holes; an assortment of saws; and many different kinds of chisels. Dickeson's inventory listed "47 carving chisels and gouges." Jefferson's joiner's shop would also have included some kind of lathe for turning wood, either a pole or treadle lathe, which operated by foot action, or a great wheel lathe with a six-foot-diameter flywheel hand-turned by an apprentice—or possibly both. (He mentioned a "turning wheel" in one of the early building designs for his dependencies.)

Carpenters and joiners who were able to create artistic paneling and furniture from tools as simple as these were products of craft training that had not changed greatly since the Middle Ages. Under the apprentice system, teenage boys were signed over by their parents, in a legal indenture contract, to a master craftsman to learn a trade. The indenture period usually lasted from four to seven years, or until the apprentice reached the legal age of twenty-one. Indenture agreements demonstrated the conflicts built into the system. Teenage boys, during the years of torrential libidinous drives, were constrained by legal contract to a life of monastic work and duty. "He shall not absent himself day or night from his said Master's Service, without his Leave, nor haunt Alehouses, Taverns, or Playhouses. . . ." The apprentice was also forbidden "to divulge the master's secrets," to play "at Cards, Dice or any other unlawful game," to "committ Fornication," or to "contract Matrimony within the said Term." The master's part in the bargain was to clothe and feed the apprentice, to teach him to read, write, and cipher, and to instruct him in the "Art, Trade, and Mystery" of his craft. At the end of the apprenticeship period, the master sent the newly minted journeyman out into the world of work with at least a new suit of clothes and a set of tools. For a carpenter, the tools would be those sufficient "to build a common Clapboard House"; in one case, these were "one Broad Ax, one Hand Saw, three Augers, one Gouge, Three Chisells & three Planes all New Tools." This meager list demonstrates the ratio of skill to tools that went into building a simple colonial house.

Since an indenture contract was in effect a term of enforced bondage, it is not surprising that apprentices, like slaves, ran away on occasion. The most famous colonial runaway apprentice was Benjamin

Franklin, who found being indentured to his older brother James more than he could take. Most apprentices, however, suffered through the experience to become journeymen, a class of workers much in demand because of the labor shortage, particularly in the South. A journeyman could either work for a master or set himself up as a master with his own shop—if he could save the capital. This was not so easily done, working at the rate of a few shillings a day. Many became itinerant worker gypsies, moving from community to community, sometimes getting into trouble and landing in debtor's prison, and often becoming alcoholics. In the South, because of the shortage of skilled craftsmen, a journeyman—whatever undesirable personal habits he might have—could usually find work.

One other source of skilled building craftsmen was the mother country. Until the Revolution, a steady stream of journeyman carpenters, bricklayers, and masons found their way from the depressed labor markets of England and Scotland to the colonial land of opportunity. In 1774, John Harrower, a Scottish clerk-merchant, came to Virginia with a shipload of 75 indentured laborers with trades ranging from glassblower to peruke maker. Their four-year indentures were sold to Tidewater merchants and planters on their arrival. Many indentured workers such as these settled in the larger coastal cities, where work was more readily available, but cheap lands to the West lured some into becoming farmer-artisans. Men such as these provided a labor pool of housewrights who were instrumental in building the villages and towns of the new nation's western migration. In Virginia, the fine interior carpentry found in many of the great plantation houses of the Tidewater had been built by craftsmen imported from England when Jefferson was still a boy. The paneling and carved woodwork of Carter's Grove is attributed to a British joiner, Richard Bayliss. Carter Burwell paid £23 for the passage of Bayliss and his family from England to Virginia. William Buckland was brought to Fairfax County from England by Thompson Mason under a four-year contract to assume "entire direction of Carpenters and Joiners work" on Gunston Hall, the seat of George Mason, one of Virginia's Revolutionary leaders. Buckland later moved on to Annapolis to become one of the outstanding architects of the colonial period. Another master builder, John Ariss, who is credited with a dozen colonial mansions, including Mount Airy in Richmond County, was born in Virginia, but learned his trade in England. Richard Taliaferro, the architect and acquaintance of Jefferson, may also have learned how to build houses as a bricklayer in England.

Jefferson attempted unsuccessfully to recruit a master builder from England early in his construction program when he was planning to get married and work at Monticello was dragging. Later, he attempted to hire a Scottish stonemason and housejoiner when he despaired at finding them locally, but he was so much of an American chauvinist, as evidenced on virtually every page of *Notes on the State of Virginia*, that he preferred American building craftsmen—preferably from Philadelphia.

Wages for workers in the building trades remained fairly stable during much of the eighteenth century until the Revolutionary War period, when inflation drove up wages and commodity prices. When Jefferson began building his house in 1768, a skilled workman in his part of Virginia made between 3 and 4 shillings a day (twenty shillings to a pound sterling, twelve pence to a shilling), with perhaps another 6 pence allowed for food and lodging. Unskilled workers averaged 2 shillings daily. Work was from sunup until sundown, approximately twelve hours a day, six days a week. Jefferson negotiated wages individually with each of his workmen; he was a canny employer who knew the going rates for wages and struck a hard bargain. The advantage he and other plantation owners like him had in hiring workers was that they could offer food and housing as part of a wage package. Hogs, corn, and wheat were raised on the plantation, and a habitable clapboard or log house could be thrown up on a piece of Jefferson land in less than a week by slave workers.

It is virtually impossible to translate the wages of colonial craftsmen into contemporary equivalents because there are so few overlays between eighteenth- and twentieth-century cultures. Assuming that a skilled American worker today makes, say, $20 an hour, $160 a day, does this mean that $160 is equivalent to the 4 shillings a colonial master worker made—an equivalent of $40 to the shilling? To answer this question it would be necessary to take into account the fact that Jefferson's skilled bricklayer or carpenter would pay no income tax, so his shilling would be worth roughly twenty-five percent more in buying power. Housing and much of his food was also included in that shilling, and these could easily combine with the absence of income taxes to double its value to $80. On the other hand, Jefferson's worker had no schools for his children, no Social Security or unemployment benefits, no hospitalization, and he worked a third to a half more time for his shilling than a modern American works. What is the cash value of these? As for the kinds of commodities each worker would purchase with his wages, there are few comparisons.

At Jefferson's plantation in 1772, a shilling would buy either four dozen eggs, three chickens, or one turkey. A shilling would purchase a one-way ferry ride across the James River, a short coach ride, a half pound of soap, four pairs of knitting needles, or a child's doll. A bushel of salt cost 3 shillings; a gallon of molasses 2½ shillings. If a 4-shillings-a-day master craftsman wanted to wear his hair in the stylish fashion, hair powder was 2 shillings; pomatum was only a shilling. A good dinner at a local tavern or ordinary could cost 5 shillings. A ticket for an evening at the playhouse at Williamsburg would cost 5 to 7 shillings, depending on the playbill, and a bowl of punch during intermission would cost another shilling. For more esoteric entertainments, Jefferson paid a shilling each to see a tiger and an alligator, and he paid 2½ shillings to see a puppet show. He paid the same amount to watch a "legerdemain man"—a traveling magician.

Clothing worn by working-class people was usually hand-sewn at home. A single yard of calico would cost a day's wages, 4 shillings; however, a yard of osnaburg, a coarse, brown linen used for work clothes, and the standard clothing for slaves, was only a shilling. A pair of shoes, if purchased in a shop, might cost from 6 to 9 shillings, boots 20 shillings; hand-knitted stockings were 5 shillings a pair. A teapot could be bought for 1 or 2 shillings, but the tea to put in it was extremely expensive throughout the eighteenth century. In 1772, Jefferson paid 22 shillings for a pound of tea, more than a week's wages for a skilled craftsman. Aside from ideological concerns, the colonists' outrage at the British tax on tea was heightened by the fact that the price of tea, even before the tax, had placed this English staple out of the reach of most working men and their families. The reason for the high cost of tea was that it was imported from the Orient to England and from thence to America, and was, moreover, a monopoly of the

East India Company. A cup of locally made whiskey could cost the same as a cup of tea.

Manufactured items imported from England as a rule were expensive. A fashionable lady's cap could cost from 15 to 30 shillings, a pair of boot buckles 12 shillings, and Jefferson paid 45 shillings for a set of chessmen, possibly the same set in use during Anna Maria Thornton's visit to Monticello twenty years later. Books could cost as little as 3 shillings for the smallest duodecimo size to 20 shillings and up for a large folio. A richly illustrated folio of natural history by the noted eighteenth-century naturalist Buffon was priced at 50 shillings, a full month's wages for most workers. Books were luxury items for colonial artisans; an average working man's library would consist of a Bible and a handful of craft handbooks or pattern books.

On balance, Thomas Jefferson was not a bad employer to work for. He paid the going rate for wages and was fair in all of his contractual dealings. Even the drunken carpenter-deserter Davy Watson was dealt with fairly when he complained to Jefferson that he was not given enough severance pay. Jefferson notified Nicholas Lewis, who was managing his affairs for him at the time, to go over Watson's account "and if any injustice has been done him, be as good as to have it rectified." Because he was a lawyer, Jefferson seldom failed to draw the terms of employment into a formal written contract. A typical contractual agreement was one he drew up in 1782 with Bartholomew Kindred, a weaver who made cloth for Jefferson's family and slaves during the Revolutionary War. Like the partnership Jefferson established with Francis Bishop, this agreement called for splitting the profit from the weaver's shop.

> Agreed with B. Kindred to continue another year without his son. I am to give him 500 lb. meat, 5 Barr. corn, ½ bush. salt & fodder as usual. He is to have half the earnings of the shop.

Jefferson was also a perfectionist employer. When he was on hand, he supervised each detail of the building process personally. The Duke de la Rochefoucauld-Liancourt, on his visit to Monticello in 1796, observed of Jefferson: "At present he is employed with activity and perseverance in the management of his farms and buildings; and he orders, directs and pursues in the minutest detail every branch of business relative to them." As a result of his concern with the "minutest detail" of the building of Monticello, during his frequent absences construction often came to a halt because workmen were unwilling to take responsibility for making mistakes. This is one reason why the house took so long to complete. Jefferson complained that his workmen could do nothing unless he was there, but until he hired James Dinsmore, a supervisor he had confidence in, he did not encourage them to work on their own. In 1797, when he was remodeling the house, he wrote, "today my workmen assemble & tomorrow begin their work, but they must suspend their work during my absence."

As Jefferson's architectural knowledge and skills increased, he became more demanding of his workers. When he started on his house in 1768, at the age of twenty-five, he was a student of architecture and of building craftsmanship. He learned much by observing his house going up. He learned even more as he continued to acquire books of architecture, and particularly when he went to France and saw firsthand not only the monuments of European Palladianism, but the new architectural styles of Paris. When he returned to Monticello and began rebuilding his house, he was a knowledgeable architect and builder who sought out the best craftsmen he could lure to Virginia and insisted that they comply with his most exacting wishes. And because "putting up and pulling down," as he put it, had become something of a passion with him by this time, he was not merely building stylish shelter, as he was in the 1770s when he rushed to finish his house for his new bride, but creating a work of domestic art. Like most artists who know what they want, he was no doubt guilty of taxing the patience of his workmen with his insistence that they execute in wood and masonry his visions of Palladian perfection. They did not give him perfection, of course, but any visitor who looks closely at the craftsmanship on display at Monticello can recognize that Jefferson coaxed from his artisans a close approximation of the level of excellence he demanded of himself.

4

To Possess Living Souls

A BRIGHT, cloudless, spring day in April of 1796 found Thomas Jefferson, soon to become Vice President of the United States, supervising a small army of workers swarming over the ruins of his house. The Monticello that he had built some twenty-five years before was now no more; its roof was partially off, the east front with its columned portico was stripped away, and workers were chipping at mortar joints in the frustratingly slow process of pulling down walls that had been built all too well. Jefferson had assembled a force of workers for his campaign to rush demolition and rebuilding of the walls so he could roof over an enlarged version of the house during the winter. This was the largest number of laborers he was ever to gather at his building site; the problems of shaping them into a smoothly functioning work team challenged the organizational skills of even Thomas Jefferson.

His neighbors were no doubt baffled at the cost and energy expended on this building project. He was tearing down what was considered one of the most stylish houses in his part of the state—for what? If, out of curiosity, they had climbed his mountain to watch his construction extravaganza, and perhaps to question the architect-builder about what in the world he had done to his house, they would have noticed that most of the workers were black. This casual observation might have passed without a thought, however, for Virginians were accustomed to seeing hard manual labor performed by blacks. But this scene, observed through the curtain of history, is a reminder that, notwithstanding the numerous free white carpenters and masons who worked on it, Monticello was built mainly by slaves. Any consideration of Monticello's labor force must take into account, therefore, the enslaved blacks who built it and maintained it.

Anton Chekhov, in *The Cherry Orchard*, wrote of a similar spring day. One of the characters, Trofimov, a perpetual graduate student, brilliant but directionless, looks out over the Renevskaya estate at a sea of cherry blossoms, breathtakingly beautiful in the Russian spring. He muses to his seventeen-year-old companion:

> Just think, Anya, your grandfather and your great-grandfather and all your ancestors owned both land and serfs, they owned living souls. Don't you see that from every cherry tree in the orchard, from every leaf and every trunk generations of human beings are gazing down at you, don't you hear their voices. . . . To own human souls—it has transformed every one of you, don't you see, those who lived before and those living today. And so your mother, your uncle, and you no longer notice that you are living in debt, at the expense of other people, at the expense of the very people you will allow no farther than the entrance to your home.

Like Chekhov's Russian aristocrats, Thomas Jefferson also lived at the expense of "his people," the slaves whose only entree to the house on his mountaintop was the servants' entrance. Beneath the white Palladian orders, the white plaster walls, the white dome silhouetted against the Virginia sky, lay black sweat, black labor, black craftsmanship.

Demolishing brick walls was, of course, unskilled labor. Many of Jefferson's workers were field hands—men, women, and boys—brought to the mountaintop to clean mortar off reusable bricks; but in an age before machine power, the greater part of any building project was manual labor. A single journeyman bricklayer would be aided by a laborer carting water, a laborer mixing mortar, a laborer hauling bricks and mortar by wheelbarrow and hoisting them atop a scaffold, and quite possibly an apprentice laying and grouting the interior bricks in the wall—all slaves. The white carpenter was also supported by at least two or three slaves. Cutting and hauling lumber was slave work; sawyers were slaves. Constructing scaffolds, hauling, carrying, and lifting timbers, planing planks, and making shingles—all slave work. The master carpenter James Dinsmore was given as helpers a slave apprentice, Lewis, and John Hemings, Jefferson's slave carpenter, who was to become the equal to Dinsmore as a joiner. Hemings was one of a number of slaves who learned building trades and were put to work alongside white craftsmen, or in place of them, at Monticello.

Jefferson most certainly realized the debt he owed to slaves— that the civilized elegance of Monticello was made possible by an institution he publicly condemned. Although he wrote that a "man must be a prodigy who can retain his manners and morals undepraved" by slavery, it is highly unlikely that he felt depraved because he was a slaveholder. Exactly what his deepest feelings about slavery were can only be guessed at, for his writings on the subject are a web of contradictions. He could write of slaves, with complete honesty:

> My opinion has ever been that, until more can be done for them, we should endeavor, with those whom fortune has thrown on our hands, to feed and clothe them well, protect them from ill usage, require such reasonable labor only as is performed voluntarily by freemen, and be led by no repugnances to abdicate them, and our duties to them.

He favored emancipation, stating that in time "it will come," but thought that freed slaves would have to be expatriated. As for intermarriage, it "produces a degradation to which no lover of his country, no lover of excellence in the human character can innocently consent."

On the other hand, although he was consistently humane and compassionate in his treatment of his slaves, he was also capable of acting like a hardened slavebreaker by having a runaway slave "severely flogged in the presence of his old companions." There is an anonymous note in his correspondence file that accused him of much worse behavior:

you will excuse the liberty when you look at my intention.
I should think it a crime to listen to the base falsehoods
utter'd against you without informing you of them. Mr. Brown
says he slept at Montecello one night and was wakened in
the morning by the most lamentable cries. he looked out and
to his utter astonishment saw you flogging in the most brutal
manner a negroe woman.

"Mr. Brown" was possibly Senator John Brown of Kentucky, whom
Jefferson had known for years, ever since his days as a law student.
Brown, whose family lived at nearby Staunton, seems to be the only
Washington acquaintance of Jefferson's by that name who may have
visited Monticello as a guest. It is difficult to assess the motivation of
the writer of the note. It purports to be friendly, revealing one of the
"base falsehoods" Jefferson has been accused of, yet it mentions by
name a man who was close enough to Jefferson to be invited to his
home. The writer appears to be attempting to discredit Brown, but
the note could also be politically inspired personal malice written under
the guise of friendship. The anonymous note merely repeats hearsay
and gossip, yet it hints at a psychological truth: that those who keep
their emotions under tight control may experience episodes of unfettered violence. In *Notes on the State of Virginia*, Jefferson himself had
written, "the whole commerce between master and slave is a perpetual
exercise of the most boisterous passions, the most unremitting des-
potism on the one part, and degrading submissions on the other."
Nevertheless, the allegation is at odds with the many known examples
of Jefferson's benevolent treatment of his slaves.

Jefferson acquired his slaves by inheritance from his father and
by marriage from his wife's dowry, but he bought and sold slaves
according to the state of his finances, always keeping such transactions
private because "I do not (while in public life) like to have my name
annexed in the public papers to the sale of [slave] property." He also
hired slaves from others and hired his slaves out. In short, slaves were
commodities and Jefferson was an economic man, attuned to the mar-
ketplace. He could discuss blacks as if they were cattle, in the language
of Adam Smith: "I know of no error more consuming to an estate than
that of stocking farms with men almost exclusively. I consider a woman

who brings a child every two years as more profitable than the best man of the farm. What she produces is an addition to capital, while his labors disappear in mere consumption." Jefferson was also a product of the Enlightenment, however, a man who believed in "moral sense," with an innate inclination to kindness, generosity, and compassion toward the underprivileged, the suffering, and the needy. He cared for sick slaves, provided for old blacks unable to work, admonished his overseers not to mistreat slaves, and did his best to keep slave families from being separated through sale or hire.

The question of his attitudes toward slaves and slavery has been further complicated by the accusations made during his presidency that he kept a slave mistress, Sally Hemings, and fathered several children by her, a scandal that subjected all of his statements about slavery to skepticism and doubt. Even if one discounts the Sally Hemings controversy, however, one of the abiding ironies of American history still remains: the man who could write with passionate conviction, "We hold these truths to be self-evident: that all men are created equal," owed his social status, his economic independence, his indulgence in scientific, literary, and artistic pursuits, to the slaves he owned until the day he died. If the mark of sanity is the ability to function comfortably in a world of moral ambiguity, then Jefferson was indeed a sane man, although he paid a price with periodic migraine headaches.

The Virginia aristocracy, of which Jefferson was a leading member, had, generations before he was born, blunted the edge of this ambiguity by creating a series of social buffers that erased all reminders that its members were indeed the owners of living souls, and perhaps depraved. The rhetoric of slave ownership removed the word *slave* from the lips of the Virginia gentry. Only in economic or legal contexts was the word used—buying, selling, recordkeeping, tracking down runaways, punishing offenders. At all other times, slaves were "the Negroes," "my people," or "my servants," the latter term echoing the respectability of service as a calling in the mother country. When Jefferson wrote in his Memorandum Book that "Willis's people left off working, having laid 14,120 bricks," it is evident that the bricklayer Stephen Willis had a team of slaves working for him.

At the same time, Virginians implanted a subtle reminder of the

A letter from the slave carpenter John Hemings informing Jefferson that the flat roof at Poplar Forest leaked. Hemings was a phonetic speller.

A letter from Jefferson's slave Hannah, housekeeper at his Bedford plantation. She was one of several of his slaves who were literate.

you will excuse this liberty when you look at
my intention. I should think it a crime to listen to
the base falsehoods utter'd against you without
informing you of them. Mr Brown says
he slept at montecello one night, and was
weakened in the morning by the most lamentable
cries, he looked out and to his utter astonishment
saw you flogging in the most brutal manner
a negro woman

---

2 Small Copper Baking pans
1 Turkish Bonnet Baking mould
3 Waffel Irons
2 Gird Irons
2 Spit ——— 1 Jack ——— 3 Cleavers — 2 hold fasts
3 Copper Laidles — 4 Copper Spoons — 1 Basing Spoon
3 Copper Skimmers — 2 Cast Iron Bakers
2 pair Tongs — 2 Shovels — 1 poker — 1 Bake Shovel
2 Large Iron pots — 2 Dutch ovens
1 Iron Chaffing Dish, ——— 21 Small Copper Baking moulds
2 Gelly moulds — 2 Freising moulds
1 Butter Tinkettle — 2 Culinders — 1 tin 1 of pewter
1 Brass Culinder 2 Graters ——— 1 old Copper fish kettle
9 wooden Spoons — 5 paste cutting moulds
1 Brass pistle & morter — 1 marble Ditto
2 wooden paste Rolers — 2 Chopping Knives
6 Iron Crevets — 3 tin tart moulds — 5 Kitchen aprons
1 old Brass Thith. — 1 Iron Candle Stick
2 Brass Chaffing Dishes

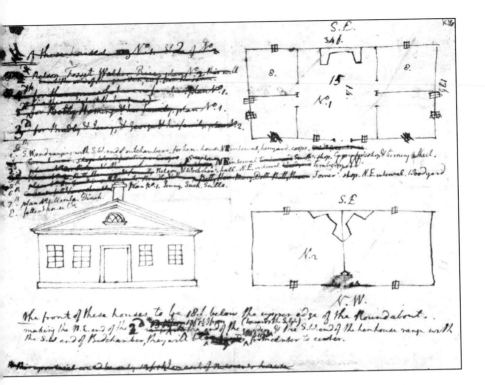

Opposite, top: *An anonymous note accusing Jefferson of "flogging in the most brutal manner a negroe woman."*

Opposite, bottom: *James Hemings's inventory of kitchen utensils.*

Above: *Jefferson's sketches for stylish slave and workmen's houses along Mulberry Row.*

Right: *One of Jefferson's typical records of slave labor: the number of loads per day, hauling stone in four carts. The stone was possibly used as fill in the construction of steps and floors of the porticoes.*

1822.	Wormly	Jerry	Isaac	Ned	Total.	
Aug. 6	24	22	23	23	92	
7			8	7	15	
8	16	20	17	13	66	
9						
10				34	34	
12				18	18	
13				24	24	
14	13	19	17	7	56	305
15	21	21	10	26	78	
16	20	15	28	26	89	
17	20	20	20	21	81	
19	19	20	20	20	80	328
20			17	18	35	
21	11	11	18	19	59	
22	20	8	22	21	71	
23	20	11	20	19	70	
24	18	18	19	19	74	309
26	16	19		14	49	
27	19	9	20	18	66	
28	20	20	20	21	81	
29	15	15	15	15	60	256
						1198

the whole interruptions amount to about 4 days work of the 4 carts, and leave 17 days for the performance of the work. there were 2 mule carts with 2 mules in each & 2 ox carts with a yoke in each: and 4 small boys & girls assisted loading. nearly the whole stone was furnished by the hill above the cooper shop.

condition of bondage by naming their slaves after biblical heroes or the gods and emperors of ancient Rome: Jupiter, Samson, Hercules, Pompey, Caesar, Minerva, and Juno were common slave names. This no doubt began as a private joke among those who shared a classical education, but to name the most powerless of human beings after the most powerful of legendary characters is also an unconscious expression of superiority or contempt. A slave named Hercules sent a repeated message to his owner, and other educated whites, about his slave status, for he was not a "living soul" with a native African or Christian name. (Virginians also went to classical Rome for the names of their blooded horses. Jefferson owned horses named Diomede, Castor, Romulus, Remus, and Tarquin.) Usually, slaveowners gave names only to those slaves purchased directly from slave traders, those who had no English names; slaves born on the plantation were named by their parents. There is something of an irony in the fact that many slaves themselves gave their offspring such incongruous names as Jupiter, Hercules, or Caesar, although it was undoubtedly done in ignorance of the classical allusion.

Slaves with last names were usually those whose fathers were known to be white men. The Hemings family is the most noteworthy of Jefferson's slaves with a white man's name, but he had several other slaves with surnames. Jefferson's slave rolls show how freed slaves acquired a surname other than that of their previous owner. Those slaves with trades were identified by first name, followed by their trade: Phill Shoemaker, Davy Carpenter, John Gardener, Phill Waggoner. The trade name distinguished the slave from others with the same given name, and was probably considered a mark of distinction by the slave.

Jefferson was not the only slaveholder who encouraged his slaves to learn useful trades; most Southern plantation owners apprenticed some of their slaves to white craftsmen for the simple reason that it was good business practice. A slave with a profession was more valuable by at least twenty percent than an unskilled field hand. During his presidency, Jefferson reluctantly offered to sell a slave to John Jordan, a brickmason who had worked at Monticello, because the slave, Brown, wished to join his wife, who was owned by Jordan. Jefferson offered to sell the slave for $500, "and think 100 D[ollars] in addition to this quite little enough for his trade." Adding a surcharge to the going price to account for a slave's additional skills was a common practice in Virginia. Slaves with trades were also hired out to provide scarce cash income. So many slave artisans were trained in the South that by the mid-eighteenth century they seriously competed with free white journeymen, leading one Southern city to enact laws limiting the number of slaves who could serve as apprentices to a master workman.

When Jefferson began building on his mountaintop in 1769, few of his slaves had occupations other than field laborer; none was capable of doing the brick and carpentry work he needed. Of the 52 "proper slaves" listed when he first started his Farm Book, only half were adults, and several of these were too old or infirm to do work of any kind. For this reason, he was entirely dependent on hired craftsmen during the initial stages of construction. However, he married Martha Wayles Skelton in 1772 and, the following year, after the death of her father, John Wayles, he came into a legacy of 135 slaves. Among these were a number of tradesmen, including two carpenters and two blacksmiths. In the ensuing years, as Jefferson brought white blacksmiths, bricklayers, masons, and carpenters to Monticello, slaves were increasingly apprenticed to them. As a result, the number of slaves who could do some kind of construction work increased as Jefferson's building on the mountaintop progressed. Three of his carpenters, Davy, Lewis, and Abram, for example, were capable of erecting a slave house "in 6 days, getting the stuff [lumber] and putting it together." By the end of his presidency, Jefferson listed twenty-two tradesmen on the Monticello slave rolls.

The senior member of the slave community at Monticello until his death in 1799, at the age of 69, was Great George. His name suggests that he was a huge man; he was sometimes referred to—no doubt jokingly with reference to the English monarch—as King George, and his wife Ursula as Queen. Thomas Mann Randolph, Jefferson's son-in-law, called him George the Ruler. He was purchased by Jefferson for £130, probably at the same time Ursula was acquired. Ursula and her two children, George and Bagwell, were purchased by Jefferson at auction in 1773, for "210£, an exorbitant price as the woman was old, and the boys infants." (She was thirty-five at the time.)

However, Martha Jefferson had set her mind on acquiring Ursula, "a favorable house woman," so her husband dutifully bid on, and purchased her. Ursula was a pastry cook and laundress, skills that Martha obviously needed. Ursula and Great George immediately moved in together as husband and wife. Great George remained one of Jefferson's most trusted slaves; from 1797 until his death in 1799 he was an overseer at Monticello. Randolph called him "steady and industrious," and made a revealing comment on Great George's independence when he wrote to Jefferson that "George I am sure could not stoop to my authority & I hope and believe he pushes your interests as well as I could."

Isaac, the son of Great George and Ursula, left a memoir that provides the most authentic account we have of slave life on Jefferson's estate. Isaac was born in December 1775, eighteen months after the death of his infant brother, Archy. As a boy, he was in Richmond when British troops arrived and forced Jefferson, then governor of Virginia, to flee with his family. Isaac recalled the scene:

> When the British came in, an officer rode up and asked, "Whar is the Governor?" Isaac's father (George) told him, "He's gone to the mountains." The officer said, "Whar is the keys of the house?" Isaac's father gave him the keys; Mr. Jefferson had left them with him. The officer said, "Whar is the silver?" Isaac's father told him, "It was all sent up to the mountains." The old man had put all the silver about the house in a bed tick and hid it under a bed in the kitchen and saved it too and got his freedom by it. But he continued to serve Mr. Jefferson and had forty pounds from Old Master and his wife. Isaac's mother had seven dollars a month for lifetime for washing, ironing, and making pastry.

Jefferson left no record of having formally freed Great George and Ursula, and he continued to carry them on his slave rolls. Isaac's statement, "but he continued to serve Mr. Jefferson" suggests that Great George and his wife may have been offered a legal manumission but refused it in favor of remaining on the estate, trusting in Jefferson's good will to be treated as free persons. George and Ursula were given rations of blankets, clothing, and food as were other slaves, but their portions were usually greater.

Although slaves were forbidden to raise wheat or tobacco ("There is no other way of drawing a line between what is theirs and mine," Jefferson wrote) they were encouraged to keep small vegetable gardens and to raise poultry. This was common on Virginia plantations where the provision allotted each slave was usually a peck of cornmeal and a pound of pork a week. Jefferson's slaves ate a more varied diet; they normally received a half pound of pork, two to four dried herring, between a half cup and a cup of molasses, a peck of corn meal weekly, plus salt for seasoning. Children received a quarter of this. The mainstay of slave diet was corn pone, a flat loaf made of corn meal, commonly called "ash cake" or "hoe cake" because it was placed on hot coals—sometimes on a hoe blade—and covered with ashes to bake. The ashes were wiped or washed off and the loaf was eaten hot. It was often used as a filler for a thick soup. Slaves supplemented this diet with vegetables grown on their own plots, particularly potatoes, snap beans, field peas, and "cymlin"—scalloped summer squash— and with eggs, poultry, and small game. They also ate fish caught in the nearby Rivanna River.

Philip Fithian, a Princeton College graduate who came south to tutor the children of Robert Carter at Nomini Hall in 1773, left a detailed diary of daily plantation living—including slave life—at one of the great Tidewater estates. On a Sunday morning in April of 1774 he recorded: "Before Breakfast, I saw a Ring of Negroes at the Stable, fighting Cocks, and in several parts of the plantation they are digging up their small Lots of ground allow'd by their Master for Potatoes, peas etc. All such work for themselves they constantly do on Sundays, as they are otherwise employed on every other Day." On another Sunday he "walked out towards evening & saw a number of Negroes very busy at framing together a small House—Sundays they commonly spend in fishing, making Potatoes etc., building & patching their Quarters." These Sunday descriptions were typical of slave-quarter activities throughout Virginia.

There were normally two slave hierarchies at every large Virginia plantation, the slaveholder's and the slave's. In the slave quarters, the most influential men and women were seamstresses, shoemakers, and carpenters, because they supplied slaves with clothing, shoes, housing, and furniture. Musicians, conjurers, preachers, and midwives were also much esteemed by slaves. House servants, on the other hand, were often perceived by their fellow bondsmen as spies and informers, and were therefore much lower in the slave hierarchy. On a plantation such as Monticello, where the house slaves were dominated by a single clan, the Hemings family, slave-quarter attitudes were probably compounded of a complex mixture of admiration, gratitude, suspicion, and envy. Hemings family members were carpenters, seamstresses, and cooks, and were in positions to distribute highly desirable favors to their fellow slaves, but they were also collaborators with the white slaveholders—no matter how benevolent the Jeffersons and Randolphs might be. If Sally Hemings was indeed Thomas Jefferson's mistress, she would have faced some trying times in the slave quarters; the slaveholder's mistress was usually held in contempt by her fellow slaves, for she was the worst kind of collaborator. Nor would her nearly white skin, and that of her children, have won her any respect; African blackness, untainted by white blood, was most admired in the quarter.

The slaveholders' hierarchy, the only one that whites were normally aware of, was based on the slave's closeness to the slaveholder. The slave who supplied the slaveholder with creature comforts, rather than economic benefits, was most esteemed. At the top of the caste were the "body servants" or "house servants" who worked as personal valets, maids, waiters, chambermaids, seamstresses, and cooks at the estate house. At Monticello, these were mostly all the sons and daughters of Betty Hemings. Great George and Ursula, because of their special circumstances, belonged to this select group. None of the house slaves ever did field work, even at harvest time when everyone else was called to the farms to get the tobacco or wheat crop in during a marathon five-day work session. House slaves were given other kinds of preferential treatment as well; they had better food because they were able to supplement their regular rations with the inevitable leftovers from the ample meals served at Monticello. They were not directly supervised by an overseer and therefore had discretionary time for themselves that other slaves did not enjoy. Their clothing was often special livery that marked them as superiors among their fellow slaves. At Monticello, Jefferson's eldest daughter, Martha Randolph, who acted as his housekeeper during much of Jefferson's later life, personally selected clothing for the house servants.

Those who took care of the horses and drove coaches and carriages—acting as the eighteenth-century equivalent of chauffeurs—ranked next in the hierarchy, although Jefferson's personal servant Jupiter was a special case. Jupiter was born the same year as Jefferson, grew up with him, and accompanied him on his various travels throughout the greater part of his life, acting not only as a coachman, but as a companion and "gofer." Jefferson's Memorandum Books record numerous borrowings of small amounts of money from Jupiter, and at times he was trusted to collect large amounts. On at least one occasion Jupiter was the subject of a rare display of anger by Jefferson. The incident was related by Jefferson's great-granddaughter Sarah Randolph:

A boy had been ordered to take one of the carriage-horses to go on an errand. Jupiter refused to allow his horses to be used for any such purpose. The boy returned to his master with a message to that effect. Mr. Jefferson, thinking it a joke of Jupiter's played off on the boy, sent him back with a repetition of the order. He, however, returned in a short time, bearing the same refusal from the coachman. "Tell Jupiter to come to me at once," said Mr. Jefferson in an excited tone. Jupiter came, and received the order and a rebuke from his master in tones and with a look which neither he nor the terrified bystanders ever forgot.

In spite of a close master-slave relationship, Jupiter was hired out to a mason when Jefferson went to France. And during the remodeling of Monticello, Jupiter was given the arduous job of blasting and hauling rock and limestone. He did not seem to reap any special privileges for his loyal service to his master. Nevertheless, at his death in 1800, Jefferson expressed genuine concern and loss. Unlike the bare, factual statements of the deaths of others, including that of his mother, his account to Thomas Mann Randolph of Jupiter's final illness and death is uncharacteristically detailed and sympathetic:

I was extremely against his coming to Fredericksburg with me & had engaged Davy Bowles, but Jupiter was so much disturbed at this that I yielded. At the end of the second day's journey I saw how much he was worsted, & pressed him to wait at Hyde's, a very excellent house till the horses should return, & I got the promise of a servant from thence. But he would not hear of it. At Fredericksburg again I engaged the tavernkeeper to take care of him till he should be quite well enough to proceed. And it seems that immediately on his arrival at home, he took another journey to my brother's where he died. I am sorry for him.

In a letter to his younger daughter, Maria, he wrote, "You have perhaps heard of the loss of Jupiter. With all his defects, he leaves a void in my domestic arrangements which cannot be filled." Shortly after writing this letter, Jefferson received from his daughter Martha an account that certainly increased his pain:

[Jupiter] unfortunately conceived himself poisoned and went to consult the negro doctor who attended the Georges [Great George and his wife Ursula]. He went in the house to see uncle Randolph who gave him a dram which he drank and seemed to be as well as he had been for some time past, after which he took a dose from his black doctor who pronounced that it would *kill or cure.* 2½ hours after taking the medicine he fell down in a strong convulsion fit which lasted from ten to eleven hours, during which time it took 3 stout men to hold him. He languished nine days but was never heard to speak from the first of his being seized to the moment of his death.

Martha reported that after Jupiter's death, the black doctor "absconded." She thought he should have been prosecuted for murder.

Slave artisans belonged to a lower level in the plantation hierarchy. Because they normally did not work at the estate house but under the supervision of an overseer, their freedom was much more restricted. At Monticello, however, because of the protracted building program, extending over decades, building tradesmen were more of an integral part of the plantation economy. Slaves usually worked as apprentices to free white carpenters and masons and therefore lived at the mountaintop during construction, a desirable arrangement from the slave's point of view because of the various perquisites that went with living close to the plantation house: this was where the food, liquor, clothing, and money were. House slaves had the greatest access to these amenities, but barter, purchase, or theft were convenient avenues of commerce for other slaves. Stealing food and liquor was common among slaves, and accepted as a matter of course by many slaveowners. "A man's moral sense must be unusually strong, if slavery does not make him a thief," Jefferson commented. Still, he expected his house slaves to be honest, and was not above placing a mark on the label of a bottle of rum "to try the fidelity of Martin." Slaves normally received no pay, but there were various sources of income. Gratuities were often passed out freely by visiting gentry. Jefferson himself seldom failed to tip slave servants during his visits to neighboring plantations. Isaac recalled how he was frequently given money by a visitor for opening a series of gates leading to Monticello (and how he was whipped if he did not do it promptly). Vegetables, poultry, and eggs produced by slaves were commonly sold to Martha Jefferson, and later to her daughter Martha Randolph, on a regular basis, providing a small, steady income.

The teenage boys who made nails in Jefferson's nail shop belonged to a special class of skilled workers. Normally, slave children, like other children in the eighteenth century, were considered to be small adults who needed only to have learning pumped into them as their bodies grew. The notion that childhood was a special state of innocence and grace, to be nurtured as something precious, was a nineteenth-century romantic idea that would have seemed absurd to educated men and women of the Enlightenment. In the case of slaves, who were economic commodities, children were capital assets who had to be kept healthy and well-fed until they matured into productive workers. Their education consisted, not of becoming literate, but of learning how to be either a docile, hardworking field laborer, or a craftsman of some kind. Female children were equally valuable, for they not only became workers, but, as Jefferson pointed out, future breeders, representing a potential increase in a slaveholder's capital.

(They did not rush into pregnancy, however; a check of Jefferson's slave rolls reveals that most of his slaves were in their late teens or twenties before having their first child.) Jefferson counted women field workers at half the labor of a man, but women also worked as weavers, spinners, cooks, and house servants. Jefferson's rule for slave children was that until the age of ten they were to be baby-sitters, or "nurses" as he termed them, while their mothers worked. He built slave cabins close together so that the aged women, who no longer did field work, could help the younger children care for infants and toddlers. "From 10 to 16, the boys to make nails, the girls spin," he recorded. Then, at sixteen years of age, slaves would either become field laborers or be apprenticed to learn a trade. Sally Hemings's son Madison reported that in practice this occurred at fourteen years of age.

Jefferson's venture into nail making was one of a number of enterprises he either considered or attempted in an effort to get some income from a plantation that owed a precarious existence to the fluctuating prices of wheat and tobacco. An ideal business opportunity, from his standpoint, would be one that required little capital and utilized the raw materials and labor resources available on his lands. At one time, he seriously considered manufacturing potash, which was used as a fertilizer and for bleaching linen, because he had the vast amounts of woodlands and the slave labor needed for it, but he abandoned the idea. He got into the business of milling flour, but as it turned out, this consumed large amounts of capital for building a canal and mill and never consistently returned a profit.

Making nails was the ideal low-capital, high-labor enterprise he was searching for. Nails were a consumer item that every farmer needed, and Jefferson was able for a time to produce them cheaper than they could be purchased from England. He sold them to various merchants in the Piedmont, and also at the Monticello shop. The rods of iron from which the nails were cut and shaped into various sizes could be purchased on credit, and Jefferson had a ready supply of teenagers to fabricate them. In good years the nail shop cleared a profit of $1,000. However, the nail business never lived up to Jefferson's expectations because of his frequent absences, inefficient management, undependable slave labor, and the difficulty of getting paid for nails that had been purchased on credit. Nails were manufactured from 1794 to

1812, until the war with Britain made it impossible to ship nail rod by sea from Philadelphia to Richmond. Because of his building schemes, Jefferson was his own best customer, so he continued making nails on and off from 1815 until 1823.

Nail making had changed little from Roman times until the end of the eighteenth century. A nail found in the Roman forum could not be distinguished from one made at Jefferson's shop. Nails were made by hand, using blacksmith's tools—forge, anvil, and hammer—in a fixed series of movements prescribed by Jefferson with the precision of a time-motion specialist: "Then he flirts the end of it against the underside of the square bit which bends it to a right angle, then he puts it through the hole in the square bit; the first stroke of the hammer discharges the but of the rod from it, & about 6 more forms the head." He kept productivity tables on his adolescent nailers, noting who turned out the most nails and which boys wasted the most nail rod. Jefferson later purchased a nail-making machine, but nails continued to be made by hand, because machine-made nails were usually too brittle to be bent with a blow of the hammer when clenching a nail to secure boards tightly.

The boys who worked in the nail shop proved to be a serious discipline problem, and one can easily understand why. Here were postpubescent young men, in the full blush of teenage vitality, working twelve hours a day, six days a week, at a repetitive, boring, mindless task. Unlike the blacksmith's craft, which changed constantly and required creativity and judgment, or even field labor with its seasonal tides, nail making at Monticello anticipated the dark satanic mills of the nineteenth century, where children worked from dawn until dusk at just such dehumanizing tasks as were done at Jefferson's nailery. As many as ten young blacks worked around two forges under the supervision of a blacksmith overseer who inspected the nails and, even more importantly, made sure the nail-makers worked, for Jefferson's corps of teenage slaves did little labor if they were not constantly watched. During Jefferson's vice presidency, Great George's son Smith George was in charge of the nail shop, but when he became seriously ill and was no longer able to supervise the nail-makers, work came to a virtual halt. Jefferson wrote to one of his nail customers, John McDowell, that "the long & still doubtful illness of my foreman together with my absence, have greatly affected my nailery, little having been done during the winter."

Smith George's successor, an illiterate overseer named Gabriel Lilly, resorted to the whip during Jefferson's absence, but Jefferson put a stop to it. "It would destroy their value in my estimation to degrade them in their own eyes by the whip," he wrote. "This therefore must not be resorted to but in extremities. As they will be again under my government, I would chuse they should retain the stimulus of character." Jefferson stimulated their character through the use, in the language of the social sciences, of positive, rather than negative, reinforcement. He gave bonuses of cash, food, and clothing to workers who performed well. Smith George and Isaac, who also supervised the nailery, were given two or three percent of the net profits. This came to a considerable sum in good years. In 1795, the two slaves were paid more than £32; in 1796, George received "2 p.c. on 2127.33 . . . [£]42.54." In his memoir, Isaac reported that the teenage boys who worked in Jefferson's nail factory on Mulberry Row received "a pound of meat a week, a dozen herrings, a quart of molasses, and a peck of meal. Give them that wukked the best a suit of red or blue; encouraged them mightily." This represented as much as twice the rations of a field worker. These rewards were confirmed by the Duke de la Rochefoucauld-Liancourt on his visit to Monticello in 1796. He wrote of Jefferson's community of slave tradesmen:

> Every article is made on his farm: his negroes are cabinet-makers, carpenters, masons, bricklayers, smiths, etc. The children he employs in a nail factory, which yields already a considerable profit. He animates them by rewards and distinctions; in fine, his superior mind directs the management of his domestic concerns with the same abilities, activity, and regularity which he evinced in the conduct of public affairs.

In this, as in so many other of his social and psychological insights, Jefferson was far ahead of his time. Yet, it did not stop the nail shop from remaining a breeding ground of "idleness," "mischief," discontent, and sometimes violence.

An attack by one of the slave nailers on another was reported to

Jefferson during his first term as President by Thomas Mann Randolph: "The boy Cary, irritated at some little trick from Brown, who hid part of his nailrod to teaze him . . . took a most barbarous revenge." Cary raised his nail hammer, Randolph reported, and struck Brown "with his whole strength upon the skull." Brown went into convulsions, then a coma, and was operated on by a local physician to relieve the pressure of a piece of skull embedded in his brain. "Warlaw and myself arriving nearly at the same time," Randolph wrote, "I acted as his assistant in the operation which he performed by means of the trephine (the saw which works both ways or with the motion of the wrist only) with the greatest boldness, steadiness and skill." Randolph immediately sent Cary to jail. Jefferson told Randolph to leave the slave there "under orders not to permit him to see or speak to any person whatsoever," until a buyer could be found so far away that "it would be to the others as if he were put out of the way by death." Cary was sold that same year. Brown recovered fully and soon learned the brickmason's trade. It was he who was sold by Jefferson three years later to the brickmason John Jordan so he could live with his wife, who was owned by Jordan.

Young male slaves, working in close proximity under sweatshop conditions, could not fail to talk of freedom—and several of them chose it by running away. The treatments of two of the boys who grew up in the nail shop, both named Jamey, represent contrasting ways that Jefferson reacted to slaves who ran away. One of them was James Hemings, the son of Critta, who was a daughter of Betty Hemings, matriarch of the Hemings clan. He was severely beaten while working in the nail shop under the direction of Gabriel Lilly. One of Jefferson's carpenters, James Oldham, described how the young slave was mistreated by Lilly: "The Barbarity that he maid use of with Little Jimmy was the moost cruel. to my noledge Jimmy was sick for thre nights and the most part of the time I rely thot he would not of Livd he at this time slepd. in the room with me." Oldham said that he informed Lilly that Hemings was not able to work "and Begd. him not to punnish him." But Lilly "whipd. him three times in one day, and the boy was rely not able to raise his hand to his Head."

Not surprisingly, James Hemings ran away. The following year, Oldham, who had set up a carpenter's shop in Richmond, wrote to

Jefferson that the young slave had been found. Oldham reported that a "Mr. John Taylor came across Jimmy," and that the two men consulted on whether to put Hemings in jail. Oldham agreed instead to take the runaway in with him "until he could heare from you." After talking to Hemings, Oldham reported that his "wish is to serve you provided he is not plaisd under the direction of Lilly, as he says the severe treatment which he experienced was the onley cause of his going of[f]." Oldham wrote that Hemings had been a sailor aboard boats running the James River between Richmond and Norfolk, and had been "living at bent Crick with a mr. James Right." The light-skinned slave was probably passing as a white laborer.

Jefferson's response was characteristic where one of the Hemings family was concerned; he was quite willing to forgive and forget. "I can readily excuse the follies of a boy," he wrote. He promised to take Jamey out of the nail shop under Lilly and place him "with Johnny Hemings and Lewis at house-joiner's work." He advised Oldham to send the young man back to Monticello by the next stage. But in fact Hemings had no intention of returning to slavery after he had tasted the life of a free man on the river. "I am sorry to inform you that James Hemings has not acted agreeable to his promis," Oldham wrote a few days later. After asking permission to leave for fifteen minutes to visit his uncle Robert Hemings, whom Jefferson had freed in 1794 and who was living in Richmond, the young man disappeared and was last seen heading up the river in a boat, Oldham reported. He was defensive about allowing the slave to escape. "His being so much affected at the thots of being placd. in confinement and expresing so grait a desir to return voluntaryly Home was the only inducement to me to befriend him," he wrote, and added, "I surmise but little good will become of him." Young James Hemings's name was removed from Jefferson's slave rolls, and unlike other runaway slaves who were hunted down with grim determination, no attempt was made to recapture him. In fact, nearly ten years later, Jefferson recorded a strange item in his Memorandum Book: "gave James Hem. [for] finding eye glass of Borda 2. D." (This was the eyepiece of a surveying instrument.) Since no other James Hemings was owned by Jefferson at the time, the notation suggests that Jamey Hemings freely returned to Monticello to visit his mother and family. If this was the case, it was an instance of Jefferson's informally freeing one of the Hemings family members without a legal manumission once he was able to work successfully in the white world. He was later to free Sally Hemings's daughter Harriet the same way. Indeed, all of the slaves freed by Jefferson, formally or by allowing them to run away, during his life or in his will, were the children or grandchildren of Betty Hemings.

The other Jamey was the son of Jame Hubbard, who was born in 1743, the same year as Jefferson; his mother was Cate, one of the original slaves inherited from Jefferson's father. Cate and Jame Hubbard had thirteen children, one an epileptic, another described by Jefferson as "an idiot." They lived and worked at Jefferson's Bedford plantation, some eighty miles from Monticello and a three days' journey. When Jefferson started his nail factory, he took young Jamey from his family to Monticello, where he lived with the other nail boys.

Jefferson's overseer Edmund Bacon recalled that Jamey Hubbard was caught stealing nails from the nail shop. After locating the nails, which had been hidden in a box in the woods, Bacon told Jefferson about it. "He was very much surprised and felt badly about it," Bacon stated. "Jim had always been a favorite servant." Hubbard was confronted by Jefferson and was "mortified and distressed beyond measure. He had been brought up in the shop, and we all had confidence in him. Now his character was gone." Hubbard wept and begged pardon "over and over again" until Jefferson said to Bacon, "Ah, sir, we can't punish him. He has suffered enough already." After talking to the slave, and giving him a "heap of good advice," Jefferson sent Hubbard back to the nailery. The shop foreman, Reuben Grady, was waiting with the whip, Bacon related, "and was astonished to see him come back and go to work after such a crime." Grady reported that Hubbard told him: "Well, I'se been a-seeking religion a long time, but I never heard anything before that sounded so, or made me feel so, as I did when master said, 'Go, and don't do so any more'; and now I'se determined to seek religion." According to Bacon's account, Hubbard subsequently asked for and received a permit to "go and be baptized." (Slaves needed a signed permit to be on the road alone.)

Bacon apparently was unaware, in relating this story, that Jamey Hubbard had run away a year before Bacon started working for Jefferson. In September 1805, the year after James Hemings fled from

Monticello to Richmond, Hubbard ran off to Fairfax County, using forged papers in an attempt to pass as a freeman. He was captured and jailed, however, and returned to Monticello. Neither Jefferson's biblical homily to go and sin no more, nor Hubbard's newfound religion kept him on the plantation permanently. Several years after the nail theft, he ran away a second time and was gone for a year before he was captured and brought back in irons. Jefferson was now past the point of sermonizing and forgiving, for Hubbard was not a member of the privileged Hemings family. He was "severely flogged" in front of the other nailers. Jefferson became convinced that Hubbard would "never again serve any man as a slave; the moment he is out of jail and his irons off he will be off himself." This was prophetic, for no sooner was he released than he ran away for the third time. Jefferson sold him in absentia to one of his carpenters, Reuben Perry, in return for carpentry and joinery work on the house at Poplar Forest that Jefferson was then building. A slave with Hubbard's history of escape obviously had little cash value.

James Hemings and Jamey Hubbard were not unique among Jefferson's slaves; a number of them were equally rebellious. Hannah's Billy, a slave born and raised at the Bedford County plantation, was especially troublesome to Jefferson. At the age of nineteen, he was brought to Monticello to learn the cooper's trade under the tutelage of Jefferson's master cooper, Barnaby. Jefferson soon reported to Joel Yancey, the overseer at the Bedford plantation, that Billy was being shipped back to him "as soon as he can make a good [barrel] band" because "he is too ungovernable." A few weeks later, Jefferson changed his mind: Billy had become so "ungovernable and idle" that he was to be sent back to Bedford as a field laborer; in the meantime, he had been taken out of the Monticello cooper shop and placed under an overseer as a field hand.

Six months later, Yancey wrote Jefferson of further difficulties with Billy, these more serious. Because of an impending frost, Yancey had ordered the slaves to cut tobacco on a Sunday, their traditional day off. Another overseer, Lewis Balling, ordered Billy to work, and he "positively refused." "A battle ensued," which Yancey later described in detail. Billy came at the overseer with a stone in each hand "and struck him several times" before Balling wrestled one of the stones from him. In the ensuing scuffle, the slave got the overseer's thumb in his mouth and "bit it severely." Billy's mother Hannah saw the battle, Yancey wrote, and she confirmed that Billy "bitt and struck the overseer" and then went looking for Yancey, presumably with the intention of attacking him as well. Not finding Yancey, Billy "made his escape." He ran off to Monticello to take his case directly to Jefferson ("they run from here to you, and from you to here," Yancey complained bitterly), but Jefferson sent him back to Bedford. Yancey wanted nothing to do with a slave as violent as Billy, and recommended that Jefferson "dispose of him." "I had at one time great hopes of reclaiming him," Yancey wrote, "but . . . I despair of making anything of him, he is certainly the most consumate, bloody minded Villan that I ever saw of his age, and he becomes more & more daring as he increases in strength."

At approximately the same time, another slave with the same name, Moses' Billy, was being jailed and tried for stabbing an overseer. He was apparently released or escaped from jail, returned to the Bedford plantation, and joined a band of runaway slaves who lived off the land. Yancey wrote to Jefferson that the runaways "are doing great mischief to the neighboring stock, considerable exertions have been made to take them, but without success." A week later he reported that "he and his comraids takes a shoat or lamb every day . . . from us." Billy was captured, tried, "found guilty of stabbing & was sentenced to be burnt in the hand and whipped." Two other slaves, Hercules and Gawen, were acquitted, "there being no positive proof of conspiracy." Hercules, also a former runaway, had been accused by some of the Bedford slaves of poisoning them. This prompted Yancey to write to Jefferson, "I am satisfied he has done a great deal of mischief, and ought to be hung."

Jefferson's response to the insubordinate slaves at his Bedford plantation was the same as he had taken in previous cases of runaway or defiant blacks—he sold them. In this case, "four prime young men, guilty of an attack on their overseer were sent, as an example, to N. Orleans to be sold." The four were not identified, but they were in all likelihood the two Billys, Hercules, and Gawen. Disposing of four troublesome slaves was perhaps made easier by the fact that Jefferson at the time was badly pressed for money, and they were sold for $2,000.

(In fact, he collected only $400 of the sale price, for two of the slaves died and one became seriously ill.)

The rebellion of Jamey Hubbard and the two Billys was an extreme example of the deep resentment to their enslavement felt by many Southern slaves, even those owned by as paternalistic a master as Thomas Jefferson. For every Great George, who reputedly turned down an offer to be set free, there was a Jamey Hubbard, who would accept slavery under no conditions, particularly those offered at Jefferson's nailery. Between these two extremes were the mass of slave workers whose acceptance of their condition depended on a wide assortment of variables, most of which constantly shifted with circumstances. It is tempting to make judgments about Jefferson's relationships with his slaves based on a handful of well-known examples—the Hemings family, Great George, Jupiter, and Burwell, the slave who served him faithfully in his old age—but these were all extraordinary cases and tell us little about the average tradesman or field laborer. These cases overlook such mutinous slaves as Jamey Hubbard, Hannah's Billy, Moses' Billy, and Hercules. Furthermore, Jefferson's history of slaveholding extends from his twenty-first birthday to his death at eighty-three. During these years, generations of slaves passed through his hands, some spending their entire lives on his estate, others bought, sold, and hired out, some coming into contact with him frequently, but most seeing him rarely. The ebb and flow of his income and his debts, the coming and going of overseers, the rise and fall of the value of slaves, and Jefferson's prolonged absences from his estate—all of these influenced the relationship of master and slave. Before the Revolution and during his stay in France, under the influence of the French Enlightenment and its philosophes, Jefferson was an ardent emancipationist. Back in his own country, with ambitious plans to rebuild Monticello and to make his estate profitable, he became a much more traditional slaveholder, concerned with labor productivity and slave commerce. In his old age, as his financial situation became more desperate, all serious talk of emancipation quietly ceased.

Like most of his fellow slaveowners, Jefferson realized that his own well-being depended upon the cooperation of his slaves. They had it within their power to destroy him economically by withholding their labor, either by running away, refusing to work, or working poorly. Slaves rebelled most commonly not in acts of aggression, but in passive refusal to give their labor. When Jefferson's nail-makers stopped working they were making a statement about bondage, about work conditions, or perhaps about personal grievances with an overseer.

The extreme decision to run away was sometimes made for purely personal reasons. It may have been a family quarrel; perhaps it was an existential choice to be free. When these kinds of escape occurred, it left even a Thomas Jefferson baffled. During his presidency, one of his blacksmiths, Joe Fosset, ran away to Washington. Jefferson recorded incredulously that it was "without the least word of difference with any body, & indeed having never in his life received a blow from any one." Fosset ran away to visit Edy, another of Jefferson's slaves, who had been sent to Washington to learn French cooking at the President's House. That a slave would run away because he was in love did not normally enter into a slaveowner's calculation of what motivated an attempt to escape. If he obeyed orders and was never beaten, he was happy. A runaway like Joe Fosset represented a threat to the slave system, for if a slave who was well-treated, trained to a trade, and seemingly content ran away, then the institution itself was suspect.

Jefferson was not alone in wanting his slaves' behavior to be rational and predictable. Virginians lived in constant fear of slave insurrection. They surrounded themselves with slaves to the point where the ratio of black to white on a plantation ran from two to one upward. It was an act of blind trust on their part that their slaves would reward humane and decent treatment with an acceptance of bondage as right and proper, and not slit their throats one night, or poison them, as occasionally happened.

A measure of slaves' disaffection with their bondage came during the Revolutionary War, when slaves were induced to join British forces with a promise of freedom. Jefferson, like many slaveholders, must have been shaken by the number of his slaves—thirty—who chose to go off with British troops. Years later, Jefferson stated that his slaves were "carried off" by Cornwallis's army, but at the time in 1781, he recorded in his Farm Book that they either "fled to the enemy" or "joined [the] enemy." It was a tragic choice, as most of them contracted smallpox or "putrid fever" (probably typhus or typhoid fever) in the unsanitary conditions of the army camps and died.

One way of discouraging slave insurrection was to prevent the communication of subversive ideas among slaves by keeping them illiterate. On the other hand, a slave artisan who was literate was more valuable; a carpenter able to read, for example, could then use the many handbooks available to the woodworking trade. Jefferson at times sent work instructions to slaves who could read. He asked Thomas Mann Randolph if he "would sometimes take the trouble to make John [Hemings] & Davy come to you and bring their written instructions, & question them as to their progress." Slaves probably learned to read or write from white master workers or journeymen to whom they were apprenticed, for there is no record that Jefferson formally taught them himself. Indeed, he was quoted as saying that slaves should be taught to "read print," but if they learned to write there was no way of preventing them from forging documents to escape. Some slaves apparently learned to read and write on their own, inspired perhaps by a desire to read the Bible. Madison Hemings reported that he learned to read "by inducing the white children to teach me the letters." There is a letter to Jefferson from Hannah, Jamey Hubbard's sister, who lived most of her life on Jefferson's Bedford County plantation and who served as his cook and laundress when he was at the house at Poplar Forest. Hannah's letter, written late in Jefferson's life, demonstrates not only her literacy, but also her Christianity. References to religious beliefs are otherwise strangely absent from all of the correspondence dealing with Jefferson's slaves. Aside from Jamey Hubbard's decision to be baptized, there are no records of how many of Jefferson's slaves were Christian or whether they attended church services, as did slaves at other plantations. Fithian reported, for example, that Robert Carter's slaves sometimes accompanied the family to church. But then, Jefferson was himself not known for being a churchgoer and he may not have encouraged his slaves to be religious. Hannah wrote to him after Jefferson failed to make his periodic trip to Poplar Forest because of illness:

> Master, I write you a few lines to let you know that your house and furniture are all safe, as I expect you will be glad

to know. I heard that you did not expect to come up this fall. I was sorry to hear that you are so unwell you could not come. It grieve[s] me many time[s], but I hope as you have been so blessed in this [life] that you considered it was God that done it and no other one. We all ought to be thankful for what he has done for us. We ought to serve and obey his commandments that you may set to win the prize, and after glory run. Master, I do not [believe] my ignorant letter will be much encouragement to you as knows I am a poor, ignorant creature. This leaves us all well.

> adieu, I am your
> humble servant
> Hannah

Several members of the Hemings family were literate. Jefferson received from his cook, James Hemings, an inventory of the kitchen utensils at Monticello, written in a clear, legible hand with unusually accurate spelling for the eighteenth century. There are fourteen letters from John Hemings, the most successful product of Jefferson's program to teach his slaves useful skills. (There are, as well, four letters to Hemings from Jefferson, mostly building instructions for the house at Poplar Forest.) John Hemings was one of the twelve children of Betty Hemings, the matriarch of the large Hemings clan. During his life, Jefferson owned thirty of Betty Hemings's children and grandchildren. Unlike the anonymity which veils the history of most American slave families, a great deal is known about the offspring of Betty Hemings. There are two reasons for this: the Sally Hemings scandal and Thomas Jefferson's obsession with keeping records. The accusations that Sally Hemings was the mother of several of Jefferson's children produced a reminiscence by one of her sons, Madison, late in life, which gives detailed information about the Hemings family genealogy. Jefferson's records reveal nothing about the Sally Hemings allegations, but they do contain much about individual members of the Hemings family— their lives at Monticello, their work, and their relationship with Jefferson.

The Hemings history is quintessentially American, for the family was rooted in one of the forbidden truths of American slavery: that slaves were not only economic property, but also sexual property. The Hemings family was the product of miscegenation. The union of the races ran through every generation of the family that Jefferson owned. According to Madison Hemings, his grandmother Betty Hemings was the daughter of an English sea captain named Hemings; her mother was reportedly a full-blooded African Negro. Betty was owned by John Wayles, the man who was to become Jefferson's father-in-law, and at whose death Jefferson acquired the entire Hemings family. Madison claimed that Wayles, after the death of his third wife in 1761, took Betty Hemings as a "concubine" and had six children by her, the youngest being Sally. Betty previously had four children, presumably by slave fathers, and, after moving to Monticello, had two more. The Wayles paternity was not only alleged by Madison, but also independently by Isaac, who claimed in his memoir that "folks said that these Hemingses was old Mr. Wayles's children."

John Hemings was born on April 24, 1776, three years after Sally; his father, according to Isaac, was "an Englishman named Nelson." This would be Joseph Nelson, or Neilson, a carpenter who worked on the original Monticello house, and who was identified by Isaac as "an inside worker, a finisher." John, or Johnny, as Jefferson sometimes called him, was not given Neilson's name, however, possibly because Hemings was a name with some prestige at Monticello. John Hemings was an apprentice to several of the carpenters who worked on Jefferson's house. The first was the British deserter and heroic quaffer Davy Watson and the last was James Dinsmore, probably the most skilled of all of the Monticello carpenters. John Hemings, in his mature years, was engaged in making furniture at Monticello, in carriage work, and in constructing Jefferson's second house at Poplar Forest. Although family tradition has it that he crafted much of the furniture throughout the numerous rooms at Monticello, none of the pieces now on display at the mansion can be positively identified as his. Edmund Bacon called John Hemings "a first-rate workman—a very extra workman. He could make anything that was wanted in woodwork. He made most of the woodwork in Mr. Jefferson's fine carriage."

One of Jefferson's great-grandchildren, Ellen Wayles Randolph Harrison, related how the children at Monticello haunted the carpenter

shop to have "Daddy" Hemings make a drawing box, a table, or a
flower box for them. A year before Jefferson's death, one of his grand-
daughters, eleven-year-old Septimia, wrote to John Hemings at Poplar
Forest, telling him about the state of Jefferson's declining health.
Hemings and two assistants were helping Jefferson's grandson, Francis
Wayles Eppes, repair fire damage to the Poplar Forest house. Although
Hemings's reply reveals a closeness between slave and child, formality
and deference are still maintained. Love is sent to her brothers, but
not to Septimia or her sisters, lest the affection be misconstrued. Given
Hemings's highly personal orthography and his lack of capitalization
and punctuation, one wonders how much Septimia could read:

Poplar Forest Augst 28.th 1825

Dear miss Septima   your Letter came to me on the 23th and
hapey was I to embreasit to see you take it upon you self to
writ to me and let me know how your grand Paw was Glad
am i to hear that he is no worst dear I hope you ar well and
all the famely give my Love to all your brothers Gorg with
Randolph speculy I shoul gite don the house on tusday that
is tining it we have all the Tarrste to do yet which is one
hundred feet Long and 22 feet 8 inches wide yesterday we
just hade one Lode of the stuff brought home fore the gutters
and that is 25 mile off where it came from I am in hope I
shal be able to com home by the 25 of Nomember Ef Life
Last

I am your obediente seirvant
John hemmings

With spelling normalized and punctuation and capitalization added,
Hemings's letter reads:

Poplar Forest, August 28, 1825

Dear Miss Septimia,
    Your letter came to me on the 23rd, and happy was I to
embrace it, to see you take it upon yourself to write to me

[123]

and let me know how your grandpaw was. Glad am I to hear that he is no worse. Dear, I hope you are well and all the family. Give my love to all your brothers, George Wythe Randolph specially. I should get done the house on Tuesday, that is, tinning it [the roof]. We have all the terrace to do yet, which is one hundred feet long and 22 feet, 8 inches wide. Yesterday, we just had one load of the stuff [lumber] brought home for the gutters, and that is 25 miles off, where it came from. I am in hope I shall be able to come home by the 25th of November. If life lasts.

> I am your obedient servant,
> John Hemmings

Septimia's brother, seven-year-old George Wythe Randolph, the youngest of Martha Randolph's twelve children (she was forty-six when she gave birth to him), was obviously Hemings's favorite. The information on the progress of work on the house was no doubt meant to be passed on to Jefferson. John Hemings was not pleased when he was sent to Poplar Forest to work, because it separated him from his wife. He was married to a slave, Priscilla, who was owned by the Randolphs. She helped raise the Randolph children, and when the family moved permanently to Monticello, "Aunt Priscilla" was given a cabin there. At her death in 1830 at the age of fifty-four, she was buried on the grounds.

The workings of Jefferson's slave apprentice system are best illustrated in the case of Isaac, whose memoir provides a rare glimpse of eighteenth-century Virginia life from the slave's perspective. In 1790, when Isaac was fifteen, Jefferson, then secretary of state, brought him to Philadelphia to be apprenticed to a hardware merchant, James Bringhurst. Isaac recalled:

> Bringhouse was a short, mighty small, neat-made man; treated Isaac very well. Went thar to larn the tinner's trade. Fust week larnt to cut out and sodder; make little pepper boxes and graters and sich, out of scraps of tin, so as not to waste

any till he had larnt. Then to making cups. . . . Isaac made four dozen pint cups a day and larnt to tin copper and sheets (sheet iron)—make 'em tin. He lived four years with old Bringhouse. One time Mr. Jefferson sent to Bringhouse to tin his copper kittles and pans for kitchen use; Bringhouse sent Isaac and another prentice thar—a white boy named Charles; can't think of his other name. Isaac was the only black boy in Bringhouse's shop. When Isaac carred the cups to his Old Master to show him, he was mightily pleased. Said, "Isaac you are larnin mighty fast; I bleeve I must send you back to Vaginny to car on the tin business."

According to Isaac, Jefferson purchased a supply of tin, and sent Bringhurst for a month's stay at Monticello to help set up the metal-working shop. Isaac reported that the metal shop, like other of Jefferson's attempts at small business ventures, failed after two years. Unlike nails, apparently tinware was not in great demand in Albemarle County. The apprenticeship served Isaac well, however, for he became an expert blacksmith, and was working at his trade when he was interviewed in 1847 at the age of seventy-two at Petersburg, Virginia. At that time he was described as "rather tall, of strong frame, stoops a little, in color ebony; sensible, intelligent, pleasant; wears large circular ironbound spectacles and a leather apron."

Isaac, his wife Iris, and two children were deeded to Jefferson's youngest daughter in 1797, but Isaac was subsequently hired to Thomas Mann Randolph. Isaac and his family lived with the Randolphs "fust and last twenty-six or seven years." Isaac was pleased with his new master, reporting that Randolph "treated him mighty well—one of the finest masters in Virginia." When Isaac moved to the Randolph estate he took possession of Smith George's old anvil and tools, and a "large new bellows." Jefferson purchased new equipment for the Monticello blacksmith shop in 1797 and reserved Smith George's much-used anvil and tools for his brother Isaac.

Among other kinds of artisan slaves on a large estate were coopers to make the barrels and hogsheads needed for transporting tobacco and flour, and shoemakers to make shoes for the plantation's slaves. Jefferson's cooper shop at Monticello was under the direction of Barnaby, a highly skilled barrel-maker. A plantation the size of Jefferson's had ample work for a full-time cooper shop, especially after the Rivanna River flour mill began production; all flour was shipped in barrels.

Jefferson began manufacturing barrels for sale in 1816 by making a contract with Mr. Colclaser, a miller who leased his manufacturing mill, to deliver 4,000 barrels a year. In order to turn out this many barrels, Jefferson had to have a work force gathering, cutting, and dressing lumber to supply the cooper shop with materials. Barnaby worked with his regular aide, Nace, and another slave helper. "I count on their setting up for delivery from 90 to 100 [barrels] a week, & they will do this at least 40 weeks in the year," Jefferson wrote to Colclaser. "Nothing but harvest or sickness will ever take them a day out of their shops." Typically, Jefferson offered an inducement to Barnaby, and later to Nace, to produce at this rate. Barnaby received the cash value of one barrel of every thirty-one produced. At the end of 1816, Jefferson paid him for eighteen barrels, his share of 563 barrels manufactured over a two-and-a-half-month period. The cooper shop continued to produce barrels for sale until 1824, when Jefferson wrote to his agent, Bernard Peyton, "the mill doing no business the last year, I lost the avails of my cooper's shop 1200 D[ollars]."

Until his death in 1809, shoes for Jefferson's slaves were made by Phill Shoemaker, who was acquired by Jefferson with the Wayles inheritance. He was also a carpenter, and was occasionally hired out. He took over shoemaking from Sandy, who was sold by Jefferson in 1773 for £100. The reason for the sale can be deduced readily by an advertisement for a "Runaway Slave" which Jefferson placed in the *Virginia Gazette* on September 7, 1769:

Run away from the subscriber in *Albemarle*, a Mulatto slave called *Sandy*, about 35 years of age, his stature is rather low, inclining to corpulence, and his complexion light; he is a shoemaker by trade, in which he uses his left hand principally, can do coarse carpenters work, and is something of a horse jockey; he is greatly addicted to drink, and when drunk is insolent and disorderly, in his conversation he swears much, and his behaviour is artful and knavish. He took with him a

white horse, much scarred with traces, of which it is expected
he will endeavour to dispose; he also carried his shoemakers
tools, and will probably endeavour to get employment that
way.

The ad shows a great deal of contempt on Jefferson's part, but slaves
who were independent or self-assertive were commonly seen by their
owners as "insolent," "disorderly," or "knavish."

The lowest members of Jefferson's slave hierarchy were the field
laborers with no skills other than the ability to do manual farm
work. These were the anonymous field hands, men and women, who
appear on Jefferson's slave rolls only as names and birth dates,
who were often sold, hired out, or shifted from farm to farm as the
exigencies of Jefferson's finances dictated. Those on his Monticello
and Shadwell farms were brought to the mountaintop on occasion
when Jefferson needed additional manual labor for his building operations.

Field hands worked under the direction of an overseer, and the
quality of their lives depended directly on what kind of man this was.
Overseers, or stewards, as Jefferson sometimes called them, managed
parts of an estate, supervised work, and reported regularly to the
owner. At any given time there might be overseers working at Monticello, Shadwell, Poplar Forest, and other outlying farms. It was a
job with a great deal of responsibility and with only moderate pay; it
is little wonder that Jefferson had difficulty keeping overseers for any
length of time. His private opinion of overseers was one that was
probably shared by many slaveholders. They are, he wrote, "the most
abject, degraded and unprincipled race, always cap in hand to the
Dons who employed them, and furnishing materials for the exercise
of their pride, insolence and spirit of domination."

Overseers often had the reputation of mistreating slaves. They
were usually uneducated men, sometimes illiterate, who found themselves with absolute power over the lives of people who had no legal
recourse from personal abuse. The only defenses a slave had against
mistreatment by an overseer were to run away or to complain to the
owner, and they did both. Jefferson was often absent from Monticello,

however, and his plantations were far-flung, so the opportunities for slaves to voice their grievances against overseers directly to their owner were limited.

One slave, Jamey Hubbard's brother, Phill, ran away from the Poplar Forest plantation to travel to Monticello with a complaint about his treatment by an overseer. The overseer, Jeremiah Goodman, would not permit Hubbard to live with his newly taken wife, "punishing her, as he supposes, for receiving him." Jefferson resolved the problem by sending the couple to another of his farms in exchange for two other slaves who wished to come to Poplar Forest. He also warned Goodman not to punish Phill for running away to complain to his master. This solution was not only humane, but economically sound as well. "Certainly there is nothing I desire so much as that all the young people in the estate should intermarry with one another and stay at home," Jefferson wrote to Goodman. "They are worth a great deal more in that case than when they have husbands and wives abroad." This was particularly so when a man married a woman belonging to another owner: the children of such a marriage were not Jefferson's. Nevertheless, such marriages did occur; a cultural commonplace of plantation life throughout the South was the Saturday evening trek by the slave husband, a sack containing gifts of food or clothing under his arm, to a neighboring plantation to spend the weekend with his wife and family. Slaves with such interplantation marriages usually pressured their masters to sell them to the owner of their spouse. Jefferson complied when it was financially convenient, or attempted to find a buyer in the vicinity. He did this in the case of one of his woman slaves: "In Albemarle I have concluded to sell Dinah & her younger children, & wrote to my brother to find a purchaser in his neighborhood, so as to unite her to her husband." In another instance, he offered to buy the wife of one of his slaves, Moses, because "nobody feels more strongly than I do the desire to make all practicable sacrifices to keep man and wife together who have imprudently married out of their respective families."

Jefferson on occasion also sold slaves to workmen or overseers, but usually only if the slaves were willing to be sold. When his Bedford plantation overseer, Joel Yancey, was leaving his employment, Yancey wrote:

Thomas Jefferson by Charles Willson Peale, 1791. The nation's secretary of state was forty-eight when this portrait was painted.

At six feet two inches tall, Jefferson dominates the signers of John Trumbull's The Declaration of Independence. *A print of the painting hung at Monticello.*

Left: *Thomas Jefferson at forty-three, when he was U.S. minister to France. This is an engraving from the Mather Brown portrait of 1786.*

Right: *Portrait of Maria Cosway. Jefferson owned a copy of this print, engraved by F. Bartolozzi from a painting by her husband, Richard Cosway.*

MARIA COSWAY

Martha Jefferson at seventeen (left), *a miniature painted by Joseph Boze in Paris, 1789, and at sixty-four* (below), *painted by Thomas Sully in 1836.*

Thomas Jefferson by Houdon.

David Rittenhouse, mathematician, astronomer, inventor.

William Short, Jefferson's secretary in Paris, painted by Rembrandt Peale in 1806.

An 1845 daguerreotype of Jefferson's slave Isaac, who left an important memoir of life at Monticello.

A pencil sketch of Jefferson attributed to the architect Benjamin Latrobe.

The second Capitol building at Williamsburg may have inspire the double portico on the first Monticello.

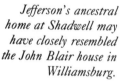

Jefferson's ancestral home at Shadwell may have closely resembled the John Blair house in Williamsburg.

George Wythe's house in Williamsburg was a model of fine craftsmanship for Jefferson.

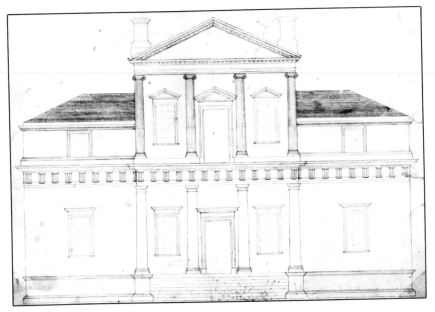

Jefferson's elevation of the first Monticello house.

An artist's rendering of what the first Monticello looked like. The upper columns and many of the decorative moldings were never installed, however.

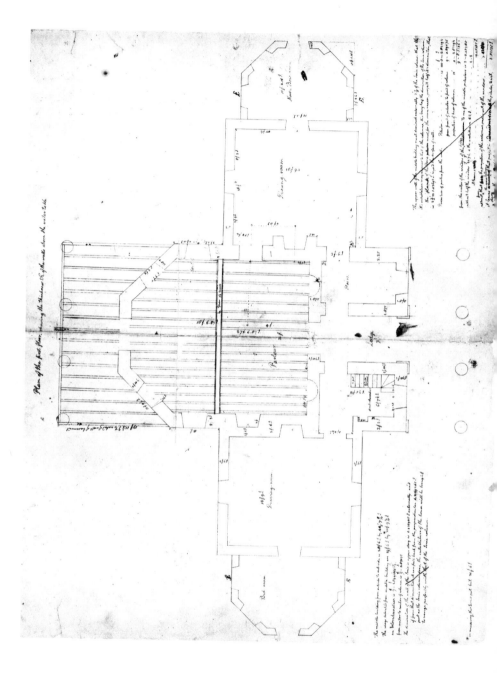

Plan of the first floor, showing the thickness &c of the walls above the water table

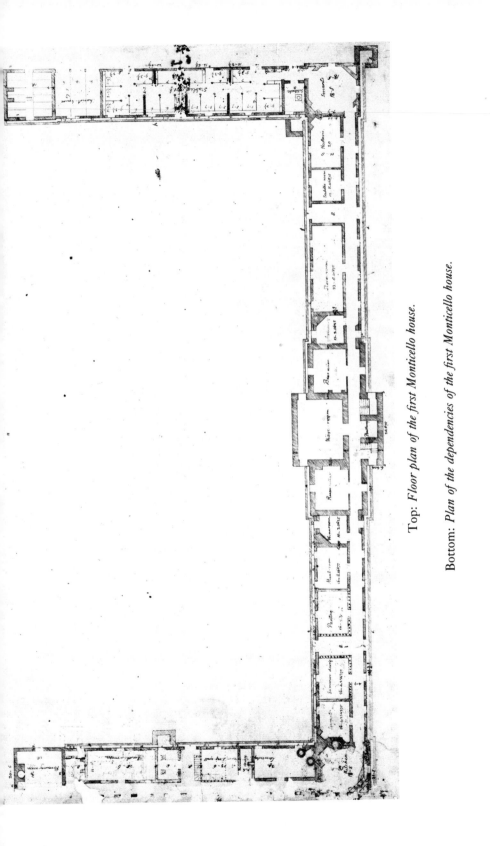

Top: *Floor plan of the first Monticello house.*

Bottom: *Plan of the dependencies of the first Monticello house.*

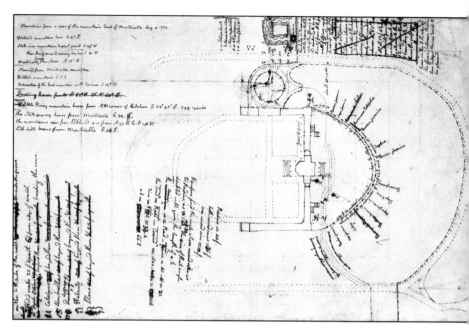

Plan of the garden and roundabout of the first Monticello.

Memorandum for Jefferson's library on the second floor of the first Monticello house, with a sketch of a folding library ladder. The floor plan of this room, drawn on the right, is the only one that exists.

We have been unfortunate in loosing 2 of our best house servants this year [by death], and we have been endeavering to supply their places out of our own stock, but have failed, could you pay me as much as would purchase a good female Servant, this winter or Spring it would be a very great accomodation to us, or if it should be agreable to you to sell, I will give a liberal price for Lucy at P[oplar]. F[orest]. as we are acquainted with her and she appears to be attached to the family, but I do not know that she would be willing to be sold.

Jefferson responded that he would sell Lucy "at a fair valuation by neighbors if she is willing to be sold, as I have little doubt she would be. She would certainly prefer the situation of a house servant under mrs Yancey and yourself and so near her friends to working in the ground under an overseer." The price agreed on was $400, and she was sold to Yancey.

Slave workers were supervised, not only by overseers, but also by what Jefferson called "headmen," blacks who were placed in charge of teams of workers. These were dependable slaves who were designated as foremen and who often labored alongside slave workers to assure that jobs were completed. The headman was a privileged worker because he had considerable authority over his fellow slaves; in many cases he was a de facto overseer. Because slaves were not motivated to work on their own, on most jobs where a white worker was not present, there would be a slave foreman in charge, usually the most experienced and responsible black among the workers. Even children had a headman placed over them. In making plans for his harvest work force, Jefferson stipulated that the "gatherers" of the cut grain should be "5 small boys & a larger for a foreman." Headmen received preferential treatment. When the Poplar Forest foreman, Nace, the brother of Jamey and Phill Hubbard, became ill, Jefferson reminded his overseer: "Nace, the former headman, and the best we have ever known, is to be entirely kept from labour until he recovers, which will probably be very long. He may do anything which he can do sitting in a warm room, such as shoemaking and making baskets. He can shell corn in the house when it is quite warm, or in his own house at any time."

Jefferson's slave workers were probably healthier than the slaves on many other plantations because he fed and clothed them better and instructed his overseers not to overwork them. His instructions to his overseer at the Poplar Forest farm are typical of his concern for the well-being of his slaves:

> If a physician should at any time be wanting for the negroes, let our neighbor Dr. Steptoe be called in. In pleurisies, or other highly inflammatory fevers, intermitting fevers, dysenteries, & Venereal cases, the doctors can give certain relief; and the sooner called to them the easier & more certain the cure. But in most other cases they oftener do harm than good. A dose of salts as soon as they are taken is salutary in almost all cases, & hurtful in none. I have generally found this, with a lighter diet and kind attention restore them soonest.

Jefferson had a poor opinion of the physicians of his age, and was often contemptuous of their treatments. He was a firm believer in the iatrogenic principle that physicians are often the cause of serious sickness, that most illnesses are self-limiting, and that diet and rest are the best ways to treat them. He disapproved of the common eighteenth-century practices of bleeding and purging, and advised his daughters to treat illnesses not with harsh medicines, but the same way his slaves were to be treated: "with a lighter diet and kind attention."

Because of his wide reading in anatomy and medicine, Jefferson was more knowledgeable about the subject than many of the practicing physicians of his period. (No formal education or degree was required to practice "physic"; one apprenticed at it like any other trade.) When he was at Monticello, he usually took care of the health problems of his slaves himself. He could set a bone, lance an abscess, or stitch a wound. He controlled one of the great scourges of his age—smallpox—by obtaining Jenner's vaccine from Boston and vaccinating his slaves himself. He kept a list of slaves who were vaccinated, indicating whether they were already immune or not. Because of his many absences, however, he had to depend on overseers to provide for the well-being of his slave workers, particularly with preventive health care. He gave frequent instructions to overseers on the distribution of clothing, the repair of slave houses, and on providing adequate food.

The infant mortality rate in the eighteenth century was high, among both slaves and free whites. Late in his life, Jefferson admonished his Bedford overseer, Joel Yancey, not to overwork nursing mothers. After the infant deaths of "5 little ones in four years," he feared that "the overseers do not permit the women to devote as much time as is necessary to the care of their children." In an age of poor sanitation, diseases of unknown cause could strike slave populations suddenly and inexplicably. Great George died of what Jefferson called "dropsy"—a general term used during this period for an abnormal swelling resulting from the retention of body fluids. His wife Ursula, their son Smith George, and Jupiter contracted and died of the same disease, most likely a parasitic infection affecting the lymph system. Jefferson's daughter Martha described it as "a constant puking, shortness of breath and swelling, first in the legs but now extending itself." Jefferson, always alert to the possibilities of contagious diseases, noted to his son-in-law Thomas Mann Randolph that "the state of Ursula is remarkable. The symptoms & progress of her disease are well worthy [of] attention."

The slaves who helped build Monticello were themselves housed mostly in log cabins, although Jefferson had better plans for housing some of them. In the 1770s, when he was building the original Monticello house, he included in his design two floor plans and an elevation for stylish cottages, to be erected on Mulberry Row below the first roundabout. They were to be used for his white construction workers and for selected slave families. The cottages were two sizes; one had two rooms, the other five. Both houses had glass windows for each room, a half-light over the doorway, gables with Tuscan moldings, and brick fireplaces. The larger five-room cottage had a center hall with a fireplace, to serve as a kitchen–living room. This was flanked on each side by two small eight-by-eight-foot sleeping rooms. The smaller house had two large rooms with a split hearth for each room. As in all of his architectural designs, the plans showed a close concern for the domestic comfort of those who would live in the houses. In the notes on the drawings, Jefferson indicated which white workman and which slaves would be assigned to each of the cottages. "Betty

Hemings and her family" were to have one of the larger houses, as were women with families, but no husbands. A smaller cottage was to go to Great George and Ursula and their children.

A total of at least eight of these cottages were contemplated. The notes accompanying the drawings were successively crossed out, however, as Jefferson redesigned and rethought his building plans. By the time of the Revolution he had scaled the plan down to a "cheaper and better way of building and arranging" the houses. Now there was only one white workman's cottage, and one for slaves, this designated for Great George and Jupiter. Apparently, none of the slave cottages was built; their priority was simply too low in a house-building program that lasted more than half a century. Like many of Jefferson's construction ideas, they were an architectural flight of fancy that had no foundation in the economic realities of slaveholding. These realities appeared on the fire insurance policy of 1796, which shows the outbuildings on Jefferson's mountaintop when he was about to begin rebuilding his house. There were four slave dwellings, described as servants' houses "of wood, with a wooden chimney, the floor earth." These were undoubtedly the same kind of log cabins that slaves lived in throughout the South. They could be raised quickly and cheaply, and the economics of slavery demanded little more than this.

Slave houses usually had a single room, sometimes with a loft, a wood-clay fireplace and chimney, a few pots for cooking, a table and several benches or chairs, a bed—often a trundle bed to conserve space—and whatever personal household items their inhabitants might add. Curiously, archaeological excavations have shown that house slaves on Mulberry Row ate and drank from imported porcelain dinner and tea service. Fragments of hundreds of pieces of this expensive tableware were found around slave cabins. These were no doubt chipped or broken hand-me-downs from the house, but they suggest that slaves, over a period of time, could collect a large number of once-elegant household items cast off by their white masters. When a slave couple married, Jefferson supplied them with a bed and a pot; any other furnishings had to be acquired on their own. The slave houses on Mulberry Row were no doubt constructed with more amenities than most slave dwellings because of their proximity to John Hemings's carpenter shop. They probably had glass windows, for example, rather than the shuttered windows on most slave cabins, which forced the inhabitants to choose between darkness or insects in the summer, and darkness or cold in the winter.

Not all of the slaves on Mulberry Row had cabins of their own; some ate and slept in the buildings they worked in. Archaeological excavations have shown that slaves lived in the smokehouse-dairy building, and in a building used to store nail rod. These buildings may also have housed hired slaves, or the slaves belonging to masons and carpenters hired by Jefferson. Cooks presumably slept in the kitchen under the south pavilion.

It was not until Jefferson's presidency, when he completed Monticello's two dependency wings, that his house slaves moved into new, improved quarters. These were the comfortable rooms beneath the terraces that Anna Maria Thornton observed during her stay at Monticello in 1802. For most of Jefferson's slaves, however, the big house on the mountaintop was as remote to their world as was the coast of Africa from which their parents or grandparents had been uprooted and which faded from consciousness with each succeeding generation. At this point in American history, they were a people stranded between a culture that denied them the legal and human rights for which it had itself fought a revolution, and a continent to which they could not return and whose values were thought primitive and barbaric. They poured their energies into an edifice that epitomized the taste and refinement of the class that enslaved them and of the man whose ringing phrases had declared freedom for all mankind. It was a monumental contradiction, and Jefferson bestrode it, not like a colossus, but uneasily, with shifting balance. His slave-built house survived, however, into an age where the gap between his words and the facts has been significantly reduced—a piece of poetic justice that Thomas Jefferson would most certainly have appreciated.

5

"Moved to Monticello"

THIRTY YEARS before Anna Maria Thornton visited Monticello on a stormy September afternoon, another young matron journeyed to the top of Thomas Jefferson's mountain under similar severe weather conditions. The season was winter rather than late summer—there was nearly two feet of snow on the ground—and the young woman was Martha Wayles Jefferson, the new bride of one of Virginia's most promising young men. At his marriage on New Year's Day of 1772, Thomas Jefferson was a burgess for Albemarle County, and had already won the respect of his fellow members of the Virginia Assembly by demonstrating the virtues that were to impress his revolutionary comrades in Philadelphia—a voracious appetite for work, an analytical intelligence, deep learning, and a facile pen. Not only was his personal career on the ascendant, he had courted and wedded one of the most desirable women of his class, a striking beauty with a rich father and great expectations. And now he was carrying her to his "new Rowanty," his hearth upon a hill where they would live a Virginia idyll in his columned and porticoed, carved and frescoed, Palladian mansion in the sky.

The only thing wrong with this arcadian vision was that there was no mansion, with or without porticoes and frescoes; there was only a construction site. The house that Jefferson was carrying his bride to was a twenty-by-twenty foot, one-room brick outbuilding, which he had been living in as a bachelor, the only dwelling completed on his mountaintop.

The wedding had taken place at the bride's home, the Forest, a two-story wood-frame Virginia farmhouse located on the James River in Charles City County, not far from the Tidewater estates of Shirley, Westover, and Brandon. The Forest could not have impressed Jefferson much; it was a house a great deal like Shadwell, and suffered Shadwell's fate by burning down in the nineteenth century. He was more impressed with its owner, John Wayles, like Jefferson a lawyer, but a more successful and much richer one, who owned extensive holdings of land and slaves. His success, Jefferson thought, resulted from "his great industry, punctuality, and practical readiness," rather than from his legal talents. He was a gregarious man, "full of pleasantry and good humor, and welcomed in every society." What Jefferson did not mention was that Wayles was also deeply involved in the slave trade from which came some of his wealth: in 1772, the year of Jefferson's marriage to his daughter, he had received, with Col. Richard Randolph, a consignment of 280 African slaves from the slave ship *The Prince of Wales*.

Jefferson had been courting Martha Wayles for more than a year before the wedding, but the romance was not the first for either of them. She had been married before, and was a widow with a young son when she married Jefferson. At eighteen, she had married Bathurst Skelton, a friend of Jefferson's from their student days at William and Mary. A year later, she gave birth to a son, and the following year her husband died suddenly at the age of twenty-four. During Jefferson's courtship, her young son died, leaving her, at twenty-three, a young woman with intensive experience in marriage, motherhood, and grief. Although she was five and a half years Jefferson's junior, her life as a wife and mother had given her a capacity for intimacy and shared emotion that Jefferson had still to learn. Whether her previous marriage and motherhood disturbed him can only be guessed at, but there is a hint that it did. He was guilty of a mental slip when he identified her on their wedding license, written in his own hand, as a "spinster."

The word was crossed out and above it, in another hand, the word "widow" was inserted. It was not the kind of error a lawyer—particularly a Thomas Jefferson—would normally make, and it suggests that he would have preferred that his wife had not been married before.

Martha Wayles Skelton was not Jefferson's first choice for a bride. At nineteen, when he was studying law under George Wythe, he fell passionately in love with Rebecca Burwell, a fetching sixteen-year-old with excellent family connections. Jefferson confided his love for her to his friend John Page in letters that have served to remind his biographers that even the most respected statesmen were once young. Rebecca is referred to by the code names Belinda, Adnileb (Belinda spelled backward), Compana in die (Bell-in-da), rendered in English and Greek, lest his friends should learn of his suit. He wanted desperately to marry her, but she would have to wait until he returned from a contemplated trip to England (which he never took). Would it be fair to ask her to wait for him? he agonized. He decided to press his suit at a dance at the Apollo Room of the Raleigh Tavern in Williamsburg. The results were reported in a "melancholy fit" to Page:

> I was prepared to say a great deal: I had dressed up in my own mind such thoughts as occurred to me, in as moving language as I knew how, and expected to have performed in a tolerably creditable manner. But, good God! When I had an opportunity of venting them, a few broken sentences, uttered in great disorder, and interrupted with pauses of uncommon length, were the too visible marks of my strange confusion!

Rebecca had other plans, it seems, for six months later she was engaged, and soon married, to Jacquelin Ambler, who was later to become treasurer of Virginia. "Well, Lord bless her, I say," Jefferson wrote to his friend William Fleming, and added one of only a few references to his own sexuality in all of his voluminous writings, and this an oblique one:

> You say you are determined to be married as soon as possible: and advise me to do the same. No thank ye; I will consider

of it first. Many and great are the comforts of a single state, and neither of the reasons you urge can have any influence with the inhabitant, and a young inhabitant too, of Williamsburg. For St. Paul only says that it is better to be married than to burn. Now I presume that if that apostle had known that providence would at an after day be so kind to any particular set of people as to furnish them with other means of extinguishing their fire than those of matrimony, he would have earnestly recommended them to their practice.

Because of the self-indulgent style of Jefferson's writing during his youth—his letters are full of learned conceits and clever displays of erudition—this is a difficult passage to read. He is responding to a letter from Fleming in which his friend gave two reasons for marrying, most probably the traditional ones of procreation and, as St. Paul put it, "to avoid fornication."

In his reply, Jefferson cites Paul's famous admonition that marriage is preferable to burning in hell for premarital sexual sins. Interestingly, in an open display of subjectivity, Jefferson misinterprets the word "burn" as meaning, not hellfire, but sexual passion. This is made clear by the following sentence where he writes "other means of extinguishing their fire." Jefferson's reading of Paul is that it is better to marry than to suffer the pains of unsatisfied sexual desire. His response is that marriage is unnecessary to supply the sexual needs of one who is young and who lives in Williamsburg, implying that there are plenty of sexual opportunities for a single man in this provincial capital.

The final sentence is the most ambiguous of all, partly because of Jefferson's tortuous syntax and confused pronoun reference. To paraphrase: God, at a later period than the early Christian era, has been kind enough to furnish "a particular set of people" with the means of extinguishing their sexual desires. If Paul had been able to anticipate this, he would certainly have recommended these "other means" rather than matrimony. The question is, what were the "other means" and who were the "particular set of people"? Prostitution is a candidate for the "other means," because the male Virginia aristocracy is a "particular set of people" who would benefit from this sexual gift of God. There is no historical record that there were prostitutes in Williamsburg, slave or white, but they existed in other large towns in the South, notably New Orleans, and there is no reason to believe that Williamsburg would be an exception. During "public times" when the assembly met, the town teemed with visiting men with plenty of money.

This is all conjecture, of course; the only thing that can be deduced for certain from the passage is that young Jefferson was obviously wounded at being rejected by the woman he loved and reacted the way young men in such situations have always reacted: the hell with marriage—I'll sow my wild oats. And he may have intended no more in his letter to Fleming than to suggest that there were plenty of other young women in Williamsburg who were willing to offer sex without marriage.

His other romance before marriage was much more serious and led to personal and political difficulties a generation later, during his presidency. In 1768, four years after the letter to Fleming, and four years before his marriage, Jefferson made sexual overtures to the wife of one of his best friends, John Walker. Betsy Walker, who had an infant daughter at the time, accused Jefferson of "improper" behavior on a number of occasions: while her husband was away on a business trip, when the couple was visiting Jefferson at Shadwell, and again at the house of a mutual friend. She told her husband that Jefferson's sexual advances went on even during his marriage. Betsy Walker did not confide these stories to Walker at the time they allegedly happened, however; she waited until 1784 when Jefferson was in France. The story became a scandal when it made the rounds during Jefferson's presidency, at which time it was coupled with the Sally Hemings "slave mistress" accusations in a full-blown campaign of political vilification. In a letter to his secretary of the navy, Jefferson admitted that "when young and single I offered love to a handsome lady. I acknolege its incorrectness. It is the only one founded in truth among all of their allegations against me." This is a lawyer's statement, subtle in its choice of language. He offered love, but he leaves unanswered whether the offer was accepted. Because Betsy Walker, for her own reasons, never admitted succumbing to Jefferson's advances, the Walker affair, like the Sally Hemings accusations, makes the question of whether

Jefferson was a sexual adventurer an historical Rorschach test: It tells more about the one making judgments than it does about the historical figure, who guarded his privacy like an anchorite.

At his marriage, however, Rebecca Burwell and Betsy Walker were behind him (although Walker was to step forward again years later), and he embarked upon what he would later describe as a marriage that was ten years of "unchequered happiness." He was nearly thirty on his wedding day, and by this time he had clearly reached a state of marriage-readiness. In the letter to Page in which he informed his friend of the burning of Shadwell, he had waxed eloquent about the married bliss of his brother-in-law, Dabney Carr. "This friend of ours, Page, in a small house, with a table, half a dozen chairs, and one or two servants, is the happiest man in the universe," Jefferson wrote. And in an aside to Page's wife Frances he assured her that he had no intention of criticizing anyone's inclination to marriage: "On the contrary, I am become an advocate for the passion."

When he finally made the leap, it was without inhibition; the wedding was a festive one, with fiddling, dancing, song, and celebration. Martha was as accomplished a musician as her husband—indeed, it was their mutual fondness for music that helped bring them together. They no doubt performed at the wedding, he on his violin, she at the keyboard. Before the wedding, he had ordered from London a new pianoforte, "worthy the acceptance of a lady for whom I intend it." Jefferson no doubt sang, with his bride's accompaniment, at the wedding party; he had a "fine clear voice," according to his slave Isaac, and was "always singin' when ridin' or walkin'."

The couple spent their wedding night at the Forest, and Jefferson not only consummated the marriage, but also apparently conceived his first child, for an infant daughter was born a few days less than nine months later. The wedding celebration went on for several days, for Jefferson gave a fiddler ten shillings on the third of January, three days after the marriage. A week later, the couple set off for a trip to nearby Shirley, the James River mansion of Charles Carter, who, like Jefferson, had been a student at William and Mary, and was one of the members of the large and influential Carter family of the Tidewater. Shirley had recently been rebuilt by Carter, and the new house must have been of particular interest to Jefferson because its exterior was similar to what he was building at Monticello. The double porticoes at the northeast and southwest ends of the house were very much like the Palladian superimposed orders Jefferson had drawn for his own house, so much so that later historians wondered whether Jefferson had a hand in designing them. The interior of Shirley was even more impressive. In the hall was an elegantly carved flying staircase, described in modern times as "one of the finest of its period in the Colonies." It lightly soared in two long flights with no visible means of support. The hall, drawing room, and dining room were paneled and decorated with moldings exquisitely carved with fine craftsmanship. Jefferson, who was attempting to find joiners to do similar work at Monticello, must have admired and even envied the Shirley interiors, and perhaps pointed them out to his bride as the kind of stylish interiors she would one day enjoy at Monticello.

While traveling to Shirley, Jefferson suffered the embarrassment every bridegroom fears—the car broke down. In this case, it was the eighteenth-century equivalent of the car—Jefferson's phaeton, a two-person carriage drawn by a pair of horses. At Shirley, he had it repaired by a slave blacksmith, John, to whom he paid 50 shillings, a princely amount. It was his honeymoon, however, and he was prepared to be generous. Back at the Forest, he lavishly tipped the servants another 50 shillings. Some of the recipients were members of the Hemings family whom he would inherit at the death of John Wayles the next year. The couple then set off for the trip west to their new home.

The journey from the Forest to Monticello was one of those honeymoon stories couples enjoy telling their children and grandchildren, and Jefferson did so with relish. On the way, they stopped at Tuckahoe, in Goochland County, the seat of the Randolph family. It was a large frame house that Jefferson knew well, for he had lived most of the first nine years of his life in it. Before his death, William Randolph had asked that Peter Jefferson move his family from Shadwell to Tuckahoe, located on the James River about ten miles west of Richmond, to take care of his son, Thomas Mann Randolph, Jr. Jefferson was only two years old when his family moved to Tuckahoe. It was here that he started his education at a small schoolhouse on the plantation, and it was at Tuckahoe that he was first introduced to a spaciousness of living he was not to enjoy again in his own dwelling until he rebuilt Monticello and doubled its size during his presidency. Tuckahoe consisted of two traditional two-story Virginia plantation houses joined together with a connecting wing to form the letter H. It had five large, high-ceilinged rooms on the ground floor and even more bedrooms on the second story. The house survives intact today, and is remarkable for its fine wood paneling and decoratively carved staircases. Whether or not these were finished when young Tom Jefferson lived there, Tuckahoe was a house that combined space and comfort. Even if it lacked the classical form he was later to demand in housing, it introduced him during his boyhood to a scale of living that he was to take as the norm for a member of his class.

The phaeton required additional repairs at Tuckahoe before the couple proceeded westward to Blenheim, eight miles from Monticello, the home of Col. Edward Carter, another member of the influential Carter family, and both a friend and a political rival in running for the Virginia Assembly. They found it occupied only by an overseer, however, so they decided to proceed on to Monticello. It was now snowing heavily—it would eventually measure three feet, the worst Jefferson had ever seen in Albemarle County—so they had to abandon the phaeton for horses. They made their way on horseback over a mountain shortcut through snowdrifts of up to two feet, and arrived at Monticello late at night with not a soul awake or a fire lit, the slaves having retired to their cabins. This was the way Martha Jefferson was introduced to her new home, what is now the small brick south pavilion at the end of the south terrace walk. She shivered at the "horrible dreariness of such a house." The story has a happy ending, however; the couple found a bottle of wine on a shelf behind some books, and ended the evening with "song, merriment, and laughter"—followed no doubt by a honeymoon romp in the expensive double bed Jefferson had bought just two weeks before his wedding.

The one-room brick building where Jefferson and his bride set up housekeeping at Monticello has since been named the honeymoon cottage because of the romantic tale of their arrival there on that snowy night. It was the first structure completed on the mountaintop and it served as an apprenticeship for Jefferson as a builder. He had decided at the very start of his construction campaign to proceed as owner-builders have ever since: to raise an outbuilding first, to provide him with a place to live during construction of his house, and to give him the experience of completing, from start to finish, a small, manageable building project. (Owner-builders today often construct a garage or storage building as their apprentice project—and live in it until their house is complete.)

Four years before his marriage, Jefferson had started accumulating the building materials for his bachelor outchamber. The most important first step was to gather lumber, have sawyers cut it, and allow it to season. In the eighteenth century, as now, no quality building could be done with green, freshly cut lumber. It had to be dried by allowing it to sit covered, each board separated, so air could circulate around it. Later, he also dried lumber in a kiln; in an 1806 survey of Monticello, a "plank kiln" is shown on the first roundabout. Palladio had directed the builder to cut timber in the winter, "in the wane of the moon"; when cut, it should be "left until it is thoroughly dry." The master warned that "neither will it in less than three years be dry enough to be made use of in planks for the floors, windows, and doors." On Christmas Eve of 1767, a team of hired sawyers rushed to complete work for the holiday season (Christmas was one of the few holidays slaves were allowed off work). They had sawed 650 feet of one-inch, and 520 feet of 2¼-inch chestnut boards. The following March, Jefferson paid 2½ shillings to have a level made. (This would be a plumb level, a straight board with a triangular projection from which hung a short plumb bob. The modern spirit level was rare in Jefferson's time; he once attempted to buy a used one.) He also paid to have 147 feet of cherry wood sawed, and ordered window glass and cord for window sashes from London. In May of 1768 he contracted to break ground for what was to be a lifetime of building: he agreed with John Moore, a prominent Albemarle County landowner who had been the steward of Peter Jefferson's estate after his death, "that he shall level 250 f. square on top of the mountain at N. E. end by Christmas, for which I am to give 180 bushels of wheat and 24 bushels of corn." Once the ground was leveled, the excavations for foundations and cellars had to be hand-dug with shovels.

Jefferson took a keen interest in how the earth was moved. On a cold winter day, for example, he hiked to his mountaintop to watch a team of four men, a boy, and two sixteen-year-old girls, all slaves, digging in the hard mountain clay. They were excavating a cellar for his house. It was so cold that the blacks had to stop frequently to warm themselves at a fire burning nearby, and they had to swing their shovels carefully to avoid hitting a makeshift shelter of loose boards erected over the pit to protect it from the snow. The dirt was hauled away as it was dug "to prevent its rolling in again." At the end of an eight-and-a-half-hour day, Jefferson was to write later in his Memorandum Book, the team had dug a three-foot hole measuring 8 by 16½ feet. He concluded from this observation that "a middling hand in 12. hours (including his breakfast) would dig & haul away the earth of 4 cubical yds. in the same soil." Later, using a two-wheeled wheelbarrow, he modified this estimate upward: "a man digs & carries . . . 5 cubical yards of earth in a day of 12 hours."

Jefferson's constant measurements of the efficiency of his labor force was an effort to reduce the variables in his construction equation to the absolute minimum. Bricks, mortar, lumber, and hardware could be accurately estimated to the final item, but labor—particularly slave labor—was a question mark. Like a modern efficiency expert, Jefferson delighted in measuring and comparing rates of labor and the effectiveness of tools and machines. He was always among the first to introduce new labor-saving machinery to his farms and was himself the inventor of a mathematically configured plow—his Mouldboard of Least Resistance—for which he was given an award by the American Philosophical Society.

Because of all of the earth that had to be moved by hand on the mountaintop, he was particularly interested in the relative efficiency of a two-wheeled versus the traditional one-wheeled wheelbarrow. The two-wheeled version was apparently built like those large garden carts mounted on bicycle wheels that are popular today. (Jefferson's two-wheeled wheelbarrow had wheels three feet in diameter.) Because the balance was in the center of the container instead of at the end, as is true of the standard wheelbarrow, the two-wheeled version could carry four times as much earth:

Julius Shard fills the two-wheeled barrow in 3. minutes and carries it 30 yds. in 1½ [minutes] more. now this is [equivalent to] 4 loads of the common one wheeled barrow, so that

suppose the 4 loads put in the same time viz. 3. minutes, 4
trips [with the single-wheeled version] will take 4 × 1½
minutes = 6 minutes, which added to 3. minutes filling =
9. minutes to fill and carry the same earth which was filled
and carried in the large barrow [two-wheeled version] in
4½ minutes.

Ergo, the double wheelbarrow was twice as efficient as the single-
wheeled version: it did the same work in four-and-a-half minutes that
the traditional wheelbarrow did in nine. A discovery such as this gave
Jefferson as much pleasure as earning £100. He copied the observation
from his Memorandum Book into both his Garden Book and Farm
Book and no doubt relayed the information to his neighbors at every
chance.

One of the highest priorities in Jefferson's construction plans was
digging a well. It was located a few yards downhill of the south pavilion,
an ideal spot, for his kitchen was to be in the basement of this building.
It was not the best location for producing water, however. One of the
serious disadvantages of building on a mountaintop was that there was
no place for water to run down from; you had to dig for it, and dig
deep. In the late summer of 1769, Will Beck, who was digging his
cellars, was given the important task of finding water. Beck was one
of those valuable men on a construction site who could do a number
of jobs dependably. Earlier that summer, in July, he had blasted rocks
with black powder to provide stone for the cellars, and during Jefferson's absences, Beck apparently supervised construction on the mountaintop, for Jefferson paid him repeatedly over a three-year period.

Beck and his slave crew labored forty-six days digging the well
sixty-five feet through mountain rock. The brickmaker George Dudley
aided in the digging operation and laid brick in the well. (On level
ground, in typical Virginia clay, thirty or forty feet was usually deep
enough to find clear water.) Although the well produced water for the
immediate needs of making mortar, and later for normal household
uses, it was not dependable. Jefferson recorded the history of the well
in his Weather Memorandum Book: from the time it was dug in 1769
until 1797, the well went dry a total of six years. Two of these years,
1773 and 1777, were during his marriage, which meant that for one-

fifth of her married life, Martha Jefferson had no readily available source of water at her house; it had to be carted up the mountain from springs lower down. Because of its position on the top of the mountain, the well was particularly sensitive to droughts and heavy rainfall. In 1791, the "dryest summer since 1755," the well failed, but in 1799 after a week of "the most constant & heavy rains in this neighborhood which were ever known in the memory of man," the well had twenty-eight feet of clear, fresh water in it. Jefferson eventually attempted to solve the problem of a dependable water supply at Monticello by building cisterns to catch rainfall from the roofs of the main house and terraces.

When Shadwell burned down on February 1, 1770, Jefferson was fortunate in that he had advanced far enough in his excavations and in assembling his building materials to finish his bachelor house that same year. When he wrote to tell Page about the fire, he commented, "If this conflagration, by which I am burned out of a home, had come before I had advanced so far in preparing another, I do not know but I might have cherished some treasonable thoughts of leaving [thes]e my native hills." With his ancestral home destroyed, his mother and sisters forced to live in an overseer's house at Shadwell, and Jefferson himself boarding in Charlottesville, he spared no expense to get the south pavilion finished by the winter of 1770. Beginning with this first intensive campaign, building at Monticello for many years to come would follow the rhythms of the seasons. Construction would start in the spring, gain momentum during the summer, take a break during the late summer and fall harvest weeks when workers and slaves were used to get the crop in from the fields, and come to an end in October. The winter months made masonry work impossible; this was the time for gathering materials for the following season's work. Jefferson was to write during his remodeling campaign, "this winter is employed in getting framing, limestone, & bringing up stone for the foundation," and these are probably the same tasks done during the winters of the early 1770s.

The exact chronology of the construction of the south pavilion and main house is difficult to determine. There are many architectural drawings and notes, but most of them are undated, and Jefferson's Memorandum Books are tantalizingly incomplete in supplying crucial pieces of information. One fairly reliable way of placing broad boundaries on his building schedule is by noting when his bricks were made and in what quantities. Using Jefferson's own notebook figures, the completed version of the first house and the south pavilion required roughly 310,000 bricks. The two wings with their octagon extensions took nearly 100,000 bricks, and the center block under 180,000. The south pavilion, the only other brick building on the mountaintop until remodeling started, used an additional 30,000 bricks.

The first batch of bricks was made by George Dudley, who arrived on the mountaintop with his crew of brickmakers in July 1769, and during the summer made approximately 45,000 bricks, for which he was paid a little less than £12, part of it in osnaburg cloth, salt, and molasses for his slaves. When Shadwell burned down, Will Beck and his crew were no doubt pushed to dig the south pavilion cellar earlier than originally planned. When finished with this relatively small excavation, they were then probably put to work on the cellars of the main building and perhaps helped to haul stone to the mountaintop as well. All of the ten-foot-high cellars of the building would be stonemasonry. Jefferson hired a slave, Phil, from one of his workmen, for £10 a year to haul rocks and lumber to the mountaintop with a wagon and team, and limestone was burned for mortar.

In the spring of 1770, Stephen Willis arrived on the mountaintop to build the south pavilion. Willis was a bricklayer, and perhaps also a housewright. (Jefferson was employed as counsel in a lawsuit against Willis for brickwork that was apparently not done satisfactorily, but this did not deter Jefferson from hiring him.) Willis and the team of slave artisans he brought with him built the south pavilion that summer—doing the brickwork and apparently the framing and carpentry as well. A skilled bricklayer like Willis, with the aid of apprentices, could lay 1,600 bricks a day; at this rate, the pavilion could have been raised in three weeks. It is quite possible that Willis also may have worked that summer on the walls of the stone cottage on Mulberry Row, although it was not completed for a number of years. This is a thirty-four-by-seventeen-foot stone building that was used at various times as an overseer's house, as house servants' quarters, as workmen's lodgings, and as a weaver's shop. It currently houses the Monticello administrative staff.

Jefferson needed a number of outbuildings on the mountaintop besides his bachelor quarters. The stone cottage used readily available building materials; stone and burned lime were being hauled up the mountain in large quantities for the cellars. Bricks, on the other hand, were precious; every brick he had was needed for the main house. The stone building used roughly fifty perch of stone (a perch is a measure 1 foot high, 1½ feet wide, 16½ feet long). At the average rate of three to five perch a day per man, the walls could have been raised by Willis's team of workers in one to two weeks. At least one slave cabin must also have been built on Mulberry Row during the 1769–70 year, because Jefferson needed housing for his personal servants when he moved into his house. His horses were probably stabled further down the mountain; Jupiter could bring them up when needed. Given the number of workers on the mountaintop during the spring and summer of 1770, one wonders where they stayed. There was a great need at Monticello for outbuildings.

In March 1770, Thomas Nelson, secretary of the Virginia Council of State, sent locks and hinges to Jefferson, the kind that were usually imported from England: "4 pr. dovetail-hinges for doors, 2 Mortise locks, 20 Pullies, and 20 pr. of Shutter-hinges." In November, Jefferson paid "for hinges &c. £4-18." By fall, Stephen Willis and his crew had departed, Willis having earned a considerable fee, more than £32. The final task to be completed before Jefferson could move into his new house was plastering. Humphrey Harwood was paid "for plaister etc. 47/" on November 8, and after allowing the plaster several weeks to dry, Jefferson recorded in his Memorandum Book on November 27, 1770, the momentous notation, "Moved to Monticello."

The house he moved into would, by today's standards, be considered a bachelor's efficiency. It was two stories, with a kitchen on the lower floor equipped with a fireplace and an oven, and probably floored with bricks. The upper floor was a mere eighteen by eighteen feet inside, with two windows, a door, and a fireplace that extended four feet into the room; the depth was necessary to accommodate the flues from the fireplace and oven on the floor below. In February of 1771, Jefferson wrote to his friend James Ogilvie in London:

Since you left us I was unlucky enough to lose the house in which we lived, and in which all its contents were consumed. A very few books, two or three beds &c. were with difficulty

[159]

saved from the flames. I have lately removed to the mountain from whence this is dated, and with which you are not unacquainted. I have here but one room, which like the cobler's, serves me for parlour for kitchen and hall. I may add, for bedchamber and study too. My friends sometimes take a temperate dinner with me and then retire to look for beds elsewhere. I have hopes however of getting more elbow room this summer.

These comments indicate that Jefferson entertained at his new house during the winter of 1771, even though he had no extra bedroom to sleep anyone overnight. His hopes for more "elbow room" at the end of the following building season also indicate that he had enough materials on hand—bricks and seasoned lumber—for the completion of the first unit of the main house, the dining room.

By this time, his courtship was in full blossom and the couple had probably made tentative wedding plans, but nothing was yet definite. He confided to Ogilvie his desire to marry, but wrote that there were obstacles, unnamed, to surmount. These were most probably Martha's young son, either his health or his legal status, and the question of property rights. Martha Wayles was due to come into a large fortune, and she would understandably be concerned that her son's future inheritance be protected. Jefferson set up an account for John Skelton in his Fee Book, with himself as guardian in behalf of Martha, his wife. But it was premature, for the boy died June 10, 1771. The boy's illness and death set back Jefferson's building plans for that summer. The time spent with Martha, on his law practice, which took him to other parts of the colony, and in his duties at Williamsburg, kept him away from the building site. More than ever before he needed a building supervisor. In June, he wrote to Thomas Adams, his agent in London, asking him "to procure me an architect" and to "send him in as soon as you can." By architect, he meant a master builder or housewright; this was the way the term was used in the eighteenth century. There is a note of desperation in his appeal, for he was falling behind schedule for the first of what was to be many times, partly for lack of someone at the site to carry out his architectural designs. It was a problem that was to plague him for years to come.

He had contracted with a brickmaker, George Bishop, to manufacture another batch of bricks, but during the following year very little money was paid to Bishop, so his brickmaking was apparently delayed for that year. By the end of the summer, Stephen Willis was on the site and stayed for three months. It is unclear where the bricks came from for his bricklaying, but in that time he could have completed the masonry for the northwest wing of the building; this was the dining room and an attic bedroom above it. This wing of the house would have been no more than a masonry shell, however, by the time Jefferson brought his bride to Monticello in January of 1772.

The house that Jefferson designed was essentially three discrete buildings; he termed them the "wings" and "middle building" on his drawings and in his notes. (The twó semi-octagon bays were added to the wings later.) It was a plan that allowed him to build any single part of the house and to use it while the rest of the building was under construction. A dining room was the most pressing need for Jefferson and his new wife. The young couple could hardly entertain in the south pavilion; it must have been jammed with furniture, clothing, and books. Anyone who came to visit them on the mountaintop had to be fed, however; and the small pavilion that was already a bedroom, living room, and study on the upper level and kitchen in the basement was totally inadequate as a dining room. When finished, the dining room wing could be closed off at the end that would later be attached to the middle building, and put to use not only for dining but also for storage in its cellar and attic. Evidence that this is what Jefferson did exists in a working floor plan of the dining room. It was drawn early in his planning for the house, but notes added later indicate that the room was used before the rest of the house was complete. One of the two doors leading to the middle building was closed off and a built-in buffet for holding dining service (Jefferson recorded it with the usual eighteenth-century spelling, "beaufet") was placed in one of the doorways. With the pavilion and the dining room wing in use, the Jeffersons could have lived comfortably, if not graciously, while construction proceeded on the rest of the house.

The dining room wing would have used all of Jefferson's available bricks. In the fall of 1772, he contracted with Dudley for another 100,000, half of them to be made in 1773, and the remainder in 1774.

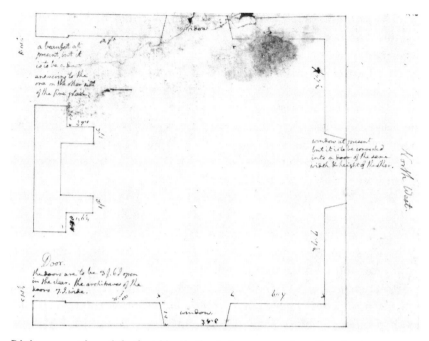

Dining room plan of the first Monticello during construction. One doorway contained a buffet; when the parlor was completed, this doorway was opened.

This schedule indicates that the building campaign of 1773 probably concentrated on completing the cellars and installing timber framing for the floor joists of the main building. The 50,000 bricks completed that year, if immediately laid that summer and fall, would be enough to raise the middle building only halfway up the first story.

As work progressed, always at a slower pace than hoped for, Jefferson continued to modify and scale down his construction plans. Some of the more grandiose features of his earlier planning, such as carrying the dependencies around the mountaintop in a huge rectangle, were abandoned. A drawing dated August 4, 1772, shows the house plan as it was ultimately built, with its octagonal bow rooms in place. The south wing was to be a dressing room, and its octagonal bow the bedroom. Because neither of the bow rooms had a fireplace, however, it is doubtful whether the one listed on his drawing as a bedroom was ever used as such in the winter.

The middle building would contain a spacious, high-ceilinged parlor with its octagonal bow windows facing westward to the mountains. Above it would be Jefferson's study where his library would be located. At the entrance to the middle building was a small "loggia" flanked on one side by a stairwell, which extended from cellar to second story, and on the other side an "anti-chamber," a six-by-eleven-foot room containing the kind of tiny, almost spiral staircase Jefferson was later to build into the remodeled house. The "anti-chamber" and main staircase were not an efficient piece of architectural design. They shared no walls with the rest of the building; as a result, they used too many bricks and took up too much floor space for their utilitarian function—a passageway, two staircases, and two virtually useless closet-sized rooms on the first and second floors. Living with these poorly designed spaces undoubtedly influenced Jefferson's decision to cut staircases to a bare minimum in the remodeled house. The second staircase in the "anti-chamber" appeared to be an unnecessary duplicate of the main staircase, but it was privately accessible to the dressing room–bedroom suite and would enable Jefferson to have the same easy access to his library that he was to have in the remodeled house.

The library, to be located on the second floor above the parlor, was getting to be a more urgent need as Jefferson continued to accumulate books at a rapid rate after the loss of his library in the Shadwell fire. In August of 1773, he took an inventory of his books and their locations. They totaled 1,256 volumes, and were housed in three bookcases and two sets of shelves. His order, a few months later, for a clothes press "high as desk & bookcase," indicates that books, desk, and clothing were still in the south pavilion. (This is not surprising. Even if the dining room had been finished at this time, he probably would have kept his books in his private quarter; he never made them publicly accessible.)

In June 1774, Jefferson ordered fourteen pairs of sash windows from London. A few months after his order, however, the Continental Congress at Philadelphia passed nonimportation agreements prohibiting the import of all goods from England. Jefferson sent a detailed letter to the Virginia Committee of Correspondence explaining that he had ordered the windows before the Congress's action and giving the Virginia Committee the freedom to dispose of his much-needed windows as it saw fit when they arrived from London. He later purchased them at auction. He had to have windows right away, however, so shortly afterward he placed orders for glass from the Tidewater.

His desire to purchase complete sash window units from London, with the glass installed and the windows ready to be hung, is a commentary on the state of American manufacture of such items just before the Revolution. It was cheaper to ship the windows from Europe than to have them made in the colonies, or at the building site. And Jefferson was no doubt convinced that the London-manufactured product was also better made.

Window glass and completed windows were expensive in the eighteenth century because the technology of glass making was still primitive. The best glass, called crown glass, was handmade by glass blowers. They began the process by first blowing a large glass bubble; the bubble was then transferred to an iron rod and the blowing tube broken off. The rod was spun and the glass worked in a furnace until, by centrifugal force, it flattened out to a uniformly even glass disk (the crown, which gave the glass its name). These "tables" of crown glass were only four feet in diameter, and when cut into rectangular window panes, all of the curved edges and the "bull's eye" where the rod had been attached were wasted. The inefficiency of this hand-made process is why colonial window panes are small and why large windows could only be made by ganging the panes, or "lights" as they were called, in a grid of wooden mullions, producing the characteristic colonial window style.

Jefferson's design specified the same standard-size window used in most Virginia plantation houses. These were double-sash windows of eighteen lights, each pane twelve inches square. The windows were three lights wide, nine in each sash. (When he remodeled, some of the windows were enlarged by using three sashes, but he kept the eighteen-light style by using larger panes of glass, six panes per sash.) The sashes were mounted in much the same way as they are today with one exception. In the eighteenth century, the top sash was normally fixed; only the bottom sash was counterbalanced with lead weights on ropes and pullies so it could be raised and lowered easily. (Modern sash windows, unless they are unusually heavy, are held in place by friction, made possible by spring-metal tracks.)

It is difficult to determine which parts of the house these fourteen windows were intended for, even though there were variations in them that corresponded to his specifications: he had specified a stronger "double flint" glass for those that would face the weather of the northwest, and the attic windows had only twelve panes, but there is no floor plan for the second story that accurately positions doors and windows, and only a single complete elevation of the house survives.

This much-reproduced elevation shows the double-porticoed eastern front, without the semi-octagon rooms at each wing. Jefferson may not have drawn an elevation for the western front of the house because he intended the double portico on that side to be a mirror image of the east portico. This changed, however, when he added the semi-octagon bay to the parlor. There is additional evidence that the surviving elevation does not accurately portray the alterations Jefferson made as his building progressed.

The main difference between the finished building and the elevation was that the house was two feet taller than indicated on the drawing. Jefferson's building notes show that when he demolished the double porticoes on the east front in 1796, the brick walls were nineteen feet on the lower story and eighteen on the upper level, a total of thirty-seven feet above the water table. On the elevation, the two levels are only thirty-five feet, including the second-story Ionic entablature. (One note indicates that he raised the lower order a foot so that the dining room could be a cube of eighteen feet. The extra foot was needed for the ceiling joists. This is one of many instances of his going to extraordinary trouble to preserve the purity of Palladian forms.) Because of these extra two feet, the building had a much more vertical appearance than the elevation indicates. Indeed, placing the two semi-octagons on each wing extended the horizontal plane of the house, producing a more aesthetically pleasing symmetry, a consideration that may have entered into Jefferson's decision to add them.

Another contingency forced him to alter the design of the upper portico of the east front, the one shown on the elevation. There is an item dated April 17, 1775, in Jefferson's building notebook indicating that when his first stone Doric column was made by the indentured servant William Rice, its diameter was greater than he had specified. Because the Palladian orders are based entirely on a module fixed by the diameter of the columns, this threw the proportions of the two orders off. Jefferson was forced to recalculate the second-story Ionic order to make the columns higher and narrower to preserve the purity of Palladian orthodoxy. He made the necessary adjustments in column height by substituting a smaller member, a zocle, for the pedestal the columns sat on.

Normally, a builder would have scrapped the column or had it recut instead of changing the entire plan of the elevation of the house, but Jefferson's decision to keep the column and change the plan is a reflection of the difficulty and expense of stonecutting in his part of Virginia. All of this trouble and expense with stonemasonry forced Jefferson to abandon stone as the medium for the columns on the west portico. These were ultimately built of specially molded curved bricks, which were laid up as columns and stuccoed to give the appearance of stone. The columns for the Ionic orders on the upper porticoes were to be of wood, but in spite of Jefferson's detailed calculations for their proper Palladian proportions, they were never made. One of the items not shown on the elevation was a railing that was to be placed on the upper porticoes, not unlike the railings on the second-story porch of Shirley, but Jefferson's railings were to be in a Chinese style.

Jefferson's records of the number of bricks manufactured on the mountaintop give some idea of the slow pace of building at the approach of, and during, the Revolutionary War period. In the summer of 1774, a new brickmaker, William Pond, was hired to make bricks at a very reasonable price, 2 shillings, 6 pence a thousand for place bricks. (He was still working in 1775, for Martha Jefferson issued him two blankets.) These bricks should have been enough to complete the middle building. In 1775, work was being done on stone foundations, most probably for the last part of the building, the south wing, and perhaps for preliminary work on the dependencies. Jefferson recorded one of those typical notes on his workers' efficiency: he wrote that two wagons brought two loads of stones round trip from the quarry to the house in eighty minutes. (The quarry was below the fourth roundabout; it took only fifteen minutes for the wagons to get to it.) A bricklayer, Randolph Johnson, was hired in the fall of 1776 at £4 a month to lay what should have been the final bricks in the middle building. These would have completed the second-story study and allowed Jefferson to roof over the middle building that year.

In the spring of 1777 yet another brickmaker, John Brewer, came to Monticello to make the final batch of bricks for the house. In 1778,

Jefferson credited him with "ninety thousand workable bricks made & burnt @ 5/ the thousand." That July and August, two of Stephen Willis's slave bricklayers laid more than 14,000 bricks. In February of 1777, Jefferson had ordered 1200 feet of "fine flooring plank" in "lengths of 19. & 25 ft." cut by John Beckley, a sawyer. These lengths would have been for the middle building, and because the lumber had to season, the finished flooring for this part of the house was probably not laid until the following year, 1778. By November 12, 1778, the middle building was apparently roofed, for on that day Jefferson recorded in his Garden Book that he took a measurement with his newly purchased theodolite, a surveying instrument for recording vertical and horizontal angles, which he placed "on the top of the house."

Two carpenters worked on the house steadily for a number of years. One was Humphrey Gaines, who was first hired for the 1774–75 year and was still there as late as February of 1778, when Jefferson records sending him on an errand to Isaac Zane's Marlboro Iron Works in Frederick County. Gaines was probably responsible for framing and roofing much of the house.

Throughout this period, the Revolutionary War years, Jefferson understandably had difficulty finding experienced labor. He wrote to his friend John Harvie in 1778 asking him to locate a house joiner. Harvie replied that they were rare and expensive to hire, and that Jefferson's best bet was to get a British prisoner who was a carpenter. Ultimately, Jefferson did the next best thing—he hired the two hard-drinking deserters Davy Watson and Billy Orr.

The second carpenter who was in residence at Monticello during the revolutionary years was Joseph Neilson (his name was pronounced Nelson, for it was also spelled that way). Isaac and Madison Hemings both refer to him in their memoirs. Isaac stated that he was an Englishman—perhaps he was also a deserter from the British army. He was still working in 1779 when Jefferson left Monticello with his family for Williamsburg to assume his duties as governor of Virginia. During his stay at Monticello, Neilson's joinery was not limited to woodwork; he also fathered, with Betty Hemings, Jefferson's talented slave carpenter, John Hemings. Indeed, there are probably still sections of woodwork at Monticello shaped by two sets of hands, father and son, white and black, free and slave, Neilson and Hemings—a continuity of craft, of generation and race, of old house and remodeled house. Such small continuities, sewn into the seams and stitches of the house by nearly anonymous workmen, have been preserved only because of the recordkeeping instincts of Monticello's celebrated designer-builder.

When Jefferson and his family left for Williamsburg in 1779, all the rooms of the house were probably habitable, but the house was far from being finished. Before he started remodeling years later, Jefferson commented that the original house had never been more than half finished. This sounds like an exaggeration, but if one considers that the dependencies were not even started, and the decorative Palladian orders he designed, not only for the exterior, but for every room of the house, were never built, the statement may be fairly accurate. (Jefferson was not in the habit of speaking hyperbolically.) When he left for Paris in 1784, two years after the death of his wife, this original version of Monticello was as finished as it would ever be.

By that time, the house had seen a number of famous visitors, but there were only scanty descriptions of what it looked like. Perhaps the most notorious visitors, uninvited, were Lieutenant Colonel Banastre Tarleton's dragoons. In June 1781, the flamboyant British officer, whose courage, daring, and insolence had made him both feared and admired by his American enemies, led a party of cavalry and mounted infantrymen on an overnight raid on Charlottesville with the intention of capturing the Virginia legislature and Governor Thomas Jefferson. After a lightning ride westward, the force arrived at the Cuckoo tavern at Louisa Court House, some forty miles east of Charlottesville, where they were observed by Jack Jouett, a bear of a man who was as fearless a horseman as Tarleton himself. Jouett, paralleling Paul Revere's feat, tore through the back trails to sound the alarm. According to the legend passed on by Jefferson's family, Jefferson fortified him with Madeira at Monticello and he then rode on to Charlottesville to warn members of the legislature. Jefferson sent his wife and family to safety at Edward Carter's Blenheim, waited until the last moment, and then rode off, leaving the house in the charge of two slaves, Martin Hemings and Caesar. Tarleton did not climb the mountain to Monticello himself, but sent a Captain McLoed and a troop of dragoons to find the governor.

As the British horsemen approached the first roundabout, Martin was passing the final pieces of silver plate to Caesar, who was depositing them under the floorboards of the east portico. Martin slammed the plank down as the first horseman appeared, trapping Caesar under the porch for the three days the British troops stayed. Martin Hemings was twenty-six at the time and had the reputation of being the sullen and brooding member of the Hemings family. The story was told that one of McLoed's men put a gun to the slave's chest and threatened to fire if he did not reveal which way Jefferson had fled. "Fire away, then," came the reputed reply. It was one of those "faithful darky" stories that were popular during the nineteenth century, and was repeated with embellishments by historians of that period. In truth, Jefferson could have lost Martin, Caesar, and Monticello during those three days, but the Revolutionary War was fought by gentlemen officers whose code of etiquette forbade the wanton destruction of the property of fellow gentlemen. Tarleton had left instructions that nothing at the house was to be touched, and McLoed complied. (General Cornwallis was not so obliging, however; he camped at Jefferson's Elk Hill plantation for ten days, and during that time his troops burned barns and crops, slaughtered stock and horses, and departed with thirty slaves—an act that Jefferson never forgot or forgave.) McLoed departed, leaving behind legends of danger and courage, but he left no description of the house he saved.

A more welcome gentleman visited Monticello less than a year later and did leave an account of Monticello. In the spring of 1782, one of the commanders of the French army in America, the Marquis de Chastellux, rode to Jefferson's mountaintop. He was one of those urbane men of the Enlightenment, a member of the French Academy, who, like Jefferson, was equally comfortable discussing the arts and sciences. He published an account of his visit to Monticello and left one of the best descriptions of the state of that first house:

The house, of which Mr. Jefferson was the architect, and often the builder, is constructed in an Italian style, and is quite tasteful, although not however without some faults; it consists of a large square pavilion, into which one enters through two porticoes ornamented with columns. The ground floor consists chiefly of a large and lofty *salon*, or drawing room, which is to be decorated entirely in the antique style; above the *salon* is a library of the same form; two small wings, with only a ground floor and attic, are joined to this pavilion, and are intended to communicate with the kitchen, offices, etc. which will form on either side a kind of basement topped by a terrace.

De Chastellux's tenses supply us with information on what was completed and still incomplete in 1782. "One enters through two porticoes ornamented with columns" indicates that both the east and west porticoes were in place, at least the lower portions. On the other hand, he states that the "lofty *salon*, or drawing room"—the parlor— "is to be decorated in the antique style." The Palladian orders in the parlor were clearly not in place, but de Chastellux had probably seen Jefferson's drawings of them. In describing the kitchen and dependencies he again uses the future tense—they "will form on either side a kind of basement"—indicating that they were not yet built. The kitchen, which was to be moved closer to the house, was still on the basement level of the south pavilion.

The comment by de Chastellux that Jefferson was "the architect, and often the builder" suggests that he not only directed labor but was willing to work alongside his artisans when needed. (Jefferson undoubtedly offered this piece of information, for de Chastellux had no other source for it.) Although some historians have been uncomfortable with the notion that an intellectual such as Jefferson also engaged in manual labor, there is ample evidence that he took pleasure in physical work. Isaac reported that Jefferson gardened ("for amusement he would work sometimes in the garden for half an hour at a time in right good earnest in the cool of the evening") and enjoyed doing metalwork and carpentry. "My old Master was neat a hand as ever you see to make keys and locks and small chains, iron and brass," Isaac recalled. "He kept all kind of blacksmith and carpenter tools in a great case with shelves to it in his library, an upstairs room. . . . Old Master had a couple of bellowses up thar." (These would be used for his metalworking.) One of his early biographers, George Tucker, who first visited Monticello in 1798, wrote that Jefferson "had acquired much practical skill" in the use of tools and that "the carriage in which he rode, his garden seat, even some of his household furniture, were the joint work of himself and his slaves." When Jefferson remodeled and enlarged the house, he kept a work bench in the piazza, just off his library. It is possible he may have made architectural models at his work bench; if so, he most certainly would have built a model of Monticello to be used in his ongoing construction operations.

Just how few of the Palladian decorative elements were installed in the first version of the house can be determined by a "bill of scantling" that Jefferson drew up, a list of wood to be cut by one of his sawyers, Flavy Frazer. The list designates specific sizes and types of wood for the orders of the exterior porticoes and interior rooms, and was written early in Jefferson's building program, for it contains materials for the orders of only six rooms and the upper porticoes. In 1783, a year after his wife's death and a year before he left for France, Jefferson came upon this list and made a note at the bottom of it. (The paper is partially mutilated, but the missing portions can be inferred.) The note reads:

[This bill of scant]lling seems to have been intended for 6 rooms Doric and Ionic. [As I now] have 10 rooms, add 2/3 to each article & it will probably do. [The other sid]e of this paper shows what each article was intended for.

June 1783

The note makes clear that the lumber had not been cut and that all the items on the list were still to be added to the house, but now with two-thirds more lumber for the extra rooms completed. (He had obviously forgotten about the list, but after finding it, decided it was still usable.) It includes materials for eight columns, seventeen feet long, to be made of chestnut, each column to be assembled of eight fluted strips joined to a core shaft. This method of fabricating the columns was dictated by the fact that there was no way of shaping them from a solid tree trunk without having the wood split badly.

The eight Ionic columns were to be installed on the two upper porticoes, but they were never made, for when Jefferson returned from France he had decided to remodel the house. The two pediments covering the porticoes were probably finished, however; they formed an integral part of the roof of the middle building. In the absence of

[171]

A lumber list showing that, in 1783, before Jefferson went to France, columns for the upper porticoes, pilasters for the lower ones, and interior decorative moldings had not been built.

the Ionic columns, they would have been held up by four temporary posts on each portico. None of the decorative Palladian orders would have been added to the pediments. From the designations of the wood to be cut, it appears that the Palladian orders around the doors and windows were probably completed, but the pilasters were not; wood for them—also chestnut—was included on the list. It seems that none of the rooms, with the possible exception of the dining room, had any cornice or frieze decorations. If any of the decorative moldings were in place, they would have been at the floor level. Perhaps dadoes or chair rails were constructed in some rooms, and the interior doors and windows may have had their orders completed. When one considers that when Jefferson left for France, Davy Watson was still working on the staircase of the house, a basic structural element, it seems highly unlikely that much of the decorative work had been done. If any single room was close to being completed, the best guess would be the dining room, the first room that was finished and the room most used for entertaining. Jefferson left a number of full-size drawings of the orders for this room, and parts of them may have been executed.

In all, it was not a very impressive building record for some fifteen years of construction, but there were extenuating circumstances. During this period, roughly from 1769 to 1784, the colonies had been transformed into a republic, and Thomas Jefferson, the amateur architect-builder of his own house, had become one of the architects of a new nation. His role as a leading figure in the Virginia delegation to the Continental Congress, and later as war governor of Virginia, the appearance of British troops in Virginia and the scarcity of labor and building materials brought about by the war—all of these conspired against an orderly and expeditious completion of his well-laid building plans. Yet, another kind of man might have finished a house in that time, even with the interruptions and contingencies of public service and war. In spite of Jefferson's constant concern with labor effectiveness, his impeccable recordkeeping, and his sharp-eyed cost cutting, there was an inherent inefficiency in his building methods. He was unwilling to commit his full economic resources in an intensive drive for completion at a fixed date. This derived in great part from his fear of going into debt. Throughout his life he commented on the absolute necessity of remaining debt-free if one were to survive in the plantation economy of Virginia. He saw credit as a constant temptation that had to be forcefully resisted. English bankers had established a system of easy credit that had kept Virginia landowners in bondage to them for generations, ultimately forcing many into bankruptcy. Jefferson was a lifelong critic of deficit financing, in large part because he was himself a victim of English creditors when he inherited the debts along with the lands of his father-in-law, John Wayles. Because of the war, he paid the debt once in inflated currency, and ended up having to pay it a second time. He lived under a threat to his economic security from this debt for decades. Throughout his career he was an implacable foe of public debt, and eventually arrived at a philosophic position which held that one generation had no right to impose debt upon the next. All debts, he argued, should be retired every twenty years.

He preached to his children the Puritan doctrine of living frugally, within one's means. After her marriage, he advised his younger daughter Maria:

> The unprofitable condition of Virginia estates in general leaves it now next to impossible for the holder of one to avoid ruin. And this condition will continue until some change takes place in the mode of working them. In the mean time, nothing can save us and our children from beggary but a determination to get a year beforehand, and restrain ourselves vigorously this year to the clear profits of the last. If a debt is once contracted by a farmer, it is never paid but by a sale.

Given this almost obsessive aversion to debt, it is not surprising that he was unwilling to go into debt to complete his house expeditiously, even in 1774 when he acquired the Wayles inheritance and doubled his capital. He insisted always that he build from his available resources and that his bills be paid promptly. He held it a point of honor that his workers were always paid in cash or with his note immediately after the job was finished. When several of them presented bills to Nicholas Lewis, who looked after his affairs while he was in France, Jefferson wrote back with some impatience:

> I made it a point of paying my workmen in preference to all other claimants. I never parted with one without settling with

[174]

him, and giving him either his money or my note. Every person that ever worked for me can attest to this, and that I always paid their notes pretty soon. I am sure there did not exist one of these notes unpaid when I left Virginia, except to Watson and Orr who were still at work for me.

He was therefore unwilling to build in the most efficient way if it meant going into debt. He could have had all of the materials assembled and ready for his workmen, for example. Instead of making bricks in batches of 50,000 or 100,000, he could have had 350,000 made at once by hiring more labor. Even the problem of finding experienced bricklayers and carpenters could have been solved if he had been willing to pay premium wages to bring them from Philadelphia. But this would have required cash, and that would have meant going into debt.

From the very beginning, Jefferson decided to finance his house on a "pay-as-you-go" basis. He utilized the cheapest local labor he could find, apprenticed his slaves to learn building trades, and used unskilled slaves as common laborers. This saved money, but it also took time. He harvested from his own plantations most of the building supplies he needed, and in utilizing labor and scarce cash resources, he fitted his building program into his overall farm economy—raising wheat and tobacco and milling flour. He was not disturbed by the snail's pace of building as much as other members of his family might have been. He took the hardships and inconveniences of living in a house in progress as an inevitable price one had to pay for insisting on the kind of quality construction he demanded. As far as his friends, neighbors, and colleagues were concerned, this work, be it building, rebuilding, remodeling, or renovating, was considered something of a status symbol, a mark that one was getting along. Besides, the code of hospitality, which demanded that every gentleman's door was always open to the most casual passer-through, carried with it the unwritten rule that visitors made do with temporary, unfinished, or crowded accommodations without complaint. And even if the house was in a state of suspended potentiality, his family and visitors ate well from ample gardens and plentiful orchards, and drank from cellars stocked with the best wine and spirits available in America. The conversation was led by one of Virginia's most brilliant and clever men, one with a talent for finding mutual interests around which to weave a web of conviviality.

For the Marquis de Chastellux this turned out to be a most improbable subject, the poetry of Ossian, the Gaelic bard whose poems were in actuality the work of their "translator," James Macpherson. With the help of a bowl of punch, the French aristocrat and his American host experienced "a spark of electricity which passes rapidly from one to the other" on discovering their mutual taste for Ossianic verse. "Soon the book was called for," de Chastellux recalled, "and placed beside the bowl of punch. And, before we realized it, book and bowl had carried us far into the night." When he left Monticello, after a four-day visit, de Chastellux was satiated with talk of politics, natural philosophy, and the arts. Mr. Jefferson, he wrote of his host with unabashed admiration, "had placed his mind, like his house, on a lofty height, whence he might contemplate the whole universe." With a "gentle and amiable wife" and "charming children," he had, wrote the French visitor, "a house to embellish, extensive estates to improve, the arts and sciences to cultivate." But this vision of his host's Virgilian future was not to be; less than five months after de Chastellux recorded these words in his diary, Martha Wayles Jefferson was dead, and Thomas Jefferson's private universe had collapsed.

6

The Mistress of Monticello

MARTHA WAYLES JEFFERSON was very much a product of her class; she was bred to be a plantation mistress, and during ten years of married life with her illustrious husband, she worked hard at being a successful one. She was physically unequal to the rigors of the task, however, particularly of bearing a child every other year; it weakened and ultimately killed her.

The mistress of a Virginia plantation was expected to assume the management of the domestic life of the plantation house. This included the normal household duties of preserving meat, dairy, and fresh foods, and supervising their preparation; knitting or sewing bedding materials, linen, and slave clothing; and manufacturing soap, candles, dyes, and—during the Revolutionary War period—cloth. She was usually the plantation physician as well; she tended to the illnesses of her own family and of the families of the household slaves. She also managed the feeding and clothing of the house servants, and was the arbiter of their disputes. Childbearing was considered to be one of her primary functions; nursing, raising, and educating children took up much of her time and energies. Indeed, during her childbearing years the plantation wife was often pregnant every other year. The size of the family of Jefferson's eldest daughter, Martha Randolph, was not uncommon; she had twelve children. Nearly half of all plantation wives in the late eighteenth century had six or more children; one of every ten bore twelve or more. Because of the infant mortality rate, however, mothers often buried as many children as they raised. Martha Jefferson's history of childbearing was not unusual. She had a total of seven children, six by Jefferson, and only two lived to maturity.

Besides these domestic and childrearing duties, the plantation wife also played an important role in her husband's business and political life, as hostess and social companion. Her education normally included music, because an ability to sing and play at the keyboard was considered a valuable social skill. She invariably studied dance with a dancing master, and was encouraged to draw or paint if she showed talent. She read verse and novels suitable for young ladies. Indeed, reading was often one of her main amusements. Robert Carter of Nomini Hall boasted that he "would bet a Guinea that Mrs Carter reads more than the Parson of the parish!" How she dressed herself was a reflection of her husband's prosperity, so her clothing was expected to be suitably stylish and tasteful. Although there were professional milliners, dressmakers, and tailors in the larger towns, and clothing was purchased regularly from England, no plantation mistress could afford not to be able to sew.

In all, the life of a plantation mistress was a challenge to the hardiest of women; even the most robust were oppressed at times by the burden of the multiple duties demanded of them. They may not have expressed their dissatisfaction as strongly as did one colonial woman, who felt that the domestic duties to which she was chained "Stagnate the Blood and Stupifie the Senses," but many plantation mistresses believed they were overworked and their labors undervalued. How much of this discontent with their plight was shared by Martha Jefferson can only be guessed at because Jefferson destroyed virtually all written traces of her existence. Only one letter by her survives, this an impersonal one. There is, however, a household journal in her hand, and for several years after their marriage Jefferson copied at the end of his own Memorandum Books his wife's yearly household accounts. From these two sources, together with third-person reminiscences by family members, an overseer, and slaves, and

Jefferson's own detailed daily record of his financial transactions during their marriage, it is possible to piece together an imperfect portrait of the mistress of Monticello.

When Jefferson brought his bride home in 1772, their future together on his mountaintop was full of promise. They had no doubt spent many hours going over the drawings of the mansion he intended to build for her, and it is likely that she took part in its design—if not the academic Palladianism, then certainly the functional decisions dealing with the utilization of space. The two semi-octagon additions to each wing of the house were added to the original plan at about the time of their marriage, and it is quite possible they were the result of Martha's appeal for more space in the dining room and bedroom wings. She could not have been too pleased with the distribution of floor space in the various rooms of the house. The dining room and bedroom were 16 by 18 feet, less than 300 square feet each, while Jefferson's study-library on the second floor over the parlor was 560 square feet. She could have argued reasonably that more space in the sleeping and dining wings was called for. The two semi-octagons joined another 150 square feet to each room. The design of the dependencies would have particularly interested her, for these were the housewife's domain. It is here that Martha Jefferson most probably asserted the greatest influence on the design of the house. Jefferson's drawings for the two L-shaped dependency wings underwent many changes, with numerous erasures and redrawings. Although the dependencies were never constructed during Martha Jefferson's lifetime, their continuing evolution on the drawing board was no doubt a reflection of shifts in her domestic management.

The two dependency wings incorporated all of the outbuildings usually found scattered about the main house of a large Virginia estate. In the southern wing was a brewing room, smoke room, dairy, laundry, kitchen, pantry, meal (grain) room, and summer dairy. On the opposite wing were stables for twenty horses, a chariot house, and a saddle room. Servants' rooms and privies were located in each wing, and a "hosterie," a room apparently to be used for the servants of visiting guests, was in the north wing. The housewife's perennial complaint about inadequate storage was satisfied by several dependency spaces specified as storerooms. Between the house and the kitchen, which was located at the L-turn in the south dependency, was a large pantry, and in the same position on the opposite service wing was an even larger "store room." Directly under the parlor was a "ware room" to be used for general-purpose storage.

An indication of how Martha Jefferson's domestic interests dictated the design of the dependencies is best illustrated by her particular pride in brewing beer. When she arrived at Monticello to set up housekeeping with her new husband, one of the first of her domestic acts was to brew a fifteen-gallon batch of "small beer." This was a low-alcohol beer probably brewed from wheat and bottled and drunk without aging as soon as fermentation was completed—usually about a week after it was brewed. During the first year of her marriage, she brewed ten fifteen-gallon casks and one twenty-gallon cask of beer, enough for 1,700 twelve-ounce cups or tankards of beer. This meant that an average of close to thirty-five servings a week were being consumed at Monticello. Martha's beer was obviously one of her specialties and was probably tasty, for, unlike some small beers, it was hopped—she purchased hops frequently. One bargain was recorded: "bought 7 lb hops with an old shirt." Jefferson was known throughout his life to prefer cider and wine as beverages, but as a young husband married to a bride who was proud of her beer-making, he undoubtedly consumed a lot of small beer. (Much later in his life, he established a beer-making operation at Monticello, but in the interim, his beverages of choice were apple cider and unfortified wine.) Significantly, Jefferson's architectural drawing for the dependencies shows that the kitchen under the south pavilion was to be converted to a brewing room with a circular masonry firebox to hold a large brewing kettle. There is little doubt that Martha Jefferson, beer-maker, had a voice in its design and location.

Unlike many colonial brides, who had little practical knowledge of housekeeping when they married—mothers then, as now, were sometimes reluctant to share the power of household management with their daughters—Martha Jefferson was a widow who brought to Monticello some experience in domestic affairs. Whether or not in her previous marriage she was in the habit of keeping accounts of her household expenses, inventories of her pantry, or records of household duties, she soon learned that her husband expected them of her. She never came close to matching the daily, detailed recordkeeping of a Thomas Jefferson, but she started her married life by emulating his business habits. She borrowed from him a leather-bound notebook in which he had, in 1768, taken notes on General Court cases. Starting at the empty pages at the back of the book, in a rather cramped handwriting, the letters separated, tight, and vertical, she made her first entry: "1772 Feb 10 opened a barrel of col: harrison's floweer." It is quite likely that Jefferson looked over her entries, for the next time she wrote *flour*, it was spelled correctly. This was followed by daily notations of what was killed for the table: pullets, turkeys, and mutton. On February 28 she took an inventory of the house linen—tablecloths, napkins, towels, and sheets. These were nearly all Jefferson's, purchased the year before his marriage, probably in preparation for it; they bore his initials. In subsequent years, she inventoried her clothing, her husband's clothes, and those of their first daughter.

Dairy products were not being produced at the mountaintop during the first two years of Martha's residence; she recorded in her borrowed household Account Book regular purchases of butter from Thomas Garth, the Monticello overseer. It was not until January 21, 1774, that she noted: "made at mottcello 3 pots of butter." (Her spelling of Monticello indicates how she may have pronounced it. Jefferson established an Italian pronunciation for the penultimate syllable, for there are contemporary references to its being spelled "Montichello." One workman, however, spelled it "monnttesello" and "mounteyselley," suggesting that there were variations in the pronunciation then, as there are now.) The butter that Martha made was not enough for the table at Monticello, however, because it continued to be purchased. By the fall of 1774, large quantities of butter were being hauled to the mountaintop from Jefferson's Bedford plantation.

Martha's first soap was made two months after her arrival: "Mar. 26 made 46 £ of soft soap." Thereafter she made hard and soft soap regularly. On January 9, 1776, she recorded the ingredients of a large batch of soap: "put in the sellar a jar that had 32 gallons of leaf fat, two firkins & two iron pots of gut fat, two store pots of sauce fat and half a barrel of craknels [cooked pork fat]. made 229 lb of hard soap, 200 lb ditto soft." Soap was produced by adding assorted fats to lye that had been made by leaching water through ashes gathered from the plantation fireplaces. (The lye was strong enough—ready for use—if an egg floated in it.) The lye and fat were boiled, usually in a large kettle over an open fire outdoors. Making soap was normally a cold-weather chore, when ashes were plentiful and pork was butchered. It was a messy job done by slaves. Hard soap, made by adding salt to the lye, was used for general-purpose cleaning as it is today; soft soap, the color and consistency of butterscotch pudding, was used for the plantation laundry.

Tallow for candles was derived from the suet of beef. It was not until more than two years after her arrival at Monticello that Martha made her first batch of candles. She recorded on March 13, 1774: "made 12 doz: candles" and two months later, she made three dozen more.

Martha Jefferson's records show that during the first two years of her marriage, extraordinarily large amounts of food were eaten for a household of two adults and an infant. Much of the killing of farm animals was for workmen, but on August 13, 1773, she recorded the staples consumed at her own table: "Eat 6 hams, 4 shoulders, 2 middlings [of bacon] in 3 weeks and 2 days. used 3 lo[a]ves of sugar in preserves, one d[itt]o in punch." This was only the pork and sugar, however; she regularly purchased poultry, fruit, and vegetables from the plantation slaves and from the construction workers and their wives. All of this indicates that, in spite of the fact their dining room was scarcely habitable, the Jeffersons were feeding a lot of guests.

During the first year of their marriage, they no doubt entertained members of Jefferson's family a great deal. They lived close by and would have been anxious to meet the former widow Skelton, now Mrs. Jefferson. There is no record of the relationship between Jefferson's mother and his young bride; the only mention of her by Martha is an item in her household Account Book, "borrowed 10 lb sugar of my mother." (She repaid it four weeks later.) Since Martha's own mother and step-mothers were dead, this obviously referred to Jane Jefferson. Calling her mother-in-law "my mother" does not necessarily suggest a cordial relationship, however; this usage was common. Maria Jefferson Eppes was later to refer to her mother-in-law as "mother." Still, it is likely that Jefferson's sisters and mother found Martha an agreeable addition to the family. Her family connections were impeccable, even for a Randolph like Jane Jefferson, and her social skills, according to reminiscences by her grandchildren, were considerable. She not only impressed a French aristocrat like de Chastellux, but, during the Revolution, she also became warm friends with the family of a Hessian baron who was a prisoner of war at Charlottesville.

Major General Baron de Riedesel was one of the officers of Burgoyne's troops who surrendered in 1779 at Saratoga. Some four thousand British and German prisoners were brought to Albemarle County, and the officers rented homes in the neighborhood, many becoming friends of the Jeffersons. Establishing close friendships with captured enemy troops may seem strange in an age of total war, where opposing soldiers are killed anonymously and described in body counts, but in the eighteenth century warfare was a game practiced by civilized men; a loss on the battlefield did not deprive one of rank or station. Losers and winners were still gentlemen, and still shared a common education, common artistic tastes, and the wealth and privilege of landed aristocracy. General de Riedesel, therefore, was not an ordinary prisoner of war; he and his wife and family rented a house close to Monticello, and proceeded to live in the style they were accustomed to. These aristocrats fell in with the rebel Thomas Jefferson and his wife as easily as if they had met at one of the courts of Europe. The de Riedesel girls became particularly attached to Martha. The Baron and his wife, a woman of Wagnerian proportions, who shocked the local Virginians by appearing in public wearing riding boots, entertained frequently. Music helped bring the Jeffersons, the de Riedesels, and other German officers together. One of the officers wrote of his impressions of Jefferson, then governor of Virginia, and his wife Martha: "As all Virginians are fond of Music, he is particularly so. You will find in the House an elegant Harpsichord, Pianoforte & some violins. The latter he performs well upon himself, the former his Lady touches very skillfully & who is in all respects a very agreeable, sensible & accomplished Lady." Indeed, a music book belonging to Martha Jefferson survives, and this book may well have been open at the harpsichord when Martha and her husband performed for the German officers. The small, leather-bound notebook is filled with romantic songs and airs, several by Purcell. The keyboard music and words are carefully copied, some no doubt by a music instructor, but a number in Martha's handwriting.

It was all very civilized—and ironic. The war which was to break the yoke of a British aristocracy and establish a republican form of government in America, brought to Jefferson and his wife, a woman who had most likely never been out of Virginia, an opportunity to live for a time the cultured life of European aristocrats. Monticello became almost an American Liechtenstein, a center of tasteful talk, good music, fine wine, and feminine charm. During eight years, from her marriage to her association with the de Riedesels, Martha had blossomed from a well-born but provincial young matron to a woman who might have held her own in the salons of Paris, where her husband would, in a few years, establish himself, but without her.

She was capable of carrying on an exchange of gossip with the French vice consul in Virginia, Charles-François Chevalier d'Anmours. A letter to Jefferson, with a witty anecdote to be passed on to Martha, shows the comfortable relationship between the French aristocrat and his charming hostess.

> On my way here I Call'd on Col. mercer, who now is Become a Compleat farmer. This piece of news is for Mrs. Jefferson, who will Scarce believe it. Yet Madam, nothing is truer. By his present appearance you Could never guess that he was once one of the first-Rate-Beaux. Red coats, Gold frogs, Gold and Silver embroider'd Jackets, Powder, Puffs, Smelling Bottles, &c. all is vanished. And if you, now and then, see some Remains of them, they appear like the Ruins of those ancient magnificent cities, which serve to show what they once were: indeed the Reformation is as Compleat as Can be imagined.

The tale of fop to farmer is classic drawing room chitchat. That this urbane aristocrat could comfortably amuse Martha Jefferson with it is a measure of her position in her husband's world. To Jefferson, D'Anmours revealed his own cynical view of war, God, and the privileged classes:

> By Calculation, there is about two hundred ships of the line, and two hundred thousand men at Sea Ready to Knock down one another. The Party that will have the Blessing of Destroying a Larger part of the human Race, will, to be sure,

thank very devoutly the Supreme Being for that Great Good Luck. And yet all this happens between the politest, and more civilized nations of the Globe, the Chiefs of which are at Versailles, L'Escurial and St. James Dancing and frolicking as Deliberately as if they were not the principal Causes of all that havock.

If Martha Jefferson the hostess was all charm, wit, and music, Martha the housewife tried to be all business. Although after a few years she stopped keeping records of how much she spent and for what, she continued periodically to enter inventories of food and clothing in her borrowed Account Book until her death. During the years she kept accounts of cash payments, she noted them on separate sheets of paper and turned them over to Jefferson, who copied them into his pocket Memorandum Book at the end of the year. All of Martha's purchases were reviewed by her sharp-eyed husband, and if she was charged too much for an item he informed her—gently, no doubt, for they were newlyweds. Indeed, she was guilty of paying too much for the very first item purchased after their marriage. On January 30, 1772, she noted: "sent to buy cyder 10/," and Jefferson, in copying it into his pocket Memorandum Book, noted for posterity "(which was 6/3 too much)." She quickly picked up his habits, however. It was not long before some of the entries in her own household Account Book could have been written by her husband. On May 16, 1774, she jotted down in precisely the same language Jefferson used in his Garden Book, "first patch of peas come to table," and as subsequent servings of her husband's favorite vegetable were picked from the garden, she noted the date. She even made one of Jefferson's characteristic experiments to determine the most efficient and economical way to measure and brew coffee.

She quickly established herself as manager of the household slaves; in June 1774, she noted the clothes given to the house servants. Ursula, Orange, Mary Hemings, and Scilla each received "2 suits of clothes," Mary and Scilla were given an apron; Ursula and Bett also received a white shift. Bob and Martin Hemings and Jupiter received shirts; Ned and James Hemings got new trousers. Two slave women too old to work, Juno and Luna, each were given a brightly dyed yellow or red "crocus coat." As only the dining room wing of the house was completed at this time, there were a lot of servants on the mountaintop to take care of a very small piece of completed shelter. Running a plantation household was labor-intensive, however. There was also a close division of labor among the household slaves; their skills were often highly specialized. An equally important reason for the large number of servants at Monticello was that the Jeffersons were slave-rich.

With the death of Martha's father in 1773, Jefferson came into her inheritance of 135 slaves (the property of a married woman was legally vested in her husband). Those who were house servants—including the Hemings family—were divided between Monticello and the Elk Hill plantation, which was included in the eleven thousand acres of land also inherited. Betty Hemings stayed at Elk Hill with her younger children; her older children, Mary, Bett, Martin, Bob, and James, were brought to Monticello. Martin, who was to stand up to the British a few years later when they charged up the mountaintop in a vain attempt to capture Jefferson, became the house butler. Bett, also known as Betty Brown, was a seamstress, and may have sewed the clothing Martha gave to the other slaves. Jupiter's wife Sukey cooked, and Mary Hemings was a pastry cook, as was Ursula, Great George's wife.

Jefferson purchased Ursula and her two children, George and Bagwell, a year after his marriage, before John Wayles's death brought the talented Hemings family of cooks and household servants to Monticello. Ursula was undoubtedly purchased for Martha because of her skills as a pastry chef. There was also a bit of serendipity in her acquisition; she became a wet nurse for Martha's sickly infant daughter shortly after Ursula arrived at Monticello. In later years, Jefferson recalled that his eldest daughter's health was recovered "almost instantaneously by a good breast of milk." Ursula at that time was nursing her third child, Archy, who died the following year. In his memoir, Ursula's son Isaac recalled the working relationship between Ursula and Martha Jefferson: "Mrs. Jefferson would come out there with a cookery book in her hand and read out of it to Isaac's mother how to make cakes, tarts and so on." This account indicates that Martha directly supervised food preparation, and was in the kitchen giving instructions when meals were cooked. Managing this many servants and supervising their duties, while nursing and caring for an infant—all in the middle of a construction site—must have taxed the energies of Jefferson's youthful wife.

She was apparently not a physically strong woman; she was small in stature and delicately featured. There is no known portrait of her; however, family tradition described her as "slightly but exquisitely formed," with a "brilliant" complexion, "expressive eyes of the richest shade of hazel," and "luxuriant hair of the finest tinge of auburn." She walked, rode, and danced "with admirable grace and spirit," and was "frank, warm-hearted, and somewhat impulsive." In his memoir, Isaac confirmed her small stature, and her beauty. In comparing the two Jefferson daughters, Martha (Patsy) and Maria (Polly), Isaac declared: "Patsy Jefferson was tall like her father. Polly low like her mother and longways the handsomest, pretty lady jist like her mother." How Martha's beauty held up under the strain of frequent childbearing and poor health is questionable. There is some hint that she may have had some difficulty with her teeth, and it is quite possible she lost some of them. Jefferson in his later life claimed that his own teeth were good. (In 1819, at the age of seventy-six, he wrote, "I have not yet lost a tooth by age.") Yet, shortly after his marriage, he paid John Baker, a prominent Williamsburg dentist, for two visits, on April 14, and May 2, 1772, a time when his wife was with him in Williamsburg. It is quite possible that Martha, then four months pregnant, suffered from calcium deficiency, with dental problems as a result. If so, a pregnancy every two years could not have improved her smile.

She transferred her own physical qualities to only one of her two surviving daughters. The eldest, Martha, was her father's daughter. Like Jefferson, she was tall, and her features resembled his—she was regarded as plain by those who described her. Anna Maria Thornton made the laconic comment in her diary, "she is not handsome." On the other hand, she found Maria Jefferson Eppes "very beautiful—but much more reserved than Mrs. Randolph." Martha inherited Jefferson's immune system, as well as his features, and passed it on to her children; in spite of the inevitable illnesses accompanying twelve pregnancies, she was physically robust, lived to be sixty-four, and eleven of her twelve children lived to maturity. Maria, on the other hand, looked like her mother and apparently inherited her mother's physical weaknesses along with her beauty. She lived to be only twenty-five and, like her mother, died from the complications of childbirth. Of her three children, only one lived to maturity.

Martha Jefferson's history of childbearing was a melancholy one; throughout much of her ten-year marriage to Jefferson, she was either pregnant, nursing, grieving the death of an infant, or sick from the complications of childbirth. That she was able to carry out the many duties of a plantation wife despite the difficult years of the American Revolution and in an unfinished house, littered with workmen's debris, while simultaneously undergoing the physical and emotional stress of multiple pregnancies and infant death, is a tribute to her strength of will and her dedication to what she perceived to be her mission in life.

The source of this dedication did not apparently come from any religious commitment on her part. There is no hint of a spiritual side to Martha Jefferson in any of the recollections of her by family members. This would not be unusual, however, for the wife of a man whose coolness to orthodox religious belief is well documented. In the paternalistic world of the Virginia plantation aristocracy, wives did not normally show a great deal of independence of thought. They were taught to accept the domination, first of a father, and then of a husband, as part of the natural order of things, as right as Newton's laws.

The way Jefferson educated his two daughters after the death of their mother is a paradigm of what an enlightened father of his generation thought the proper training of a plantation mistress should be. Martha and Maria were unusually well educated, although it was a specialized schooling for an American woman. He told Martha that he wished to see her "more qualified than common" among women of her class. Jefferson outlined his educational plans for Martha to the Marquis Barbé-Marbois, who had offered to procure a French tutor for her:

The plan of reading which I have formed for her is considerably different from what I think would be most proper for her sex in any other country than America. I am obliged in it to extend my views beyond herself, and consider her as

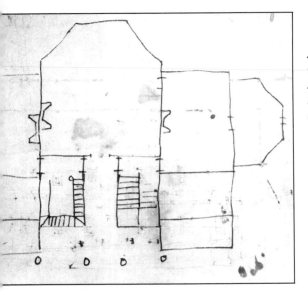

Jefferson's sketch of the first version of Monticello showing how he considered enlarging the house by adding rooms on each side of the east portico.

The first page of Martha Jefferson's household Account Book, started soon after her marriage on January 1, 1772. On February 27, she brewed the first of many casks of small beer.

1772
Feb 10   opened a barrel of col: harrison's flower
13   a mutton killed
17   two pullets killed
22   a turkey killed
27   a mutton killed
   a cask of small beer brewed   15 gallon cask
28   a list of the house linen
   6 diaper table cloths
   10 ditto damask
   12 diaper napkins marked T I 71
   12 ditto towels T I 71
   6 pr of sheets 5 pillow-cases T I 71
Mar 1   opened a cask of of butter weight 20 ℔
10   a turkey killed
   a shoat killed
12   a cask of small beer brewed
20   a mutton killed
26   made 46℔ of soft soap
27   a turkey killed
29   two pullets killed
   made 12℔ of hard soap
July 1   bought of garth a ℔ of butter
3   ditto 4℔
   brewed a cask of beer
4   bought of garth 2℔ of butter

Above: *Jefferson's Memorandum Book* records the whiskey drinking of two of his workers.

In 1782, Jefferson recorded in his *Memorandum Book*, "Sep. 6. my dear wife died this day . . ."

possibly at the head of a little family of her own. The chance that in marriage she will draw a blockhead I calculate at about fourteen to one, and of course that the education of her family will rest on her own ideas and direction without assistance. With the best poets and prosewriters I shall therefore combine a certain extent of reading in the graver sciences.

Both girls were placed in a fashionable convent while Jefferson was in France, and Martha in particular absorbed the language and culture of pre-revolutionary Paris. She spoke French fluently and read the classics. Both young women were taught music, dance, literature, languages, drawing, and needlework. The latter, Jefferson thought, was particularly useful for a plantation wife. "In the country life of America," he stated, "there are moments when a woman can have recourse to nothing but her needle for employment." When one is in dull company and it is poor taste to read, or simply leave, "the needle is a valuable resource." Besides, how can a plantation mistress direct the sewing of her servants if she is not herself skilled in needlework?

The more mundane domestic skills of cooking, cleaning, and household management were not neglected, however. Jefferson was concerned that his daughters could not learn them at the convent of Panthemont in Paris. He wrote to his sister-in-law Elizabeth Eppes that Martha's education was progressing well, with one exception: "She will need, however, your instruction to render her useful in her own country. Of domestic economy she can learn nothing here, yet, she must learn it somewhere, as being more solid value than anything else." When he returned to America with his daughters, he wrote to Maria, who was staying with Elizabeth Eppes, wanting to know "how many hours you sew? whether you have an opportunity of continuing your music? whether you know how to make a pudding yet, to cut out a beefsteak, to sow spinach? or to set a hen?" Maria was then not yet twelve. And Martha, after her marriage, sent a long letter to Jefferson detailing her daily management of the household at Monticello during his absence in Philadelphia. She followed it with a letter announcing the birth of her first child. Jefferson responded enthusiastically: "Your last two letters gave me the greatest pleasure of any I ever received from you. The one announced that you were become a notable housewife; the other a mother. The last is undoubtedly the key-stone of the arch of matrimonial happiness, as the first is its daily aliment."

Like most men of his age, Jefferson believed women's interests were to be confined chiefly to housekeeping and childbearing. In particular, he thought women should keep out of politics, which was a masculine realm. "The tender breasts of ladies were not formed for political convulsions," he wrote. After Martha's marriage, his letters to her were about domestic and health matters, the grandchildren, his affection and love for her; political news was directed to her husband, Thomas Mann Randolph. (During his presidency, Jefferson sometimes forwarded political news and gossip to her, but this was the exception.) In spite of her father's disapproval, Martha was interested in politics; even when she was at Panthemont, she passed on political tidbits about the French court in her letters to her father. (He pointedly let them pass without comment.) Maria was much less concerned with politics; she was a reluctant reader and writer as a child and seemed to her father to be intellectually lazy. In spite of her beauty, she was shy and seems to have felt inferior to her older and brighter sister. As is often the case with children close to each other in age, she chose not to compete with Martha intellectually because she could not hope to win. Unfortunately, the one superiority she had over her sister, her physical beauty, was undervalued by a father who made it abundantly clear that reading, writing, and brilliant conversation—skills attained by hard work and diligent practice—were more to be admired than the chance accident of physical beauty. (This is not to say that he was not attracted to handsome women; on the contrary, all of the women he was associated with romantically during his life were noted for their beauty.) He also felt strongly that women, plain or fancy, brilliant or dull, had a single purpose in life, marriage and subordination to a husband. And he taught this to his daughters. At Martha's marriage, for example, he wrote to her, "the happiness of your life depends now on continuing to please a single person. To this all other objects must be secondary; even your love to me."

If his letters to his daughters are any indication, Jefferson's letters to "Patty," his affectionate name for his wife, were true love letters— one reason why they were destroyed. Although Jefferson was aloof to strangers and friendly but formal to his male friends, he was effusively expressive of his love to his daughters. He courted them in his correspondence as shamelessly as a lover. When he was in Philadelphia as secretary of state, he wrote to Maria, "Would to god I could be with you to partake of your felicities, and to tell you in person how much I love you all, and how necessary it is to my happiness to be with you. . . . Tell [your sister] from me how much I love her. Kiss her and the little one for me." During his vice presidency he wrote to Martha: "I value the enjoyments of this life only in proportion as you participate [in] them with me. All other attachments are weakening, and I approach the state of mind when nothing will hold me here but my love for yourself and your sister, and the tender connections you have added to me."

The oral tradition passed down by the family to Jefferson's early biographers would have us believe that Jefferson and his wife lived a life of perfect marital harmony; nineteenth-century American hagiography did not permit stains on its icons. We now know the inevitability of pigeons roosting on statuary. Jefferson wiped away any traces of marital strife, however, when he destroyed his correspondence with Martha.

There are some suggestions of the kinds of marital disagreements the couple may have had in the advice he offered his daughters about marriage. Shortly after Maria married her cousin John Wayles Eppes, Jefferson wrote her a long letter advising her on how to achieve a happy marriage. The primary goal was marital harmony: "Nothing can preserve affections uninterrupted but a firm resolution never to differ in will," he wrote. When differences between husband and wife occur, he observed, each piece of strife is placed in a private pouch until, when the pouch is filled, love is destroyed. He also cautioned against bickering—"a constant stream of little checks and obstacles"—and criticizing one's mate before friends: "Nothing is so goading." How much of this advice was based on his own marriage is conjectural, but he had strong opinions about the damage done to a marriage by quarreling over trivialities, and it is possible this reflected his own experience.

Although he cautioned his daughters to be economical in the management of household and plantation affairs, he advised them never to be parsimonious about clothing. Dressing for one's spouse is important, he wrote, for it is an essential part of continuing to please each other. As we age, he noted, there is a tendency to "become slovenly in proportion as personal decay requires the contrary." Jefferson was fastidious about cleanliness and grooming in women, even though he was himself accused during his presidency of being careless and shoddy in his dress. During his marriage, however, he dressed fashionably, and his wife Martha spent a considerable amount of money on clothing. When Jefferson went to Philadelphia in 1776 for the Second Continental Congress, he used the opportunity to buy the latest fashion accessories for her, including six pairs of shoes, seven pairs of gloves (purchased on July 4) and £18 worth of "sundries." (He also bought toys for young Martha, then approaching her fourth birthday.) Perhaps the most forceful expression of his distaste for carelessness and uncleanliness in women's dress was in a letter he wrote to his eldest daughter shortly after the death of her mother. Martha, then only eleven, was told that her clothes must at all times be "clean, whole, and properly put on." Do not wait until clothing is visibly dirty, her father warned; "you will be the last to be sensible of this." A woman must be freshly and cleanly dressed at all times:

> Some ladies think they may under the privileges of the dishabille be loose and negligent of their dress in the morning. But be you from the moment you rise till you go to bed as cleanly and properly dressed as at the hours of dinner or tea. A lady who has been seen as a slut or a sloven in the morning, will never efface the impression she then made with all the dress and pageantry she can afterwards involve herself in.

This may seem to be strong language to use on an eleven-year-old girl, but Jefferson obviously had strong feelings about cleanliness in women. The word "slut" in the eighteenth century was commonly used to describe a woman of dirty or untidy habits or dress, without suggestions of sexual promiscuity; nevertheless, the vulgar meaning was also current, and Jefferson's use of the term in a letter to his daughter is revealing. He was obviously deeply offended by a lack of cleanliness in women, and he no doubt insisted upon it in his wife.

"Nothing is more disgusting to our sex as a want of cleanliness and delicacy in yours," he told his daughter. Women must dress to please men; therefore "from the moment you rise from bed," he wrote, "your first work will be to dress yourself in such a stile as that you may be seen by any gentleman without his being able to discover a pin amiss, or any other circumstances of neatness wanting."

For a man of Jefferson's compulsive need for order, a desire for neatness in women would be expected, but calling indelicacy of personal habits "disgusting" suggests that he may well have been one of those men whose compulsive personalities lead them to associate women's sexuality with filth. Men who hold this vision of women often sublimate their disgust for physical sexuality by idealizing love as pure, transcendental, and romantic. Jefferson admired women who were "soft," passive, modest, and chaste, and who possessed such artistic talents as made them ornaments of a masculine world. As mothers and housekeepers they were domestic workhorses, but as sexual objects they must be delicate and beautiful, living works of art existing in an imaginative world of romantic, sentimental love. Martha Wayles Jefferson was such a woman, as was his other known mature love, Maria Cosway, the petite and beautiful artist-musician he was to meet in Paris after Martha's death.

This view of women reduces them to either ladies or sluts—clean and chaste, or filthy and sexual. Conflicts arise when one marries a lady and finds her sexuality sluttish. The close resemblance of Jefferson's personality to the compulsive-retentive profile, together with the revealing letter to his daughter, hints at the possibility of marital conflicts over sexuality, but if so, they have been blown from history with the ashes of burned letters. All we know of Jefferson's penchant for cleanliness is that Martha Jefferson made large amounts of soap at Monticello, and that Jefferson, in remodeling the mansion, installed an ingenious waste disposal system that took a great deal of planning and inventiveness. Indoor privies, one in Jefferson's bedroom, dropped waste down to the ground level, where it was removed by slaves. An elaborate underground air shaft ran up the interior walls to help eliminate offensive odors. The system removed from eye and nose that ubiquitous reminder of the union of sex and excrement, the chamber pot.

Whatever Jefferson's sexual proclivities may have been, his marriage demonstrates that he was very much a sexual creature. In ten years, he fathered six children, several of them at times when Martha's health should have precluded pregnancy. But Jefferson was as unwilling as any male of his class to deny himself the pleasures of the marital bed because of his wife's poor health. And Jefferson, who was as knowledgeable about health and medicine as any layman of his age, appears to have made no attempt to practice contraception or child planning. It seems unlikely that the colleague of scientists such as Benjamin Franklin and David Rittenhouse, the owner of one of the largest private libraries in the country, the man who was to become president of the American Philosophical Society, was not familiar with contraceptive devices. Although the syringe and sponge were not to come into common use until the turn of the century, Moreau de St. Mery, a Philadelphia bookseller and printer, was selling "certain small contrivances"—probably condoms—in his shop in 1794. (Jefferson recorded the purchase of at least two syringes in his Memorandum Books, one in 1786, and another in 1800, both after the death of his wife. Although the instrument could be put to a number of uses other than contraceptive douching, it could have been obtained for this use.) Women in the late eighteenth century practiced a form of contraception by prolonging infant nursing. The normal time of weaning was twelve months after birth; wives sometimes nursed their children for two years or more, using the contraceptive effect of lactation for child spacing. Although this method has been discredited as unreliable in modern times, it was the only way eighteenth-century women could exert control over the endless, debilitating, and ultimately killing cycle of pregnancies. Neither Martha Jefferson nor her two daughters seem to have practiced this method, however.

Martha Jefferson's terminal illness, like her youngest daughter's, was a lingering one, following a pregnancy. On May 8, 1782, she gave birth to a daughter, Lucy Elizabeth, named for another infant who had been born only eighteen months before and lived for only four and a half months. Early death was the sad fate of four of Martha's six children by Jefferson: a daughter, Jane Randolph, born in April 1774, lived for only seventeen months; a son, born in May 1777, died seventeen days later (the fact that he was not named suggests that he was given little chance of survival at birth, perhaps because he was premature or defective in some way); and her final daughter who died of whooping cough at two and a half years.

Martha had once before—in the summer of 1776—been so seriously ill that her life was feared for. Jefferson, in Philadelphia for the Second Continental Congress, had become frantic about her health. He wrote to Richard Henry Lee, who was to relieve him as a Virginia delegate, "For god's sake, for your country's sake, and for my sake, come. I receive by every post such accounts of the state of Mrs. Jefferson's health, that it will be impossible for me to disappoint her expectations of seeing me." Although her illness was not specified, it is quite possible that, like her daughter Maria, she suffered a miscarriage—it was more than two years since she had last become pregnant, and during her entire marriage to Jefferson she never at any other time went more than two years without conceiving a child. Whatever the extent of her illness, it did not prevent Jefferson from getting her pregnant immediately upon his return to Monticello in September 1776. Their son was born less than nine months later.

During her final illness Jefferson was again under pressure to be separated from her, but he steadfastly refused to leave her bedside. Less than two weeks after the birth of the second Lucy Elizabeth, Jefferson had announced the child's arrival to James Monroe with an ominous postscript: "Mrs. Jefferson has added another daughter to our family. She has been ever since and still continues very dangerously ill." During the week of the infant's birth he had been, against his wishes, elected Albemarle delegate to the Virginia legislature. In spite of his refusal to serve, he was threatened with being forcibly taken to Richmond by the sergeant-at-arms; a delegate could not legally be excused from serving unless he first appeared at Richmond and formally requested leave. In a letter to Monroe, Jefferson raged against the idea that one could be forced into public service as a lawmaker for an indefinite period. "Nothing could so completely divest us of . . . liberty as the establishment of the opinion that the state has a *perpetual* right to the services of all its members," he wrote. In spite of the pressures from Richmond, for the final four months of his wife's life he stayed with her at Monticello. As his daughter Martha was to recall, "when not at her bed side he was writing in a small room which opened immediately at the head of her bed." This would be the "anti-chamber," the small room between the entrance hall and the Jefferson bedchamber. Although this space was not a good piece of architectural design, it was perfectly suited to the use to which it was put at this time. It could be closed off from the hall and bedroom to provide Jefferson with a small sanctuary where he could be close to his wife and working at his writing desk at the same time. With his sister, Mrs. Dabney Carr, and his wife's sisters, he nursed her, fed her food and medicine, and sat up with her during her final months.

Shortly before her death, Martha copied some lines from one of Jefferson's favorite books, Lawrence Sterne's *Tristram Shandy*:

> Time wastes too fast: every letter
> I trace tells me with what rapidity
> life follows my pen. The days and hours
> of it are flying over our heads like
> clouds of a windy day never to return. . . .

The passage was completed in Jefferson's hand:

> —and every
> time I kiss thy hand to bid adieu, every absence which
> follows it, are preludes to the eternal separation
> which we are shortly to make!

This moving exchange—the only writing of any kind between them that has been preserved—was kept by Jefferson with a lock of Martha's hair entwined around it.

Edmund Bacon, Jefferson's overseer at Monticello for sixteen years, from 1806 to 1822, recounted the deathbed scene as it was reported by the house servants to Mrs. Bacon. At Martha's bedside with Jefferson and other family members were Betty Hemings and four of her children, Betty Brown, Nance, Critta, and Sally; and Great George's wife Ursula. It may seem strange that slaves would be allowed to participate in a ritual so personal and private as the death of a loved one, but the ceremonial gathering of the favorite house slaves about the deathbed of their owner was not uncommon in the South. It was one of many signs of a deep affection that often existed between master and slave in an institution which, by all rational measures, should have created only hatred and suspicion. The Hemings family, too, was a special case; six of Betty Hemings's children allegedly were fathered by John Wayles; if so, they were Martha Jefferson's half-brothers and sisters. Aside from statements by Isaac and Madison Hemings in their memoirs, the most convincing evidence of the truth of the allegation is that Jefferson treated the Hemingses as if they were free white servants rather than slaves. The presence of the Hemings women at Martha's deathbed, therefore, was of special significance, for they were in all likelihood considered to be members of the family in blood as well as in the extended use of the term "family" to describe household servants. There is not the slightest hint that Martha's feelings for Betty Hemings and her family were anything but warm and affectionate. The best record of this is the deathbed scene itself. Martha's final words to her husband, described by Bacon, were uttered openly before the Hemings women:

> . . . when Mrs. Jefferson died they stood around the bed. Mr. Jefferson sat by her, and she gave him directions about a good many things that she wanted done. When she came to the children she wept and could not speak for some time. Finally she held up her hand, and spreading out her four fingers, she told him she could not die happy if she thought her four children were ever to have a stepmother brought in over them. Holding her other hand in his, Mr. Jefferson promised her solemnly that he would never marry again. And he never did. . . .

This was a remarkable request for a dying woman to make to her husband, particularly in an age when many married men outlived several wives. The deathbed promise, before witnesses, placed a heavy burden upon Jefferson to respect his wife's last request, and as Bacon stated, he did. Yet, the question remains, why would a wife wish to extract from her husband a promise such as this? A clue lies in the reason she gave, that she feared a stepmother would be "brought in over them." Martha was herself a stepchild. Her own mother, also named Martha, died shortly after she was born, and she was raised by two stepmothers. The first had three children of her own, so Martha, the only living child of John Wayles's first marriage, was raised with three younger half-sisters. It was a Cinderella scenario, and although Martha's relationship with her half-sisters was close in her adult life, as a child she may have chafed at being a stepdaughter and may indeed have been treated less lovingly than her half-sisters by her stepmother. Her second stepmother married Wayles when Martha was twelve, and died a year later. Thereafter, she was quite possibly raised by Betty Hemings, a surrogate stepmother, reputedly her father's mistress. Ironically, it may have been the slave "stepmother" who was the most loving and loved, which would explain in part the uncommon position of the Hemings family at Monticello, and Jefferson's preferential treatment of the Hemings children throughout his life. They were a tenuous hold on the memory of his beloved wife.

Jefferson's reaction to the death of Martha also revealed something of his own emotional state at the time. His daughter Martha described his reactions: "A moment before the closing scene he was led from the room almost in a state of insensibility" and taken upstairs to his library, where he "fainted and remained so long insensible that they feared he would never revive." For the next three weeks he kept to his room and "walked almost incessantly night and day, only lying down occasionally, when nature was completely exhausted, on a pallet that had been brought in during his long fainting fit." When he left his room, Martha recalled, she accompanied him on long horseback rides during which she was "a solitary witness to many a violent burst of grief." The extremity of Jefferson's grief circulated among his friends and caused some concern. Edmund Randolph, who was later to become Jefferson's secretary of state, commented in a letter to James Madison: "I ever thought him to rank domestic happiness in the first class of the chief good; but scarcely supposed that his grief would be so violent as to justify the circulating report of his swooning away whenever he sees his children." (Madison thought this rumor to be "altogether incredible.") A month after Martha's death, Jefferson wrote to her half-sister Elizabeth Wayles Eppes that he was "unable to attend to anything like business," that life was "too burdensome to be borne," and that if it were not for his children he "could not wish it's continuance a moment."

Jefferson's uncharacteristic loss of emotional control might be more easily understood had Martha died suddenly and unexpectedly. Her death, however, came after a four-month decline and was certainly anticipated for some time. Normally, in such extended terminal illnesses, loved ones work out their grief by the time the dying spouse has gone through the denial-anger-acceptance phases of the familiar mourning pattern. Martha's instructions to her family were evidence that she had accepted her death and was putting her affairs in order. When the long-anticipated death finally came, Jefferson's violent physical reaction suggests that there were fundamental conflicts left unresolved. The two most common dynamic emotions in cases of violent bereavement are guilt and anger. He may well have felt, at a subliminal level, anger at his wife's being taken from him. In her tombstone epitaph he used the expression "torn from him." Grief is an irrational response, of course, but for a man like Jefferson, who attempted to order his life according to rational certainties, the random abduction of a loved one by death shook the very roots of his being. Rebellion, war, political strife—all had been riddled with risk, but Jefferson had threaded his way through them to what appeared to him to be a safe haven. As Chastellux had pictured it, he had a "gentle and amiable wife, charming children whose education is his special care, a house to embellish, extensive estates to improve, the arts and sciences to cultivate—these are what remain to Mr. Jefferson." Martha's death shredded that future. Perhaps if she had tried harder, fought harder. But if, indeed, his thoughts had run in that direction they had inevitably to confront a terrible fact: her death was ultimately caused, not by Martha's weakness of will or lack of determination to survive, but by the pregnancies resulting from the sexual demands of her husband.

Jefferson could not help but face this conclusion and hold himself responsible for his wife's death. Throughout his life he had practiced a stoic control over his passions, but the liberties of the marriage bed were a temptation he was unwilling or unable to check—even though he knew the inevitable pregnancies placed her seriously at risk. During his wife's long illness, he had ample time to brood over his own complicity in her condition and to generate a monumental weight of guilt. It may well have been aggravated by a conviction that he had also failed to provide her with the amenities he had promised, including the finished house they had planned together. In the room

Martha died in, Jefferson could look up at the bare walls and unadorned windows and doorways for which he had drawn decorative Palladian orders a decade before, but which had never been built. And he could have recalled with pain Martha's attempting to maintain some semblance of domestic order amid the scaffolding, dust, mud, noise, and debris—the sheer ugliness of a house forever being built around her. It was by his own admission a house only half finished, and this was the only Monticello she knew. The Monticello of Jefferson's precise architectural drawings and of their mutual planning simply did not exist during her lifetime. She lived in a dwelling that, were it not for the dream of its one day becoming the elegant mansion of her husband's imagination, was depressingly ordinary inside. There were, of course, the outlines of a stylish house, but the elegance of Palladian architecture is derived from the detailed articulation of its parts, in particular its interior rooms, each of the orders crafted in plaster and wood. Martha Jefferson died in a skeleton house, the exterior, with its half-finished double portico, announcing—with the exception of the dining room—an empty Palladian shell. The dependencies were not even started; it was like living in a modern house without laundry, garage, or closets, and with the kitchen a half-block away. Jefferson could blame his failure to finish their house on revolution, war, assuming the governorship of Virginia, on a scarcity of labor—but these were rational explanations. They ignored the simple emotional reality that he had not given her what the wife of Thomas Jefferson should have enjoyed. And because the house one builds is a mirror of what one is, flawed shelter equaled a flawed husband.

These personal failures were reinforced by the accusations of public failure that occurred at the same time. Jefferson had been accused of misconduct in office during his two years as war governor of Virginia. The public spectacle of legislative delegates, and the governor himself, fleeing westward before Benedict Arnold's troops and Tarleton's raiders had led to charges of poor military preparedness. The accusations were politically motivated, and after an inquiry he was exonerated by the Virginia legislature, but the charges deeply humiliated him. In the letter to James Monroe in which he revealed Martha's severe illness, Jefferson wrote of his shock and dismay on learning of the accusations. The affections of his countrymen were all he ever desired from public service, he declared, and now he had "even lost the small estimation I before possessed." The incident, he wrote, "had inflicted a wound on my spirit which will only be cured by the all-healing grave." The spiritual wound was followed closely by the coup de grâce, the death of his wife. If Jefferson did indeed meditate upon these private failings and public slights during Martha's long illness, it would help explain the violence of his grief at her death.

Jefferson recorded in his family bible, which gives births and deaths for four generations: "Martha Jefferson died Sep. 6 1782 at 11-45 a.m. aged 33y - 10m - 8d." She was buried in the eighty-square-foot graveyard Jefferson had set aside on his mountaintop in 1773, a year after his marriage. The graveyard had been cleared from the surrounding forest to receive the body of his boyhood friend and brother-in-law, Dabney Carr, who died suddenly at twenty-nine of "bilious fever." The spot selected for the graveyard was a sentimental one; the two young men had read and talked together under a great oak at this spot and had made a pact that they would both lie there in death one day. Typically, Jefferson, while suffering grief at the loss of his closest friend, found time to observe and write in his Garden Book a useful piece of information on worker efficiency: "2 hands grubbed the Grave Yard . . . in 3½ hours so that one would have done it in 7 hours, and would grub an acre in 49 hours = 4 days." When Martha was interred, Jefferson placed on the grave a slab of white marble with her birth date and the lines: "Intermarried with Thomas Jefferson January 1st, 1772; Torn from him by death September 6th, 1782: This monument of his love is inscribed." This was followed by two lines from the *Iliad*, in Greek, which read in translation, "Nay, if even in the house of Hades men forget their dead, yet will I even there remember my dear comrade."

Five days after his wife's death, in the midst of the violent outbursts of grief his daughter Martha was to recall, Jefferson recorded this observation in his Garden Book:

Sep. 11. W. Hornsby's method for preserving birds.
Make a small incision between the legs of the bird; take out the entrails & eyes, wipe the inside & with a quill force a passage through the throat into the body that the ingredients

may find a way into the stomach & so pass off through the mouth. Fill the bird with a composition of ⅔ common salt & ⅓ nitre pounded in a mortar with two tablespoonfuls of black or Indian pepper to a pound. Hang it up by its legs 8 or 10. weeks, & if the bird be small it will be sufficiently preserved in that time. If it be large, the process is the same, but greater attention will be necessary. The seasons also should be attended to in procuring them, as the plumage is much finer at one time of the year than another. . . .

That Jefferson should copy, a few days after the burial of his wife, a piece of clinical information such as this on ornithological taxidermy seems on the surface to be in questionable taste, and to belie the accounts of his deep feelings of loss. Like the notes on grubbing the grave of Dabney Carr, however, the method for preserving birds reveals a lifelong ability to sever his rational, mathematical, and scientific attitudes from his emotions and instincts, or, as he was later to write in one of the most famous love letters in American history, to bisect the head from the heart. He was a man of consummate self-discipline, and was able, even during moments of severe emotional distress, to continue the daily habits of list-making, classifying, account-keeping, note-taking, and agricultural and scientific observations, which were the very heart-tick of his intellectual life. Indeed, in times of stress, these mind-gates and fences may well have retained his sanity.

A closer examination of this entry suggests a deeper insight. It deals with rendering a beautiful, natural object timeless through the art of taxidermy, of preserving a dead bird from decay by giving it a permanent beauty and life. Days before, Jefferson had lost his once-beautiful wife to death; now, in an oblique, scientific note on how to stuff a bird, he perhaps revealed a fantasy of halting death by preserving and immortalizing a beautiful object. The same sentiment was expressed more directly four years later when he related the death of his wife and children to a friend he had not seen in years. "My history, since I had the pleasure of seeing you last," he wrote, "would have been as happy a one as I could have asked, could the objects of my affection have been immortal."

The loss of his wife would not be the last death of a loved one suffered by Jefferson. His youngest daughter Maria was an even more saddening example than her mother of the toll taken by frequent pregnancies. She married John Wayles Eppes at nineteen and, before her death at twenty-five, had three children and a miscarriage—four pregnancies in six years of marriage. Only one child lived past three years, a boy, Francis. Like most men of his class, Eppes was highly solicitous of his wife's health, and poured out his worries in letters to his father-in-law. He kept Jefferson informed of the ups and downs of her sicknesses, and like his father-in-law, believed exercise and diet to be more beneficial in the treatment of illness than bleeding, purging, or medicines. He thought the miscarriage after the birth of Maria's first child was particularly injurious: "to that unfortunate accident I attribute her ill health for the last two years." Maria's older sister, Martha, came to her aid two years later after the birth of her final child, by nursing the infant for her. Eppes reported to Jefferson: "Her child is well also from the kindness of Patsy who has nursed it with her own—Maria during her illness has lost her milk entirely." Maria's health declined steadily, however; Eppes wrote of a "rising in her breast," and then an inability to take nourishment: "she is extremely thin, a mere walking shadow." Four weeks later she was dead. Several poignant letters from Maria to her husband survive and they show a close, loving relationship between them. One was written by Maria while Eppes was in Washington serving as a congressman:

I find it often hard to bear up against sickness, confinement & a separation from you, for since my last to you my health has been growing gradually worse. I have puked up a great deal of bile which I suppose is the cause of it, but am afraid to take anything in my present situation. Tho my stomach is so weak that it scarcely retains anything, do not however be uneasy my dearest husband. The hope that in a week or two, for it can last no longer, I shall be able to give you the intelligence most interesting & most desired, makes me support it with patience. To present you when we meet with so sweet an addition to our felicity would more than compensate for allmost any suffering. . . . Dear Francis is well & so much improved in speaking that he will be able to keep up a conversation with you when you return. He has been begging very hard for a pencil to write you & talks too much of you, I think, to forget you. Adieu once more best beloved of my soul. I live but in anticipation of the happiness I shall feel when we meet again. I hope it is not a little increased in knowing that it will not be followed by another separation. Yours ever with tenderest love

M E

On the day before Maria's death, her brother-in-law Thomas Mann Randolph wrote to a friend to inform him of "the dismal doom which at this time envelopes the domestic scenes of Monticello." Slaves had carried Maria on a litter four miles from the Randolph home at Edgehill to Monticello, where Jefferson personally attended her in a vain effort to restore her failing health. In the overblown rhetoric common among educated Virginians of the period, Randolph described the physical deterioration of the dying young woman: "This fairest flower which my eyes ever beheld to blow in the Parterre of female beauty has allready lost all its enchanting appearance." He wondered how the President would survive the death of his daughter: "I can tell you how he bears it now. He passed all last evening with her handkerchief in his hand."

Jefferson's grief at the loss of Maria was great, but unlike his behavior after the death of his wife, it was a private, controlled emotion, one typical of men of his generation. There was no guilt associated with her loss, as there had been with the death of his wife. He announced her death to one of his closest friends, James Madison, with one line in a letter otherwise filled with governmental business: "On the 17th instant our hopes & fears here took their ultimate form." The death of his daughter, which came during Jefferson's first term as President, was particularly shattering because it deprived him of a fantasy he had increasingly enjoyed as the burden of his office weighed ever more heavily upon him: that he would retire to Monticello like one of the patriarchs of old with his two daughters and their families embosomed about him. He wrote to his old friend John Page that now his hopes for future happiness were suspended "on the slender thread of a single life"—that of his remaining daughter Martha. The loss also faced backward in its echoings of the death of Martha Jefferson. The daughter who so much resembled her mother in life was to die her mother's death.

Ultimately, as all men must, Jefferson accepted the finality of his wife's death. His acquiescence was aided by an opportunity for a change of scene. Two months after her burial, he accepted an appointment from Congress to aid in the peace negotiations in Paris. The appointment was withdrawn, however, when it was learned that a provisional peace treaty had been signed. It was not until another year and a half had passed that he was to embark for France. In the interim, however, he returned to public service as a delegate to Congress. At Annapolis, where Congress met, he threw himself into committee work and drafted a total of thirty-one papers, including a plan for creating fourteen new states from the western territories, and another for creating a decimal coinage. His "Notes on the Establishment of a Money Unit, and of a Coinage for the United States," was largely responsible for the dollar-and-cents system we now use. In May 1784, he was once again appointed minister to France, this time to negotiate commercial treaties with European nations. In July, after leaving Maria with her Aunt Elizabeth Eppes, he sailed from Boston aboard the *Ceres* for France with his daughter Martha and James Hemings.

In the twenty-two months between Martha's death and the departure for France, work had continued on the house at Monticello, even though Jefferson was gone most of the time. During Martha's four-month terminal illness all interior carpentry was undoubtedly suspended, but three months before her death Jefferson had looked over an old list of various kinds of lumber to be cut for the interior decorative orders and the missing columns on the upper porticoes. He was still making plans for finishing the house. The British deserter Davy Watson was doing carpentry work at Monticello during this time and continued on even after Jefferson left for France.

Jefferson had also considered the possibility of enlarging his house. At the death of Dabney Carr, he had assumed responsibility for raising his sister Martha Carr's six children. By 1781, a year before Martha Jefferson's death, the Carr children had come to live at Monticello, placing considerable pressure on the available space. It may have been at this time that Jefferson drew a rough sketch of the floor plan of the house with four additional rooms added, two small rooms stacked against the dining room next to the east portico, and a balancing pair of rooms fronting the dressing room. He retained this idea while in France, for during his stay he recorded in a building notebook a list of all of the rooms of Monticello, which included "4. new rooms." It would have been relatively easy to add the four rooms, but aesthetically it would have been a disaster, breaking the unity of the central-block-and-wing design. Furthermore, the rooms would have had no hall or corridor access and would therefore have been of little practical use. When Jefferson began seriously to consider adding more space to his house, he did so after he had closely studied the latest architectural fashions of Europe and had restructured his thinking, not only about domestic housing, but about domestic living. These new ideas would produce the version of Monticello that now stands majestically atop his mountain.

7

"The Sublimated Philosopher" in Paris

A PLEASANT Paris day found Thomas Jefferson, *ministre plénipotentiare des États Unis d'Amérique*, perched on a wall of the Tuileries Garden overlooking the Seine. He stared across the river, bustling with small boat traffic, at a building under construction, the Hôtel de Salm, one of the elegant new residences of Paris. He had been so "violently smitten" with the house, he was later to write to his friend and confidante Madame de Tessé, that he would visit the Tuileries Garden almost daily to watch the work progressing, straining his neck "to view the object of my admiration." As he gazed across the river, he could see the construction site teeming with workmen—masons in their leather aprons cutting and dressing the great blocks of white stone that faced the building, carpenters constructing scaffolding, carters hauling supplies, and, at the periphery of the site, women selling food and drink to the workers. (An unknown artist captured the scene from the same perspective as Jefferson's perch on the riverbank. In the foreground of the painting, a French poodle, in a wry commentary by the artist, lifts its hind leg.) The Hôtel de Salm, designed for the Prince de Salm-Kyrborg by Pierre Rousseau, was a new style of building. As Jefferson explained to a friend later, the newer houses of

Construction of the Hôtel de Salm, the Paris residence Jefferson was "violently smitten" with, by an unknown artist.

Europe were sixteen to eighteen feet high, with the public and entertainment rooms full height, and the bedrooms stacked, "two tiers of them from 8 to 10 f. high." This kind of house was not only more practical, and more aesthetically pleasing because it hugged the earth, but it was also, Jefferson argued, less expensive to build.

The Hôtel de Salm, however, was hardly inexpensive—or small. Its cost beggared its owner and stretched its construction time to five years. It was a sprawling residence with one courtyard front facing the Rue de Bourbon, and another facing the river. The river front was a rectangular block with a semicircular columned bay, decorated with antique statuary and capped with a dome. When Jefferson began to redesign Monticello, the image of this domed, riverside elevation of the Hôtel de Salm was to be on his mind.

The Hôtel de Salm was but one of a number of buildings that were to influence Jefferson's architectural taste during the five years he spent in France. His European experience gave him an opportunity to see for himself some of the antiquities of the Roman empire he had previously admired only in books and to examine firsthand the most stylish examples of French Palladianism. The house he leased for four years in Paris, the Hôtel de Langeac, was perhaps most influential of all, for here he enjoyed the amenities of this new architecture, not by studying it but by living in it.

The house was situated on what were then the western limits of Paris at the intersection of the Champs Élysées and the Rue de Berri, a location that made it a balcony to one of the great seasonal spectacles of eighteenth-century Paris—the *Promenade à Longchamp*. Every Easter week, the elite of Paris mixed with workers in their best clothing for a procession up the Champs Élysées, across the Bois de Boulogne to the Abbey of Longchamp, presumably to listen to Lenten music at the abbey, but in truth to gawk and be gawked at; most of them never made it to the abbey. Splendid carriages, bejeweled and begowned ladies and courtesans, gallants with their blooded horses—all joined in a three-day procession with the gaiety, intoxication, and revelry of a Rio or New Orleans Mardi Gras. Jefferson's Hôtel de Langeac provided orchestra seats for the spectacle, and on at least one occasion was almost the stage for a French farce. Jefferson's secretary, William Short, a handsome young Virginian with exceptional intelligence and poise, related the events to Jefferson, who was on an extended trip to the south of France. Jefferson had invited several of his women friends, including Madame de Tessé, to use the house to view the promenade, but in the meantime, his landlord, the Count de Langeac, invited himself to the house. On the first day of the promenade, he showed up and ensconced himself in an upstairs room with three ladies whom Short politely informed Jefferson "I did not know," and was apparently not introduced to. The nonplussed secretary expected the worst when Madame de Tessé and her woman friend would arrive to find the count with his harem, but as in all good French farce, the doors opened and closed at the right times, the proper people avoided the improper ones, and the proprieties—the *provenances*, as Short put it—were maintained.

When Jefferson was at home at Langeac, entertaining was much less dramatic. Except for an occasional formal dinner for special guests, he preferred informal "family soupes" with a select group of American émigrés or intellectual friends. This is not to say the Hôtel de Langeac was a Parisian boarding house; on the contrary, it was an elegant establishment, even by Parisian standards. Indeed, until this period of his life, it was probably the most splendid house Jefferson had ever lived in, including the Governor's Palace in Williamsburg and Monticello itself. It would have been difficult for him not to compare Langeac with his own home in Virginia and conclude that by French measures, his own design and construction were provincial and gauche.

The Hôtel de Langeac was situated at a sharp angle between the Champs Élysées and the Rue de Berri, so the architect was forced into an unusual trapezoidal floor plan. The problem of how to insert geometrical Palladian forms into this odd-angled house was solved by the use of two highly fashionable architectural shapes, the circle and ellipse. The public rooms on the ground floor were dominated by a large, elliptical entrance hall, one end formed by a semicircular bay. The entrance hall led to a circular salon with a large skylight. This room, except for a circular rather than an octagonal shape, may have looked something like the dome room that Jefferson was to build at Monticello. The second floor housed the private quarters: three spacious bedrooms with attached *cabinets*—small dressing rooms—walk-in closets or *garderobes*, and a *lieux à l'anglais*, an indoor privy. Jefferson apparently converted a large *cabinet* to another bedroom so his daughters, when visiting from the Abbaye de Panthemont, could have adjoining *chambres à coucher*. (It was a common practice for him to alter even the rented houses he lived in. Virtually every house he ever resided in, including the Governor's Palace in Williamsburg, was remodeled.) The bay on the second floor overlooked the garden and formed an oval salon, which Jefferson apparently used for his library-study. This room, with Jefferson's adjoining bedroom and *cabinet*, formed a private suite, not unlike the one he would construct for himself at Monticello.

Jefferson furnished the Hôtel de Langeac with pieces he had purchased for his previous Parisian residence, a town house he leased on his arrival in France, located on the Cul-de-sac Taitbout. Much of this furniture was later shipped to America and some found its way to Monticello. He also hired a staff of servants for the Taitbout house, including a *maître d'hôtel*, a *valet de chambre*, and a floor polisher (floors were waxed by placing brushes on the feet of the *frotteur*, who skated around the floor in a series of gyrations that never ceased to amuse visiting Americans). His servants were all brought to the Hôtel de Langeac, and a permanent coachman was hired, because Langeac included a stable and Jefferson had purchased horses and a carriage. James Hemings, who had been brought to Paris with Jefferson, was apprenticed to a series of caterers to learn the secrets of French cooking, and Sally Hemings, who later accompanied Jefferson's daughter Maria to France, served as a maid. Jefferson soon became convinced that his maître d'hôtel Marc was overcharging, so he fired him and promoted Adrien Petit to the post. Petit stayed for the remainder of Jefferson's term in France and was eventually lured to America, where he was in charge of the domestic staff during Jefferson's term as secretary of state in Philadelphia. He became homesick and returned to France in 1794. Petit was intelligent, dependable, honest, and trustworthy, traits that Jefferson searched for in domestic servants and rewarded when he found them.

The establishment at the Hôtel de Langeac suited Jefferson perfectly and he quickly grew fond of his rented house. Langeac taught Jefferson a number of architectural lessons that he was to carry back with him to Virginia. He learned that interior rooms without windows could be adequately illuminated with skylights, and that these could be made waterproof; that small private staircases (Langeac had two, plus a formal staircase) provided great convenience for the amount of space they took; and that indoor toilets were functional and highly desirable.

Another architectural lesson learned in Paris was associated with Jefferson's love affair with Maria Cosway, a woman he was infatuated with the moment he set eyes on her. It was perhaps inevitable that he would fall victim to her charms; she was a woman much like his late wife—delicately beautiful, impetuous, and a talented artist and musician. She was married to the miniaturist Richard Cosway, and was herself a painter who had established a reputation in the fashionable circles of London. After her marriage to Cosway in 1781, she exhibited nearly every year at the Royal Academy. She and her husband were introduced to Jefferson by the American painter John Trumbull, who was a frequent visitor at the Hôtel de Langeac. The meeting occurred in September 1786 at the Halle aux Bleds, the magnificently domed grain market, which Jefferson was visiting with an eye toward using its design for a public building at Richmond. It was there that Trumbull introduced him to the Cosways and he fell under the spell of the exquisite Maria. The foursome spent the rest of the day sightseeing, which ended in a visit to the Parc de St. Cloud where, after Jefferson hastily sent a messenger to cancel a previous dinner engagement, they dined and admired the gardens. Afterward, they took in a fireworks display on the Rue St. Lazare, and then ended the evening with a musicale at a friend's house.

Jefferson managed to see the Cosways, and Maria in particular, almost daily. It may have been on one of their excursions that, showing off his horsemanship, he attempted to leap his mount over a fence, fell, and dislocated his wrist. An ineffectual French surgeon merely worsened the injury, rendering his right hand useless for months; it never completely healed. Shortly afterward, the Cosways left Paris for Brussels, and, after bidding them farewell, Jefferson spent the following days composing, and painstakingly copying with his left hand, one of the most remarkable letters he was ever to write.

The letter, which runs to some four thousand words, was in the form of a popular eighteenth-century literary genre, the dramatic dialogue: "Seated by my fire side, solitary and sad, the following dialogue took place between my Head and my Heart." In the dialogue, the Heart expresses its unqualified admiration for Maria, and describes the effect she had on its tender emotions. "How gay did the face of nature appear! Hills, vallies, chateaux, gardens, rivers, every object wore its livliest hue! Whence did they borrow it? From the presence of our charming companion." The Head chastises the Heart for the "scrapes into which you are ever leading us," and proceeds to give the Heart an Epicurean lecture on the superiority of intellectual over physical pleasure:

> The art of life is the art of avoiding pain. . . . Pleasure is always before us; but misfortune is at our side. . . . The most effectual means of being secure against pain is to retire within ourselves, and to suffice for our own happiness. Those, which depend on ourselves, are the only pleasures a wise man will count on: for nothing is ours which another may deprive us of. Hence the inestimable value of intellectual pleasures. Ever in our power, always leading us to something new, never cloying, we ride, serene and sublime, above the concerns of this mortal world, contemplating truth and nature, matter and motion, the laws which bind up their existence, and that

external being who made and bound them up by these laws. Let this be our employ.

To which the Heart replies:

Let the gloomy Monk, sequestered from the world, seek unsocial pleasures in the bottom of his cell! Let the sublimated philosopher grasp visionary happiness while pursuing phantoms dressed in the garb of truth! Their supreme wisdom is supreme folly. . . . Had they ever felt the solid pleasure of one generous spasm of the heart, they would exchange for it all the frigid speculations of their lives.

The Heart proceeds to counterlecture the Head on the several virtues of their "divided empire." When nature gave them the same residence, the Head was allotted science, the Heart morality; the latter was "too essential to the happiness of man to be risked on the incertain combinations of the head." The Heart recalls several occasions where it unwillingly gave in to the Head but later regretted it. It concludes with an impassioned plea for an acceptance of Maria by both Head and Heart as an object of their mutual adoration. (Cosway is included as a formality; the lady was, after all, married.) "Know then my friend," the Heart declares, "that I have taken these good people into my bosom, that I have lodged them in the warmest cell I could find: that I love them and will continue to love them thro life. . . ." After closing the Head-Heart dialogue, Jefferson concludes his letter with some topical news and a personal note: "As to myself my health is good, except my wrist which mends slowly, and my mind which mends not at all, but broods constantly over your departure."

The Head-Heart letter has been justly described as one of the notable love letters in the English language. Its distinction, however, derives not only from what it reveals about Thomas Jefferson, but from what it discloses about those who read it. Like most works of art, it is richly ambiguous, arguing with equal persuasiveness for the ascendancy of intellect and of feeling. The conflict between head and heart is like modern warfare, where victory by either side is destruction for both. Either a triumphant intellect that strangles emotion, or victorious feelings unfettered by rational controls, can each lead to misery and unhappiness. Modern psychology has taught us that the only resolution of the head-heart conflict is a synthesis that recognizes that human personality must engage in a creative interplay between reason and emotion. The art of Jefferson's letter lies in its refusal to resolve the contest and declare an undisputed winner. Because he was writing a love letter, it would have been easy for him to stack the argument in favor of the heart. But he was honest with himself in writing to Maria Cosway, and this is what is most revealing about the Jefferson character. He had obviously fought this battle many times before, and argued its pros and cons to himself—and perhaps to others. It was, for a man whose life had been conducted by the eighteenth-century rules of proper living, and by his own compulsive personality, a very real dilemma. What is the role of emotion in life? Is it inferior to the life of the mind? Are one's sense of morality and of sympathetic feelings for others, of altruism, of a belief in social justice—those qualities that contributed to making Jefferson a political revolutionary—are these inferior and secondary to the life of reason? Jefferson's response to this question is, in effect, "I don't know," for he gives equal weight to each cause, arguing for each as persuasively as he can. The result is a psychological filter that allows us to either pass through or retard whichever side of the conflict satisfies our own needs for reassurance and supports our own personality style. Most works of art do no more than this: shore up our own psychic beaches against the tides of hopelessness and despair, and, from a haven of security, offer visions of human happiness.

If there is an identity theme to Jefferson's personality—a kernel statement that summarizes his adaptive strategies—it is contained in the Head-Heart letter. Such a theme might be stated this way: the need for a tight rational control over life's exigencies must be balanced by an ability to feel and express love. It was only within the framework of family relationships—his wife, daughters, and grandchildren—that Jefferson was able to strike this balance. He attempted it briefly with Maria Cosway, but quickly concluded that a lasting relationship was impossible. All of Jefferson's biographers have noted that he was a deeply domestic individual. This domesticity was a close part of his identity core, for it provided the locus for his need to express love.

This is also why Monticello grasped his imagination at an early age and held it tenaciously throughout his life. It was the physical environment, the bosom, the nest, where love flourished. Even the brief infatuation with Maria Cosway was brought into the Monticello landscape. His most ecstatic description of his mountaintop was written in the Head-Heart letter: "She wants only subjects worthy of immortality to render her pencil immortal. . . . Our own dear Monticello, where has nature spread so rich a mantle under the eye? mountains, forests, rocks, rivers. With what majesty do we ride above the storms." The sublimity of Monticello was immediately joined to his passion for his new love. He built the original home for the great love of his life, his wife Martha, and continued building it for his daughters and grandchildren, and insisted, successfully, that they come and live with him at every opportunity. Physically, the house was also a mirror of his identity theme, balancing Palladian rationalism with his sensory needs for love, comfort, and ease. Because so many of us share the same desires, Monticello has touched the heads and hearts of millions of Americans.

There can be little doubt that much of the Head-Heart letter was lost on Maria Cosway; she was a native of Italy and her knowledge of English was inadequate to grasp the nuances of Jefferson's debate. Nevertheless, her letters show she most certainly recognized that it was an artful declaration of love, addressed to a married woman. Ultimately, it was her married state that dictated the form of Jefferson's Head-Heart letter. By having the Head retract each statement of love voiced by the Heart, Jefferson tiptoed a fine line between propriety and offense—and maintained a perfect balance. Had Maria Cosway been single, the letter would probably never have been written in this form, for he could have expressed his infatuation for her without reservation. There can also be little doubt that Jefferson was well aware that his letter possessed some literary merit. He carefully preserved a press copy of it among his papers, allowing it to survive, even while he destroyed his correspondence with his wife. He was no doubt convinced that it was in no way incriminating, and that he had succeeded in disguising, behind the convention of a dramatic dialogue, that he had fallen in love.

Maria Cosway was later to return to Paris alone, but the ardor of their first series of meetings was not repeated. Whether the love affair was consummated has been debated exhaustively by Jefferson's biographers, mainly because it is the one relationship after the death of his wife that is documented with an extensive exchange of letters. It is possible that, while in Paris, where morality among the aristocracy was notoriously lax and marital infidelity was a social sport, he may have dallied sexually with any of a number of attractive women he was acquainted with—including Maria Cosway. All of this could have occurred without leaving any telltale correspondence. He did leave one tantalizing trace in one of his letters to Maria, however. After returning from a trip to Holland and the Rhineland, he wrote: "At Strasbourg, I sat down to write to you. But for my soul I could think of nothing at Strasbourg but the promontory of noses, of Diego, of Slawkenburgius his historian, and of the procession of the Strasbourgers to meet the man with the nose. Had I written to you from thence it would have been a continuation of Sterne upon noses."

The chapters on noses in *Tristram Shandy* are a bawdy tour de force of sexual innuendo. In particular, Slawkenburgius's history is an extended double entendre, with Diego's elongated nose a thinly veiled reference to an extraordinarily long penis. The procession of the Strasbourgers to meet "the man with the nose" includes virtually every woman in town, all intent on touching a nose "six times as big" as a normal one. Jefferson, who knew his *Tristram Shandy* as well as any American, and whose exchange of passages from the book with his wife are the only known surviving piece of correspondence between them, was certainly well aware of the sexual meaning of noses in Sterne. That he chose to include this oblique sexual comment in his letter to Maria Cosway suggests that if the relationship was not physical, Jefferson wanted it to be. If he thought that Maria would catch the allusion, he was mistaken. In her reply, after she fumed at him for not writing, she commented on his reference to noses: "Many things to say, and not One word to write, *but on Noses?*" (She may have deceived him by telling him she had read *Tristram Shandy*, for he made the reference to the "promontory of noses" without mentioning the book's title, apparently assuming she was familiar with it.) Interestingly, Jefferson used a similar sexual innuendo from Sterne in attempting to induce Angelica Church, another married friend, who was also a confidante of Maria Cosway, to accompany him on the trip from France to America. This was an allusion to the final chapter of *A Sentimental Journey*, where Sterne creates a long sexual tease by placing Yorick in the same bedroom with a handsome lady and her serving girl. Jefferson wrote to Mrs. Church: "Think of it then, my dear friend, and let us begin a negociation on the subject. You shall find in me all the spirit of accommodation with which Yorick began his with the fair Piedmontese. We have a thousand inducements to wish it on our part. On yours perhaps you may find one in the dispositions we shall carry with us to serve and amuse you on the dreary passage."

Whether or not Jefferson was physically intimate with Maria Cosway, the place where he met her, the Halle aux Bleds, provided him with architectural and engineering ideas he took back to America and put to use in building the dome of Monticello. What was remarkable about the dome of the Halle aux Bleds was that its architects, J. G. Legrand and Jacques Molinos, had spanned 130 feet with ribs constructed of a series of small, matched and shaped boards that were ingeniously interlocked with sections of lath—"a parcel of sticks and chips," as the Heart expressed it in the letter to Maria Cosway. Separating the wooden ribs were rays of glass running the full arc of the dome, from lantern to base, bathing the interior with light. When constructing the Monticello dome on a much smaller scale, Jefferson used a modified Halle aux Bleds system.

One other building seen by Jefferson in France influenced his architectural sensibilities, although it did not have a direct effect on his construction of Monticello. This was the Maison Carrée at Nîmes. He visited it during his trip to southern France and northern Italy in 1787, and spent a day gazing at it, as he wrote to Madame de Tessé, "like a lover at his mistress." It was then, and still is, the best-preserved example of a classic Roman temple in existence, and Jefferson, even before his visit to Nîmes, thought it would be a perfect model for the new capitol building to be constructed at Richmond. He contracted with, and aided, the French architect Charles Clérisseau, who adapted the Maison Carrée to an American public building. It is this plan that, after numerous modifications, was ultimately built. But Jefferson had to contend with the news that a foundation had already been laid for another architectural plan for the capitol. He wrote immediately to James Madison and told him to have construction halted, and then proceeded to lecture his fellow Virginians on the role of public architecture in a new nation. "How is taste in this beautiful art to be found in our countrymen, unless we avail ourselves of every occasion when public buildings are to be erected, of presenting them models for their study and imitation?" he asked. The clincher to the argument was that Clérisseau's design would only cost two-thirds as much as the competing one. The principle that the public buildings of the infant American republic should be patterned after the best models from antiquity was established almost singlehandedly by Jefferson from his remote outpost in Paris. Later, he was to be instrumental in promoting the Classical Revival style in the new capital city of Washington.

Although Jefferson's five-year stay in Paris made him a Francophile, it did not make him a master of the language. He never became completely fluent in French, at least not to the extent that his secretary William Short or his daughter Martha did. On arriving in Paris with Jefferson, Short moved to a small town and boarded with a French family, there learning to speak conversational French quickly and fluently. (He also had a love affair with one of the young women in the family.) Jefferson's advice to his future son-in-law, Thomas Mann Randolph, who was in Europe for an education, was to learn French the way Short did: "Fix yourself in some family where there are women and children. . . . You will learn to speak better from women and children in three months, than from men in a year." His daughter Martha, when placed in the Abbaye de Panthemont where French was the spoken language, picked it up quickly and in later life taught French to her children.

James Hemings, like Jefferson, also had difficulties learning French. Jefferson brought Hemings to France with him for one purpose, to apprentice him to a chef to learn French cooking. (He had obviously developed a taste for French food even before going to Paris.) Apprenticing his young mulatto slave to learn how to prepare French cuisine was in keeping with his philosophy of training his slaves to do the skilled plantation work that would otherwise be performed by free white workers. A year and a half after he arrived in Paris, Jefferson wrote jokingly about Hemings's difficulty with the language, "he has forgot how to speak English, and has not learnt to speak French." Jefferson attempted to help Hemings by getting him a tutor; this, however, ended in a seriocomic scene when the tutor tried to collect his back pay. In a letter of complaint to Jefferson, the French tutor, Perrault, related how he tried to induce Hemings to pay a debt for teaching him French grammar. Instead of his pay, he received only the harshest abuse (*"Sotisses Les plus durs"*). When he went to Jefferson's maître d'hôtel Petit for his pay, Jimmy (*"Gimme"*) Hemings was there in a truculent mood. Hemings beat and kicked the teacher (*"m'accablé De coup de pied Et De coup de poing"*) and tore his coat. Now, he wrote, he was bedridden and, with no coat to protect him from the January weather, he was unable to go outdoors. How can he make a living? There is no record that Jefferson paid the debt, but in ticklish cases such as this, he usually took the easiest way out and paid.

Hemings was a better student of cooking than of language. After getting over a serious illness contracted on his arrival in Paris, he was apprenticed to several cooks and a *pâtissier*. Eventually he took over as *chef de cuisine* at the Hôtel de Langeac and was put on the payroll, as was his sister Sally. Jefferson had something of a problem keeping two slaves in France with him, however. According to French law, slavery was illegal, and they could petition for their freedom. During his tenure in France as U.S. minister, he received a query from an American couple about the legality of bringing a slave servant into the country. He replied that he had "made enquiries on the subject of the negro boy, and find that the laws of France give him freedom if he claims it, and that it will be difficult, if not impossible, to interrupt the course of the law. Nevertheless I have known an instance where a person bringing in a slave, and saying nothing about it, has not been disturbed in his possession." This person was, of course, Jefferson himself, who brought James Hemings with him. Jefferson advised the Americans to take the same course; the slave was young and "it is not probable he will think of claiming freedom."

It is unlikely that James Hemings remained ignorant of his status under French law; he was nineteen when Jefferson brought him to Paris and twenty-four when he and his sister Sally returned to America with Jefferson and his two daughters. Jefferson no doubt used all of his arts of persuasion to convince Hemings that a life of bondage as Thomas Jefferson's cook was preferable to freedom in Paris. He would never be permitted to return to America, or to see his family again, for example. Jefferson's trump card would have been a promise of future freedom. It was a pledge he drew up into a formal document in 1793: if Hemings returned to Monticello from Philadelphia, where he was serving as cook during Jefferson's tenure as secretary of state, and if he taught another slave his culinary skills, he would be emancipated. Hemings taught his brother Peter how to cook, and Jefferson kept his promise and freed James Hemings in 1796.

Hemings's life as a free man was to end tragically. At his emancipation, Jefferson gave him $30 to pay for his transportation to Philadelphia, where he had friends. From there he quite likely went briefly to Paris. On June 8, 1797, Jefferson wrote to his daughter Martha from Philadelphia, "James is returned to this place, and is not given up to drink as I had been informed. He tells me his next trip will be to Spain. I am afraid his journeys will end in the moon. I have endeavored to persuade him to stay where he is and lay up money." As it turned out, Jefferson was wrong about the drinking. Four years later, Hemings returned briefly, reluctantly, to Monticello as a cook at $20 a month. He was, Thomas Mann Randolph reported, apprehensive about having to be "among strange servants." For one who had lived for five years in Paris and was now a free man, the kitchen at Monticello must have seemed like a return to bondage. After only a month and a half, Jefferson paid him $30 wages and he left Monticello; whether he quit or was fired is not known. Several weeks later, he committed suicide at the age of thirty-six. At Jefferson's request, a friend in Baltimore investigated Hemings's death: "The report respecting James Hemings having committed an act of suicide is true. I made every inquiry at the time this melancholy circumstance took place. The result of which was, that he had been delirious for some days previous to his committing the act, and it was the general opinion that drinking too freely was the cause." There is little historical evidence on which to attempt to fix an underlying motivation for James Hemings's suicide. The bare facts of the five years of his life after he was emancipated, however, point to two powerful causes—rootlessness and alcoholism. After leaving the security of Jefferson's benevolent paternalism, he was appar-

Exterieur de la Halle au Bled

The Halle aux Bleds in Paris (top), with its lightweight, wooden dome. Jefferson used the same "sticks and chips" construction method for the dome of Monticello.

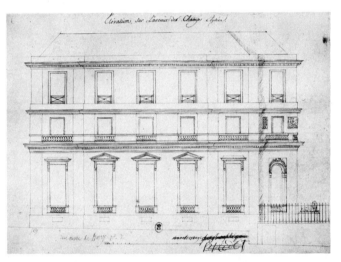

Élévation sur l'avenue des Champs Élysées

Elevation (above) and floor plan (right) of the Hôtel de Langeac, Jefferson's Paris residence.

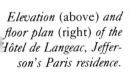

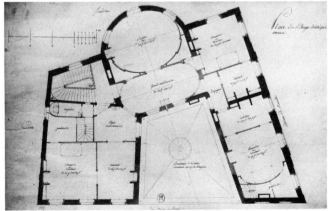

A plaster model of the Virginia State capitol, based on the Maison Carrée, *which Jefferson sent to Richmond from Paris* (top). *The building today, even with its added wings, is still Jefferson and Clérisseau's design* (bottom).

Right: *Two of the recipes Jefferson brought back from France. The ice cream recipe is believed to be the first written example of this quintessential American dessert*

Ice cream.
2 bottles of good cream.
5. yolks of eggs.
½ lb sugar
mix the yolks & sugar
put the cream on a fire in a casse-
-role, first putting in a stick of vanilla
then near boiling take it off &
pour it gently in to the mixture
of eggs & sugar.
stir it well.
put it on the fire again stirring
it thoroughly with a spoon to
prevent it's sticking to the casse-
-role.
then near boiling take it off and
strain it thro a tamis.
put it in the Sabotiere.
then set it in ice an hour before
it is to be served. put into the
ice a handful of salt.
put ice all round the Sabotiere
i.e. a layer of ice a layer of salt
for three layers.
put salt on the cover lid of the
Sabotiere & cover the hole with
ice.
leave it still half a quarter of an
hour.
then turn the Sabotiere in the
ice 10 minutes.
open it to loosen with a spatula
the ice from the inner sides of
the Sabotiere.
shut it & replace it in the ice
open it from time to time to de-
-tach the ice from the sides.
when well taken (prise) stir it
well with the spatula
put it in moulds, justling it
well down on the knee.
then put the mould into the
same bucket of ice.
leave it there to the moment
of serving it.
to withdraw it, immerse the
mould in warm water,
turning it well till it
will come out & turn it
into a plate.

To make biscuit de Savoye.
12 eggs.
12 table spoonfuls of sugar}
separate the yolk & white perfectly
grate the peel of one orange.
mix the whole, & beat them very well.
6. spoonfuls of flour put thro a searce.
beat well the whites separately.
mix the whole gently.
grease the mould with butter
powder it with sugar.
put in the mixture & put it in
the oven, of the same heat as usual
taking the edge of the macaroon,
take care not to shut the oven till
the biscuit begins to swell up.
then close the oven.
a half an hour suffices to bake
more or less according to size.
       Blanc Manger.
4. oz. sweet almonds, with 5. or 6 bitter
almonds. pour boiling water on them
to take off the skin.
put them in a mortar & beat them
with a little cream.
take them out of the mortar & liquify
them with cream little by little, (near a
pint) stirring them.
4. oz. sugar not to be put in.
have ready some
say 1. oz. in boiling water & pour it
into the preceding mixture,
stir them well together
strain it thro' a napkin
put it into a mould, & it is done.
       Wine jellies.
take 4. calves feet & wash them well
without taking off the hoofs. (or in-
-stead of that 1. oz. isinglass, or 1. oz.
of deers horns)
these feet must be well boiled the
day before they are wanted.
let them cool in order to take off the grease
after taking off the grease put the jelly
in a casserolle. put there 2 oz. sugar
cloves, nutmeg, boil all together
take 6. whites of eggs, the juice of 6 le-
-mons, a pint of milk, a pint of madeira
stir all together.
pour it into the jelly & boil it.
strain the whole thro' flannel
taste it to see if sweet enough, if
not, add powdered sugar.
strain it 2 or 3 times thro' flan-
-nel till clear.
put it in glasses or moulds.

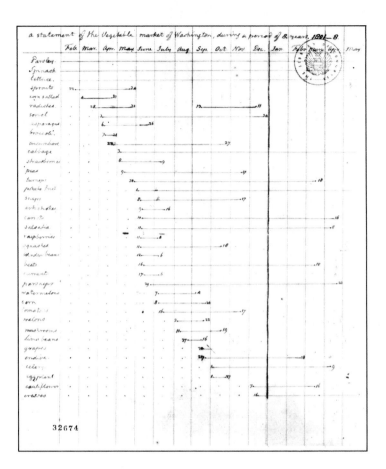

Above: *Jefferson's eight-year record of the appearance of thirty-six fruits and vegetables at the Washington vegetable market.*

Jefferson's memorandum and sketch of an Italian extrusion device for making macaroni.

A section of the record Jefferson kept of the number of guests he had to dinner at the President's House in Washington. In one fifteen-and-a-half-week period, he entertained 564 people.

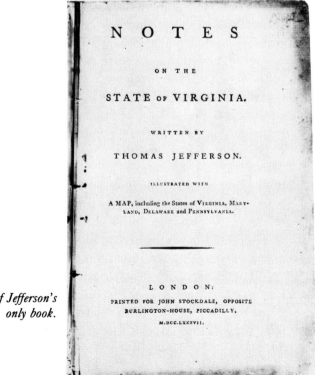

Title page of Jefferson's only book.

ently unable to find a niche in either the white or the black worlds. His return to Monticello indicates that he had failed to find productive and creative work, and that his self-esteem had suffered badly. Excessive drinking was not uncommon among slaves; alcohol, whenever it could be obtained, was the universal opiate of enslaved peoples. In the case of Hemings, his legal freedom ironically became license for self-destruction. Jefferson's effort to discover the facts of Hemings's death suggests that he may have pondered his own role in the failure of a talented young man, trapped between the races, to survive as a free person. Whatever James Hemings's personal feelings of failure were, he left his mark on the plantation where he was raised; he acquired and brought to Monticello one of the most prized trophies of civilized European society, the art of French cooking.

French haute cuisine was already legendary in Paris by the mid-eighteenth century; given time, staff, and money enough, a talented French chef could produce miracles of culinary splendor. He could also make virtually anything palatable. There is the story of a French caterer who, lacking meat, took an old pair of water-buffalo gloves, shredded them, stewed them with onion, mustard, and vinegar, and served them to his unknowing diners with resounding success. By the second half of the eighteenth century, there was a reaction to the extravagances of haute cuisine, with its elegant stocks, rich sauces, exotic ingredients, and theatrical effects—a reaction not unlike the contemporary turn from classic French recipes to *la nouvelle cuisine* and *cuisine minceur*. Rousseau, in *Émile*, had argued for a simple diet of fresh vegetables, salads, eggs, and milk; meat made men cruel and barbarous, he proclaimed. The effect of Rousseau on many of the philosophes of Paris was to lead them to *cuisine à la bourgeoise*, a style of cooking that was simple, intimate, and refined. This was a kind of dining that would predictably attract Jefferson, for it combined moderation with delicacy. What he admired about the French "pleasures of the table" was that "with good taste they unite temperance." It also appealed to his vegetarian bias; he had always preferred the balance of his diet tipped in the direction of fresh fruit and vegetables.

The French cooking that Jefferson brought back to America with him was essentially *cuisine bourgeoise*. Indeed, he gave to his daughter Martha a copy of one of the most influential books on this style of food preparation, Menon's *La Cuisinière Bourgeoise*, a work written expressly for women. To assure that the cooking expertise that had been acquired by James Hemings in France would not be lost, Jefferson also compiled, in his own hand, a list of menus and recipes, some, no doubt, from a woman cook he employed at the Hôtel de Langeac. The menus were, like most of Jefferson's lists, encyclopedic; just about every kind of meat and vegetable was included, as well as numerous pastries and desserts. Jefferson wrote the menus in French, but occasionally included an English annotation, as with a veal-olive dish which was breaded and fried in butter: "paupiette de veau tranch panné, et frit au beur, slices of veal, broken bacon with meat rolled up." Some classic French sauces are there, such as sauce Robert, and piquante sauce. So, too, is the favorite, then as now, French fries: "pommes de terre frite" served "a toute sorte de sauce." Vegetables are usually prepared simply, with either a plain white sauce, a butter sauce, or a brown sauce with onions ("sauce roux aux oignons"). Some of the more exotic dishes from the French culinary canon are included, such as stewed pigeons, boned and stuffed rabbit, fresh pigs' feet breaded and broiled, and "boudin noir," or blood sausage, still a favorite in southern Louisiana. These are balanced by such standard French desserts as fruit tarts and petits fours (the recipe for these includes sixteen eggs to one-half pound of flour and a pound of sugar).

Macaroni was a highly fashionable food in late eighteenth-century Paris, and Jefferson not only enjoyed the dish but also commissioned William Short to purchase a machine for making it. The machine was later shipped to America. Jefferson also investigated the manufacture of macaroni during his trip to northern Italy and drew a sketch with detailed notes on the extrusion process. When Short was in Italy, he sampled the local product and concluded that the cooks of Paris made better pasta than he could get at Naples. Apparently, the macaroni machine that Short bought was either not durable or unsatisfactory, for in later years Jefferson imported macaroni and Parmesan cheese from Marseilles for his use at Monticello. While in France, he also copied a recipe for making macaroni ("Nouilly a maccaroni") without a machine. This recipe makes clear that what was eaten as macaroni was what Americans today would term spaghetti—the dough was rolled thin and cut into strips, and each strip was then rolled with the hands into a noodle shape.

Jefferson copied other recipes; the one for brandied peaches ("peches a l'eau de vie") was in French, those for meringues and macaroons were half French, half English. There were also recipes for sponge cake ("biscuit de Savoye"), blancmange, wine jellies, and ice cream. Indeed, the first written recipe for this archetypical American dessert is in the hand of Thomas Jefferson. It was made in much the same way homemade ice cream is made today, with a custard mixture packed in ice and salt. The main difference was that without a mechanical ice cream maker, the frozen cream had to be scraped from the sides of the container manually with a spatula. When it was firm, the ice cream was placed in a mold, further frozen in ice-salt, and demolded when served. Collecting recipes, such as those he copied in France, was a habit Jefferson kept during his entire life. When a new, enjoyable dish was presented to him, he took detailed notes from his hostess about how it was prepared.

Jefferson also purchased in Paris the necessary accompaniments to French cuisine: silver service, pewterware, dishes for hors d'oeuvres, porcelain cups, saucers, plates, soup tureens and bowls, serving platters and casseroles, crystal goblets, "wine tumblers," decanters, a tea urn, and a coffee pot. For the kitchen, there were various kinds of kettles, saucepans ("28 round saucepans—19 copper saucepan covers"), frying pans, food warmers, chocolate molds, ice molds, pie pans, spoons, ladles, cleavers, knives, and a pair of kitchen scales. On a trip to Holland, he acquired a taste for waffles and purchased four waffle irons to make them. Most of these articles were eventually brought back to Monticello, where they augmented an already ample supply of dining and kitchen implements. Indeed, Jefferson's kitchen could have matched that of a French caterer in its supply of specialized cooking and baking ware. James Hemings, before his freedom was granted in 1796, wrote out, in a neat, legible hand, with remarkably accurate spelling, an inventory of the Monticello kitchen utensils. It included many of the items that were shipped back from France.

The list reveals a great deal about how cooking was done at Monticello. It is easy to forget, when admiring the menus and recipes Jefferson accumulated, that these dishes were cooked either in an open fireplace or on a small iron stove, and baked in a primitive masonry oven. The collection of "kitchen furniture," as Jefferson termed Hemings's inventory of utensils, is extensive, but it conceals the fact that pots were hung over hot coals on hooks, cranes, and trammels, that pans, pots, chafing dishes, and skillets were usually equipped with three short legs so they could sit over a bed of hot coals, and that meat and fowl were roasted on a spit placed in front of the fire and turned by a clockwork mechanism. (Before the invention of mechanical spit-turners, meat was often turned by a small "turnspit dog." The dog was trained to walk on a treadwheel which turned the spit.) Gridirons with legs of varying heights were used to adjust the heat of the coals placed beneath them.

Jefferson brought a number of cast-iron stoves back from France. He shipped a total of five stoves (one was a "sheet-iron camp stove"); two of them were equipped with "stone bases" for insulation. Several of these may have been small cooking stoves or "stewholes," bottom-less cast-iron boxes with a grill on top. When filled with charcoal they could be used as a controlled heat source for sautéeing or preparing delicate sauces. After his presidency, Jefferson had a Georgetown ironmonger make a set of stewholes in three sizes for the Monticello kitchen.

Tongs, shovels, and pokers were necessary for preparing the fire for cooking and were usually long-handled, as were waffle irons, spoons, skimmers, and frying pans—the heat from an open fireplace demanded a certain distance, especially in the summer. Detachable wooden extension handles were common. Cooking was not for the frail, weak, or aged. Many of the large iron or copper kettles listed on James Hemings's inventory weighed up to thirty pounds empty, and twice that full. Much of the cooking was done bending over, stooping, or squatting, and hours spent before the heat of the fireplace or iron stove were debilitating.

Hemings did all of his cooking at Monticello in the old kitchen beneath the south pavilion, the same kitchen that Martha Jefferson had cooked in. The kitchen that visitors to the mansion view today, located at the turn of the south dependency wing, was not constructed until Jefferson built the dependencies during his presidency. The new kitchen has two ovens built into the masonry wall on either side of the fireplace; the old kitchen probably had only one originally, but Jefferson had another oven built after his return from France. The oven was nothing more than a brick recess in the thick masonry wall with a cast-iron door and a flue running to the chimney of the fireplace. It was heated by placing coals in it until the bricks were hot; the coals were then removed and the oven was ready for breads or pastries. Regulating the heat for delicate pastries was something of an art. In his recipe for macaroons, Jefferson indicated how to test for what we would today term a "slow" oven of about 300 degrees. The oven should be "not too hot, but hotter than after taking out the bread," he wrote. "You prove the proper heat of the oven by holding in it a bit of white paper. If it burns, it will burn your macarons, if it just browns the paper it is exact."

The style of cooking and the menus and recipes Jefferson brought back from France became part of the kitchen heritage at Monticello for the remainder of his life. Generations of granddaughters and great-granddaughters copied these recipes into cookbooks and passed them on to their children. Jefferson's daughter Martha recorded two favorite recipes in the record of court cases that Martha Jefferson had borrowed from her husband to use as her household Account Book. Martha Randolph used the blank pages remaining in the book for her own accounts of eggs, poultry, and vegetables purchased from the household slaves. Among the accounts was a recipe for her father's favorite vegetable, peas, and another for boiled fish. The peas were sautéed briefly in butter, then simmered in stock with onion, cloves, and a little sugar. The onions and cloves were removed, and the stock was thickened with flour and egg yolks into a sauce. The boiled fish was served with a sauce of butter, cream, and nutmeg. The French influence on these two dishes is apparent, with their rich sauces and delicate flavorings.

Another of Martha Randolph's recipes, this one for bread pudding, has also been saved. The pudding was simple enough—two loaves of crumbled bread, two quarts of milk, and eleven eggs, all well-beaten together. This mixture was boiled for four to five hours in a cloth bag. There was no sugar in the pudding itself; the sweetness came from a sauce of sugar, flour, butter, and lemon juice, labeled "all important" by Martha. This dessert was obviously a favorite at Monticello, for it was recorded as "the famous sunday pudding."

The taste for French cooking acquired in Paris was brought to Washington during Jefferson's presidency. He entertained frequently, dining with close friends or members of Congress or the diplomatic corps nearly every evening. Indeed, dining was an important part of the political process for Jefferson; it allowed him to meet with both political friends and enemies in an informal, pleasurable atmosphere. He spoke of dinner parties as "campaigns," and gave them two or three times a week when Congress was in session. Both Republicans and Federalists were entertained, but rarely together, for Jefferson's strategy was to use dining as a way of creating political accord rather than dissent. His dinner parties were so well oganized that he compiled a master chart listing every dinner given, with the names and sometimes the home states of those attending. He invited from twelve to fifteen guests; usually members of his cabinet were included with congressmen and senators. Each member of Congress could be expected to dine at the President's House two to three times a year. Dinners were normally all male, but periodically he invited visiting wives and women family members, more frequently during the summer months when Congress was not in session. To assure that no one was inadvertently forgotten, his lists were indexed by name, and after each name he wrote the dates each guest had dined. He compiled, in his entertainment lists, a summary of the dinners from November 5, 1804, to February 22, 1805, a total of 110 days. He gave forty dinners, with 564 guests.

Dining on such a scale could be wearisome for the host. At the end of his first term, he wrote to his daughter Martha that he dreaded the forthcoming social season "on account of the fatigues of the table in such a round of company, which I consider as the most serious trials I undergo." These dinners were not the casual "family soupes" of the Hôtel de Langeac in Paris, but elegant affairs with the best of French cuisine and wine. One of his guests, Louisa Catherine Adams, described a "handsome" dinner she attended at the President's mansion: "French servants in livery, a French butler, a French cuisine, and a buffet full of choice wines." The French cook during Jefferson's presidency was Honoré Julien, who was hired in Philadelphia. The maître d'hôtel was Etienne Lemaire, who was Jefferson's equivalent in Washington of his Hôtel de Langeac housekeeper, Petit. It was not uncommon for Jefferson to accompany Lemaire to the produce market at Georgetown to help select groceries and to check for the earliest appearance of various fruits and vegetables. He would later record these on his chart listing the first and last dates of the appearance of thirty-seven different fruits and vegetables.

As might be expected from the scale of entertaining, his food and wine bills were astronomical. During one year of his presidency, the amount spent for provisions and groceries came to more than $6,500, excluding wines. How much money this would amount to today can be judged from the fact that his French chef Julien, who prepared these foods, received $300 a year.

The cost of the wines served at Jefferson's presidential dinners that first year was $2,797. Jefferson considered fine wines "a necessity of life," however, and money spent for them was paid cheerfully. He was one of the most knowledgeable wine connoisseurs of his age; his enthusiasm for wine and viticulture was boundless. During his five-year stay in France, he not only became familiar with that nation's premier Burgundies, Bordeaux, and champagnes by drinking them at the best tables of Paris, he journeyed to the regions of France where they were produced to learn how they were made, how the vines were grown, and which winemakers produced the finest vintages. In 1788, he also toured the Rhine Valley and did the same kind of meticulous research on the fine wines of Germany. His philosophy on the selection of wines for his own table was the aristocrat's maxim—get the best no matter what it costs. This was his advice for choosing all luxury items: horseflesh, timepieces, scientific instruments, and wine. "Be kind enough to supply the best available in this class of wine," he wrote to his wine agent, M. Parent. "I always trust you for quality, and let the price [be] whatever it should be, while still considering quality rather than price." Whenever possible, he ordered wine directly from the producer to prevent it being diluted by wine merchants, a common practice in France. In 1787, he purchased from the Marquis de Lur Saluces 250 bottles of the Grand Premier Cru of Sauternes, Chateau d'Yquem. He drank the Premiers Crus of Bordeaux—Chateaux Margaux, Lafite, Latour, and Haut-Brion—wines that were as renowned by the connoisseur then as now.

When he returned to America from France, he was acknowledged to be a wine expert who knew which wines to buy, where, and at what price. He served as wine adviser to three presidents, Washington,

Madison, and Monroe, and during his own presidency, he purchased and served wine on an extravagant scale. He helped make champagne fashionable in Washington by serving it at most of his dinners. In France it was drunk *non mousseaux*, nonsparkling, but in Washington the preference was for bubbles, and slightly sweet. Jefferson went through rivers of it; in 1802 he wrote in his Memorandum Book "a hamper of Champagne of 50. bottles opened Dec. 7. is finished Dec. 19 in which time 125. gentlemen have dined, which is 2. bottles to 5. persons." In 1804, he noted that there were forty bottles of champagne left from an order of 247 bottles: "The consumption then has been 207. bottles, which on 651. persons dined is a bottle to $3\frac{1}{7}$ persons. Hence the annual stock necessary may be calculated at 415. bottles a year or say 500. . . . ."

Unlike most of his countrymen who preferred sweet, fortified wines like Madeira, sherry, or port, Jefferson liked unfortified wines with a taste he described as "silky." Silkiness in wines, he explained to a merchant, is "a compound in their taste of the dry dashed with a little sweetishness, barely sensible to the palate." The best wine he ever tasted, he affirmed, was a "wine of Bellet," produced near Nice, which was "silky and a little astringent."

Jefferson was temperate in his use of wine, as he was in all of his habits, but this does not mean that he did not get slightly intoxicated from it. He stated late in life that he drank three glasses of wine daily, and four or five with friends. This is a half bottle or more of wine, enough to produce a slight intoxication, especially if it follows alcoholic cider or beer, commonly served during meals. For a man as reserved as Jefferson was, the mild euphoria offered by wine was an emotional doorlatch that released his innate charm and conviviality. Wine encouraged lively conversation, one of his greatest pleasures; this is probably why he served it after dinner, to encourage and prolong table talk. "No wine drank till the cloth is removed," Anna Maria Thornton reported.

His opposition to hard liquor for his workmen and slaves was coupled with an advocacy of wine for the working classes. He favored reducing duties on the importation of wine because high duties raised the price and condemned Americans to "the poison of whiskey, which is desolating their houses." "No nation is drunken," he argued, "where wine is cheap; and none sober, where the dearness of wine substitutes ardent spirits as the common beverage. It is in truth the only antidote to the bane of whiskey." Who would not prefer wine to whiskey, he asked rhetorically, if wine were cheap enough?

His observation of viticulture in Europe led him to oppose raising grapes to produce wine in America, however. "The culture of the vine is not desirable in lands capable of producing anything else," he wrote. He called it a "species of gambling" because if the crop is too heavy, prices are poor, and if it is light, not enough wine is produced to make a profit. "The middling crop alone is the saving point, and that the seasons seldom hit." He observed too that laborers in the vineyards of France made less than ten sous a day, only pennies by American standards. He favored raising wine grapes for personal consumption, however, particularly during the embargo, when wine imports were halted. He had experimented with raising grapes from his earliest years at Monticello; before the Revolution, he encouraged the Italian, Philip Mazzei, a man not unlike William Thornton in his range of interests, to raise grapes on a plantation near Monticello. Mazzei imported Italian vignerons and established a vineyard, only to have it fall into ruin during the Revolutionary War. (It was Mazzei's house, Colle, that General de Riedesel and his family lived in.)

Jefferson imported vines from Europe in an attempt to raise vinifera grapes, those that produce the great wines of Europe, but this, and all such attempts, were doomed to failure. It was not known then that the hot, humid climate of the Southeast United States harbored the deadly phylloxera root louse, which, in the mid-nineteenth century, was accidentally carried to Europe and wiped out the wine industry of France. (Grafting vinifera grapes onto native American rootstock allowed it to recover.) It was not until modern times that disease-resistant rootstocks, anti-fungal sprays, and insecticides have made vinifera wine growing possible at Monticello; indeed, Virginia now nurtures an infant wine industry.

Jefferson ultimately recognized that if wines were to be made in the Southeast they would have to be produced from native grapes, muscadines and scuppernongs, which are immune to the diseases that decimated European varieties grown in America. "I think it will be well to push the culture of . . . [American grapes] without losing time & effort in search of foreign vines, which it will take centuries to adapt to our soil & climate," he wrote. Despite a lifetime of trying, Jefferson never succeeded in making a bottle of fine wine at Monticello. At his death, even though he was virtually bankrupt, his cellar contained a modest variety of European wines and scuppernong from North Carolina.

During his stay in France, Jefferson became enamored of French culture, art, architecture, science, food, wine—as well as of the Italian Maria Cosway—but he did not lose his love for his native land; if anything, it was increased. It was in France that he published the only book he ever wrote, *Notes on the State of Virginia*, a love song to his home state in the form of a scientific treatise. The work was written in response to a questionnaire sent in 1780 by François Marbois, secretary of the French legation at Philadelphia, seeking geographical, historical, demographical, social, political, and commercial facts about each of the American states. Jefferson, then governor of Virginia, was given the list of twenty-two queries to respond to. In 1781, he retired to his plantation at Poplar Forest to recover from a fall from his horse, carrying with him from Monticello books and notes he had been gathering over the years about the flora, fauna, geography, and history of Virginia. He wrote in a few weeks a draft of what was to become a classic of American literature. After sending a copy of the manuscript to Marbois, he continued working on it sporadically for the next few years, showing it to friends and adding new data to it. When he went to France, he took the manuscript with him, by now three times the length of the original, and had a private edition of two hundred copies printed without his name, as was common among gentlemen authors of his age. (Jefferson never swerved from the rules of the class he identified with: Gentlemen never wrote for money or vanity; books were to be written from motives of the purest social interest, for their scientific or literary value.) The copies of *Notes* were distributed to friends in France and America. A poor French translation was subsequently printed, and after Jefferson learned that a pirated English edition was planned, he published the book in London in 1787 under his own name, complete with a map based on the one drawn by Joshua Fry and his father, Peter Jefferson.

The book was widely respected among intellectuals on both sides of the Atlantic, and it established Jefferson's reputation as a philosopher and man of letters. The literary value of the work rests not on its collection of facts about Virginia and its inhabitants, even though these demonstrate Jefferson's close and accurate scholarship. Rather it is his moral, social, and political judgments, and the directness, clarity, and felicity of their expression that have given the book a life beyond his own. *Notes on the State of Virginia* is full of passages that illustrate these qualities, but perhaps none quite so lyrically as the following description of the violence of the elements, followed by a homely observation on human nature.

> The passage of the Patowmac through the Blue ridge is perhaps one of the most stupendous scenes in nature. You stand on a very high point of land. On your right comes up the Shenandoah, having ranged along the foot of the mountain an hundred miles to seek a vent. On your left approaches the Patowmac, in quest of a passage also. In the moment of their junction they rush together against the mountain, rend it asunder, and pass off into the sea. . . . This scene is worth a voyage across the Atlantic. Yet, here, as in the neighborhood of the natural bridge, are people who have passed their lives within half a dozen miles, and have never been to survey these monuments of a war between rivers and mountains, which must have shaken the earth itself to its center.

This is yet another reminder of how forcefully the sublimities of nature impressed themselves on Jefferson's sensibilities, and how much the landscape of his native land defined what he was. France may have won his head—its philosophes reinforcing his beliefs in scientific progress and liberal politics—but his heart was rooted in Virginia, and in his long-abandoned Monticello. In 1787, he had written to George Gilmer: "All my wishes end, where I hope my days will end, at Monticello. Too many scenes of happiness mingle themselves with all the recollections of my native woods and fields, to suffer them to be supplanted in my affection by any other. I consider myself here as a traveler only, and not a resident." It was to Monticello, after five years in France, that he returned in 1789, determined to build once again.

8

"A Shelter to Unite Under: O Welcome Hour Whenever!"

WORMLEY WAS only an eight-year-old plantation urchin on that memorable day, two days before Christmas, when Thomas Jefferson and his daughters returned home from France to Monticello. More than seventy years later, however, he recalled the event well. The Jefferson ménage had spent a leisurely month traveling westward after landing at Norfolk, visiting family members and friends along the way. When word was sent to the overseer to get the house ready for their arrival, news traveled instantly to every slave cabin on the plantation. The Christmas holiday, always anticipated as one of the truly happy and festive times in a life otherwise dominated by manual labor, would be augmented by the return of the Master of Monticello. It would be holiday heaped upon holiday, a rare occasion.

From the slave's point of view, the return of Jefferson to Monticello was much to be desired, for life was always better when he was in residence. Without the presence of a humane owner, a slave's fate was completely in the hands of an overseer whose self-interest, ignorance, or cruelty could make life hell. Jefferson was accessible to his slaves, and his paternalism acted as a buffer between slave and overseer. Moreover, during his five-year stay in France, slaves had been hired out to other plantations; they would now come home to families and friends. Jefferson's return, therefore, was a genuine cause for celebration, and the Monticello slaves were caught up in the fever of the occasion. In his eighties, Wormley remembered preparations for the homecoming. All of the slaves from the surrounding farms had been granted the day off, and men, women, and children were dressed up in their Sunday best for the trip to the foot of the mountain to line the road where the carriage would appear. As they waited and the hours dragged on, the throng kept moving farther down the road, until they were near Shadwell, some two miles from the house. At last, the carriage, pulled by four horses, with a postilion riding a forward mount, came into view and a shout went up from the slaves. As the carriage slowed down, they surrounded it and ran alongside as it began to climb the steep ascent up the mountain. Finally, Wormley recalled, the slaves detached the horses from the carriage and it was dragged, pulled, and pushed the last half mile to the lawn of the house.

Martha Jefferson, watching the scene excitedly from the carriage, also remembered it vividly: "The shouting, etc., had been sufficiently obstreperous before, but the moment [we] arrived at the top, it reached the climax. When the door of the carriage was opened, they received him in their arms and bore him to the house, crowding round and kissing his hands and feet—some blubbering and crying—others laughing." Being carried on the arms of his slaves was certainly a first for Jefferson—indeed, it is doubtful whether many other slaveowners ever matched that experience—and he had to be flattered by it. The episode is a commentary on how slavery shaped the behavior of a people; pleasure at the return of a slaveowner was expressed in ritual acts of subservience: taking the horse's place in pulling the master's carriage, and carrying him bodily in one's arms. Martha and Maria, dressed in their Parisian frocks, were treated with more deference, as Wormley remembered. The crowd of blacks broke when the girls stepped from the carriage, and a path was formed to greet them as they walked to the once stately but now badly decayed portico of Monticello.

During Jefferson's five-year absence, he had placed his affairs in the hands of a friend and neighbor, Nicholas Lewis. For an annual fee of £50, Lewis acted as general manager of the plantation, collecting income from the various farms and paying bills, but little else. As a result, income from the estate had declined, and the economic base needed to support a style of living Jefferson found increasingly costly to maintain had seriously eroded. In France, his salary had not matched his expenses; at home, his farms did not generate enough income even to begin to pay off the debt he had inherited with his wife's lands and slaves. That debt, with its ever mounting interest, ate into his capital like a silent weevil, leading to the day when he would finally be brought to financial ruin.

The only ruin now apparent, however, was his house. For five years it had been completely neglected, and as Jefferson walked around its exterior and observed the flaking paint, the warped wood, the still-unfinished porticoes, and the dependencies that existed only on paper, his head was full of ideas for improvement, plans he had conceived during homesick days and nights in France. These plans were to be strung out interminably, however, by the demands of public service. He was soon called on by President George Washington to serve as secretary of state, and this office was to take him from Monticello for another four years. Before leaving, however, he presided over the wedding of his eldest daughter, Martha, to the son of his boyhood friend, Thomas Mann Randolph of Tuckahoe.

In France, Jefferson had corresponded with Randolph, Jr., while the young man was studying at Edinburgh, offering him avuncular advice on his education, on his choice of career, and on books to read. Exactly how Randolph and Martha, who were second cousins, met and fell in love is unclear because it happened so rapidly. Although they knew each other as children, they apparently met for the first time as adults while the Jeffersons were traveling from Norfolk to Monticello in December. They saw each other soon afterward when Randolph traveled to Monticello. They were married on February 23, 1790, exactly two months after Martha arrived home with her sister and father. Some of her acquaintances and family members may have raised their eyebrows at news of so hasty a marriage, but if they were looking for scandal they were disappointed, for the Randolphs' first child did not come until a year after the wedding. The rushed marriage came about because Jefferson, having accepted the appointment as secretary of state, was forced to leave for the nation's capital, New

York, by March 1, and he had no intention of missing his daughter's wedding.

Randolph must have thought himself fortunate to have won Martha Jefferson so easily. Although she was no beauty (one observer called her "rather homely, a delicate likeness of her father"), at seventeen she was as polished, poised, and accomplished as any young Virginia woman her age. A miniature of her done just before she left Paris shows a stylishly coiffed, full-busted young woman. She had spent the last five years of her life in Paris, spoke French fluently, and in her final year in France had circulated among the salons of Jefferson's intellectual friends and associates. She was unusually well-educated; she had attended the most fashionable girls' school in Paris, read the classics, and was seriously interested in the life of the mind.

Randolph, who was twenty-one at his marriage, was somewhat in awe of his new father-in-law, one of Virginia's most prominent citizens, now about to take his place on the national stage. Jefferson had won his affection by treating him as an adult and as an intellectual peer, and by drawing him into his closest confidence. Still, Randolph could not help feeling that he was competing with his new father-in-law, for his wife worshipped her father, and made no secret of it. Jefferson had been wooing his two daughters ever since he lost his wife, and his continuing rise in political power and prestige, combined with his unrestrained expressions of love and affection, bound them to him, Martha more than the younger Maria.

Physically, Randolph was tall, lean, and swarthy, an excellent athlete and horseman. Family tradition had it that the Randolphs of Tuckahoe were descendants of Pocahontas. In Jefferson's papers, there is a "Genealogy of Pocahontas" compiled by Randolph, starting with Pocahontas and John Rolfe, and descending to the Randolphs, who were supposedly one-thirty-second Indian. The line of descendants includes "John Bolling married to Miss Jefferson." This was Jefferson's older sister, Mary. Randolph was certainly not the "blockhead" Jefferson feared his daughter would marry, but he did not wear his learning as casually as his illustrious father-in-law; his letters to Jefferson were often stilted, pedantic, and stuffy. His most serious fault was considered to be his temper, a defect that would not have been overlooked by Jefferson, who seldom raised his voice and rarely showed anger. One of Jefferson's best-laid plans was threatened when Randolph's rage was directed at his father during negotiations for the purchase of a 1,500-acre farm at Edgehill, near Monticello. Jefferson and Martha very much wanted young Randolph to complete the purchase of the property, but a violent argument, during which young Randolph "took fire" and showed his "tempestuous temper," almost alienated his father irrevocably. Wounded feelings were eventually salved, however, and Jefferson was delighted to see the young couple eventually move to within three miles of Monticello. Jefferson's dowry to his daughter was a thousand acres of land from his Bedford County plantation and twenty-seven slaves. Randolph, Sr., had bestowed on young Randolph 950 acres in the lowlands of Henrico County below Richmond, and forty slaves. These lands, combined with the Edgehill farm, would appear to assure the couple a prosperous living, but Randolph's career as a farmer, like that of many Virginians, including his father-in-law, was reduced to a constant struggle against debt and nagging creditors.

Jefferson attempted to diversify his plantation from its sole dependence on the uncertainties of growing wheat and tobacco to a steady income from subsidiary enterprises. Nail making was one of the most successful; manufacturing potash never got started. Milling wheat was a high-capital business that showed promise of profit, but it consumed large amounts of his income, time, and energy, and never recovered the costs. Because his Shadwell estate was on the Rivanna River, Jefferson owned an ideal site for a mill. His father, Peter Jefferson, had constructed a toll mill in 1757, and Jefferson inherited it, but it was washed away by a spring flood in 1771. Even before leaving for Paris, Jefferson had started digging a canal for this mill; on his return from France, he was determined to finish both canal and mill. Like all of his business enterprises, however, it suffered from absentee management; he was never at home long enough to give the project the close personal attention it needed. As a result, building the dam, canal, and mill house dragged on for more than a decade before it ever ground a bushel of wheat. During Jefferson's presidency, he started construction on a larger "manufacturing mill," which included a grain elevator. This began operating in 1807 and was leased to a number of tenants, but because of poor management, controversies with the

A nineteenth-century print of Jefferson's Shadwell mill.

lessees, and the constant need for repairs, it never recovered the large investment Jefferson put into it.

The mill construction projects, which were designed to relieve Jefferson's financial difficulties, came into direct conflict with his housebuilding plans, for they both used slave labor and scarce capital. Much of the delay in remodeling Monticello resulted from not having materials and labor available when needed because work on the canal and mill were given first priority. Initially, Jefferson thought he could carry on his mill projects and his housebuilding simultaneously, but limited resources of capital and labor, and particularly his absences from Monticello, forced him to change his mind: "I had digested a plan of operation too complicated to be pursued by any one less interested in it than myself," he wrote to young Randolph in the spring of 1792. "There seems to be no way to save myself from great loss & disappointment but to change the order of the objects, and to take up first that one which is the most simple and important, I mean my canal." He then gave Randolph detailed instructions for utilizing the plantation slaves to dig the canal. Work on the house was to be postponed, but only until later that year. He asked Randolph to have the slave work crew gather timber, stone, and limestone for house construction when they were finished with the canal work.

But each postponement was followed by another as long as he was away and could not supervise the work himself. During the nearly four years that Jefferson served as secretary of state, from the beginning of 1790 to the end of 1793, he did little but make plans and collect building materials for the remodeling of Monticello. In 1792, a year before he resigned his cabinet position, he had written to the man who had been responsible for building much of the first house, Stephen Willis, to see if he was available for work again. In his letter he outlined his building timetable:

> Having long ago fixed on the ensuing spring for the time of my retiring to live at home, I did, when [at Monticello] last fall, endeavor to put things into a train for resuming my buildings. This winter is employed in getting framing, limestone, & bringing up stone for the foundation of the new part to be first erected. The demolition of the walls wherein the present staircase is run up, & of the Antichamber (about 60,000 bricks) will, with about 20,000 new bricks which I possess, suffice I hope for the first summer's construction, building to the water table with those. I shall begin about the first of April to dig my cellars, & then do the stonework, and as far as I can judge I shall be in readiness after that to do the brick-work.

This schedule, as it turned out, was wildly optimistic; he did not begin to do brickwork until four years later. In the meantime, however, there was building to be done to make Monticello a more comfortable and functional house to live in.

Jefferson's failure to construct any of the carefully planned dependencies for the original house was now a serious embarrassment. Randolph and his bride were staying at Monticello until they could establish their own household, and they soon became acutely aware of the shortcomings of the dependencies. In particular, there were no stables on the mountaintop, no laundry, and the food preparation facilities were poor. In the fall of 1790, Jefferson sent instructions to Nicholas Lewis, who was still acting as steward of the plantation, to add a series of outbuildings to those already located on Mulberry Row. He directed that the slave carpenters build a wash house, two smoke-houses for meat, "one of them for me, the other for Mr. Randolph and the passage between for their dairy," and a stable "on the same plan with the meat house." All of these buildings were to be con-structed "of logs, covered with clapboard." This was a clever form of building. The logs were the structural members and could be raised quickly and easily by semi-skilled slave carpenters. The clapboard siding not only added weatherproofing, it also placed a civilizing cos-metic coat on the raw logs of the wilderness. Had all the buildings on Mulberry Row been constructed this way, and then joined with a fence of palings as Jefferson indicated on his fire insurance policy of 1796, it would have produced a neat and attractive plantation street.

Neither the stables nor the slave cabins were apparently covered with clapboard, however. The reason was an increasing scarcity of lumber, particularly lumber that had been sawed into boards. Two years after the instructions for having them built were issued, the stables were not yet started. In a memo to his new overseer at Monticello, Jefferson gave new directions for building the stables: five log houses were to be constructed "of chestnut logs, hewed on two sides and split with the saw, & dove-tailed." This would produce two timbers from every log, each D-shaped, with three flat sides and a rounded one. If the hewed sides were placed log to log, the rounded side inside, and the sawed side outside, a tight wall would have resulted, with only half the material normally used in a log cabin. The flat exterior wall of the cabin could then be covered easily with clapboards. The dovetailed corner, still used in log-house construction, is one of the most secure ways of joining logs. It produces a square corner without log overhang, a necessity if clapboards are to be added. Three of these log houses were to be equipped with wooden racks and feeding troughs for stables; the other two, with wood and clay chimneys, were to be slave quarters. Jefferson's log cabins were to be a significant improvement over traditional slave housing. Each of these buildings had a loft made of "slabs," the curved edge cuts produced when the pit saw or saw-mill made a square timber of a log. These were often waste cuts, although they could be shaped with a maul into clapboards.

Slabs were usually readily available in quantity, but not so when Jefferson needed them. "The store of them which you saw at the sawmill was exhausted by a neighboring blacksmith who took it into his head to make charcoal of them," Randolph reported. Jefferson's slave carpenters did not complete the stables until the fall of 1793. The two slave cabins were not even started because, as Randolph wrote, "the men having been so much deceived in the quantity of timber required for the stables," they ran out of lumber.

But delay and a shortage of materials was the norm rather than the exception during Jefferson's long construction campaign. He had ordered poplar timbers cut and set aside to dry for window frames, and had put Jupiter to work at quarrying limestone. During Jefferson's absence in France, Jupiter had been hired out at £25 a year to a brickmason and he had become proficient in extracting limestone. Jefferson had directed him to quarry one thousand bushels of limestone to be used for brick and stone mortar. In January of 1793, Randolph reported that "Jupiter from what I can learn had not raised more than ¼ of the limestone you ordered. He is now at work with two assistants." The stone for the new basements of the house—150 perch— was also slow in being hauled to the mountaintop from the quarry below the fourth, or lower, roundabout, in what had formerly been the deer park. Jupiter had also been given this task.

Young Randolph found himself more and more involved in superintending the gathering and preparation of building materials. Besides bringing lumber, stone, and limestone to the top of the mountain, sand for mortar had to be hauled by oxcart from the Rivanna River. On rainy days the slave carpenters worked at splitting, planing, jointing, and rounding shingles. After reporting on the progress made in sawing timbers for floor and ceiling joists, Randolph uttered the owner-builder's classic lament: "Picking and hewing this timber so as to leave only the heart has consumed much more time than I had any idea of." He also found that slave labor was not always as skillful as necessary. One of the slave carpenters, Davy, was ordered to make three-foot-diameter wheels for the wheelbarrows, but the wheels he made, Randolph wrote, were worthless: "Davy can use the wheelwright's tools but has no rule in working: he cannot make a wheel with all the fellows [spokes] in the same plane."

In the meantime, Jefferson was trying unsuccessfully to hire a stonemason to work on his columns. He still hoped to place stone columns on both porticoes of his house. Through a master mason in Philadelphia he made arrangements for a mason and a housejoiner to come from Scotland, but he had the same lack of success in acquiring a stonemason for his remodeling as he did in hiring one for the first house—at the last moment, the Scotsmen changed their minds. The failure to get a Scottish housejoiner, however, was a blessing in disguise; he searched instead at Philadelphia and found one of the best workmen he ever hired, James Dinsmore.

Another worker he failed at hiring was a loss, not only to Jefferson, but also to history—a woman brickmaker, Nanny Brewer. In 1794, Jefferson wrote to Thomas Pleasants, the neighbor from whom he purchased dried fish for his slaves, to "engage Nanny Brewer to come to Monticello immed'ly after harvest to make 100,000 bricks & to fix her wages. I to send a horse for her." Nanny Brewer was the wife of John Brewer, one of the brickmakers who made bricks for the first house. While Brewer was making 90,000 usable bricks on the mountaintop, she accompanied him. She obviously learned the brickmaking trade from her husband, and learned it well, for Jefferson would not have considered hiring her unless she was competent. Apparently, Brewer either died or was unable to work, and his wife took over his trade. She was certainly one of the few professional woman brickmakers in Virginia, indeed, in the nation. For whatever reason, she was not available, and did not come to Monticello.

When Jefferson resigned as secretary of state and returned to Monticello in 1794 to assume the management of his plantations, he had a well-defined plan for enlarging and remodeling his house. His motivations for plunging once more into a prolonged, expensive construction project were even more complex than those that directed his first housebuilding efforts. To his initial psychological needs for maternal comfort and security were added those of the accomplished designer-builder. His stay in France and his travels through Europe had cast a vision in the architect's eye. Much of what he saw became a template to be overlaid upon his own country, his own lands, his own home. He returned to America alive with new architectural ideas, and his unfinished house was the creative anvil on which they would be forged.

He was no longer the novice apprentice who designed and built the first house, however; he now needed no books or workmen's advice to tell him how to build. He was a journeyman housebuilder who needed only a keyboard on which to practice his architectural studies. Like generations of housebuilders who would follow in his footsteps, he had learned how to build, so he would continue to practice his skills; architecture had become a creative compulsion that would last a lifetime. During the second term of his presidency, when Monticello was nearing completion, he threw himself into a new building project, a country house at his Bedford County estate, Poplar Forest, and when this was finished he took on his final and most ambitious architectural project, the University of Virginia. Between these building enterprises, he designed various houses for friends; indeed, from the time he took up his pen and drew his first floor plan for a one-room bachelor's house atop his "little mountain" until his death at eighty-three, he was either planning to build or actually involved in building something.

His plan for remodeling and enlarging Monticello was arrived at with the same kind of internal logic that infused the best of his political writing. He began with two facts and a pair of aesthetic principles, and from these he worked through a series of logical deductions and compromises that resolved facts and principles. The first fact was that he was not starting with a tabula rasa; he had a house already sitting on his preferred building site. Fact two: the house was too small for a man for whom hospitality was virtually a disease. The first aesthetic principle was that the most fashionable Palladian houses—the only kind he would consider building—were one-story, or gave the appearance of being one-story. The second was a corollary of the first: a dome provides an elegant cap for a stylish Palladian residence. These facts and principles led to several design choices:

First, remodeling involved not simply altering, but significantly enlarging the present house. In order to make the house larger, he had to build outward rather than upward. He already had two stories, one too many.

Second, there was only one way to build out, in the direction of either the east or west porticoes; adding rooms to the wings would produce what later generations would recognize as a series of Pullman cars rather than a house.

Third, adding a set of rooms to the center block and wings required a hallway between the old rooms and the new ones, to avoid having to walk through private rooms or bedrooms to get to the ends of the house.

Fourth, this hallway, which would run through the horizontal axis of the house, suggested that he oppose the old rooms with matching new ones, producing a symmetrical floor plan.

And fifth, a circular dome could have been built on the new addition to the house, but the old house already had a two-story octagonal bow on the west portico, just the right size for a dome. The law of parsimony prescribed that an octagonal dome be placed there, particularly since Jefferson was partial to the octagonal shape.

Although these sets of facts and principles narrowed the range of Jefferson's choices, they did not dictate on which side of the house the addition would be placed. There was a compelling reason to build it on the west side: by doing so, he could arrange to place the dome directly in the center of the house, the position of choice in Palladian architecture. His reasons for selecting the east side instead were practical and aesthetic. The placement of the two-story-high stairwells on the east front of the original house demanded that this entire wall be demolished no matter which side he built on. This became the logical side for the additions, since it would have to be rebuilt anyway. The dome, on the other hand, could be placed atop a wall that would remain virtually intact. Jefferson obviously decided that constructing the dome on one side of the house and placing a traditional Palladian portico on the other was as aesthetically satisfying a compromise as could be made, given the physical constraints of the existing house.

He was aware, however, that his new architectural plan did not conform strictly to the Palladian principles he admired so much. In later years he apologized to Benjamin Latrobe when the architect of the Capitol in Washington made his first visit to Monticello: "My essay in architecture has been so much subordinated to the law of convenience, & affected also by the circumstance of change in the original design, that it is liable to some unfavorable & just criticism."

The term "convenience" was a favorite one with Jefferson. His Washington friend and admirer Margaret Bayard Smith reported that "his local and domestic arrangements were full of contrivances or *conveniences* as he called them, peculiarly his own and never met with in other houses." Mrs. Smith referred to comforts such as the alcove beds and indoor privies, but also to the kind of domestic gadgetry that so fascinates visitors to the house today—the dumbwaiters, the cannonball clock, the weathervane, and the glass doors that open and close in tandem. Jefferson was sensitive to the fact that these clever amenities were not in conformity with Palladian orthodoxy. When he spoke of a "law of convenience," however, he implied that domestic ease came before architectural purity. This was certainly the case in his use of classical decorative elements; in his own house, if not in public buildings, he felt free to break the Palladian rules. Late in life, when he was finishing the interior of his house at Poplar Forest, he wrote to William Coffee, the sculptor who executed some of his decorative friezes: "In my middle room at Poplar Forest I mean to mix the [decorative motifs of] faces and oxskulls, a fancy which I can indulge in my own case, although in a public work I feel bound to follow authority strictly."

But the term "convenient" was also used in a specialized way by Palladio in the second volume of his *Four Books of Architecture*, and in writing to a fellow architect, Jefferson may well have alluded to Palladio's meaning. "That house only ought to be called convenient," the master wrote, "which is suitable to the quality of him that is to dwell in it, and whose parts correspond to the whole and to each other." The houses of great men, Palladio declared, "and particularly those in a republic," should be spacious and well-adorned, while those of "a meaner station" should be of less expense and have fewer ornaments. Jefferson always considered Monticello to be a country house, one suitable for a Virginia farmer. Did he intimate to Latrobe, however, that he may have erred in the direction of simplicity, subordinating his construction too much to what is appropriate for a gentleman farmer? The Palladian decorations could have been much richer and more ornate, the orders might have been Ionic rather than Doric, there might have been decorative ceiling murals, and more expensive materials rather than locally manufactured ones might have been used. Even if Jefferson had desired a more luxuriant Monticello, however, he was handicapped in achieving it by the difficulty of bringing master craftsmen to Monticello. As for the faults resulting from "the circumstance of change in the original designs," he would no doubt have pointed out to Latrobe without prompting that his failure to design stairs for the dome room rendered it useless.

There is evidence that he intended to provide staircases for access to the dome, and it seems highly unlikely he would purposely design such a room without a comfortable way of getting to it. One of his granddaughters stated that Jefferson had intended to use the dome room for a billiard room (the four-foot glass oculus would have illuminated the table perfectly), but that a law was passed before the dome was completed prohibiting public and private billiard tables in the state. As a result, she claimed, the staircases intended for it were never constructed. These were to lead from the balcony in the entrance hall to the dome room. Jefferson may well have intended putting in two staircases, one from each side of the entrance hall, to the balcony (it is perfectly constructed to allow this), and then have a single staircase lead from the balcony to the dome room above. This would have converted the dome from a private chamber to a public room, accessible from the public rooms below. His granddaughter's account also explains why Jefferson did not simply eliminate the floor of the dome room and make the dome a spacious ceiling of the parlor below: because he was an absentee builder, his construction program was fixed to a vast wheel of inertia, which prevented him from shifting plans when circumstances changed. The dome, therefore, remained an aesthetic principle when viewed from the outside; from within, it was Monticello's appendix—a useless architectural appendage.

In spite of all the compromises Jefferson was forced to make, however, the enlarged house plan was commodious, comfortable, and handsome. His solution to the problem of producing a one-story house with sufficient bedroom space for family and visitors was to build a mezzanine floor, which was concealed from the outside by cleverly designed, elongated windows, an idea he picked up in France. The mezzanine provided six bedrooms, four of them containing one of Jefferson's favorite architectural motifs, alcove beds, also borrowed from French examples. The small, square windows in the bedrooms, the ones Anna Maria Thornton thought so strange, were located at floor level to create the illusion of a single story from outside, where they appeared to be the upper sash of the window on the first floor below them. Above the mezzanine floor, tucked into the attic space in the center of the house, were three more bedrooms illuminated only by skylights. These were undoubtedly inhabited by Jefferson's numerous grandchildren when they were in residence at Monticello. (The Randolphs had eleven children.) The dome room, or "sky room," as Jefferson called it, was also on this top level, and for want of any other use probably became a children's playroom.

The remodeled ground floor was more than twice the size of the original house. Facing the original parlor, which remained virtually intact, was a new, spacious entrance hall with a balcony or gallery. The balcony was an inspired solution to a very real problem: how to provide access, for those in the bedrooms on the north side, to the privy on the south side of the mezzanine floor. The two-story-high entrance hall, which separated the north-side sleepers from their south-side relief, was bridged by a balcony that was not only functional, but also decorative. Jefferson designed the balcony into a semi-octagonal architectural shape with thin, straight, closely spaced balusters, topped with a delicate mahogany rail. The artistic effect of viewing the balcony from the hall is to create architectural interest immediately upon entering the house. The vertical balusters accentuate the height of the room and contrast with the Palladian cornice behind them. The semi-octagonal shape of the balcony alludes to the many uses of the octagon throughout the house. The balcony is one of the many instances of the architect's creating virtue of necessity—or in this case, of a necessary.

The rooms on either side of the entrance hall in the new section of the house were rough mirror images of the rooms in the first house. Opposite the original wings, which were Jefferson's dressing room on the south side, and the dining room on the north side, were two new bedrooms. Balancing semi-octagon rooms were placed next to these, matching symmetrically the octagonal rooms in the original building. These new pairs of octagons on each end of the house were joined in the center by large semi-octagonal piazzas. The south piazza was enclosed with glass and served as Jefferson's workshop and greenhouse.

The finished floor plan was a rampant self-indulgence in octagonality: four semi-octagon rooms, two semi-octagon piazzas, a semi-octagon balcony, a full octagon bedroom (the northeast chamber), and an octagonal dome. He was obviously infatuated with the octagon form, but why? Aside from the octagon's maternal allusion, which suggests the deeper psychological geometries of this shape, there were also more easily recognizable motivations. Like the most notorious of his spiritual descendants, the phrenologist Orson S. Fowler, who set off a fad of octagon housebuilding in America in the mid-nineteenth century, Jefferson was a convert to the architectural potentials of the octagon. Fowler was to go to a great deal of effort to attempt to prove a principle that Jefferson arrived at independently generations earlier—that the optimal shape for a room is octagonal rather than square. The major advantage of the octagon over the square in an age before electricity was that it eliminated dark corners. The corner of a square room in an eighteenth-century house was lost space for anything requiring decent light. Candles or oil lamps were seldom used during daylight hours; reading and handwork were done in front of a window. The octagon eliminates dark corners by allowing a window on each of its short walls. The parlor and tearooms at Monticello are perfect examples of the superiority of the octagon shape in admitting light. Each of these rooms, one a spacious public room, the other an intimate room for dining, is bathed in light from its arc of windows.

The trade-off is that windows not only admit light, but also heat and cold. In winter, Jefferson closed off the tearoom with a pair of sliding glass double doors. Most of the windows of the house were fitted with indoor wainscot shutters, which are completely concealed when folded back. These were closed at night during cold weather. In spite of the problems of heat loss through doors, windows, and skylights of glass, Jefferson's design, with its light-admitting semi-octagons, was remarkably modern. Ever since the Crystal Palace, built to house the London Exhibition of 1851, architects have had a love affair with light. The Crystal Palace, little more than a vast greenhouse of cast iron and glass, rendered interior darkness and shadows anathema. Palladianism, on the other hand, with its deep porticoes, large interior halls, and minimal fenestration, did not normally produce brightly lit rooms. But Jefferson, along with his commitment to Palladianism, was an advocate of light.

From his earliest youth he had developed lifelong sleeping and work habits that were tied to the sun. He awoke at sunrise and immediately began reading and writing; after sunset, his time was mostly devoted to socializing and conversation. The technology of artificial light in Jefferson's age was so inferior to natural light for reading and writing, his two most important work and leisure activities, that he avoided using candles or lamps whenever possible. Unfortunately, his preferred style of architecture, Palladianism, did not normally furnish the natural light he required. The town houses of Paris, including the Hôtel de Langeac, had proved to him, however, that Palladianism and light were not necessarily incompatible. One reason he was so taken by the Halle aux Bleds in Paris was that its dome, with its alternating rays of glass, flooded the interior of the grain market with an un-Palladian brilliance. In remodeling his house, then, he used every possible architectural trick within the orthodoxy of the Palladian code, including all-glass French doors with half-lights above, to illuminate his rooms with always more sunlight. In this respect, his design for Monticello took a step in the direction of twentieth-century architecture.

Another modern convenience Jefferson designed into his house was privacy. In the eighteenth century, domestic privacy was rare. Houses were invariably overcrowded—particularly the bedrooms—and floor plans made most rooms public spaces. In the South, house servants were ubiquitous. The first version of Monticello had been designed with privacy in mind: the Jeffersons' bedroom–dressing room wing was isolated, and Jefferson's second floor library-study over the parlor could be closed off to intruders. The remodeled house created three open, spacious, public areas—the hall, parlor, and dining-tearoom—and kept the rest of the rooms private. The transverse hallways, one on each wing of the house, separating the old from the new rooms, made this privacy possible. Like the modern central hall plan, which revolutionized domestic architecture by separating private bedroom-bathroom areas from living-dining-kitchen spaces, Jefferson's two passages made the four bedrooms on the first floor and those on the mezzanine and attic levels completely private; most bedrooms had a single entrance with double doors and latches. The two narrow staircases, located midway at each passage, led to hallways on each floor rather than to public rooms and made it possible for individuals as well as servants to move about the house without unintentionally entering public spaces and making unwanted contact with others. Staircases in Palladian houses normally connected public rooms on each floor; the small, private staircase was an innovation Jefferson had observed in the new houses of France. In building the narrow, cramped staircases of Monticello, however, Jefferson transformed the virtue of privacy into a dangerous inconvenience.

Jefferson also attempted to assure privacy while dining, constructing a lazy Susan serving door at the end of a dining room alcove. Food could be placed on shelves and turned into the room on the center-pivoting door without having a servant enter. He also built dumbwaiters on each side of the dining room fireplace for bringing wine up from the cellar without an intruding servant. Both of these devices, which have fascinated millions of Monticello visitors, were attempts by Jefferson to insulate himself, family, and guests from the ears of black servants, who usually listened with interest to the conversations of their white masters. (Where house servants were numerous, as they were at Monticello, there were few secrets concealed from the plantation slaves.) The rooms with the greatest amount of privacy were those in Jefferson's bedroom-library suite on the south end of the first floor, which included the original dressing room and octagon bedroom from the first house, plus the new octagon room, the south square room, and the piazza.

Jefferson was one for whom solitude was not merely an occasional luxury, but a necessity. The pains he took to escape the social traffic of living were sometimes remarkable. In France, when the pressures of society interfered with his need for seclusion, he retired to a hermitage of lay brothers at Mont Calvaire in Paris. He would stay for a week or more, usually working on a mass of papers and correspondence he brought with him. These retreats were not an opportunity for meditation and psychic renewal for Jefferson; they were intensive work sessions carried on in pleasant surroundings without interruption. This need for a solitary retreat, a haven from other people, became almost obsessive as Jefferson entered increasingly into public life, and more demands were made on his time. Much of the governmental work he did required research and study, and his correspondence was oppressively large. Intellectual labor of this kind is of necessity solitary; the demands of work therefore dictated that ever longer periods of his time be spent in seclusion. When he became secretary of state, he went to a great deal of expense and trouble to design and have constructed a special room where he could enjoy personal privacy in his rented house in Philadelphia. It was to be "a place to retire and write in . . . unseen and undisturbed even by my servants, and for this purpose it was to have a skylight and no lateral windows." What he got instead was one of those comedies of errors that occur so often when construction projects are poorly supervised: "When I returned from Virginia I found the garden house made with a window-door at each end, no sky-light, and a set of joists which were in the way." The room was eventually used for what it was, a closet.

It is understandable that when he remodeled Monticello he was determined to provide an island of complete privacy within what was often a turbulent sea of domestic activity. When, during his presidency, even his private quarters were no longer a barricade against the increasing demands on his time from family, friends, and casual visitors, he built his final retreat, Poplar Forest, the nation's first octagon-shaped house, in the isolated back country of Bedford County. Here, the geographical isolation of the house itself supplied his necessary privacy.

Before Jefferson could begin to build his newly designed Monticello, he had some tearing down to do, and that proved to be much more than he bargained for. As he outlined in his letter to Stephen Willis, the east front of the central block of the original house had to come down; this space would become half of the new entrance hall. The roof of the entire house also had to be removed; the old library-study walls over the parlor were to be lowered to ten feet, and the dome would sit on top of them. The attic floor and roof of the original wings would also have to be removed. These extensive demolitions involved two time-consuming complications: the brick walls had been built a lot stronger than Jefferson was aware of, and his plan to reuse the bricks from the old wall did not take this into account. Cleaning old mortar from bricks—especially well-made mortar—is slow work. ("The walls are so solid," he wrote Randolph, "that 7 men get down but between 3 & 4000 bricks a day. They would make new ones as fast.") The tenacity of the mortar also meant that he could salvage fewer bricks than he thought because of breakage. He originally hoped to get 62,000 used bricks, but the actual number was 29,000 whole bricks and 15,500 half bricks.

He started taking the house apart soon after he retired as secretary of state. In October of 1794, he wrote to George Wythe, "we are now living in a brick-kiln, for my house, in its present state is nothing more. I shall recommence my operations on it in the next summer." This comment seems to indicate that the porticoes and cornices had been removed from the house, leaving only the raw brick walls and a roof. In 1795, little was done on the house. His energies and capital were expended instead on getting his nail business started, and on running his farms. Earth was turned over in preparation for making bricks, and contracts were made with two sawyers to prepare for cutting structural timber. At the start of 1796, he was in search of a stout rope to lower the drums of the stone columns from the east portico. "We cannot proceed either to demolish our walls or dig our cellars till the columns are taken out of the way," he wrote. The rope finally arrived at Charlottesville, but in the meantime, he had "fallen on an easy & quick method of taking down our columns, which was but the work of one day." He failed to mention what the method was, but without a rope for a block and tackle, the most likely method would be to build a scaffold and an inclined plane, and slide the drums down to the ground.

Once the columns were down, his crews went at the brick walls. When the bricks were pulled away and he got a look at the timbers supporting the roof and floors, he concluded that "it was high time" his remodeling commenced, for some of the wood was eaten with dry rot. By now the house was a full-fledged construction site, with men, women, and children picking, scraping, hammering, and hauling. Working on it was dangerous in an era before hard hats: "The tumbling of brick bats keeps us in constant danger," Jefferson informed Randolph. "We have as yet but one accident to a man knocked down." The danger was brought closer to home the following year, however, when his daughter Maria took "a tumble thro' the floor into the cellar, from which she escaped miraculously without hurt." She was not so lucky in a later accident; during her honeymoon, she fell out of a door, sprained her ankle, and was immobilized for a time. There was a fatality during the construction of Monticello, however. John Holmes, a skilled housejoiner from Philadelphia, described as a "Sober Genteel young man" who "understands drawing," fell from a scaffold in the winter of 1801 and died from his injuries.

The noise, dirt, and hazards did not prevent Jefferson from continuing to invite guests to the mountaintop. "I have begun the demolition of my house, and hope to get through its re-edification in the course of the summer," he wrote to William Giles. "But do not let this discourage you from calling on us if you wander this way in the summer. We shall have the eye of a brick-kiln to poke you into, or an Octagon to air you in." The Duke de la Rochefoucauld-Liancourt, in exile from the French Revolution, left a written account of his visit, one of the most detailed of all contemporary descriptions of Jefferson and his mountaintop estate. He thought his host had a "mild, easy and obliging temper," but, like many acquaintances, he found him "somewhat cold and reserved." Liancourt's portrayal of the house was mostly in the future tense, for the "brick kiln" that it resembled in 1796 when he arrived gave him little idea of what it had been or would be. The French aristocrat, using the interior evidence of the original rooms and Jefferson's architectural drawings, somewhat generously concluded that "Monticello, according to its first plan was infinitely superior to all other houses in America, in point of taste and convenience," in spite of the fact that Jefferson's knowledge of architecture was acquired "in books only." Now that his artistic tastes have been honed by his travels in Europe, Liancourt observed, his newly enlarged house "will certainly deserve to be ranked with the most pleasant mansions of France and England." Monticello's "apartments will be large and convenient," he wrote; "the decoration both outside and inside, simple yet regular and elegant." Liancourt, echoing his host's confidence, announced that the enlarged and remodeled version of the house, "already much advanced," would be completed "before the end of next year." He was off by about a quarter of a century.

Jefferson also sent an invitation to another friend from France, Count Constantin François de Volney, with the caveat: "the noise, confusion and discomfort of the scene will require all your philosophy and patience." (De Volney gathered up his patience and philosophy, traveled to Monticello, and stayed for three weeks.) He had advised de Volney to "find comfort in a comparison of our covering with that of an arabian tent," which suggests that the part of the roof removed when the east portico was demolished was replaced with temporary canvas to keep out the weather. The remainder of the roof was not removed until later.

Jefferson's joking reference to brick kilns showed the subject was once more on his mind. His brick kiln was set up beside a spring on the southeast side of the mountain. The old question, posed when he built the first house, of whether to carry water to the mountaintop and make bricks there, or to make bricks where water was available and haul the bricks to the building site, was finally resolved: bricks were manufactured at the spring, stored there and hauled up the mountain as needed. Most of the bricks for the remodeled house were made by Henry Duke, a local brickmaker. The bricks that Duke made were durable but rough, uneven, and somewhat porous. Later, when Richard Richardson, an Albemarle mason who did bricklaying, stonemasonry, and plastering at Monticello, went to Philadelphia, he asked Jefferson to "send mr Duke a brick from this place as a model, & proof how much too careless our workmen are in making theirs."

By April 1796, the walls were down, the cellars dug, and Jefferson was ready to build the stone foundations and cellars for the new part of the house, but he had no stonemason. He appealed to a neighbor, Archibald Stuart in Staunton, to hire "as cheap as we can" Felty Millar, whom he had heard was a good workman. It was Millar who did much of the rubble stonemasonry work on the remodeled house, with help perhaps from another local mason, Joseph Moran, and from Richardson, who later accompanied Jefferson to Philadelphia to get inoculated against smallpox and to learn stonecutting and plastering. The lime for mortar was burned by Will Beck, who had done the same job on the original house.

By late summer, the stone foundations were completed and Jefferson was ready to begin on the new brickwork, but again there was delay, this time because of "perpetual rains which give only broken intervals of work," and the "fever and ague" of Stephen Willis, "on whom solely I depended." Willis was at Monticello two weeks after this complaint, however, with two bricklayers, John Shell and a slave, Ned. Jefferson had also rehired Davy Watson, the hard-drinking housejoiner–carriage-maker who had worked on the original house.

One of his jobs was probably to make window sashes; the remodeled house, with its numerous windows, many of them with triple sashes, required framing for five hundred panes of glass. (During the demolitions, some of the window sashes in the original section of the house had been broken and had to be replaced.) Jefferson had continuing difficulties getting glass in the size, quantity, and quality he needed. He purchased most of the glass that went into Monticello's windows from Joseph Donath of Philadelphia. He had to refuse some of Donath's glass, however, "on account of the size, and its not being 1½ thick, as in the high situation of my house, the winds make a very stout quality of glass necessary."

Because the decorative frames and mullions in a window had to be hand-shaped with a plane, manufacturing sashes in the quantity needed for Monticello was a formidable piece of carpentry. Some of the woodwork done at Jefferson's joinery shop on Mulberry Row for a number of years involved window making. He thought that sashes for the circular windows of the dome room were beyond the skills of his joiners and glazers, however. He purchased them from a Philadelphia sash-maker, Daniel Trump, in mahogany frames at an exorbitant price of $2.14 per pane. The sashes for the half-lights in the dome, porticoes, and piazzas, however, were made by James Oldham after he set up his own business in Richmond.

Jefferson's bricklayers worked into the winter of 1796, running a race against the thermometer in an attempt to bring the walls to roof level so the roof could be completed by the following spring. The race was lost, however; Jefferson reported to Randolph that it was "so cold that the freezing of the ink on the point of my pen renders it difficult to write. We have had the thermometer at 12 °. My works are arrested in a state entirely unfinished, & I fear we shall not be able to resume them." He was right, for he wrote to James Madison on December 17 that "the severest weather ever known in November" had "arrested my buildings very suddenly, when eight days more would have completed my walls."

The bitter cold snap, which made masonry work impossible, cost Jefferson much more than eight days, however. On November 4, he was elected Vice President of the United States, and this, with his subsequent two-term presidency, took him away from Monticello for the greater part of the year for the next dozen years, slowing construction work to a crawl. (It is a telling historical commentary to contrast Jefferson's election to the vice presidency in 1796 with modern presidential elections; during the campaign, Jefferson never left Monticello.) With masonry work halted, Jefferson paid off the workers who had, in a three-month span, built most of the brick skeleton for the remodeled house.

On February 20, 1797, Jefferson set out for Philadelphia to assume his duties as Vice President. He was away for less than two months, however, and by April he had once more assembled his workmen to finish the brick walls. It was important, he explained in a letter to de Volney, that he get the work finished while he was still at Monticello (he had to return to Philadelphia in May) because his work team "must suspend their work during my absence." His house plan was too unorthodox, he wrote, "to trust them with its execution in my absence." His intention was to "uncover all but two middle rooms" on his return to Monticello in July. The two rooms with a roof remaining would be the library-study on the second floor and the first-floor parlor. The bedroom and dining room wings of the original house would be roofless and therefore uninhabitable. In March, he put his bricklayers back to work and hired Henry Duke to make bricks. In mid-June, still in Philadelphia, he was concerned with how many slave helpers the bricklayers would need from the crews preparing to harvest crops. He feared he would be short-handed for the all-important harvest, during which virtually everyone on the plantation went to the fields. The bricklayers "should reserve for the harvest season that sort of work which will require the least attendance [in slave labor]," he wrote Randolph. He advised him to allot to the bricklayers as helpers the "most indifferent" harvesters. In late summer he was back at Monticello inviting family and friends to pay one last visit "before we uncover our house." His timetable for removing the roof was behind schedule, however; in early August he informed de Volney "it will probably be a month now before we take off the roof of our house." By the end of 1797, the roof still had not been completely removed, and Jefferson was now compelled to spend more time in Philadelphia. As a result, it was to be a long time before he was to get Monticello under the shelter of a new roof.

During two years of tearing down much of the original house and constructing a shell of the new, family life managed to go on at Monticello, although it was hardly the tranquil, ordered existence Jefferson preferred. The most pleasant family event was the marriage of his youngest daughter Maria to John (Jack) Wayles Eppes, a half-cousin she had known most of her life. When Jefferson went to France after the death of his wife, he had left Maria, then six years old, in the care of his sister-in-law, Elizabeth Eppes. Aunt Eppes became virtually a mother to the child, and the Eppes estate in Chesterfield County near Petersburg was home to her. While Maria was virtually a member of the Eppes family, Jack Eppes was no stranger to Jefferson. When Jefferson was secretary of state, he assumed responsibility for Eppes's education and allowed the young man to stay in his house in Philadelphia. Before Eppes left for Philadelphia, Jefferson had offered his mother some practical advice to pass on to her son: "Load him on his departure with charges not to give his heart to any object he will find there. I know no such useless bauble in a house as a girl of mere city education. She would finish by fixing him there and ruining him." Eppes had little time for such romantic entanglements, for Jefferson enrolled him at the College of Philadelphia, directed his reading in history, government, and the law, and put him to work in Jefferson's own office. Ultimately, Eppes followed his mentor's advice on marriage and settled on a fine country girl, who appropriately enough happened to be Jefferson's daughter. Jefferson learned of the engagement of the couple, not from Maria or Jack, but by letter from his oldest daughter Martha. If he was offended by the breach of decorum in Eppes's not asking his permission, he did not show it. "She could not have been more to my wishes, if I had the whole earth free to have chosen a partner for her," he wrote to Martha. To Maria, he declared that in his opinion Eppes "possesses every quality necessary to make you happy and to make us all happy."

The couple married on October 13, 1797, at Monticello, amid the debris and scaffolding of the brickmasons, undoubtedly in the parlor, which was to become the traditional room where weddings were performed at Monticello. It was now one of the few rooms still habitable in the house. (One wonders where the wedding guests stayed, and how anyone got to the second floor with the staircases demolished.)

The bride and groom were a striking couple. Maria, at nineteen, was a beautiful young woman by all contemporary accounts. The ex-slave Isaac termed her a "pritty lady jist like her mother." Eppes was twenty-five at his marriage; Isaac called him "a handsome man but had a harelip." Whatever the psychological effects of this birth defect in an age before corrective surgery, it did not appear to affect his personality, which was described as "sunny" and "warm." And if there was any speech defect associated with his cleft lip, it did not prevent him from becoming one of the Republican leaders of Congress, reputedly an effective debater. It is interesting to note, however, that the words "hare" or "rabbit" were never afterward used by any of the Jefferson family members in their correspondence, even though Isaac reported that rabbits were raised at Monticello and served at the table.

Of his two sons-in-law, Jefferson appeared to favor Eppes over Randolph, but he was scrupulously careful to show no overt preferences. Although he succeeded in chaining the Randolphs and their numerous children to him with bonds of land and slaves, he failed to get the more independent Eppes to establish himself near Monticello. Jefferson gave his younger daughter a nine-hundred-acre plantation at Pantops near Shadwell as her dowry with the hope that the couple would settle there, a short distance from Monticello. But the estate had no house on it, and because of his own building schemes, Jefferson was not able to assist them in building one, although he did design one for them—the octagonal house he later built for himself, Poplar Forest. As a result, Eppes and his bride eventually took up permanent residence near Eppington at Bermuda Hundred, an Eppes estate that was deeded to Jack Eppes on his marriage. In this case, Jefferson lost a daughter by marriage, even though she visited Monticello frequently and never failed to express her love and devotion to her father.

Unlike Maria, Martha never placed her husband above Jefferson in her affections. Eight months after Maria's marriage, Martha, anticipating Jefferson's arrival home, wrote to her "Dearest and adored Father" with "raptures and palpitations not to be described": "The heart swellings with which I address you when absent and look forward to your return convince me of the folly or want of feeling of those who dare to think that any *new* ties can weaken the first and best of nature."

[264]

One wonders what Randolph would have thought of this letter. Maria's first love became her husband; the tender love letter she wrote to him shortly before her death is evidence that the magnetic pole of her affections shifted from Monticello to Eppington after her marriage.

By February 1798, the house was still roofless except for the still-covered parlor-library section of the old central block. Jefferson wrote from Philadelphia to Martha inviting her to use these two rooms and the south pavilion for her family. She was living temporarily at Belmont, six miles from Monticello, and heavy rains had filled the basement of the house, making it damp and unhealthy. In the meantime, Jefferson was becoming increasingly uneasy about the delay in putting a roof on his house. He wrote to Randolph, "I begin to feel with great anxiety my houseless situation."

The new roof for Monticello was not an easy one to construct. Jefferson had designed a compound roof, a combination of hips and gables, making the framing unusual and tricky, particularly for workmen in his part of Virginia. He further complicated the roof design by adding a balustrade to circumscribe the entire house at the edge of the roof line just above Monticello's massive cornice. At the top of the roof, a Chinese railing was added as a parapet. Although these adornments were not installed until much later, they added a great deal of finished carpentry work to the house, each of the thick balusters having to be turned on a lathe. The balustrade and railing were not entirely decorative; they served a functional purpose—to partially conceal the shake roof and skylights. (Except for its stepped plinths, which were tinned, the original dome was also covered with shakes.) The rusticity of wooden shakes clashed violently with the formal symmetry of Palladian architecture, yet when the first house and the remodeled version were built, shakes were the only building material available to Jefferson. It is unclear when Monticello was completely covered with a metal roof. In 1807, Jefferson ordered sheet lead, the traditional European roof covering used by those who could afford it. In 1825, however, a year before Jefferson's death, John Hemings reroofed the house with tin, a roofing material that was being used on the buildings of the University of Virginia. The dependencies were stripped of their shakes and covered with sheet iron in 1808. It is questionable whether the balustrade and Chinese railing would have been added to the house if Jefferson had been able to use metal roofing, with its clean, geometrical surfaces, when the roof was first installed.

Aside from aesthetic considerations, a metal roof was an important deterrent to fire, always a fear at Monticello. Lightning was particularly dangerous because the house was the highest point on the mountain. Isaac recalled that it was once struck by lightning; after that, one of Franklin's lightning rods was attached to one end of the house. "Old Master used to say," the ex-slave stated, " 'If it hadn't been for that Franklin the whole house would have gone.' "

The roofing of the original house was a simple gable over the central block with separate hip roofs over each wing. The fact that it consisted of three discrete roofs made it possible to remove each one separately while living under the part of the house still covered. This is what Jefferson did, and this is why the family was able to inhabit Monticello during its prolonged pulling down and putting up. The last roof to be pulled down, the middle section, was replaced in part by the dome. When this final roof was removed, it was necessary for Jefferson to move his books, probably to the only shelter still available, the south pavilion.

He hired a sawyer-carpenter, William Davenport, to work on the new roof during his stay in Philadelphia as Vice President. Davenport was a poor choice, however, for he proved to be undependable when not closely supervised. Jefferson had urged him to keep a "strong force sawing sheeting plank and getting and preparing shingles" so that with the first good weather of spring, the roof could be started. He had also given his two most experienced slave carpenters, John Hemings and his helper Davy, instructions for carpentry work. He had hired a housejoiner, a Mr. Arnold, one of many workmen contracted for who failed to show up. Arnold was to have worked on the frames for the doors and alcoves of the house. These were necessary to "enable us to close [the rooms] & make them inhabitable," Jefferson explained. John Hemings was to work under Arnold's guidance in preparing and finishing floorboards. The housejoiner who finally executed these instructions when Arnold failed to appear was James Dinsmore, whom Jefferson hired in Philadelphia, and who arrived at Monticello in July 1798. He was to remain there for more than a decade.

At the beginning of May 1798, Jefferson wrote to Randolph, "I am in hopes from Davenport's account that I shall find the house nearly covered, and that we shall not be long without a shelter to unite under. O welcome hour whenever!" His euphoria was quickly deflated, however, when, a few days later, he received word from Randolph that "Davenport has done nothing at Monto since your departure— he is not at work there now—he has got 3000 Chestnut shingles for you & has cut a number of Stocks at Pouncey's but has not yet begun to saw them." Over a period of six months, all of Jefferson's feverish instructions, his worrying over workers, and his detailed directions for work schedules had produced virtually nothing in tangible results. The reason was not because he was unwilling to spend the money necessary to get the work done, as was the case with the first house. Although he was still heavily in debt, he now had the salary from the vice presidency and his income from his flourishing nail business to support his construction, and he had the cash to pay for labor and supplies. The reason, simply enough, was that he was an absentee builder, attempting to supervise a complex, unconventional housebuilding project by correspondence. He depended on Randolph for informal supervision of his workmen, but this was impeded by Randolph's own construction enterprise. He was building a modest, two-story house at Edgehill, a few miles from Monticello, using many of the craftsmen who had recently worked at Monticello. This house, not unexpectedly, had been designed by Jefferson. Randolph did not have time for both construction sites; he had enough trouble with delays on his own house. (He and his family did not move to Edgehill until early in 1800.)

When Jefferson returned to Monticello on July 4, 1798, he again took control of his building operations. He set Dinsmore to work on the interior door framing, with John Hemings as helper, and by August, work was well under way on the architraves of the doorways. He hired William McGehee, a local carpenter, to work on the roof, and progress was made on covering the south end of the house, where Jefferson's new bedroom-library suite was located. He hoped that the entire roof would be finished by the end of the year. As usual, this was an overconfident estimate. When McGehee was paid off on December 17, only the south half of the house was covered with a roof. And when the architect-builder left Monticello for Philadelphia the next day, construction stopped. The following March, he wrote to Maria that "scarcely a stroke has been done toward covering the house since I went way, so that it remained open at the North end another winter." In the meantime, floors were being constructed for the new sections of the house, but this work also met with disappointment and delay. Thomas Buck, the carpenter who was working on the floors, unexpectedly quit, leaving many of the newly roofed rooms in the south part of the house unusable.

Throughout this snail's-pace construction schedule, Jefferson blithely continued inviting family and friends to Monticello on his return visits from Philadelphia, as if he had decent quarters to lodge them in. Martha and her children joined him in the summer of 1798, but Maria was prevented from coming because of illness. (Jefferson apologized for not visiting her when she was ill, but his workmen, he wrote, "cannot proceed an hour without me.") In the summer of 1799, Martha's family and Maria were in residence, as well as Dr. William Bache, who was moving to a six-hundred-acre farm near Charlottesville. The accommodations could not have been very comfortable. Jefferson's strategy, as it had been in constructing the original house, was to finish each room in serial order, making one room inhabitable and then moving on to another. The new rooms were not yet plastered and nothing was painted, however, and even though windows were probably installed, there were few doors, and hence little privacy. Before the entire house was completely roofed, there was no dining room—this was located in the north section, the last to be covered. Food was probably served in the parlor. (The dome above the parlor was not constructed until later; it probably had a temporary gable roof installed over it to protect the rooms below.)

The patience of Martha, who was in residence during most of Jefferson's return visits to Monticello during his vice presidency, was nothing short of heroic. The summer of 1799 was a particularly trying one for her: she had three small children, aged four, seven, and eight, and was about to give birth to a fourth. Managing to keep her brood from serious injury while playing on the attractive hazards of a construction site, acting as hostess to her father and his visitors—all during the final months of a pregnancy—must have severely strained her natural cheerfulness. She was later to express to her father her feelings about the hectic visits to Monticello when Jefferson insisted on gathering his friends about him no matter how unsuited his house was for entertaining. His visits home provided little time for real intimacy and closeness, she complained: "I never had the pleasure of passing one sociable moment with you. Always in a crowd, taken from every useful and pleasing duty to be worried with a multiplicity of disagreeable ones which the entertaining of such crowds of company subjects one to in the country." Jefferson's reply indicates how deeply the rituals of hospitality were embedded in him. "The manner and usages of our country," he reminded Martha, "are laws we cannot repeal." To refuse to honor these laws would be "revolting conduct which would undo the whole labor of our lives." They are changing, he noted, and the time will come when "the eternal presence of strangers" will be reduced to "the visiting hours of the day, and the family left to tranquility in the evening," instead of having visitors move in for weeks at a time, as was the case at Monticello. In the meantime, he advised her to "view the pleasing side" and "consider that these visits are evidences of the general esteem which we have been . . . all our lives trying to merit."

An unwritten corollary of the law of hospitality which "we cannot repeal" was that it was supported by the institution of slavery. A houseful of guests who paid prolonged visits was made possible by a large staff of slave servants to do the necessary housekeeping, laundry, food preparation, and meal serving. The tradition of unlimited hospitality had been imported to America from England, where inherited estates and a pool of cheap domestic labor supported the large staffs of servants necessary for running an open house for all visitors. The plantation system of the American South did not produce the wealth of the English aristocracy, and a labor shortage did not support a class of free servants, but the institution of slavery made it possible for the Southern gentry to open their doors as wide to friends and casual acquaintances as any English baron. When Jefferson took his lifelong habits of hospitality to Washington, where servants had to be paid, and food purchased instead of being supplied by slave field hands, he quickly found himself in financial difficulties. Indeed, the steady decline of his economic fortunes from the time he began his career in national politics can be traced in part to his inability to adjust the slave-supported hospitality of Monticello to the quite different social economies of Paris, Philadelphia, and Washington.

By the turn of the century, Jefferson's house was under cover of a roof and he was faced with the considerable task of finishing the flooring. Like the roof, the floors were not easily constructed. The floor joists in the parlor, for example, were heavy, hewed timbers spaced sixteen inches apart and inserted into joist-holes in the brick walls. Ledgers were nailed to each side of the joists to support short, inch-thick wood battens. These ran perpendicular to the joists and provided a sub-floor for the nogging of brick, clay, and straw, which was packed up to the top of the joists. Lath was run under the joists and an inch and a quarter of plaster was troweled over the lath to create the ceiling of the room below. On top of the joists, heart-of-pine boards, finished to a fine smoothness, were laid tongue-and-groove for the flooring. This floor required large amounts of lumber and a great deal of labor to build. Jefferson purchased some of the lumber already cut to size from local sawyers or sawmills, but his own crews of sawyers and carpenters, white and slave, were left with the final kiln-drying, cutting, fitting, and finishing, all with hand tools that seem primitive by today's standards. Hauling and putting in place a hundred tons of nogging also consumed an enormous number of slave work hours. Constructing floors went on for years.

In March 1800, Jefferson sent word to Richard Richardson, the bricklayer who was then supervising construction, that his bedroom was to be plastered by the time he returned to Monticello. Richardson immediately began putting up the lath and possibly worked on the plastering himself, a skill he had studied in Philadelphia. Most of the initial plastering at Monticello was done by Hugh Chisholm, who was a brickmaker and bricklayer, but who also plastered, as was often the case with brickmasons. Jefferson later hired a professional plasterer in Washington, a German, Martin Wanscher, possibly because he was not completely satisfied with Chisholm's work. Martha made a comment on the quality of the plastering in November 1801: "The plaistering at Monticello goes on, not as well as the first room which was elegantly done but better than the 3d and fourth, the two I think you would have been most anxious about," because they were on the first floor. This suggests that Jefferson was finishing off rooms on the mezzanine and ground floors simultaneously, no doubt because bedrooms were needed every bit as much as the public rooms on the first floor.

There is no clear indication of when the dome was started, but construction of its laminated ribs was underway in 1800. In November, Jefferson noted in his Memorandum Book, "settled with Reuben Perry. I owe him for all work to this day, exclusive of dome £20-6-9½." This would suggest that Reuben Perry, brother of John Perry, one of the carpenters who was also working on the house, built the structural members of the dome and was given premium pay for it. In later life, Jefferson stated that James Dinsmore built his dome, but earlier he commented that the structural system of Philibert de l'Orme, which was used for the dome, was so simple and cheap "it is used for barns in France. A very coarse & uninformed carpenter is making mine, who never heard of a dome before." This would not be Dinsmore, who was well versed in Palladian architecture. Dinsmore's letters to Jefferson are literate, befitting a housejoiner trained in Philadelphia. Reuben Perry, a local carpenter rather than a housejoiner, was probably given the task of building the dome's structure and of sheathing and shingling it, while Dinsmore supervised construction and, over a period of years, finished the interior.

The framing trusses of the dome were fabricated of 1-by-12-inch oak boards a little more than five feet long—not quite the "sticks and chips" of Jefferson's Head and Heart letter, but they were still small pieces of lumber for structural framing. The boards were sawed and planed down to the curve of the dome, reducing them to nine inches wide. (A template was undoubtedly used to make these curved boards in quantity.) Four of them were nailed together in staggered layers to produce 4-by-9-inch laminated oak trusses which ran from the base of the dome to the collar of the oculus, a four-foot-diameter opening at the top. When the trusses were put into place, they were joined by 1-by-9-inch bulkheads running concentrically around the dome every thirty-nine inches. The sheathing for the outside of the dome was ½-by-5-inch boards bent to fit the curve; the inside was lath and plaster combined with decorative paneling.

In February 1801, Jefferson was elected President after a campaign that ended with the electoral college tied at seventy-three votes each for Jefferson and Aaron Burr. This sent the contest to the House of Representatives where it also became deadlocked. After thirty-six ballots, the tie was broken, and on February 17, Jefferson was named third President of the United States. The effect on his building campaign of his election to the presidency was to reduce even further the amount of time he had to personally supervise his workmen. This was mitigated, however, by the fact that his visits to Monticello were made regularly and could be planned for. He wrote to his daughter Maria shortly after his election that he expected to make a short visit of two or three weeks in April to Monticello, "and two months during the sickly season in autumn every year." The sickly season was late summer and early fall, when those who were able to, moved from the coastal regions of the South to healthier climates further inland. The chief danger was malaria, known as intermittent fever, marsh fever, or autumnal fever. It was not yet known that it was transmitted by mosquitoes. Washington, which became the nation's capital in June 1800, was considered particularly unhealthy because it was situated on a swamp. Congress closed shop from August to October, allowing Jefferson regular fall visits to his mountaintop. In spite of the unhealthy climate of Washington, Jefferson was pleased by the capital's being moved from Philadelphia, for it brought him closer to home and eased the burden of travel over terrible roads.

As he began a presidency that was to last two terms, the house Jefferson had been putting up and tearing down for more than thirty years was in no more livable condition than it was at the beginning of the American Revolution. Its size had more than doubled, but probably fewer than half of the rooms had plastered walls and many still did not have finished flooring. The dependency wings, which Jefferson and his wife Martha had planned together during the earlier years of their marriage, were just now being started, but in a greatly simplified version. During the first two years of his presidency, however, building moved rapidly because Jefferson now had at least one dependable workman, James Dinsmore, who was capable of supervising construction during his absences. Nevertheless, it would not be until he retired as President that the interior of Monticello would be finished, and many years after that before the exterior of the house looked like the Monticello we know today.

east portico of Monticello.

Above: *Anna Maria Thornton's watercolor
of the west lawn of Monticello, painted during
her visit in 1802.*

Right: *Monticello's stairs were described by Mrs. Thornton as "a little ladder of a staircase . . . very steep."*

Below: *A pivot window on the second floor of Monticello. Anna Maria Thornton may have slept in this room.*

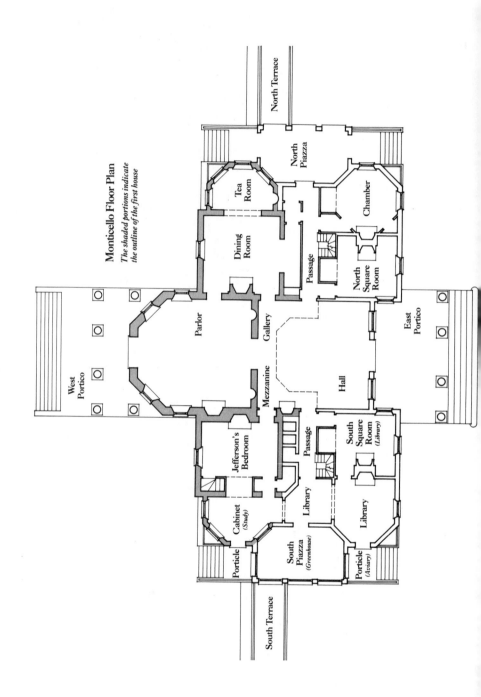

Monticello Floor Plan
The shaded portions indicate
the outline of the first house

North Terrace

North Piazza

Tea Room

Dining Room

Chamber

Passage

North Square Room

Parlor

Gallery

East Portico

West Portico

Mezzanine

Hall

South Square Room
(Library)

Jefferson's Bedroom

Passage

Cabinet
(Study)

Library

Library

Porticle

South Piazza
(Greenhouse)

Porticle
(Aviary)

South Terrace

...e kitchen, *located beneath the south terrace.*

...nticello entrance hall with the Great Clock over the doorway and its cannonball *...ights in the corner. During Jefferson's life, this room, filled with Indian arti-* *...ts, was known as the Indian Hall.*

*The entrance hall. The double glass doors leading to the parlor
open together when one is pushed.*

*The parlor, with its cherry and beech parquet floor. Many of
Jefferson's paintings were hung here.*

*Jefferson's library. The bookcases were individual boxes
stacked on top of each other.*

*Jefferson's bedroom. The alcove bed was enclosed with a screen during his
lifetime. Above the bed is a clothes closet ventilated by three oval openings.*

The dining room. Dumbwaiters built into the side of the fireplace delivered wine from the cellar.

The dining room, looking into the tea room. Double glass doors closed off the tea room in cold weather.

The tea room, a semi-octagonal room connected to the dining room. This "most honorable suite" contained busts (left to right) of Franklin, John Paul Jones, Lafayette, and Washington.

The dome room at Monticello.

A Rumford fireplace and alcove bed in the south square room, next to the library. The bed was converted by Jefferson into a book alcove, and the room into a sitting room.

The south terrace, Chinese railing, and south pavilion, with the dependencies below cut into the side of the mountain.

The columns on the west portico are stuccoed brick. They were not constructed until 1823, three years before Jefferson's death.

The south pavilion "honeymoon cottage" at Monticello, where Jefferson brought his bride on a snowy night.

The south terrace with a chimney, in the shape of a Doric pedestal, emerging from the smoke room below.

*e south piazza, connected to Jefferson's bedroom-library suite,
s used as a workshop and greenhouse.*

*small pavilion rests atop the mortarless rock retaining wall
it supports the garden terrace.*

9

A Single Example of
Chaste Architecture

IF THERE IS a signature to Palladian architecture, it is the columned portico, echoing the majestic temples of Rome and, even more distantly, the Parthenon of Attica. The columns of a Palladian portico are a stately fanfare, capable of sounding a trumpet voluntary of Corinthian pomp and grandeur, or a simpler note of Doric truth. The columns are pure geometry, a Platonic realization of idea and form, harmoniously proportioned in diameter, length, and distance between shafts. Imagine, then, the utter horror and disbelief experienced by Thomas Jefferson when he learned that the columns newly erected for the portico of Monticello—were crooked.

The workman responsible for this nightmare was Richard Richardson, the jack-of-all-trades who had been given the task of reassembling the columns from the original house. The stone drums that made up the shafts had been taken down in haste, and when they were hauled away for storage no one took the trouble to mark the position of each drum on its column. When Richardson gathered the twenty drums before the east front of the remodeled house in preparation for reassembling them into four columns, he had not the slightest notion of which drum belonged on which column. By carefully measuring each drum, he was able to determine its place in the column shaft, and he thought the rest would be easy. He erected two columns, only to have Jefferson return from Washington and discover that they were not parallel. Richardson may well have argued that they were straight enough, but for a builder like Jefferson who measured his drawings to a thousandth of an inch, and who could position a surveyor's transit to provide optical proof, "straight enough" was not straight. He left for Washington after issuing orders to dismantle the two errant columns and put the four up perfectly straight.

Richardson dutifully took down the two columns and began reassembling the other two. When one-and-a-half columns had been erected, these too, in the words of Thomas Mann Randolph, were found to be "not perpendicular, I suppose from the wrong placing [of] the pieces of the shaft." Randolph may have been secretly pleased at this, for he disapproved of Richardson, who apparently was something of a dandy when he was not doing construction work. Randolph had earlier derided him to Jefferson for "dressing and gal[l]anting." In any case, three days before Christmas an exasperated Richardson had written to Jefferson and explained his predicament with the columns: because they were unmarked, he "never experience[d] so troublesome a job in [his] life" in trying to put them back up. He "found they must be put together before they are put up, to mark them, as they are to stand." The problem was obviously in the way William Rice, the original stonecutter, had cut the drums; each was shaped to fit accurately in only one position, and Richardson had to rotate each drum on the one below it until he discovered by trial and error what its position was. This had to be done on the ground before the drums were raised into position on the column. The entire process was both frustrating and time-consuming. In the meantime, "the weather proving very cold . . . the mortar freesed," so Richardson sent his workmen away and postponed the job until spring. By then, Jefferson would be back at Monticello to supervise the work himself and assure that the columns were placed with precision. All of them were not erected, however, for two more years. In 1803, Jefferson paid a mason, Robert Hope, $20 to finish the job. The fiasco of the leaning columns of Monticello was a textbook case of how Jefferson's well-laid plans met with constant interruptions. Absentee supervision, carelessness in

A stone column on the east portico, its joints chipped and battered from Richard Richardson's repeated failure to get the columns up straight.

working with salvaged materials, and undependable labor all contributed to a delay of three years in erecting four columns. This meant that during that time, work was probably suspended on the portico that the columns were to support.

In spite of the delays caused by the columns, during the first year of his presidency Jefferson made a determined effort to push work on the house with some urgency. The office of the nation's chief executive opened new avenues for acquiring skilled craftsmen to work on Monticello; he quickly hired a housejoiner and a plasterer from the Washington area and sent them to Virginia to work under James Dinsmore's supervision. James Oldham, the housejoiner, started working in March 1801 at $240 a year and continued in Jefferson's employment for a number of years. Martin Wanscher, a German plasterer, "started from the citey Washington to mounteyselley," as he recorded it, on August 17, 1801. He did much of the difficult plastering in the large public rooms of the house.

During Jefferson's absence, Dinsmore was in charge of all construction work; he also handled the accounts for the nailery and acted as a guide for the visitors who showed up at Monticello even when Jefferson was not there. His salary was $480 annually, twice that of Oldham, his fellow joiner. He was literate, honest, dependable, and a master craftsman capable of executing the most unorthodox of Jefferson's architectural plans. During 1801 and 1802, Dinsmore worked on the dining room, one of the most carpentry-intensive rooms in the house. Not only did it have a massive entablature, as did other rooms on the ground floor, but the walls were also wood-paneled to a height of eight feet from the floor. And to add to Dinsmore's challenge in this room, there were two arches, a skylight, and a floor to construct.

The entablature was the jeweled crown of interior Palladian architecture. The essential principle of interior decoration was to imitate in each room the major parts of exterior Palladian style. The entablature—the architrave, frieze, and cornice of the exterior roof line—was repeated around the intersection of wall and ceiling in the interior rooms. The triangular pediments of the exterior porticoes were placed above doors and windows; columns were imitated by engaged, rectangular pilasters, placed next to doors, room partitions, windows, and fireplaces. Interior Palladian decoration was not limited to a single style, as was the case with the exterior. Each room could be decorated in a version of the three major orders: Doric, Ionic, or Corinthian. Where Jefferson was limited to the simple Doric style for the exterior of the house because of the impossibility of finding craftsmen to execute the more decorative orders, this was not the case with the interior. By simply abandoning columns and pilasters, with their difficult fluting and intricately carved capitals, he was able to decorate his rooms with a variety of Palladian styles.

He turned to the engraved plates of the architectural folios of his library for models. One of these books has survived the Library of Congress fire of 1851, which destroyed most of the volumes Jefferson sold to Congress. It is *Parallèle de l'Architecture Antique avec la Moderne, Suivant les Dix Principaux Auteurs qui Ont écrit sur les Cinq Ordres*, by Charles Errard and Roland Freart de Chambray, revised by C. A. Jombert, published in 1766. Jefferson marked in pencil in this folio a number of entablatures from the temples of Rome with corresponding rooms at Monticello where they would be installed. His goal was to have a fine example of all of the Palladian orders in the public rooms of his house. "The internal of the house," he later commented to a visitor, "contains specimens of all of the different orders except the composite which is not introduced. The Hall is in the Ionic, the Dining

Room is in the Doric, the Parlor in the Corinthian, and the Dome in
the Attic. In the other rooms are introduced several different forms
of those orders, all in the truest proportions according to Palladio."
For his bedroom, he copied an Ionic entablature from the Temple of
Fortuna Virilis. The frieze details, taken from another of his folios,
Antoine Desgodets's *Édifices Antiques de Rome*, depict an ox skull, garlands, and a cherub. One might wonder about the propriety of using
skulls to decorate a bedroom, but Jefferson was aware that the decorative elements of Roman temple architecture were symbolic rather
than literal. Ox skulls, their horns festooned with ribbons, were icons
suggesting the sacrifices of bulls to the gods in exchange for fecundity
and prosperity. In the parlor, a Corinthian frieze adapted from the
Temple of Jupiter the Thunderer uses an ox skull, knife, pitcher, and
decorative helmet, all related to rituals of religious sacrifice. Swagged
garlands, symbolic of festivity, and possibly fertility, were also a much-
repeated motif.

As in all of his architectural choices at Monticello, the cornice
and frieze details had to be matched to the skills of his workmen.
With the arrival of James Dinsmore as his chief joiner, he had a craftsman capable of fabricating and installing whatever wood moldings were
required for the three Palladian orders. He was also fortunate in locating in Washington an artist-manufacturer, George Andrews, who
carved the ornate elements of the cornice and frieze, cast molds for
them, and reproduced them in quantity in plaster composition. For
the Corinthian orders, for example, Jefferson commissioned Andrews
to reproduce specialized sections of the entablature: modillions for the
cornice, egg and anchor ovolos, roses for the soffits, and the entire
frieze. The composition ornaments were shipped to Monticello and
mounted by Dinsmore. Once painted, it was impossible to tell the
wooden from the composition elements.

Acquiring well-executed composition ornaments was an essential
part of producing Palladian interiors. During the end of his first term
as President, Jefferson came to the aid of James Oldham when the
housejoiner, who had established himself in business in Richmond,
needed ornaments for a job he was doing. "I observe you are fitting
up a Corinthian room for mr. Gallego," Jefferson wrote. "I am glad
to learn it, because a single example of chaste architecture may guide

the taste of the city." This is especially true, he added, when it is found that well-executed Palladian interiors cost "no more than the barbarous & tawdry fancies of each individual workman, and generally not so much." Jefferson introduced Oldham to Andrews and suggested that Andrews use the same molds for Oldham's job as he had carved and cast for the entrance hall of Monticello. Oldham had asked to have the ornaments from the parlor reproduced, even though they "are done in the Juish [Jewish] stile but I imagine that will make no difference with Mr. Galligo." Jefferson, however, decided otherwise. "The ornaments for your Corinthian frize are now in hand," he later wrote. "They are made in the same moulds with those of my Hall, far handsomer than those of the Parlour." The entrance hall frieze consists of winged griffins, urns, colonettes, and ornate floral motifs, and they are indeed arranged in a much more unified pattern than the rather disparate elements of the frieze in the parlor. Jefferson performed one more service for Oldham: a small baluster, part of the Corinthian modillion, if made of plaster composition, would have required that two halves be glued together. "As they warp a little in drying," Jefferson wrote, it "would make a bad job." He had one of the carpenters working on the President's House in Washington make the pieces of wood by turning them on a lathe. He then paid the carpenter and mailed the small decorations to Oldham. This act of generosity was typical of Jefferson. It was also perhaps an indication of how important he thought it was that Mr. Gallego's Corinthian room be finished with the finest workmanship possible, to "guide the taste" of Richmond.

During the year 1802, a time when Jefferson found the "steady and uniform" business of the presidency was keeping him at his writing desk "10 to 12 & 13 hours a day" with only "4 hours for riding, dining & a little unbending," he still managed to maintain a running Monticello construction correspondence with James Dinsmore. Jefferson had undoubtedly asked Dinsmore to report his progress regularly by letter, a request he was to make of his overseers, and even of John Hemings when he was working on the house at Poplar Forest. Dinsmore was an able correspondent; those of his letters that have survived show him to have been a close and detailed reporter. He is also shown to have been a craftsman confident in his abilities to solve the most

Letter to James Oldham, one of Jefferson's housejoiners: "A single example of chaste architecture may guide the taste of the city" of Richmond.

obstinate problems of carpentry. In constructing the paneling for the dining room, for example, he found that the method he had devised for joining the boards was defective, "on account of the tongue & groove giving way." Another way would have to be found for mounting the panels, Dinsmore wrote, although he was not yet certain "what method of putting them together will have to be substituted." There was no doubt raised, however, that a solution would be found; it was simply a matter of time.

A measure of Jefferson's maturity as a builder was his increasing willingness to allow his workmen more independence in making construction decisions. Part of this was necessity; once he assumed the presidency and was limited to twice-yearly visits to Monticello, he was no longer able to supervise the driving of every nail and the laying of each brick. To assure that steady progress was made, he was forced to give his workmen autonomy in the execution of their crafts. He provided them with detailed architectural drawings and the necessary materials and labor required, but because he was an absentee builder, he expected them to solve problems on their own. In an engineering decision so basic as the size of the ceiling joists for the dependencies, for instance, Jefferson wrote Dinsmore, "I leave this to yourself to decide," with the admonition, "let there be no danger of failure for want of due strength." He was, however, unremitting in his demand for accuracy and quality craftsmanship; hence, when Richardson put the columns up less than perfectly true, he insisted that they be taken down and placed correctly. But it was left to the workman to determine how it was to be done.

Correcting mistakes rather than allowing them to stand is a practice every owner-builder learns quickly; but mistakes sometimes do not appear until it is too late or too expensive to correct them. Jefferson recorded in his Construction Notebook, for example, that "a 7 I[nch]. architrave having been put [up] by mistake instead of one of 8 ½ I. the frize and cornice must be proportioned to the 7 I." In this case, the error, probably Dinsmore's, was allowed to remain. The composition ornaments for the cornice and frieze had probably not yet been ordered, and the sizes could be changed. In another instance, when Dinsmore discovered that some of the ornaments which had already been made for the cornice of the room were two inches too large, he asked Jefferson to replace them with ornaments the correct size. In this case, the ornaments were apparently initially ordered in the wrong size, a fault that probably rested with the architect.

Construction disagreements between Jefferson and Dinsmore sometimes took years to resolve. One such incident involved not handcrafted items such as entablature ornaments, but as common an object as sash weights. Early in 1802, Dinsmore received a shipment of sash weights Jefferson had sent from Washington. The weights, which were needed to counterbalance the heavy sash windows at Monticello, were made of iron instead of lead. Dinsmore reported that they did not fit "any of the new [window] frames." He contended that the weight-to-size ratio of lead was essential; iron weights had to be so large that they would not fit into the space allotted them. The difficulty for Jefferson was money; lead cost three to four times as much as iron, and was scarce. The sash weight problem remained unresolved for five years, which meant that during that time, the windows were raised and lowered with great difficulty, and had to be propped open. (Slaves, of course, suffered this inconvenience.) Finally, a decision had to be made; Jefferson tried to purchase a thousand pounds of lead in Richmond, but could find only fifty, and that was much too expensive. He asked Dinsmore once again to consider iron: could the weights be cast to the proper size in iron? The carpenter replied that some cutting and fitting could be done on the window boxes in which the weights were concealed, but there was no guarantee that there would not be obstructions. Jefferson decided to check in Washington whether they could be successfully cast in iron. He learned that they would be "so small & long that the small degree of warping which happens in their cooling will probably render them useless." After five years of procrastinating, Jefferson acquiesced to his construction foreman, paid the price, and ordered lead weights. Dinsmore replied tactfully that he was glad Jefferson had decided on lead; "it will answer much better."

This was not the first time that Jefferson's refusal to pay the market price for building materials caused him needless delays and personal anxiety. He agreed to purchase lumber from a neighbor, John B. Magruder, who operated a mill on the Rivanna River, but, as was often the case, no price was agreed on. When he received Magruder's bill for the plank, he refused to pay it, asserting that it "transcended all the bounds of moderation." Jefferson wrote Magruder that he was in the habit of paying six pounds per thousand board feet "for the finest flooring plank of the greatest lengths"; Magruder had asked three times this price. The normal way differences such as this were resolved in Virginia was through arbitration, by "good men of our mutual choice," as Jefferson put it. He asked that his overseer Gabriel Lilly and the carpenter John Perry attend the arbitration session because "they know nearly all the plank I have ever bought for my house, & the prices of it."

The arbitration decision favored Magruder, so Jefferson chose, instead of paying Magruder's price, to replace the lumber and receive back the partial payment he had already made. Five years later, after Jefferson had returned to Monticello from his second term as President, he had not yet replaced the timber, and Magruder was badgering him for it. He wrote to Perry in 1810 and asked him if he would cut the timber and return it to Magruder. Perry replied that no timber of the quality that Magruder had supplied was located within a reasonable distance. Jefferson offered to pay the price to haul it. Two years later, Magruder had still not received his lumber, and was understandably growing more impatient. In exasperation, Jefferson implored Perry to hurry with the lumber "that I may at length be done with it." Perry at last agreed to cut the timber—eight years after Magruder had first presented his bill.

This incident was exactly the kind that Jefferson deplored; it damaged his reputation for fairness in dealing with his neighbors and involved him in a conflict that lasted many years. It resulted from his long absences from Monticello, which kept him out of touch with market conditions and convinced him that local merchants and workers habitually overcharged him. In many cases he was right in this assumption, but he was also stubbornly unwilling to allow prices paid to local merchants and farmers to rise beyond what he had been paying for the past decade. This was one of the continuing reasons for the delays in his construction. When he thought a supplier had overpriced cherry wood to be used for the famed parquet floors of Monticello, he wrote to Thomas Mann Randolph, "Mr. Hudson, who was to supply the cherry wood, must therefore be declined and mr Dinsmore must finish his rooms without the floors, leaving them till we can supply ourselves with cherry at the usual price."

While Dinsmore was coping with delays such as this in finishing the interior of the house, work was proceeding with the dependencies. The extensive plans for the dependencies that Jefferson had developed with his wife Martha—none of which were built—had been considerably simplified for the remodeled house. The major change was the elimination of the many rooms intended for the passageways that ran from the house to the right angles forming an L. What had originally been planned as storage rooms or servants' quarters were reduced to bare underground tunnels. The north dependencies, anchored by the north pavilion, now contained carriage rooms, horse stables, a laundry, and an icehouse at the angle. On the south side of the house, the kitchen was located at the angle; along the passage to the south pavilion were a smoke room, dairy, and servants' quarters. In the basement of the house itself was a wine room, rum cellar, beer cellar, cider room, storage room, warming kitchen, and servants' rooms.

These dependencies required extensive excavations and stone work. Richard Richardson may have supervised digging on the south wings; the work was undoubtedly done by slave field hands and perhaps by some of the nail boys. The overseer Gabriel Lilly directed excavations on the north wing. The walls of the dependencies were made of field stone, laid mostly by the stonemason Joseph Moran, who worked on them for several years before quitting unexpectedly

Instructions to James Dinsmore on how to construct the Monticello icehouse.

at the end of 1801. In the spring and summer of 1802, Jefferson sent Dinsmore two long sets of instructions about such diverse subjects as how the partition walls of the dependencies were to be built, how many doors to place in the north dependency "necessary" (there was an outhouse in each dependency wing), and how to excavate for the coach house to assure it was high enough—nine feet—for a carriage. He also sent instructions for building his icehouse, one of the conveniences he had become accustomed to in the President's House in Washington.

Before the age of electrical refrigeration, ice was collected in winter and stored in the earth; if the supply was well managed, it would last through a summer of food preservation, cooled drinks, ices, and ice cream. An icehouse was not merely a luxury at Monticello, but an important item of economy. In 1809, Jefferson cautioned his overseer Edmund Bacon to be certain to fill the icehouse. "It would be a real calamity should we not have ice to do it," he wrote, "as it would require double the quantity of fresh meat in summer had we not ice to keep it." The rather simple technology of the icehouse had been known since antiquity; wine and fruit juices were cooled at the

Sir   Washington Dec. 30.08.

By Davy you will recieve a bundle containing 2. bells, & 4. bell-levers, the planes you wrote for, & 2 kneebolts. in a sepa--rate roll is the sand-paper you desired. the folding mahogany sash which closes the alcove of my bed is too heavy & troublesome. I with you to make a folding frame to fit the alcove & to be covered with paper on both sides. the frame must consist of 3 parts united by a pr of hinges, in this manner (observing first that it is to open vertically, and not horizontally as the mahogany one does) the piece a is in place of a stud, only to be thin, & of such breadth as to give it suf--ficient strength, & it will need very little. it is to be bolted at bottom into the floor, & at top into the rabbet of the architrave. to it are to be fasten--ed on each side the two wings b. &c. by hinges on which these wings will open easily so as to let them get at the bed to make it up. when open they will stand thus ☐ alcove ☐ the piece a remain--ing fixed. the two bolts which for the piece a but by mistake were got as knee bolts & therefore will not do. but I recollect to have seen in the stores at Mil-ton & Charlottesville round bolts of the same kind, but not kneed, which therefore I would pray you to get. they ought to be much smaller than these. you will find paper for this object in my cabinet there are 2. rolls, & I think they lie on the book shelves of the Eastern angle. if not there, they are somewhere in the cabinet. my best wishes attend you.

Mr. Dinsmore.   Th: Jefferson

Instructions to Jefferson's carpenter James Dinsmore for a folding screen to enclose his alcove bed. The screen, "to be covered with paper on both sides," replaced a "folding mahogany sash."

A *photograph of Monticello, taken about 1890, showing the restored "porticles"
in front of Jefferson's bedroom-library suite. They were later removed.*

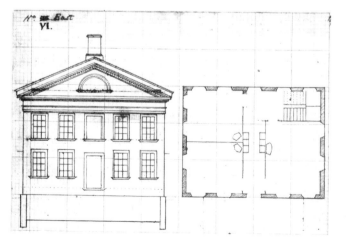

*Jefferson's drawing
of pavilion VI of the
University of Virginia,
showing stoves on the
second floor.*

...ferson's sketch for hanging blinds between the columns of the porticoes of Monticello. The ...ch indicates the blinds were possibly intended to fold into recesses in the ceiling.

Below: *Jefferson's sketch for one of two "porticles"—small louvered verandas that provided privacy for his bedroom-library suite.*

Jefferson's calculations for the number [of] bricks to make the six columns of the w[est] portico.

Below: *An inventory of "Carpenters tools belonging to Mr. Jefferson" prepared by James Dinsmore when he was leaving Monticello after working there for ten years.*

palace of Nero in ancient Rome by snow brought from the Alps and stored underground. Jefferson had designed an icehouse for the original Monticello, but like most of his ambitious plans for this house, it was never constructed. In the original plan, the icehouse was to be placed far from the dependencies, on the other side of Mulberry Row. In the remodeled version, the icehouse was located at the angle of the north offices where it was much more accessible. It was a sixteen-foot hole in the ground, its interior eight feet in diameter, lined with a stone wall that extended four feet above the ground, making the entire cistern twenty feet deep. The above-ground section had a door in the side for access and was covered with a wooden top on which was placed a layer of earth for insulation.

There was only one problem associated with an icehouse such as the one Jefferson designed—how to get rid of melted ice water. It was probably not until 1807 that Jefferson procured a pump to remove the water from the bottom of the icehouse. He wrote to his overseer Edmund Bacon in November of 1806 that "a pump maker at Charlottesville promised to fix a pump for me in the icehouse." From 1802, when the icehouse was completed, until 1807, water had to be removed manually. Jefferson contrived one of his typical ingenious devices for hauling the water out. He instructed Dinsmore to make a six-inch-square tube, long enough to run from the bottom of the icehouse out through the top. Then he was to make a square bucket with a hole in the bottom to fit inside the tube. "Nail a bit of stiff leather as a valve" over the hole in the bucket, he wrote, "so that when it goes down it may fill up with water." The filled bucket, guided by the interior walls of the tube, would then be hauled up with a rope. As an afterthought, he added that the tube and bucket might be tighter and work better if they were made round rather than square. "In this do as you think best," he informed Dinsmore. In May 1804, Jefferson sent instructions to have his blacksmith William Stewart "make Joe draw off the water from the icehouse twice a week. I at the same time supposed that mr Wanscher taking his water from thence might keep it always down." This gives some idea of how rapidly the ice melted in the warmer months. (Normally it lasted until September or October.) It also demonstrates the chronic scarcity of water on the mountaintop; for his plastering needs, the German plasterer Wanscher was to use melted ice water.

The icehouse was filled as soon as the weather became cold enough to form an inch of ice on the Rivanna River. When Jefferson first constructed the icehouse, it was filled exclusively with river ice, which was not edible. Later, he built another icehouse by the Rivanna River, filled it each winter with river ice, and probably used it primarily for food preservation. The icehouse at Monticello was then filled with snow, which was edible, and could be used directly in drinks or ices. Jefferson filled the Monticello icehouse for the first time in the winter of 1803. He recorded in his Garden Book on March 12, "my ice house here has taken 62. waggon loads of ice to fill it, have 1. foot thickness of shavings all around. the whole cost including labour, feeding, drink etc. has been 70. D." Filling the icehouse was given a high priority. In the winter of 1806, Jefferson notified Bacon to have the wagons from the various farms converge "at a moment's warning, laying aside all other work." The icehouse could be filled, he wrote, in four days. "Ice of 1¾ I. thick from a pond 50. yds square will fill it." The method Jefferson used for insulating the ice in its cistern was essentially the same technique described in Diderot and d'Alembert's *Encyclopédie*, a work he owned and often referred to. The bottom of the icehouse was to be latticed with boards and these covered with a bed of straw. As the ice was poured in, the walls were to be lined with straw and the ice tamped to form a solid mass. The top of the ice was then covered with a thick insulation of straw. Because of the carpentry work being done at Monticello, wood shavings were an abundant waste product and were substituted for straw by Jefferson. To retrieve a portion of ice from the Monticello icehouse, a ladder was lowered into the cistern, and one of the slaves would brush aside the shavings and chop a block of ice with an ax.

Not only did Jefferson construct a cistern for holding ice, he built four others for storing rainwater. These were also placed at the angles of the dependencies, convenient locations for capturing the runoff water from the roofs of Monticello and its dependencies. A ready source of water was necessary, not only for drinking, but also for fire protection. (The north pavilion caught fire in 1819 and the blaze was kept from spreading by covering the adjoining terrace with snow from the icehouse.) Before Jefferson's cisterns were built, he had instructed Dinsmore to install gutters on the terrace eaves "so that we may hereafter lead the water to the terras easily into tubs . . . to hold a sufficient supply of water for a case of fire." A permanent storage system was obviously needed, and Jefferson went about designing it with typical thoroughness. He calculated the total roof area of the main house, pavilions, and dependencies, multiplied them by the average yearly rainfall at Monticello—a figure he arrived at after years of daily observations—and concluded that four cisterns, each an eight-foot cube, would furnish him with six hundred gallons of water a day. The brickwork for the cisterns was completed in 1810, but it was to be many more years before they held any rainwater. The problem was finding a waterproof plaster for the cisterns.

Jefferson queried virtually everyone he knew in an attempt to learn what material was suitable. Not surprisingly, William Thornton offered not one, but two solutions. Thornton wrote Jefferson a long letter describing the two methods for making hydraulic cement, one using a volcanic ash, pozzolana ("the Roman Baths are made in this way"), and another using an unlikely mixture of molasses, lime, and sand. He also enclosed a finely drawn sketch of a homemade filter that he had invented for clearing cider, but which, he assured Jefferson, could be used to render water "perfectly sweet." If Thornton's cement formulas were tried, neither worked.

William Coffee, the New York artist-sculptor who did terra-cotta busts of two of Jefferson's granddaughters and carved the interior frieze ornaments for the house at Poplar Forest, supplied Jefferson with the solution to his cistern problem. In 1818, he sent a detailed set of instructions for the use of Roman cement, a hydraulic mortar imported from England and commonly used in New York City. He even offered to supervise its installation. "My only reward for two or three days Inspection," he wrote, "will be two glasses of good wine every day after dinner." Coffee came to Monticello as promised and "instructed a bricklayer, a black man," how to use the Roman cement. In the summer of 1822, twelve years after the cisterns were first constructed, Jefferson recorded measurements in one of them and noted that an inch of rainfall raised the water nine inches. Even with Coffee's supervision and assistance, however, the cisterns were not entirely free of leaks. In fact, during Jefferson's lifetime, only two of the four cisterns at Monticello consistently held water.

Jefferson's experience with his cisterns demonstrates one of the limitations of the owner-builder method of construction. He could not duplicate at Monticello what Roman engineers had perfected 1,500 years before and what was being done routinely in cities such as New York. Even after Jefferson acquired the necessary hydraulic cement for lining his cisterns, his workmen did not have the skill to apply it competently. Professional workmen who repeatedly perform construction tasks master them through the traditional ways of the hand, the harmony of motion, tool, and material that is acquired only with time. This is why the medieval guild system demanded an apprenticeship period of years to teach crafts that could be superficially acquired in months. An owner-builder, even an experienced one such as Jefferson, who does a job only once or twice, must learn by trial and error what is accomplished routinely by professional builders. This was even more true of the slaves who had to execute Jefferson's architectural and engineering plans. They had gone through no formal apprenticeships; their skills were usually picked up from a number of transient workmen, and they had limited opportunity to practice them. Such tasks were usually finished satisfactorily—unlike the cisterns—but there was a heavy cost in time, an important reason why Monticello took a lifetime to build.

There was one other design problem connected with the dependencies. Jefferson had demonstrated splendid architectural ingenuity in placing on the roof of the dependencies a wooden deck that served as a promenade and gave an unobstructed vista from the house. But what was to be done with the chimneys coming from the rooms below the terrace, particularly the kitchen? From Jefferson's earliest plans for the original house, this problem "troubled him greatly," as Fiske Kimball put it, because chimneys "were likely to be excrescences no matter how formed." He first situated the rooms requiring fireplaces at the corners of the dependencies, or adjacent to them. He then considered several ways of concealing the chimney flues. These included hollowing out columns, building an obelisk with holes near the top, or using iron pipes to carry the smoke a distance away. None of these was practical, so he settled upon a straightforward approach: bringing the chimney flues up through the terrace, "the shafts to be no higher than the balustrading." This solution violated a principle that was to be formulated in a later age by John Ruskin. In a cottage, a chimney is "a beautiful accompaniment," Ruskin wrote, "but in buildings of a higher class, smoke ceases to be interesting." The associations aroused, he declared, "are not dignified; we may think of a comfortable fireside, perhaps, but are quite as likely to dream of kitchens, and spits, and shoulders of mutton." Not dreams, but odors wafted from Jefferson's kitchen and smokehouse chimneys, both facing his own bedroom suite on the south side of the house. The chimneys were handsomely shaped as Palladian Doric pedestals, but because they were only four feet high, they must have blown smoke into the house, a frequent occurrence in the summer when all the windows were wide open.

The chimneys on the main house presented no such problem, for they were raised well above the roof level. The fireplaces in the house, however, not only smoked on occasion, they gave off very little heat. Monticello was not unique in having inefficient fireplaces; most eighteenth-century fireplaces were poorly designed—a rectangular masonry box with a chimney coming straight out at the top. Even a roaring fire merely sent its heat up the chimney while pulling cold air into the room from uninsulated walls, floors, doors, and windows. Not only did fireplaces fail to heat rooms; if cold air came down the flue, they smoked. The problem of getting more heat from a fireplace was most successfully solved in the American colonies by Benjamin Franklin with his famous stove. The Franklin stove was a cast-iron fireplace insert designed to channel air from the room through the stove, heat it and then release it back into the room. Smoke traveled a greater distance by passing down a flue in the back of the stove, and then up into the chimney. This helped prevent smoking. The effectiveness of the stove was due in part to its reducing the firebox and chimney throat, thereby controlling combustion and giving off radiant heat. Franklin's stoves would not fit all fireplaces, however, and manufacturers modified them considerably, often making them aesthetically more acceptable, but less efficient.

In Europe, improved fireplace design was associated with Benjamin Thompson, Count Rumford. An American born at Woburn, Massachusetts, in 1753, Rumford was a farmer's son who rose spectacularly to become a count of the Holy Roman Empire. At the age of nineteen, he took the first of a number of opportunistic leaps that would lead him from obscurity to fame and riches, marrying a wealthy widow fourteen years his senior. This introduced him to the circle of Governor John Wentworth of New Hampshire and established him politically as a loyalist. At the outbreak of the Revolutionary War, he became a Tory spy and was eventually forced to leave the country. Establishing himself in England, he acquired a powerful patron, Lord George Germain, secretary of state for the colonies, largely, according to London gossip, because of a homosexual liaison between the two men. He rose quickly to power and affluence and, during the waning years of the war, he returned to America as a Lieutenant Colonel in the British cavalry, engaging in several skirmishes at Charleston and Long Island, actions that would not improve his reputation with the author of the Declaration of Independence. After the war, he returned to London and was knighted, but, Lord George Germain then being out of power, he attached himself to the elector of Bavaria in Munich. It was there that he rose to the height of his personal power, becoming minister of war, minister of police, and grand chamberlain to the elector. And it was in Bavaria that he engaged in many of his experiments on the properties of heat, which later led him to practical applications in the design of fireplaces and cooking apparatus. He ultimately settled in France, marrying the wealthy widow of the celebrated chemist Lavoisier.

His life was unquestionably that of an adventurer and soldier of fortune, but he was also one of those inquisitive, creative intellectuals that the Enlightenment produced in abundance. From his earliest years he had engaged in scientific experimentation and had become a fellow of the Royal Society by the age of twenty-seven.

The device that won him an international reputation as a scientist and benefactor of mankind was his Rumford fireplace. He developed a method for altering a standard masonry fireplace to make it smaller and to throw more heat into the room. To "Rumfordize" a fireplace, the sides, or "cheeks," were sharply angled to radiate heat outward into the room; the rear was brought forward to reduce the volume of the burning chamber, and, most importantly, the throat—the opening into the chimney flue—was reduced to four inches, creating a ledge behind it. This "smoke shelf," as it is termed today, prevents cold air from pouring, without obstruction, down the rear of the flue into the firebox, one of the main causes of a smoky fireplace. If a damper were to be added to the throat of the firebox, and the top third of the rear wall angled forward, Rumford's fireplace would be essentially what is now found in tens of millions of houses all over the world.

A number of manufacturers took Rumford's designs and built cast-iron stoves that were inserted into a fireplace in the same manner as Franklin's stove. This eliminated the necessity of obtaining a mason knowledgeable enough to construct a brick Rumford fireplace. Jefferson, who owned a copy of Rumford's works, which included detailed instructions on how to build a Rumford fireplace, converted two of his fireplaces, those in the two ground floor "square room" bedrooms, into brick Rumford fireplaces by extending the fireboxes forward into the room. He also decided to design his own cast-iron Rumford fireplaces and have them built. These turned out to be failures. They "smoke so," he commented, "that I am obliged to give them up. I should be afraid to try others." In their place, he asked the architect Benjamin Latrobe to select for him at Philadelphia three "of the handsomest stoves, of the kind called Open stoves, or Rittenhouse stoves, which are in fact nothing more than the Franklin stove, leaving out the double back and flues formed in supplying warm air." There was no practical reason for adding this piece of historical information in a request for a purchase, but Jefferson wanted his architect friend to be made aware of certain priorities: "the Rittenhouse stove," he lectured, "is the one commonly used in Philadelphia, and was the model & origin of the Rumford fireplace, which is a Rittenhouse stove in brick instead of iron." The clear suggestion is that Rumford stole an American idea and passed it off as his own without credit. The astronomer David Rittenhouse, of whom Jefferson had written, "as an artist he has exhibited as great a proof of mechanical genius as the world has produced," had improved the Franklin stove by simplifying it. In the 1790s, it replaced the Franklin stove in popularity. The Rittenhouse stove was an advance over the Rumford stove in that not only were the sides sharply angled, but the back plate was also angled forward to the throat, directing radiant heat downward into the room.

Rumford, in his writings on chimneys and fireplaces, does indeed fail to credit either Rittenhouse or Franklin for their work in this field, even though, as his biographer notes, "it is pretty clear from careful reading of Rumford's essay that he had Franklin's paper very much in mind while writing his own." Franklin's *Observations on the Cause and Cures of Smoking Chimneys* was well known in Europe and his scientific authority was unimpeachable. It was not mere American chauvinism that prompted Jefferson to attack Rumford's precedence in this field, however; the attack was undoubtedly also based on personal dislike for the man. When Rumford was still Benjamin Thompson in London, he was responsible for having the American artist John Trumbull jailed on suspicion of treason when he voyaged to England during the war to study painting with Benjamin West. It was Trumbull who introduced Jefferson to Maria Cosway when Jefferson was in France, and Jefferson almost certainly learned from him the full story, not only of Thompson's anti-Americanism, but also of his scandalous career in London. Rumford later expressed a desire to return to America and received permission to do so from President John Adams. Rumford changed his mind, but it is questionable whether the same welcome would have been offered by Adams's successor, President Thomas Jefferson.

Even with the improvement of a cast-iron stove insert, a fireplace was a poor method of heating a room. A freestanding stove, connected to the fireplace flue with a stove pipe, is vastly more effective; it radiates heat in all directions from its cast-iron plates. The aesthetic disadvantage of the freestanding stove, as Franklin recognized, is that you cannot enjoy watching the fire. The stove itself is often dirty, unsightly, subject to rusting, and requires that the fireplace opening be blocked off. Jefferson was sometimes willing to forgo aesthetics for comfort, however. As early as 1795, he wrote Thomas Mann Randolph, asking for black lead for "cleaning our stoves, which we have set up much to our comfort & the economy of wood, for I think we have double the heat with half the wood." An undated note in his Memorandum Book mentions a "10. plate stove in my room," quite possibly one of those he needed the black lead for, and one of the five stoves he brought back from France. (A ten-plate stove is a rectangular box stove, named after the number of iron plates used in its construction. It usually has tall legs to protect the floor it stands on from excessive heat.) And in 1809, he sent to a Georgetown iron monger, Henry J.

Foxall, a model for a freestanding stove. The stove was built and delivered three years later, and Jefferson was delighted with it. "I have set it up and find it to answer perfectly. The room is very small where it is placed, and it is fully warmed by it in a few minutes," he wrote. The "very small" room would appear to be the tearoom, one of the coldest rooms in the house in the winter, because of its arc of windows. In a floor plan of Monticello drawn by Cornelia Randolph, one of Jefferson's granddaughters, there is a reference to a "Niche in the Tearoom intended for a statue but with a stove in it." Because this tiny room had no fireplace flue, the stove pipe would have had to be vented outside the house, an unsightly expedient.

Jefferson also asked Foxall about a larger stove for the dome room. Still another reason why this room was virtually useless was that it had no heat source, obviously because there was no way of providing a chimney flue without marring the appearance of the dome from the exterior. Apparently no stove was ever installed in it.

In the architectural designs Jefferson executed after his presidency, his recognition of the superiority of the freestanding stove over the fireplace can be readily seen. In plans for Barboursville, a house he designed for James Barbour of Orange County, Virginia, the public rooms show fireplaces, but the second-story bedrooms have freestanding stoves connected to concealed flues. And in his drawings, done late in his life, for the pavilions of the University of Virginia, freestanding stoves are also indicated for the upstairs rooms.

The function of the fireplace is not the only concern in fireplace design, however. In Palladian interiors, the mantel of the fireplace normally imitates in miniature the frieze decorations of the architrave of the room and is an integral part of the overall aesthetic. Jefferson imitated the frieze designs of the hall and parlor on the fireplace mantels of those rooms. In the dining room, he altered this pattern by setting into the mantel frieze two oval medallions and a plaque depicting Greek muses from the *Apotheosis of Homer* in the British Museum. They were in Wedgwood, their pale blue background matching the dining room walls.

Stylish fireplace openings were usually bordered with marble. The marble fascias of the fireplaces of Monticello were not installed until 1825, less than a year before Jefferson's death. In ordering them a year earlier, he sent a detailed set of measurements to Thomas Appleton, the American consul at Leghorn, Italy, who had for two decades been sending plants and seeds for Jefferson's gardens. Appleton had commissioned an Italian sculptor to make marble capitals for the columns of buildings at the University of Virginia. This gave Jefferson an opportunity to have fireplace decorations made economically for Monticello, replacing wooden fascias with elegant marble ones. They could be shipped to Virginia with the university marbles. He sent dimensions for plinths, uprights, and horizontal sections for eight fireplaces, three large and five small, "with one of the three larger ones a handsome marble." The three large fireplaces were in the parlor, dining room, and Jefferson's bedroom. Appleton reported that "no pains were spared, either in procuring beauty of marble, or in their execution." Seven were of the best "common marble," the eighth, at double the cost, was "from a new quarry lately discover'd, of a beautiful variety of colours." Termed "Venato Nuvotato" by Appleton, this is the marble—black with multicolored grain—that adorns one of the most striking of all Monticello's fireplaces, that commanding the central space of the parlor.

Jefferson gave particular attention to the interior decoration and furnishings of the parlor, the symmetrical focal point of the house and its most spacious public room. The twin glass partition doors from the hall to the parlor, for example, were meant to be a conversation piece from the time he installed them, and continue to be so to visitors today. When one door is pushed, both doors swing open, apparently by magic, for there is no visible mechanical connection between them. This piece of architectural legerdemain defied analysis until the mansion was restored extensively in the 1950s and the floor boards were pulled up to disclose its simple chain-and-pulley mechanism. On the bottom pivot corner of each door is a rod that runs through the floor and is attached to a small metal drum, which acts as a pulley. A hand-wrought chain in the shape of a figure eight is affixed to the two drums; when a door is pushed, the rotation of its drum, through the motion of the chain, causes the other drum to rotate in the opposite direction, swinging the door open. Jefferson is probably responsible for the design of this simple mechanism, but the parts were undoubtedly crafted by his master blacksmith, William Stewart.

The mahogany-framed glass doors themselves were made by James Oldham, the joiner who befriended the young slave James Hemings and allowed him to escape. After working at Monticello for several years, Oldham had gone to Richmond in 1804 to establish himself in business. Jefferson wrote him a letter of recommendation, citing him as an "able workman in housejoinery, skilled in the orders of architecture, honest, sober, and industrious. He wishes to get into business on a larger scale than that of merely monthly wage, and I have recommended Richmond to him."

Oldham found that there was no work in Richmond, so he wrote to Jefferson asking whether there was any employment for housejoiners in Washington. Jefferson replied that nothing was available, but that he needed a number of doors and window sashes made and was willing to have Oldham do the work at Richmond. Oldham quickly accepted. During the next two years, he produced twenty-five interior doors, including the glass partition doors for the parlor, as well as semicircular window sashes for the exterior pediments, and the five large, arched windows of the piazza-greenhouse in Jefferson's private suite. Oldham's account of the trials he underwent in making these doors and sashes provides a paradigm for construction practices in Virginia during the early American republic and helps explain why delays were as common as sawdust.

Oldham promised Jefferson he would immediately "procure Lumber for to begin your worke," and asked for "money to pay for the Lumber as my circumstances will not admit of a beginning on my own footing." He quickly discovered, however, that on visiting "all the sawmills in the cuntery within Twelve miles round" there was no seasoned lumber to be found. "The Lumber that is maid use of in this plaice is all green." This would prevent him from making Jefferson's doors and sashes—unless Jefferson was willing to wait a year, for in that time he "could procure good Lumber for the purpose." Jefferson offered the opinion that if Richmond builders "do all their housejoinery with green stuff they are much behind even what I had expected." He inquired whether kiln-dried lumber would not serve as well as air-dried, seasoned lumber, and agreed to wait a year. Oldham reported back that kiln-dried lumber was indeed just as serviceable as air-dried, but "there is no such thing as a Kiln for drying Lumber in Richmond." He intended to build his own, however.

Three months later, Oldham informed Jefferson that he had acquired "very nice plank for the purpose of making your doors and sashes," and had prepared a kiln to dry it. Two weeks after writing this, he had bad news to report: "Unfortunately for me Last nite about Twelve Oclock my plank kiln took fiar and was intirly consumd." The lumber intended for Jefferson's doors and sashes was in the kiln, but Oldham would take the financial loss himself. In the meantime, he needed money to purchase more lumber to try again. Another two months passed, however, before Oldham wrote that he had "just finished drying plank for your worke." Exactly how he dried it was not made clear. A month later, Oldham announced that he was building a workshop and asked Jefferson for $100. "Your doors are now in hand," he declared, "and shal proceed to finish them as fast as possible." He also sent suggested drawings for the greenhouse sashes, but Jefferson responded with a long letter detailing exactly how he wanted these sashes made: "I took these measures with great accuracy, and as the rest of the work is doing on the same measures, I wish your sashes to conform to them."

Two weeks later, June 30, 1805, Oldham informed Jefferson that he was shipping fourteen doors, but he did "not have a sufficiency of Lumber to compleat the hole of the doors as early as I could wish owing to my calculating the quantity two scant." He reiterated the difficulty of finding seasoned lumber that could be planed to 1½-inch thickness, the width of Jefferson's doors; the doors in most houses were 1¼ inches thick. Even door hinges proved to be a problem. Jefferson ordered his agent in Richmond to supply Oldham with two dozen door hinges, but Oldham could find only one dozen.

In October 1805, a year after Oldham accepted Jefferson's order for doors and window sashes, the joiner wrote: "Your dores and sashes are not all in redyness as yet owing to the difficulty of getting seasoned Lumber. In a few days I expect to get a plank-kiln erected of my own when shal be enabled to proceed much better." Jefferson replied four months later with an ultimatum: "It is now become very material that the whole doors should be finished & got to Monticello as speedily as possible, as my painter will otherwise have left me. He is a most capital hand, & should he not paint them, it may be years before I have another opportunity." This had the desired effect, because in six weeks Oldham wrote that he had shipped twenty-five doors and the sashes for the greenhouse windows; the semi-circular sashes for the pediments would soon follow. "The largest portion of the work was executed by myself and am persuaded in belief you will be pleased."

The correspondence between Jefferson and Oldham is revealing, not only for its insights into the difficulties of producing quality craftsmanship in rural America in the early nineteenth century, but also for its demonstration of the egalitarianism born of a shared commitment to the craft. The emergence in the twentieth century of Jefferson as one of the nation's foremost architects has obscured the fact that he was also a builder with a professional understanding of the construction crafts and their craftsmen. His involvement with his workers in the construction of Monticello sliced through political, economic, and class barriers and allowed builder and artisan to communicate, not as President of the United States and a hired hand, but as professional equals. Jefferson was generous to Oldham when he needed generosity and tolerant when he experienced difficulties and delays. He aided Oldham in getting work and material for other jobs, gave him financial advice, and even collected money for him in Washington. He deferred to the housejoiner's superior knowledge of his craft, but asserted an employer's prerogatives in setting deadlines and demanding that they be met. His willingness to allow Oldham to make the doors and sashes at Richmond was a combination of generosity and self-interest, common components of any professional relationship: he gave work to Oldham when he was between jobs and needed money, but in return he received, at a very good price, quality carpentry—some of it in mahogany, an imported wood not readily available in Albemarle County.

Oldham paid the proper deference to Jefferson's social rank and political office, but he did not hesitate to ask the nation's President to look after his business interests in Washington. One could not imagine the head of state of any nation of Europe establishing this kind of relationship with a carpenter. There was no doubt a certain amount of paternalism on Jefferson's part; he considered all workers at Monticello—slaves and craftsmen alike—a part of his extended family, to be cared for and protected. But in the case of Dinsmore, Neilson, Stewart, Chisholm, and Oldham, artisans who had reached the peak of their crafts, he exhibited the same professional equality shown to the scientific friends and colleagues with whom he exchanged theoretical or useful knowledge. Professional skill seldom failed to win Jefferson's admiration and respect, particularly if it was a skill he needed. It also gained entrance into his extensive circle of correspondents, with both the privilege of asking favors and the obligation of executing them. These were the courtesies gentlemen had always shown each other in the far-flung plantation economy of the South, where lending and borrowing, carrying messages, dropping off packages, purchasing items, and seeking out useful information was asked for or proffered as a matter of course. To refuse such requests was a breach of an unwritten code of etiquette. Jefferson extended these privileges to his craftsmen, not as a theoretical exercise in democracy, but because he considered their knowledge the equal to any. A house-joiner such as Oldham, who was literate, to whom he loaned one of his precious editions of Palladio (and whom he tried to aid in buying one for himself), was not a mere employee, but a fellow builder, and as such was due all the goodwill, benefits, and emoluments enjoyed by Jefferson's numerous friends and correspondents.

Oldham was not without his faults; he was quick-tempered and did not get along with his fellow workers. "His temper is unhappy," Jefferson wrote of him, and disclosed the reason Oldham left Monticello: because of "disagreements with his brother-workmen . . . without any displeasure between him and myself." The particular workers Jefferson referred to were Gabriel Lilly, the overseer at Monticello, and the carpenter John Perry. In a long letter to Jefferson, Oldham claimed that Lilly called him "one of the moost vilest reches on earth," and refused to allow him to return to Monticello for his tools and clothing. Lilly, he wrote, threatened to "blow me thro if I attempted to pass." He further accused Lilly and his "purgered brother-in-law John Perry" of getting "beastly drunk" on Jefferson's wine, of falsifying lumber charges, and of stealing flour and pork. He fell out with Lilly, Oldham reported, within six weeks after his arrival at Monticello when he refused to aid the overseer in punishing Lewis, John Hemings's and Oldham's slave assistant. "Luis went off from me twice," Oldham wrote, "but it is well [k]nown that I never punished him, and have many a time wishd that I had of never seen him." A more serious charge leveled by Oldham was that Lilly plotted with

Perry and others to murder Jefferson's tenant, John Craven, a plot that was thwarted, according to Oldham, when he learned of it.

Jefferson's response to Oldham's shower of accusations was an Olympian refusal to get involved, with an admonition against "bickering" reminiscent of the one he gave to his daughter Maria at her marriage:

> It is my rule never to take a side in any part in the quarrels of others, nor to inquire into them. I generally presume them to flow from the indulgence of too much passion on both sides, & always find that each party thinks all the wrong was in his adversary. These bickerings, which are always useless, embitter human life more than any other cause: and I regret that which has happened in the present case.

Like Dinsmore, Neilson, Chisholm, and Perry, Oldham later worked at the construction of the University of Virginia. After Jefferson's death, he opened a tavern at Staunton and his aggressiveness emerged once again: he shot a neighbor's son in a tavern altercation, but was never indicted for it.

Jefferson could have been particularly sympathetic with Oldham's report of the loss of his first kiln; the year before, his own lumber kiln at Monticello burned to the ground. His daughter Maria reported to her husband the "misfortune that has happn'd at Monticello, the burning of the plankhouse just after it had been completely fill'd with flooring plank & timber for the cornices." Jefferson's granddaughter Anne Cary Randolph informed him of the fire. The kiln contained, she wrote, wood for "the floor of the hall and the Music gallery." Jefferson had been kiln-drying lumber at Monticello for some time. After his kiln burned down, Jefferson immediately instructed Dinsmore to construct a fireproof kiln made of brick. It was designed so that its opening could be closed to smother flames in case of a fire. This is probably the kiln that appears on an 1806 survey of the property, at the northeast arc of the first roundabout.

Fortunately, the burned kiln did not contain the cherry and beech wood used for the parquet floor in the parlor. This floor, one of the first of its kind in America, was laid by John Hemings and Lewis over a subfloor of two-inch oak. A family member described its practical beauty:

> The floor of this room is in squares, the squares being ten inches, of the wild cherry, very hard, susceptible of a high polish, and the color of mahogany. The corner of each square, four inches wide, is of beech, light-colored, hard, and bearing a high polish. Its original cost was two hundred dollars. After nearly seventy years of use and abuse, a half-hour's dusting and brushing will make it compare favorably with the handsomest tessellated floor.

Jefferson, who had seen parquet floors in France, made drawings of several patterns, quite possibly in an effort to find the best way to make a virtue of economy. The expense of cherry wood and his refusal to pay the market price for it may well have influenced his decision to design a floor that used small, less expensive and more available pieces of cherry wood. The pattern he chose used more than twice as much beech as cherry.

Even more striking than the parquet floor, perhaps, were the floors of the entrance halls and dome room. They were painted in a fashionable color of the period—grass green. Jefferson sent to Dinsmore a swatch of paint showing the precise color he wanted. It came from no mere house painter, but from the pallet of Gilbert Stuart. Jefferson was at Stuart's studio and they were discussing Stuart's enthusiasm for green floors "which he had himself tried with fine effect." Stuart "observed that care should be taken to hit the true *grass* green, & as he had his pallet & colours in his hand I asked him to give me a specimen of the colours, which he instantly mixed up . . . and I spread it with a knife in the enclosed paper." Jefferson added that "the painters here [Washington] talk of putting a japan varnish over the painted floor and floor cloth," indicating he planned an additional covering over the painted floor. A visitor to Monticello late in Jefferson's life reported that the entrance hall was "covered with a glossy oil cloth."

The floors were given their green coat by Jefferson's master painter, Richard Barry, who painted the entire house over the course of more than two years. Barry was hired by Jefferson from the Washington area at $30 a month, and he stayed at Monticello for two periods, 1805–06 and 1807–08. Two years seems an extraordinary amount of time to paint a house, but Jefferson was either unwilling or unable to hire more than one painter, and there was a lot of painting to do at the mansion. Barry took as his apprentice Jefferson's personal servant Burwell. After Barry left, Burwell became Monticello's painter during the remainder of Jefferson's life.

House painting during the late eighteenth and early nineteenth centuries took much more skill than is required in our age of manufactured paints and high-speed application techniques. Paints and varnishes were mixed by hand, and colors were created by eye. The only method of application was by brush or spatula. Like most of the building trades, painting technology had changed little in hundreds of years. Paint was made possible by the properties of certain vegetable oils, particularly linseed oil, which is derived from pressed flax seed. When most other oils are spread thin and allowed to dry, they form a sticky, gummy residue, but boiled linseed oil will spread into a hard, tough film. If resins are added, it becomes varnish; the addition of white lead and pigment produces paint. Master painters such as Barry were expert at mixing linseed oil, white lead, color pigment, and turpentine into a high-quality paint. They were also skilled in applying paint, not only in single colors, but in an imitation of grained wood, marble, or stone. Barry painted imitation wood grain and stone at Monticello, and quite possibly artificial marble for the fireplace fascias, which were later replaced by the real thing. Some of the finest painting done by Barry was on the interior doors that had been made by James Oldham in Richmond. Pine doors on the ground floor of the house were painted to simulate the wood grain of fine hardwood. This *faux bois* or French grain effect has been recently restored on Monticello's paneled doors.

Imitation stone was also painted on the four stone columns of the east portico. Richard Richardson had wrestled with these columns in an attempt to erect them perfectly straight. By the time the drums of the columns were finally placed in position, their edges had been chipped and worn, and no amount of patching with mortar could reproduce the appearance of a shaft of stone. The solution was to fill the joints with mortar and then paint artificial stone color on the columns. Until a few years ago, the columns were painted white, but restorers determined that a tan imitation of stone was what Jefferson had ordered from his painter. This is confirmed by a comment in a letter from Jefferson's mason, Hugh Chisholm: "the Plarstring is all finished and I am at this time sanding the colloms for Mr Barry to paint."

In painting the interior and exterior woodwork, Barry used four coats of paint, probably two prime coats and two finish coats. He gave an estimate before moving to Monticello of the amount of paint needed to cover the interior, exterior, and roof of the house: 424 pounds of white lead, 127 gallons of linseed oil, and 85 gallons of turpentine, at a cost of $240. This was exclusive of pigments, varnishes, and, of course, his labor. These figures were grossly underestimated, however, for the amount of white lead alone was triple Barry's estimate. His original estimate failed to take into account, for example, the large amount of paint necessary for the terraces.

Besides the oil-based painting, there was also much water-based whitewashing to be done. Whitewash, made by slaking quicklime in water, was frequently applied to walls and ceilings of houses during this period as a sanitary measure. At Monticello, plastered ceilings and walls were whitewashed, or in some cases the plaster was left unpainted. Whitewash was also mixed with pigment to give various tints to the walls. Although white was the dominant color for the interior decorative moldings, at least one of the entablatures was painted in color. Jefferson's granddaughter Ellen Wayles Randolph, after seeing the newly painted entrance hall for the first time, wrote, "I think the hall with its gravel coloured border is the most beautifull room I ever was in." She added that the portico columns were "rough cast and look very well."

Early in his remodeling plans, in 1792, Jefferson had intended to decorate the plastered walls and ceilings of the public rooms of the house—hall, parlor, and dining room—with fresco paintings. He attempted to lure a New York fresco painter named Schneider to Monticello, but was unwilling to pay the painter's price of 2 dollars a day. Even if Jefferson had decided to hire Schneider at his asking wage, it is unlikely the wall would ever have been painted with frescoes;

Jefferson's anticipated time schedule was much too optimistic for the actualities of his construction. The walls of Monticello were not ready for plastering for more than another decade, and by that time he had accumulated enough paintings, prints, maps, and archaeological curios to fill most of the wall space available.

A relatively cheap way of decorating walls—the application of wallpaper—was not exploited by Jefferson. Although he brought back 145 rolls of wallpaper from France, little of it found its way to the walls of Monticello; most of it was used in his residence in Philadelphia. Only the north octagonal room was papered—with a "Lattice and Treillage" pattern that he had purchased in Paris.

Because of the ephemeral nature of housepainting, Richard Barry's craftsmanship, unlike that of Monticello's housejoiners and masons, has vanished beneath subsequent coats of varnish and paint. Through the art of twentieth-century technology, however, solvents have probed beneath 180 years of accumulated paint and dirt and have enabled restorers to reveal, and in some cases duplicate, Barry's original colors. Barry's hand can still be seen in Oldham's greenhouse sashes, and in the famed parlor partition doors, for, like most painters of the period, he was also a glazier, and cut or installed the glass in these doors and windows.

Jefferson provoked Barry's anger by postponing the painter's second trip to Monticello from the spring of 1807 to September, "as the most important thing you have to do here is to finish the floor of the hall & to paint the floor of the Dome room exactly in the same way." Barry responded indignantly, "I have had four applications to me within these two months past, I have rejected them all in order to comply with my engagements with you in returning as soon as I would finish here [in Washington]. Mr Calverts of Blandenburgh was the last, which I have accepted. Intend going out there this day to commence work."

This did not sour the relationship between worker and employer, however. Barry, for example, was quite willing, as were other Monticello craftsmen, to defer payment for his work when Jefferson informed him at the end of his presidency that "on winding up my affairs in Washington I fell considerably in arrears." Jefferson asked him to consider the $243 debt as capital being kept at interest "and laid by as it were for future investment." Jefferson heard that Barry had attempted to discount his note, a common practice in a period of money scarcity, and asked Barry to spare him the embarrassment of having his paper placed in the hands of strangers where payment could be called for at any time. Barry replied that it was all a mistake. "I can assure you Sir," he wrote, "if it was one hundred times the sum and that I was without a coat to my back I would never put your paper into the hands of any man[,] *even* to limit you to a time of payment." Jefferson responded with gratitude for the "kind dispositions" shown by Barry and assured him, "I shall ever be ready to render you any service in my power from motives of real esteem." Moreover, if Barry was ever in "real want" Jefferson would get his money to him. A year later, Barry's time of "real want" arrived. "As I now intend to build myself a House to live in for the first time in my life," he wrote, "and Knowing it will be necessary for me to collect my little earnings together to meet with the demands of it, you'l much oblige me by letting me have the money due me the 20th of March next." It was not as simple as that; Jefferson had no ready cash. He promised Barry he would send the money in April, but sent only $100 with a pledge of another $100 shortly, and the $75 balance when the harvest was in. By the end of the year, Barry still had not received the balance due him, but by the last of January, Jefferson promised to send it in three or four weeks. The final letter of the exchange came from Barry: a reminder that the settlement did not include $8.80 for a glazier's diamond—a small diamond set in a handle, used for cutting glass. Barry had earlier described the diamond as "glorious" and "a remarkably good one," and advised Jefferson to have "whoever is to use it at your place . . . practice on it every leisure hour he can spare," cutting glass with a glazier's diamond obviously requiring a degree of skill. He also requested a recommendation for a job.

Although Jefferson prided himself on paying his workmen promptly, once the $25,000 annual salary of the presidency was lost, he found himself increasingly in financial difficulties. Barry was only one of many workmen whose pressure for payment forced Jefferson ever more deeply into debt. Indeed, the construction of Jefferson's architectural masterpiece was completed only by adding to its massive foundations an indebtedness as heavy as Monticello itself.

The floor-to-ceiling greenhouse windows that Barry glazed and painted were some of the most carefully thought-out structures in the house. Jefferson, as avid a gardener as he was a builder, decided early in his construction plans that the piazza adjoining his library suite had unusual possibilities. Its five arched openings boxed the compass to the south, capturing sunlight throughout the seasons. If glassed in, the piazza would make an ideal greenhouse for "oranges, Mimosa Farnesiana & a very few things of that kind." One reason why Oldham had such a difficult time with the windows for these openings—and why his lumber had to be perfectly dry to prevent warping—was that each of the double sashes was five feet wide by four feet high, an unusually large, heavy sash, but one that allowed the room to be drenched with sunlight. The sashes could be raised from the floor into a space at the fanlight above to create an opening five by eight feet. When all windows were raised, the greenhouse became an open porch. When closed, however, the piazza-greenhouse presented Jefferson with a serious problem of temperature control. As anyone who has ever done any greenhouse gardening knows, some way must be found to regulate the amount of sunlight admitted to a closed glass house. Jefferson's solution was the use of louvered shutters. He wrote to Oldham from Washington that the windows "are to have Venetian blinds of a particular construction, now in hand here under my own eye."

Louvered blinds, which had been introduced into Virginia in the mid-eighteenth century, were perfectly suited for Jefferson's style of architectural design. However, these were not what we term venetian blinds—frameless, cloth-connected laths that can be raised and lowered—but louvered shutters. "Venetian blind" was a term applied during this period to any louvered window covering. He wrote to Dinsmore in 1807 that he liked the interior venetian blinds in the windows of the President's House and wanted some for Monticello if they could be made to fit, as they were in the President's House, in the concealed recesses of the window jambs where solid wainscot shutters normally went. They were to go in the windows and doors of the hall, square rooms, and his cabinet; all these openings looked out on public spaces and required blinds for privacy. Dinsmore replied that he had measured the windows and the recesses, and the blinds would not fit. "The only windows in the house where they could be used are those of the Parlor," he wrote, "& for them the [solid] shutters are already made, besides they have outside blinds."

The outside blinds Dinsmore referred to were louvered shutters placed on all of the ground floor windows. Jefferson's infatuation with these louvered shutters went as far back as the early 1770s when he ordered six pairs for the first house, probably for the parlor, chamber, and dining room windows, all facing southwest. In Paris, he acquired five more pairs, then five in Philadelphia, and six in New York. All of these found their way back to Monticello and were installed on various windows. There were still a number of windows and doors needing shutters; these were made by a Washington joiner, Peter Lenox, and shipped to Monticello. Some of the shutters made by Lenox had "fixed laths, folding together with a rabbet at the meeting"; others had "laths moving on 2. pivots." Most ground floor windows of the house, therefore, had inside and outside shutters, the louvered "Venetian blinds" on the exterior, and solid wainscot shutters, the traditional window covering of Georgian architecture, hidden behind deep reveals on the inside.

Louvered interior shutters were also placed on the skylights of the dining room and Jefferson's bedroom. In a reply to Benjamin Latrobe, who had sent him a drawing for venetian blinds for the windows of the dome of the Capitol, Jefferson wrote, "I know that the method proposed in your letter for keeping out the sun would be effectual and convenient, because I have hit on the identical device for my skylights." Besides having strings to operate the movable louvers, "my blinds open up on hinges, as in the winter we want both light and warmth of the sun."

As shocking as it seems, Jefferson also planned to put louvered blinds between the columns of the porticoes. In his Remodeling Notebook, he gave the dimensions for louvered shutters to be hung between the shafts of the columns, with one set fixed at the top, and two sets attached by hinges so they could swing upward behind the fixed shutter. Later, he revised this idea; two long shutters would hang the length of the columns, the bottom one folding up into the upper one. They would both swing up parallel with, and possibly be recessed into, the portico ceiling. Whether Jefferson ever installed these shutters on the porticoes is conjectural. There is no contemporary mention of them by visitors to the house, but calculations by Jefferson in his notebook suggest that he actually took measurements of supporting fixtures of blinds already installed on the east portico. Jefferson's willingness to hang shutters between the portico columns of Monticello—somewhat like fitting the entrance of the White House with awnings—indicates the extent to which he would go for privacy. Although the porticoes were used as social gathering places by Jefferson, the family, and guests in summer (according to his grandson Thomas Jefferson Randolph, he would "read for half an hour in his public rooms or portico"), the east-facing portico did not require blinds for protection from the sun; the western portico was the sunny one. The eastern portico, however, faced the entrance road to Monticello, and it was here that "sitting in the shade of his porticoes to enjoy the coolness of the approaching evening, parties of men and women would sometimes approach within a dozen yards, and gaze at him point-blank until they had looked their fill, as they would have gazed at a lion in a menagerie." It was the insensitivity of strangers traveling to Monticello to be able to say that they had seen the great man that caused him to consider the extreme defense of placing a shuttered screen across the portico.

He also decided to build two structures that, aside from the narrow staircases, are the most questionable architectural decisions he made at Monticello. On either side of the greenhouse he built small, seven-foot-square, louvered verandas, or "porticles" as he termed them. On January 30, 1808, Dinsmore wrote Jefferson, "we have finished the shutters & sashes of the Hall Parlour & Dining Room and are now engaged at the venition work adjoining the green house." He wanted to know whether Jefferson wished Chinese railings around the roofs of the two structures. Jefferson responded, "I do not propose any Chinese railing on the two Porticles at the doors of my Cabinet, because it would make them more conspicuous to the prejudice of the Piazza & its pediment as the principal object. The intention was that they should be obscure as possible that they might not disturb the effect of their principal."

Architecturally, the two porticles were a disaster, even though they were competently made by John Hemings, who was instructed to build them. Jefferson attempted to integrate them into the design of the piazza by building complementary ornamental arches in the louvered work, but they still appeared to be a pair of garden lath-houses attached to the piazza-greenhouse. They are in complete conflict with the Palladian style of the exterior of the house: their wooden lathwork is at odds with the arched piazza next to them, the red brick of the walls behind them, and the classic entablature above them. Besides, their presence on one side of the house breaks its otherwise perfect Palladian symmetry. Jefferson was obviously aware of this, as his comment to Dinsmore about rendering the structures as "obscure as possible" makes abundantly clear. Why, then, did he build them?

If Jefferson was willing to ignore the code of Palladian orthodoxy on the exterior of the house where it was embarrassingly visible, he must have had a powerful incentive. One possible motivation is that he wanted lath-house extensions to his greenhouse to serve as plant nurseries and a protective environment for ferns and shade-loving plants. This is clearly not the case, however; Jefferson never used his greenhouse for serious gardening, only for storing a handful of specimen plants. In response to a query from one of his gardening correspondents, he replied, "You enquire whether I have a hot house, greenhouse, or to what extent I pay attention to these things. I have only a greenhouse, and have used that only for a very few articles. My frequent & long absences at a distant possession [Poplar Forest] render my efforts even for the few greenhouse plants I aim at, abortive. During my last absence in the winter, every plant I had in it perished." In all of his extensive correspondence on gardening or farming, there is not a single mention of the porticles as garden lath-houses.

The single important function that they served was unrelated to the adjacent greenhouse; they were constructed primarily as privacy screens for Jefferson's bedroom-library suite, although one of them was made into an aviary. The terrace that extended from this suite made it possible for servants or visiting strollers literally to look through his cabinet door into his bed, an intolerable assault on the privacy of an extraordinarily private man. He had earlier attempted to address this problem by erecting a partition with windows on the library side of his alcove bed. This, however, proved to be unsatisfactory. He wrote to Dinsmore complaining that "the folding mahogany sash which closes the alcove of my bed is too heavy & troublesome. I wish you to make a folding frame to fit the alcove & to be covered with paper on both sides." He included instructions and a sketch. Dinsmore replied that he did not understand exactly how it was to be made, whether it should be solid wood covered with paper or simply a "light frame," somewhat like a window sash. Jefferson sent another sketch of a double screen, hinged on a center dividing post, "to be mearly a light frame . . . covered with paper on each side." In effect, the study side of his alcove bed was shielded from curious eyes by a pair of Japanese shoji screens, covered with wallpaper, that could be swung open for ventilation and closed for privacy.

By erecting the two louvered porticles between his sanctum sanctorum and the public terraces and gardens, Jefferson permitted air and light to be admitted, but vision denied. The porticle in front of the library room, on the southeast corner of the house, was constructed as an aviary by John Hemings. It undoubtedly was designed for mockingbirds, Jefferson's favorite bird. He had always admired the song of this bird, and at various times purchased mockingbirds. It was not until he went to France, however, that he was able to compare it to the legendary song of the nightingale. He advised his daughter Martha to become acquainted with the nightingale's song "that you might be able to estimate its merit in comparison with that of the mockingbird. The latter has the advantage of singing thro' a great part of the year, whereas the nightingale sings but 5. or 6. weeks in the spring, and a still shorter term and with a more feeble voice in the fall." During his presidency he kept mockingbirds at the President's House. Margaret Bayard Smith described his affection for one of them: "He cherished [it] with peculiar fondness, not only for its melodious powers, but for its uncommon intelligence and affectionate disposition. . . . He allowed the bird to fly around the room when he was alone," she reported, "and it would perch on his shoulders and take food from his lips. . . . How he loved this bird!" It was undoubtedly for the mockingbirds he kept in Washington that Jefferson decided to make one of his porticles an aviary. On his return to Monticello, he wrote to his steward at the President's House, Etienne Lemaire, "My birds arrived here in safety & are the delight of every hour."

The other porticle, the one in front of his cabinet, made it possible for him to leave the doors to this room open for ventilation without extending an invitation to anyone strolling on the terrace to invade his privacy. The porticle had a hinged, folding shutter door of its own which could be closed and latched. The porticle offered him the equivalent of that southern architectural institution, the screened porch: a place in which he could read or write in comfortable shade on mornings when the eastern sun was flooding his suite. Aside from this small, private veranda, there was no location where he could sit outside in solitude, although he was later to build a small garden pavilion for this purpose.

There are those who will view Jefferson's porticles as yet another strand in the web of circumstantial evidence linking him to Sally Hemings: the porticles were constructed to conceal her presence in his bedroom and to allow her to slip more easily in and out of his sleeping quarters. It is true that the timing of their construction supports this allegation: they were seemingly designed, and certainly added, after the Sally Hemings scandal broke upon him in 1802. A much more likely explanation for the timing, however, is the addition of the terrace walk outside of his bedroom. With the construction of this public promenade directly in front of his bedroom-library suite, he realized the full impact of what he had inadvertently wrought—an orchestra seat to his private life for anyone who cared to view it. This serious flaw in his design could have been avoided by simply extending the width of the piazza-greenhouse seven feet on each side. The piazza then would have supplied the privacy of the porticles, while still retaining the integrity of his Palladian plan. It would have been necessary to make this decision, however, during the initial stages of the rebuilding of Monticello. Once the piazza was in place, the only solution to the problem of privacy in his personal quarters was the kind of architecturally unsatisfactory one he arrived at.

The two porticles can no longer be seen at Monticello; after 1890, they were removed by the owner of the house, Jefferson M. Levy. This is unfortunate; not only were they designed and constructed during Jefferson's presidency, and were therefore an integral part of the second house, but they reveal more about his character than all of his Palladian ornamentation combined. They were the best demonstration to be found at Monticello that the "law of convenience" took precedence over any absolute standard of architectural purity. Jefferson believed that a house existed primarily to be lived in comfortably, and if conflicts arose between comfort and aesthetics, compromises favored comfort. He could not be comfortable without privacy, which was more than a necessity for Jefferson; it was an obsession, one that found its expression in a rather simple piece of construction technology, the louvered shutter.

His history of collecting shutters over a span of three decades indicates that he placed them on the windows of virtually every house he lived in, even temporary residences. There was obviously something about the venetian blind that appealed to him deeply. Windows were an architectural paradox for Jefferson; they admitted the light and ventilation that he found essential for work and comfort, but they also denied him solitude and privacy. The venetian blind, with its adjustable louvers, was a filter that allowed him to control light and air without being seen. Blinds were at once a functional, utilitarian device and a symbol of the Jefferson personality. He was a man who revealed to others only what he chose to; he remained fixedly concealed behind what we would call his defenses—observing all but seldom revealing. Only with his close family, in the confines of the walls of Monticello, did he allow himself to be seen, to reveal his needs for, and his capacity to show, love and affection. These private feelings were not for public display; therefore as Jefferson's fame grew during his presidency, and Monticello became increasingly an inn, his need to control his privacy intensified. His bedroom-library sanctuary, protected by locks and blinds, gave him a measure of control; when this was not enough, he built another house at Poplar Forest and periodically disappeared from Monticello, where he was on public exhibition, to the rural solitude of his Bedford plantation. Loss of control of his privacy was one of Jefferson's few real fears, so he took extraordinary efforts to assure that this would not happen. When it did, during the Sally Hemings scandal, for instance, it caused him excruciating pain. Public scrutiny of his private life made him all the more determined to protect his privacy by such architectural shields as blinds in his windows, screens at his bed, louvered porticles at his doors, and even a wall of shutters across his portico that would have made the sainted Palladio shudder in his grave.

Jefferson's willingness to destroy the perfect symmetry of Monticello with the two porticles was all the more significant considering the extraordinary effort and expense he had undergone to maintain the balance of the two dependency wings. He designed the north pavilion differently from its sister structure, the "honeymoon cottage" south pavilion. Based on his own experience of living in the south pavilion, he modified fireplaces and doors and added windows in an effort to make the two pavilions, if not more commodious, more efficient and comfortable. His new design, however, required that he rebuild the south pavilion to make the two buildings identical.

Earlier, Jefferson had flirted with the idea of placing porticoes with Tuscan orders on the two pavilions, but abandoned it, as he did many grandiose ideas for the dependencies. Instead, he designed the two pavilions as simple two-story brick buildings, with an entrance door on the terrace leading to a comfortable single-room apartment. The floor below on each building was a utility room. Early in 1808, as Jefferson was making plans to leave Washington for permanent retirement at Monticello, he pressed his workmen to complete these two "outchambers," as he termed them. The north pavilion was to be used by Thomas Mann Randolph, whose residence there in later years was to prompt the family to call the building Colonel Randolph's Study. In March 1808, Jefferson wrote Dinsmore, "I presume mr Perry has laid the floor of the North Pavilion so that . . . it may be in readiness for Mr Randolph to use." He was particularly anxious for the south pavilion remodeling to be completed because he was sending all of his books from Washington and planned to store them there. His library suite was obviously already cramped for space.

The remodeling was being done by the "very good-humoured" mason Hugh Chisholm, who probably also did the brick work for the north pavilion. At the end of 1807, he had written Chisholm that since there were no bricks left to do the south pavilion, "I conclude to make them." He gave explicit directions for turning over and removing stones from the brick earth in preparation for molding "24,000 bricks of our usual size of the neatest make." Two months later, he wrote Chisholm again, informing him that his trunks of books would soon be arriving at Monticello; they had to be opened to avoid becoming mouldy. It was imperative, therefore, that the south pavilion be quickly finished. "I wish you to take every possible care not to injure the floor," he admonished. He gave directions for "waste plank" to be laid over the finished floor "so that no lumps of brick may get in to scratch it." As little plaster as possible was to be removed from the walls, and Dinsmore was to have "doors, sashes, chairboards etc" in readiness. "In every other respect," he advised, "it is to be finished on the model of the North pavilion except the fireplace below is to be large enough for a work house, say 4 f. 6 I wide." When finished, the room was to be whitewashed. Dinsmore wrote and suggested that if a new roof was to be put on the building, "it would be advisable to have it done before you move your Books in there." Jefferson instructed him that "a new coat of shingling is all that is wanting."

Remodeling the south pavilion was an emotional closure for Jefferson. Nearly forty years before, he had brought his bride to the small brick cottage sitting unimpressively on the frozen earth of his mountaintop. It had been their cramped living quarters during the early years of their marriage, and was the room where their first, and now their only surviving, child was born. It was the last vestige of the original Monticello to be altered into something new. When he returned to Monticello from Washington on May 11, 1808, for his annual spring visit, he must have viewed what his workmen had wrought with mixed feelings. His eight trunks of books were safely stored in the south pavilion, ending his anxieties about them. But as he ran his eyes over the freshly plastered and painted room with its new windows in strange locations, he could not help but experience a loss; the familiar intimacy of his honeymoon cottage had vanished forever and a door had quietly shut on one of the happiest times of his life.

During the final year of his presidency, Jefferson pressed forward with determination to complete Monticello by the time he returned from Washington for permanent retirement. The crew at work on the house was by now a smoothly functioning unit, with Dinsmore, Neilson, John Hemings, and Lewis doing joinery, John Perry structural carpentry, and Chisholm masonry. Dinsmore gave a progress report in April 1808: he was making the final window sashes for the house, "Mr Perry has got the roof on the S. E. offices & covered way ready to lay the [terrace] floor on & Mr. Chisholm has got the most of the rooms plaistered & Bricks ready to raise the Chimneys." The chimneys were those from the kitchen and smokehouse fireplaces, emerging on the terraces.

The previous winter, Perry had reroofed the south dependencies

The accordion-pleat roof with the wooden terrace deck removed.

with sheet iron, making an accordionlike pleated roof, which Jefferson had designed in an effort to prevent the flat roofs of the dependencies from leaking. The integrity of this roof was jeopardized, not only by its flatness, but by the terrace deck that rested on top of it. Reroofing the south dependency presented a hardship for the servants whose living quarters were in this wing; the old roof had to be taken off. In deference to the servants, Jefferson decided to wait until spring to do this job, but John Perry had all of his materials ready in December. "It would suit me much better to go on with the work this winter than to wait untill Spring," he wrote. He proposed doing half of the roof "& then if the weather is bad stop untill a good spell of weather to do the ballance." He thought the roof would be uncovered no more than two weeks, but was silent about the plight of the house servants whose living quarters would be roofless during at least two of the coldest weeks of the year. Jefferson's main concern, on the other hand, was for the comfort of the house slaves. He gave Perry permission to continue the roof that winter if he finished half of it completely, "then, while you are about the residue, the families in it can live in the Washhouse & kitchen, till their own apartments are done again."

In July 1808, Dinsmore reported, "we are engaged at the Chinese railing." This was a Chinese trellis railing serving as a parapet around the top, flat section of the roof of the house and around the terraces of the dependencies. John Hemings was given the task of building it. Although Chinese ornamentation on Palladian architecture seems incongruous, it was popular in the eighteenth century, particularly in France, where Jefferson might have first encountered it. He had also seen Chinese architectural designs in England. During a tour of English gardens in March and April of 1786, he visited Kew Garden and saw William Chambers's famed Chinese Pagoda. The greatest influence on the popularization of chinoiserie in England was Chambers's *Designs of Chinese Buildings, Furniture, Dresses, Machines and Utensils*, published in 1757. Jefferson owned a copy of this folio, and it influenced his Chinese railing designs. He built outdoor benches for the terrace and porticoes using a pattern similar to the railing design. Whether the Chinese railings that now appear on the terraces were completed by Jefferson is questionable. Although one visitor's account mentions a Chinese railing around the terraces, two contemporary watercolors depict a simple vertical-rail fence. Jefferson's Remodeling Notebook shows sketches, notes, and a lumber list for a simple picket fence for the terrace, dated June 23, 1824. (It is possible that an earlier Chinese fence deteriorated and this was for a replacement.)

The final work finished under Dinsmore's direction was completing the balustrades and then the north piazza. This piazza, which joins two rooms on the north side of the house, the tearoom and an octagonal guest bedroom, was a duplicate of Jefferson's greenhouse-piazza, except that its ceiling reached to the top of the mezzanine, and its arched openings were not enclosed with window sashes. In February 1809, Dinsmore installed the final pieces of the egg-and-dart cornice on the interior of the piazza, and Chisholm plastered the walls.

When Jefferson arrived at Monticello on March 17, 1809, on his last trip from Washington—a triumphant return celebrated by family, friends, and the citizens of Albemarle County—he must have been pleased by what he saw. The remodeling campaign he had started more than a dozen years ago was nearly finished. The smell of fresh carpentry and paint filled the air, and Monticello bowed before him, displaying its new dependency wings, pavilions, and terraces. There was but one major piece of unfinished business on the house, and ironically it was so glaringly visible that it could not help but disturb its architect-builder. Neither of the porticoes was completed; there were only temporary wooden steps leading up to the platforms, and the platforms themselves were unpaved wooden porches. They stayed in that condition for many years. As late as 1823, a visitor complained that he "entered the [east] portico by a narrow flight of wooden steps of a very gentle ascent. This is very unworthy of the elegance of the interior." Even worse, the pediment of the west portico was held up not by the six Doric columns Jefferson had designed for it, but by what one visitor called "the stems of four tulip trees." Augustus John Foster, British Minister to the United States from 1810 to 1812, who had visited Monticello in August 1807, had rhapsodized over the beauty of the temporary tulip tree columns: "when well grown [they are] as beautiful as the fluted shafts of Corinthian pillars." But for Jefferson they were unsatisfactory substitutes for six Doric columns matching the four on the east portico. The four tulip tree columns in all likelihood had supported the west portico of the original house, for there would have been no reason to discard four finished columns for temporary ones when he remodeled. This means that the west portico never had columns until a few years before Jefferson's death.

After his difficulties with the stone columns of the east portico, Jefferson had committed himself to making the six columns of the west portico not of stone, but of circular-molded brick stuccoed to resemble stone. In 1804 he had written to Latrobe suggesting that the interior columns of the Capitol in Washington would best be made "of well burnt brick moulded in portions of circles adapted to the diminution of the columns." This method, Jefferson wrote, had the imprimatur of Palladio: "Ld. Burlington in his notes on Palladio tells us that he found most of the buildings erected under Palladio's direction & described in his architecture to have their columns made of brick in this way and covered with stucco." Jefferson stated that he knew of a building in Virginia with columns "20. f. high well proportioned and properly diminished executed by a common bricklayer." An added comment explains why his own columns had not already been built of brick by Hugh Chisholm, who constructed the columns at Poplar Forest exactly this way: "the bases & capitals would of course be hewn stone."

In spite of his success in procuring competent artisans from Washington to work at Monticello, Jefferson had not been able to acquire a stonecutter. The masons he used were either bricklayers like Chisholm, or stonemasons who worked with uncut fieldstone. Therefore, the west portico remained unfinished until such time as he could acquire a competent stonemason to cut the bases and capitals for his columns. By 1814, he had still not found a stonecutter, and the west portico was still not finished. In that year, his friend and longtime correspondent Elizabeth Trist needled him about the incomplete portico: "I have been questioning Francis Gilmer as to the improvements at Monticello," she wrote. "He tells me except for an observatory everything remains as when I left it. What exclaim'd I, are not the Porticoes completed. No." She added that she feared that if Jefferson did not finish his house it "will stand a poor chance of ever being completed."

It was not until 1822, in his seventy-ninth year, four years before his death, that Jefferson launched his final building campaign, one that would complete construction work on Monticello. He hired a stonecutter who had done much of the stone work at the University of Virginia, John Gorman, to quarry and cut stone needed for the bases and capitals of the west portico columns. Gorman, whom Jefferson termed "sober, skillful and industrious," also quarried, cut, and laid stone and slate on the platform floors and steps of both porticoes. Only with the completion of these two porticoes could one say that Jefferson's house was finally finished.

Jefferson gave Gorman as an apprentice one of his slaves, Thrimston; he also supplied him with "two additional hands for quarrying my work." By the time the team had quarried, cut, and carved the Doric bases and caps for the six west portico columns, Gorman had made Thrimston, as he put it, "a tolerable good stone cutter." Before Gorman was hired, Jefferson had made a detailed list of the number of specially molded curved header and stretcher bricks he would need to construct the shafts of the six columns—a total of 4,320. Another thousand common bricks were needed to "fill the hollows" of the columns. In the summer of 1822, Gorman and his crew set the bases in place, and started laying up the bricks, a row of stretchers followed by a row of headers. (The tulip tree columns that had been holding up the pediment had to be removed and temporary supports placed under it while the new columns were being constructed.) After taking the columns to two-thirds of their height, their diameter was diminished by three inches, according to the Palladian standard for the Doric order. Jefferson had smaller bricks made for the final diminished third of the columns, but the gradual transition to the diminished section of the columns required considerable skill on the part of the bricklayer and stucco plasterer. Jefferson certainly supervised this part of the construction closely, for the finished columns are smoothly and uniformly diminished. When the bricks were brought to the top of the column shaft, Gorman set the capitals in place.

After finishing the columns, Gorman made an agreement with Jefferson to do the stone work on the portico floors and steps, "if you will Board me while laying and Cutting." Jefferson struck a hard bargain: he would allow Gorman to keep the now-skilled Thrimston as his helper, but Gorman would now have to pay to hire the slave by the day. After the work began, Jefferson modified the agreement to allow Thrimston "half of every Saturday" off, so that the slave worked five and a half days a week—Thrimston's bonus for his newly acquired skill as a stonecutter.

In April 1809, Jefferson wrote to his successor, President James Madison, "Dinsmore and Neilson are set out yesterday for Montpelier. If mrs. Madison has anything there which interests her in the gardening way, she cannot consign it better then to Neilson. He is a gardener by nature, & extremely attached to it." James Dinsmore and his housejoiner-gardener colleague, John Neilson, an Irishman who came to America to make his fortune, were leaving Monticello for Montpelier to work on the Madison house. Their departure must have been an emotional one for them, for they had been working at Monticello long enough to become virtual family members. Dinsmore had lived there for ten years; Neilson four. Little is known of the personal lives of these itinerant bachelor craftsmen. Dinsmore, who reportedly was also an Irishman, had a brother and, on at least one occasion, he returned to Philadelphia to visit his family. The two workmen probably lived in the upstairs rooms of Monticello while Jefferson was in Washington during his presidency, when the house was otherwise empty. There was plenty of space on the second and third floors. On one occasion,

Dinsmore advised Jefferson he was working on the dining room at night, suggesting that he was living in the house. When family and friends descended on the house during Jefferson's visits from Washington, the two housejoiners may have moved to Milton, the village located three miles away on the Rivanna.

Passing his two housejoiners on to Madison when they were finished at Monticello was typical of Jefferson; he was an architectural cornucopia to his friends and neighbors. He drew plans for their houses and supplied them with architectural and engineering information, nails from his nail shop, and skilled artisans from Philadelphia and Washington. Madison hired Dinsmore and Neilson to remodel and enlarge his house and Chisholm to stabilize the foundations and replace the columns of the portico.

Jefferson used his connections in Washington to attempt to get Dinsmore and Neilson work when they finished Madison's Montpelier. He wrote letters of recommendation to Benjamin Latrobe praising the two men for having "done the whole of the joiner's work of my house, to which I can affirm I have never seen any superior in the U.S." Latrobe was in charge of rebuilding the Capitol building, which had been burned and gutted by the British in 1814. He responded with a long, apologetic letter explaining how workmen already living in Washington had been given the available jobs—but that he would attempt to obtain a position for Neilson and "promote his interest." If Neilson worked in Washington, it was only for a short time; he was back in Petersburg when Jefferson wrote to Dinsmore to offer the two joiners work at Central College, shortly to become the University of Virginia. Both men worked for years at the university, as did Chisholm and Perry. It was, indeed, Perry's land that was purchased as the site for Jefferson's "academical village."

One reason Jefferson continued to look after the interests of his workers when they left Monticello was that he was their debtor. By lending him their wages, his workmen helped finance the construction of Monticello. Jefferson was able to induce several of his workmen, as he did the painter Barry, to lend their wages back to him. They drew only enough cash to cover their living expenses and allowed Jefferson to keep the balance at the established six percent interest. Jefferson noted in his Memorandum Book on May 16, 1802, for example, that on settling his account with Oldham, $232.40 was due him, "which he chuses should be in my hands. I promised to settle interest on it as I do on Dinsmore." Oldham withdrew all of his money from Jefferson's Monticello bank when he left for Richmond, however. Perry and Chisholm demanded their pay when it was due, but Dinsmore and Neilson both allowed Jefferson to keep sizable amounts of their pay for a number of years, even after they left Monticello. Jefferson settled his debt to Dinsmore in 1813, paying $159 interest on $618 principal, but as late as 1820 he renegotiated a note with Neilson for principal and interest amounting to $843. He refused to give compound interest on these debts; six percent interest in four years was calculated as twenty-four percent of the principal. When Neilson complained about his not compounding the interest annually, Jefferson replied that he had always paid simple interest of six percent, and that if compounded, the interest rate would have to be no more than four or four and a half percent.

Some of the wages paid to his construction workers was in bartered goods rather than cash. Unlike the overseers, who were supplied with pork, beef, flour, and a house as part of their contract, construction workers normally had to supply their own food and lodgings—to "find themselves," as it was put. Jefferson ran what was, in effect, a company store; he supplied his workers with foodstuffs from the plantation when they were available, and deducted the cost from their wages. He also paid workers with slaves on occasion, something he was willing to do when he had an abundance of slaves and a scarcity of cash. John Perry purchased a slave with £125 deducted from his earnings, and Reuben Perry received the runaway slave Jamey Hubbard in exchange for carpentry work.

Jefferson continued to be a clearinghouse of information about his workers for years after they left his employment. He kept track of them through their occasional letters, and passed on information about them to inquiring relatives. The plasterer Martin Wanscher instructed his friends in Germany to send their letters to Jefferson, and Richard Richardson's father corresponded with Jefferson in an attempt to learn his son's whereabouts.

Of all his workmen, perhaps Richardson was most indebted to Jefferson, who had hired him as a bricklayer in 1796 at the age of twenty-one. A year later, at Jefferson's urging, he went to Philadelphia to learn stonecutting and plastering, two skills Jefferson sorely needed. On his return to Monticello, he became overseer for a time, and it was then that he wrestled with the east portico columns in an unsuccessful attempt to get them up straight. Jefferson had noticed an item in the *Richmond Examiner* reporting the death in Jamaica of a Joseph Richardson, with the additional news that the dead man's estate had been left to his nephew Richard Richardson. President Jefferson obtained a passport for him, signed by Secretary of State James Madison, wrote a letter verifying his identity, paid him travel money, and offered him some advice: bring the legacy money back to Virginia and buy a farm as an investment. Richardson did not take this advice, for he had inherited an extensive sugar plantation. He returned to the United States in 1804 and wrote to Jefferson twice, inquiring about the wisdom of purchasing sugar lands in the Orleans territory. He decided to return to Jamaica, however, and married and raised a family there. He wrote to Jefferson from Jamaica once more in 1809, but after that neither Jefferson nor his family in the United States heard from him. He died in Jamaica.

James Oldham was a better correspondent; he dutifully wrote to Jefferson when he left Richmond for St. Louis in 1818 to make his fortune on a housebuilding scheme. He was backed by a speculator with ambitious construction plans, having sent "10 hands, sawyers & hewers," along with "a large quantity of iron mongery" ahead of Oldham. But by the end of the year, Oldham had returned to Virginia, "much disappointed in my engagements." His backer had broken the contract with him "on account of the embarest state of his afares in Richmond."

When Jefferson was asked his opinion about resettling elsewhere, he counseled his workmen, as he had Richardson, to stay in Virginia. Dinsmore inquired whether he should buy land at Opalousas in the Orleans territory. His brother, who had settled there, informed him that the land and climate were good and that the price of land would certainly rise when the embargo was lifted and agricultural products could once more be shipped. After swearing Dinsmore to secrecy, Jefferson responded with a long letter informing him that western lands could never be converted back to cash, and were therefore not a good investment. (The request for secrecy was for political reasons: Jefferson's advice contradicted the government's official position, which was to encourage the settlement of western lands.) He advised Dinsmore to purchase land around Albemarle, where it had steadily increased in value and could be more easily sold. Furthermore, he warned, in case of hostilities with Spain, western lands would become a war zone. Dinsmore took his advice, remained in Virginia, and prospered.

Even after the release of his two professional housejoiners, Jefferson was not without skilled construction resources. The team of John Hemings and Lewis, under the tutelage of Dinsmore and Neilson, had become, if not their equals as woodworkers, then close to it. With most of the major carpentry in the house completed, Hemings and Lewis set about making furniture for Monticello's numerous rooms. Jefferson's retirement from public life now gave him the leisure to turn his attention to making his house and its surrounding grounds the comfortable country gentleman's estate he had always intended it to be. He had already made some improvements on the grounds, but there were still ambitious plans on the drawing board for enhancing the gardens, walks, roads, and outbuildings on the mountaintop. He was to discover, however, one of the permanent truths of the builder's art; when one finally finds the time for a long-planned construction task, the money to pay for it and the inclination to finish it seem somehow to have vanished.

10

The Guardian Spirit
of the Place

I placed a jar in Tennessee
And round it was, upon a hill. . . .
The wilderness rose up to it,
And sprawled around, no longer wild. . . .
It took dominion everywhere. . . .

—Wallace Stevens,
"Anecdote of the Jar"

THE MOST insignificant human artifact, when placed in primitive nature, the poet tells us, transforms the landscape before our eyes; the simple geometry of an ordinary jar is capable of imposing itself upon, and taming, a wilderness. Stevens sees civilization as a contagion infecting all it surveys, an idea that Thomas Jefferson would have grasped immediately, for his lifetime of building was an attempt to bring civilized order to an awesomely raw America. Like Stevens's jar, Monticello took dominion over its surrounding wilderness.

From the moment Jefferson decided to shave his mountaintop and adorn it with a Palladian crown, he was aware that the forest could not be allowed to sprawl about his porticoes. It was necessary to transform the encroaching woods into gardens, parks, walks, and groves where the sublimity of the surrounding mountains could be enjoyed in ease and comfort. Exactly how this was to be done was a problem that perplexed him from the very beginning.

The landscape tradition that Jefferson inherited in Virginia was the formal garden. It was laid out in geometrical patterns, with symmetrical flowerbeds surrounded by walks—the familiar parterres—with straight poplar alleys, and with boxwood topiary clipped into cubes, cylinders, and spheres. This is the way the College of William and Mary and the Governor's Palace were landscaped, and it was how the gardens of the James River plantation houses Jefferson was familiar with—Shirley, Rosewell, Carter's Grove, Westover—were laid out. It was undoubtedly also the kind of garden Jefferson knew as a boy and young man at Tuckahoe and Shadwell.

The formal garden should have appealed to Jefferson at his deepest level. His love of mathematics and geometry, his skill at surveying and mechanical drawing, his study and practice of the law, his infatuation with rule-bound Palladian architecture, his penchant for classification, for tables, lists, indexes, and catalogues, the very logic and system of his mind—all argue for his eager acceptance of a traditional landscape design based on formal pattern and symmetry. But from the very beginning of his interest in building a house of his own he abandoned all notions of formal gardens in favor of the informal, "picturesque" landscape, *le jardin anglais.*

The English picturesque garden of the early eighteenth century was an offspring of the Whig enlightenment, particularly of Richard Boyle, Earl of Burlington, and his neo-Palladian circle. The names usually associated with this style of gardening are Alexander Pope, who built a much-admired boutique garden of 3½ acres on the Thames at Twickenham; William Kent, painter, landscape architect, and protégé of Burlington, who was credited with the observation that "all nature is a garden" and with the introduction of the free-form, natural garden in England; and the Royal Gardener Charles Bridgeman, who introduced one of the thematic elements of picturesque gardening, the sunken fence or "ha-ha," and created at Stowe perhaps the most famous informal garden of the first half of the eighteenth century. At the time of Jefferson's birth, the term picturesque in gardening had already become associated with a landscape that was natural rather than artificial, with irregular and asymmetrical patterns, with curved rather than straight borders, and with trees and shrubs in their natural contours—all the very antithesis of the formal garden. By the time Jefferson began building at Monticello, he had been thoroughly converted, through his reading, to this fashionable new garden style.

It was paradoxical, of course, that the British aristocrats who clutched

Palladio's architectural rules to their bosoms, abandoned all notions of rational formalism when they stepped into the gardens of their Palladian villas. The epoch was full of such contradictions, however. It produced the sentimental novel as well as the *Encyclopédie*, and Rousseau's *Confessions* along with Dr. Johnson's *Dictionary*. As Jefferson was to demonstrate in his Head and Heart letter to Maria Cosway, the Apollonian Enlightenment found it necessary to forge its Dionysus. Deism begot Methodism, Fragonard cohabited with the Poussinists, *The Spectator* kindled the primitive heroics of Jefferson's favorite poet, the spurious Ossian, and topiary inspired the tea rose. Indeed, it is no accident that the informal garden reached its popularity during the age of sensibility; the Palladian Head required its passionate Heart.

Jefferson had absorbed in his youth the moral sense philosophies of Francis Hutcheson, had read Edmund Burke on the sublime, and identified with the sentimentality of Sterne. He wore his *sensibilité* on his sleeve when he went courting Martha Wayles Skelton in 1771, and if he had not destroyed his correspondence with her, posterity would likely have discovered in him a surprising capacity for expressing emotion—love, pity, sympathy, and melancholy. He revealed some of this romantic sentimentality when he recorded in his Memorandum Book in that same year how he planned to landscape his mountaintop.

He described first the burying ground, "some unfrequented vale in the park . . . among antient and venerable oaks," interspersed with "some gloomy evergreens." With echoes of the graveyard poets, he quoted lines he had earlier copied in his commonplace book from Nicholas Rowe's *The Fair Penitent*: "no sound to break the stillness but a brook, that bubbling winds among the weeds; no mark of any human shape that had been there, unless the skeleton of some poor wretch, Who sought that place out to despair and die in." There was to be a "small Gothic temple of antique appearance," with an altar in the middle. "Very little light, perhaps none at all, save the feeble ray of a half extinquished lamp." He ended with four lines of Latin verse to his dead sister, Jane Jefferson, *puellarum optima*. This extravagant plan for a graveyard was never executed; two years after copying it into his Memorandum Book he fenced off a small square plot a short distance from the end of Mulberry Row, and it became Monticello's permanent burial ground.

At the site of a spring located on the north side of the mountain he contemplated another ambitious gardening project: he proposed leveling the ground so that the spring water could fall in a cascade. A temple would then be erected on the level terrace. Close to the spring he would place "a sleeping figure reclined on a plain marble slab, surrounded with turf," and on the slab Latin verses addressed to the *nympha loci, sacri custodia fontis* (nymph of the place, guardian of the sacred spring). Near the spring he would fix a metal plate with more Latin verses, these the *beatus ille* lines of Horace's second epode, extolling the joys of a simple, arcadian life, free from the cares of the city. Beech, aspen, honeysuckle, and jasmine would be planted, and a vista opened to "the millpond, river, road etc."

Then with a characteristic second thought—something he frequently did in his memoranda—he decided on a better plan: instead of leveling the ground around the spring he would excavate into the steep earth and create a grotto guarded by a sleeping nymph. "Build up the sides and arch with stiff clay," he wrote. "Cover this with moss, spangle it with translucent pebbles from Hanovertown, and beautiful shells from the shores of Burwell's ferry. Pave the floor with pebbles." The spring water would be allowed to fall into a basin in the grotto, and the statue of the nymph would be placed on a "couch of moss." Pope's translation of the *nympha loci* verses would then be more appropriate, he thought. Pope, in his rhymed couplets, had freely transferred the nymph from her Latin *fontis* to the poet's garden grotto:

> *Nymph of the grot, these sacred springs I keep,*
> *And to the murmur of these waters sleep;*
> *Ah! spare my slumbers! gently tread the cave!*
> *And drink in silence, or in silence lave!*

The lines from Pope and the description of the proposed grotto make it clear that Jefferson's imaginative garden was much indebted to Pope's famous garden and grotto at Twickenham. The grotto under Pope's house was decorated with shells and colored stones, and had a spring much like the one on Jefferson's mountain. The "nymph of the grot" verse was composed for a statue such as Jefferson desired. The peek into Jefferson's deeper desires provided by his proposed moss-covered, jewel-like grot is revealing. He was a young man in love, anticipating his forthcoming marriage, and it is not surprising that his thoughts ran to reclining nymphs and their mossy grottoes.

These early imaginative notes indicate that the sources for his ideas about gardening, like those about architecture, were entirely literary, and remained so until he went to Europe and saw for himself many of the renowned picturesque gardens of England. Indeed, literature was to figure even more directly in his projected garden. The rocks and trees themselves were to be annotated with "inscriptions in various places, on the bark of trees or metal plates, suited to the character or expression of the particular spot." These bits of verse or classical sententia, which were placed at vistas or points of interest in English gardens, were meant to capture a mood by alluding to a familiar literary work. They obviously appealed greatly to the bookish young Jefferson, whose classical education was a lifelong source of pride.

The work on landscape theory that influenced him most was Thomas Whately's *Observations on Modern Gardening*, a book he acquired in 1778. It is understandable why Whately impressed Jefferson: he anatomized the English picturesque garden by establishing landscape categories, and derived from these a system of rules for creating an English garden. Whately was attempting, in effect, to do for free-form landscaping what Palladio had done for classical architecture. He took the four elements of the landscape—ground, water, rocks, and buildings—broke them down to their constituent parts, and described how each was to be used in four kinds of landscape setting: an ornamental farm, a park, a garden, or a riding. Each produced its particular aesthetic effect: "*elegance* is the peculiar excellence of a garden; *greatness* of a park; *simplicity* of a farm; and *pleasantness* of a riding." Whately's book would have been little more than a Linnaean classification of landscape types if he had not illustrated each of his categories with a detailed description of an English estate that demonstrated a successful application of each of his landscaping principles. Whately's *Observations* was therefore not only a theoretical work, but a tour guide through some of the most famous picturesque gardens of England. It was precisely the kind of book that Jefferson loved, one that combined analysis and theory with practical solutions to design problems.

When he and John Adams went on a tour of English gardens in

1786 during Jefferson's stay in Europe as minister to France, he carried a copy of Whately in his pocket. As he walked through the gardens, he was impressed with the accuracy of Whately's descriptions. He found them "so justly characterized . . . as to be easily recognized, and saw with wonder, that his fine imagination had never been able to seduce him from the truth." He made this pilgrimage, however, not merely as a connoisseur. The notes he took did indeed show an eye for garden aesthetics, but they were also concerned with the economics of gardening on a grand scale: the costs of constructing various garden settings and the labor force needed to maintain them. "My inquiries," he wrote in his Memorandum Book, "were directed chiefly to such practical things as might enable me to estimate the expense of making and maintaining a garden in that style." He noted, for example, that the grotto at Paynshill was "said to have cost 7000.£"; Blenheim required 200 people "to keep it in order"; the waters at Wotton produced "2000. brace of carp a year"; and William Shenstone, who "had but 300£ a year," ruined himself by turning his farm, the Leasowes, into a picturesque garden. "It is said he died of heartaches which his debts occasioned him," Jefferson wrote sympathetically.

The one necessary addition to any gentleman's estate that Jefferson did manage to build was a deer park. As early as 1769, he had noted in his Memorandum Book a park on the north side of the mountain, but this was either abandoned or moved to the south side. The new park was located below what was to become the fourth roundabout on a large piece of land that was partially a meadow with a stream meandering through it. At considerable effort and expense, he enclosed his park "two or three miles round" with a high paling fence, "twelve rails double-staked and ridered," according to his slave Isaac. He purchased deer for it, and in time they became tame. The Marquis de Chastellux wrote that there were some twenty deer in Jefferson's park; "he amuses himself by feeding them with Indian corn of which they are very fond, and which they eat out of his hand." On his return from France, Jefferson decided that a deer park was a luxury he no longer desired or could afford, so he converted his park into cropland. It may well have been that his deer park, like some of his other garden ideas, had existed mainly to impress and amuse his wife, and with her death he lost all interest in it.

Aside from the deer park, Jefferson's fanciful garden plans came to nothing during the ten years of his marriage and his construction of the original Monticello. He built the first two roundabouts, the roads needed for access to farms and utility areas, and planted a vegetable garden and orchards, but that was all. Like the house, which was never completed during Martha Jefferson's lifetime, the romantic garden plans of the young man who courted her remained mere reveries until the day of her death. Where revolution and public service had merely interrupted construction on the house, they had forced him to abandon completely any extensive landscape work.

During his stay in France, however, Jefferson designed a garden in the English style, although on a diminutive scale. Attached to the Hôtel de Langeac was a "clever garden," as Jefferson termed it, of about three-quarters of an acre. He drew two working sketches and a final plan for turning it into an English garden. His design included many of the features of the picturesque garden: serpentine paths, short vistas, a mound with a spiral walk leading to the top such as Pope had at Twickenham, statuary, a pond, and a parterre. How much of this was executed at Langeac is unknown; Jefferson's precise measurements for some of the walks suggest that these were actually in place. He was known to have a vegetable garden where he raised Indian corn for his own consumption, and there were trellises for grapevines. It is unlikely that much of this imaginative plan was ever built, however. When Jefferson moved into the house, the garden was virtually all trees. (He fired de Langeac's gardener, claiming he had nothing to do because the garden was *"tout en arbres."*) It is improbable that the Count de Langeac would have allowed Jefferson to cut down his trees to create what for de Langeac would have been an eccentric English garden. Besides, Jefferson could not justify the considerable expense of attaching such a garden to a rented house. When he settled his bill with the Count, the only credit he received for work done on the house was for placing bars on the ground floor windows and installing some doors. There was no mention of garden improvements, nor did he receive credit for any.

Though it was never constructed, Jefferson's garden design for the Hôtel de Langeac, which has been termed "the earliest surviving plan by an American for a *jardin anglais*," suggests that even before returning to America he was itching to try his hand at creating an English garden. At the same time he was indulging himself in this playful landscape design, however, he was engaged in the more substantive business of producing a plan for an enlarged and remodeled Monticello. This project, which became Jefferson's first priority upon his return to America, forced the postponement of any serious landscaping on his mountaintop for another twenty years.

This does not mean that he completely abandoned gardening until Monticello was completed. On the contrary, he began planting trees, vines, grass, and a kitchen garden even before he moved into his one-room bachelor cottage. He was a gardener from his earliest youth; he started his Garden Book in 1766 at the age of twenty-three at the family house at Shadwell with what has become one of his most quoted notes, "Mar. 30. Purple hyacinth begins to bloom." He continued to garden throughout his life with increasing pleasure. "No occupation is so delightful to me as the culture of the earth," he wrote to the artist Charles Willson Peale in 1811, "and no culture comparable to that of the garden. . . . But though an old man, I am but a young gardener."

The location of his house on a mountaintop dictated that his orchards, grapevines, and vegetable garden would be planted on the south slope of the mountain where they would receive the full benefit of the sun. This placed them below Mulberry Row, and it was here that he planted his first fruit trees and kitchen garden. The vegetable garden was subsequently redesigned at the end of Jefferson's presidency when he put in a retaining wall and leveled its gentle slope.

In an effort to discover the history of Jefferson's gardening activities on this section of the mountain, with a view to re-creating his garden as it existed after 1809, the relatively new science of landscape archaeology has recently been employed at Monticello. Under the direction of archaeologist William M. Kelso, who had previously excavated the grounds at Carter's Grove and Kingsmill, a neighboring plantation near Williamsburg, Monticello's orchards, vineyard, vegetable garden, and the remains of the outbuildings along Mulberry Row have been excavated. "By applying the principle of natural soil stratigraphy—whereby earth and artifacts are uncovered and recorded carefully by separate layers in the order in which they were originally deposited," Kelso explains, "even fragile signs of long vanished wooden fences or planting beds can be dated and recorded." At Monticello, in spite of Jefferson's carefully documented gardening history, the physical remains had largely vanished. Under Kelso's direction, excavations have discovered the locations of fence posts and gates, planting beds, terracing, and even the regularly spaced trees and vines of Jefferson's orchards and vineyard. These have been restored with the same varieties of fruit trees and grapevines Jefferson planted. One of the more significant findings from the archaeological excavations was that, as Kelso put it, "so much of what had been constructed during the first forty years of Jefferson's development was changed at the time of or soon after his retirement from the presidency in 1809."

The major change on the sloping ground below Mulberry Row was the construction of a level, 80-by-1,000-foot terrace, held in place by a stone retaining wall. In an era before power-driven earthmoving equipment, this was an enormous undertaking. Jefferson had built a stone garden wall as early as 1774, recording in his Garden Book one of his typical notes on worker efficiency: "in making a stone wall in my garden I find by an accurate calculation that 7½ cubical feet may be done in a day by one hand who brings his own stone into place and does every thing." (The reference suggests that a mortarless dry wall was being built by unskilled slave labor.) This wall apparently enclosed a garden located at the eastern end of Mulberry Row, below the stable. He continued to garden on this plot for decades, but during his presidency he decided to enlarge it by building a retaining wall, which extended the garden to the size of more than three modern football fields. The orchards and vineyards were placed below and to the west of the garden terrace. The overseer Edmund Bacon was given the task of building the wall and leveling the earth, using hired slaves as well as some from the nailery. "We had to blow out the rock for the walls [with black powder]," he recalled, "and then make the soil." Rocks were removed from the earth and used for the walls, and a rich garden loam was produced by heavily manuring the terraces. Once the work got underway, Bacon discovered that the slope of the mountain was not regular along its east-west axis, and that in order to keep the terrace level, the retaining wall was going to have to get increasingly higher, and the amount of fill dirt increasingly greater. "Were we to go on reducing the whole to the same level we have begun with," Jefferson wrote, "the labor would be immense." Instead, he advised Bacon to step the terrace into four level platforms; Bacon was able to level the terrace with three platforms, each roughly 80 by 330 feet. The terraces were subdivided into twenty-four squares of approximately one-twenty-seventh of an acre each, with a grass-covered walk running the length of them. The garden, orchard, and vineyard were then enclosed with a ten-foot-high picket fence, tall enough to keep out deer, and with palings close enough "as not to let even a young hare in."

Jefferson's motivation for creating a vegetable garden of this size can only be guessed at, but serving hundreds of guests at regular dinners at the President's House certainly had much to do with it. The Washington vegetable market, the produce of which he charted so painstakingly, made it possible for him to place on his table unlimited quantities of fresh fruit and vegetables. But there was no such market in Albemarle County (nor could he have afforded its expense if it had existed), and as the number of visitors to Monticello increased during his presidency, he saw that he was going to have to supply fruit and vegetables from his own gardens. When he finally enlarged his garden at the end of his presidency, he did so with some urgency, for by that time his fame, coupled with his compulsive hospitality, had opened a floodgate of visitors to Monticello, all arriving with country appetites. Jefferson also experimented with new varieties of fruit, grains, and vegetables, and exchanged plants and seeds with an extensive number of correspondents. These agricultural experiments also required garden space. (Like the orchards and vineyards, the vegetable garden is now restored and is planted annually with Jefferson's favorite vegetables.)

Jefferson constructed a small brick pavilion on the center terrace of his garden. Of a number of such structures planned, it was the only one built. It disappeared after Jefferson's death, but archaeological explorations uncovered its foundations, and it has now been restored. The pavilion, built in 1812, is a simple, twelve-foot-square structure with windows and a pyramidal roof. It was undoubtedly the "observatory" mentioned by Elizabeth Trist in her letter to Jefferson in 1814 chiding him for his delay in completing Monticello. It was reportedly

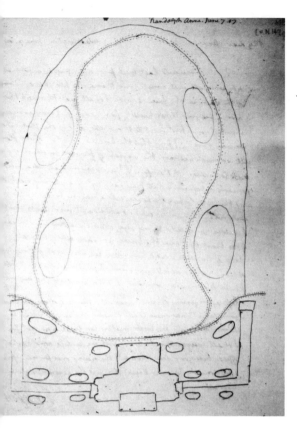

Jefferson's sketch of the west lawn, serpentine walk, and flowerbeds. Its contour is similar to his plan for the garden of the Hôtel de Langeac.

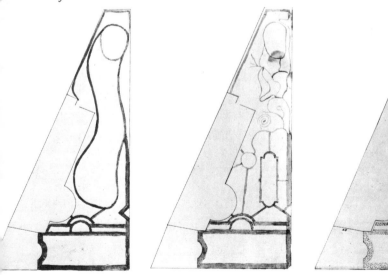

Jefferson's drawings for an English garden the Hôtel de Langeac. The house is out- ed on the left.

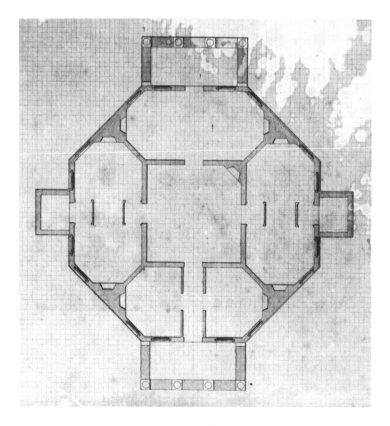

*ne of Jefferson's most Palladian designs, the rotunda of the
niversity of Virginia.*

pposite: *Floor plan* (left) *and elevation* (top)
*Jefferson's octagonal house, Poplar Forest, as
awn by his granddaughter Cornelia Randolph.*

Jefferson at seventy-eight, five years before his death, by Thomas Sully.

a favorite place for him to sit and read. Protected from sun and rain, he could look over his orchards and vineyards to the mountains beyond.

In the course of his long building campaign at Monticello, Jefferson considered, and even drew plans for, a variety of other garden structures. In 1804, he composed a memo, "General ideas for the improvement of Monticello," which included "a turning Tuscan temple," "Demosthenes' lantern," and two copies of "the Chinese pavilion of Kew garden" to be located at the angle of Monticello's offices. (This was one of a total of five different designs he at various times considered for this location. None was constructed.) Along the garden wall, he proposed a four-building history of some of the more celebrated styles of architecture, much as he later designed for the lawn of the University of Virginia. There was to be a model of the Pantheon, and one of "cubic architecture" such as the Maison Carrée, as well as examples of Gothic and Chinese styles. Then, in one of his typical afterthoughts, he concluded that a kitchen garden was no place for "ornaments of this kind." "These temples will be better disposed," he wrote, "in the pleasure grounds."

In actuality, they were disposed in the files of his library with other unbuilt drawings and plans. There were a number of reasons why these decorative garden pavilions were never built, not the least of which was the economic one. When, after his presidency, Jefferson's finances fell into a steady decline, such unnecessary building projects as garden pavilions could easily be postponed indefinitely. Jefferson, however, seldom denied himself anything he really wanted, whether he could afford it or not, so a lack of money was no real reason for not building these pavilions. After all, he had slave workmen capable of doing much of the labor on such structures, so the costs could be minimized. The most likely reason they were not built was that he decided that they were no longer desirable at Monticello.

All of these projected structures were public buildings to be enjoyed by visitors walking or riding over the grounds. Their effect would be to encourage more visitors to Monticello at a time when Jefferson had already found his privacy uncomfortably compromised. Casual passers-through were increasingly making a detour to Monticello, hoping for a glance at its famed sage. A granddaughter told Jefferson's biographer, Henry Randall, of the aggressive rudeness of some of these unwanted visitors. "Swarms of impertinent gazers," Randall wrote, ". . . without permission or any ceremony whatsoever, thrust themselves into the most private of Mr. Jefferson's out-of-door resorts, and even into his house, and stared about as if they were at a public show." Turning the gardens into a sightseeing attraction by constructing decorative pavilions would certainly not discourage this practice. The Southern code of hospitality, which was like Newtonian law for Jefferson, forbade him from excluding visitors and guests, but he was not compelled to make Monticello into a Virginia version of the English estates he and Adams had visited on their garden tour. For a small coin anyone could stroll through the grounds and visit the pavilions— and even peer through the windows of the manor house. Clearly, this was not the kind of garden Jefferson wanted at Monticello.

What he wanted was an ornamental farm that combined functional agriculture with pleasure gardens, a *ferme ornée* somewhat like the one he had seen at Woburn Farms in England. But because his house was located on top of a mountain, it presented him with problems not found at typical English country retreats. In 1806, he sent a plea for help to William Hamilton, whose estate near Philadelphia, the Woodlands, in Jefferson's opinion rivaled the gardens of England. In a long letter to Hamilton, Jefferson assessed Monticello's "very difficult" landscape. The mountaintop site, he wrote, "takes away from me the first beauty in gardening, the variety of hill and dale, & leaves me as an awkward substitute a few changing hollows & ridges." The climate of Virginia was also an enemy of the landscape designer. He compared the "sunless climate" of England with the "beaming, constant and almost vertical sun of Virginia." "Shade is our Elysium," he wrote. His solution for landscaping under conditions of too much sunshine was to cut the lower branches from lofty trees and plant clumps of shrubs and bushes underneath them. (This is what he attempted to do on a wooded eighteen acres he termed the "grove," located on the west side of the mountaintop.) The single virtue of this lofty site was the "rich profusion" of vistas: "Mountains distant & near, smooth & shaggy, single & in ridges, a little river hiding itself among the hills so as to shew in lagoons only, cultivated grounds under the eye of two small villages." The difficulty, he wrote, "is to prevent a satiety of this."

The landscaping conundrum he had created for himself forty years earlier by choosing to build on a mountain instead of alongside a river was, of course, one that admitted no solution. Even Thomas Jefferson could not prestidigitate a mountain into Salisbury Plain. There could be no extended serpentine walks that discovered new vistas at every turn, or glens and hillocks to surprise and delight the eye with constant changes in elevation. Lakes were not possible, nor rustic bridges to span them. These were denied to a landscape that was essentially the shape of a derby hat. Yet, the compromises he was forced to make in landscaping the grounds of his estate were no different from those he made in constructing his house. The building materials at hand and the availability of skilled labor dictated many of the choices in the design of both Monticello houses, the original and the remodeled version. Jefferson's willingness to modify theory in the face of fact was characteristic of him, for in neither his political nor his artistic life was he an idealist who placed abstract principles beyond the reach of practical considerations. In the most important accomplishment of his presidency, the Louisiana Purchase, for example, he ignored the serious questions of constitutionality, and in an act of naked pragmatism, pushed a ratification treaty through Congress. Architectural principles were no more sacred. And in landscaping, he ultimately accepted the fact that even though a Woburn Abbey or Leasowes on his mountaintop might be desirable, the site, his finances, and his need for privacy made it impossible.

The one place where Jefferson was able to execute his landscaping ideas with complete freedom was within the confines of the first roundabout, the lawns and gardens immediately surrounding the house. In June of 1807, he wrote to his granddaughter Anne Cary Randolph, who shared his enthusiasm for gardening, "I find that the limited number of our flower beds will too much restrain the variety of flowers in which we might wish to indulge, & therefore I have resumed an idea . . . of a winding walk surrounding the lawn before the house, with a narrow border of flowers on each side." He included a rough sketch of the serpentine walk and flowerbeds to be located on the perimeter of the lawn stretching before the west portico. The gravel walk, flowerbeds, and a reflecting pool were laid out the following year. The oval flowerbeds proved to be a great source of joy for Jefferson and his grandchildren. Ellen Randolph Coolidge wrote an account of how the grandchildren would help Jefferson plant hyacinth and tulip bulbs with such exotic names as "Roman Empress," "Queen of the Amazons," "Psyche," and "God of Love," and anxiously await "the surprisingly beautiful creations I should see arising from the ground when spring returned."

The serpentine walk that Jefferson laid out was little changed from one he designed for the original house in the 1770s. It was also much like a walk he designed for the garden of the Hôtel Langeac in Paris a decade or more later. The scale at Langeac was smaller, but the pattern is remarkably similar. It demonstrates the durability of some of his architectual ideas, particularly those that reached into the core of his personality, such as his attraction to sexual contours in many of his designs. The sinuous garden path, with its oval flowerbeds and a pond tucked into its convexities and concavities, brought the English landscape style to the very doors of Monticello, consummating a love affair Jefferson had carried on with picturesque landscaping for nearly forty years.

Once inside Monticello's doors, however, the obverse side of Jefferson became apparent, for in the furnishings and interior decorations of Monticello, he gave expression to his intellectual, scientific, and mechanical interests, his commonsense practicality, and his acquisitiveness. (We would today be tempted to say he landscaped with his right brain and furnished with his left.) His practicality has already been seen in the way he designed his library, using modular bookshelves that were inexpensive and portable. The library was also the most obvious evidence of his acquisitive instincts; he was a compulsive collector of books, statutes, letters, drawings, notes, memoranda, and records of every sort. Not only did he collect, he also indexed, classified, and systematized. He would be expected, therefore, to own what every gentleman of the Enlightenment possessed—a natural history cabinet. He had certainly seen many of these private museums at the residences of his scientific acquaintances in France: collections of animal skins or skeletons, fossilized bones and shells, rare rocks and gems, and artifacts from primitive cultures. Jefferson not only had a natural history collection, it was one of the most extensive of its kind in the nation. One visitor declared, "It is supposed there is no private gentleman in the world, in possession of so perfect and complete a scientific, useful and ornamental collection."

Jefferson's curios included a variety of Indian artifacts, so many that the entrance was often called the Indian Hall. There were bows, arrows, poisoned lances, peace pipes, wampum belts, moccasins, dresses, and cooking utensils. An English visitor reported seeing "the belt and shot pouch of the famous Tecumseh." Among the more prized items were a pair of seated Indian figures, carved of stone, which were excavated in Tennessee and "supposed to be of great antiquity." (One visitor, the Baron de Montlezun, commented that the figures were "sculptured by savages," and "very hideous.") There were also two buffalo-hide wall hangings, one depicting a battle between the Panis and Osage tribes, the other a map of the Missouri Territory.

Jefferson's interest in the American Indian went back to his youth. At eighteen, he had gone to see one of the great Cherokee chiefs, Ontasseté, and was filled with awe by the Indian's moving farewell oration before members of his tribe. Jefferson studied Indian cultures throughout his life. In *Notes on the State of Virginia*, he wrote a brief history of American Indian tribes and their folkways with an attention to detail that marked all of his scientific work. He made a collection over the years of the vocabularies of more than thirty Indian tribes (the trunk it was stored in was stolen en route to Monticello and the collection lost), and during his presidency, he met with tribal chiefs, played White Father to them, and smoked their peace pipes with obvious enjoyment.

In contrast to his attitudes toward black African slaves, whom he thought to be genetically inferior to whites, he romanticized Indians as Rousseauistic noble savages. He was impressed particularly by their native eloquence, their courage, and their stoicism, traits that were the same Roman virtues he had himself absorbed through his classical education. Jefferson's Indian artifacts were, therefore, more than a collection of scientific specimens; they were tokens of admiration acquired by one who sentimentalized the Indian, much as later generations were to do. In his old age, he would repeat to visitors Thomas Mann Randolph's claim that his grandchildren were distant descendants, on the Randolph side of the family, of the legendary Indian princess Pocahontas. Coming from a man who detested royalty of every kind, it was a rare illustration of how totally he was captive to the reach and power of Indian myth.

Included in Jefferson's natural history collection were mastodon fossils from the famous paleontological cache at Big Bone Lick, Kentucky. Jefferson had commissioned William Clark of the Lewis and Clark expedition to excavate at the site, at Jefferson's own expense, for fossils to be sent to the American Philosophical Society in Philadelphia and the Museum of Natural History in Paris. He kept some of the fossils from Clark's horde of bones "for a special kind of Cabinet I have at Monticello." These included parts of a mastodon head as well as tusks from an elephant and a mastodon. Jefferson was particularly proud of these fossils, considering them prize items in his natural history collection.

Like the Indian artifacts, the fossil collection at Monticello was an overt manifestation of a covert daemon. One of the reasons Jefferson wrote and published *Notes on the State of Virginia* was to refute a claim by the eminent naturalist, the Comte de Buffon, that human and animal life in America was degenerative and therefore inferior to the life forms of Europe. Buffon believed, Jefferson wrote in his *Notes*, "that nature is less active, less energetic on one side of the globe than she is on the other." Jefferson added, with more than a hint of sarcasm, "as if both sides were not warmed by the same genial sun," and launched into a lengthy refutation of Buffon's hypothesis with convincing evidence that animals are actually larger in America than in Europe. The mastodon, or mammoth, was his clincher; Europe had produced no animal to match this behemoth. More than two decades after his disagreement with Buffon, he was still anxious to add supporting evidence for the preeminence of American over European fauna; his shipment of mastodon fossils to Paris, therefore, was not entirely Enlightenment altruism; it was also a final salvo in a scientific war.

In spite of a display of gentlemanly modesty about his numerous personal achievements, Jefferson never doubted his own social and intellectual superiority. And because his self-esteem was identified totally with place—Monticello, Virginia, the United States—any affront to his pride of place was also an affront to him. Throughout his public career, therefore, he remained sensitive to European claims that the young American republic was in any way an inferior nation. His refusal to be treated as a second-class subject by George III and the British Parliament helped make a rebel of him; Buffon's suggestion that infant America was nature's retardate drove him to collect the ancient bones of the mammoth. He actually thought it possible to find a live one, for he did not believe animals or vegetables became extinct. "I think therefore still," he wrote in 1818, "there is reason to doubt whether any species of animal is become extinct." But the bones proved at least that the mastodon had indeed trod the soil of the American continent. When he received his fossils, he catalogued them carefully and precisely, as was his habit, sending them off to Philadelphia for admiration, and to Paris for edification. He kept a few choice specimens, however, for his Monticello museum—trophies of a sort in commemoration of a private victory in the battle of New World versus Old.

Along with the Indian artifacts and the fossil collection was an assortment of "petrifications, chrystalizations, minerals, shells etc," together with mounted heads of an elk, deer, buffalo, and mountain ram. This miscellany must have created an impression of dense clutter in the entry hall, especially since the remaining available wall space was covered with paintings, and much of the floor space with sofas, tables, and statuary.

George Ticknor, who was later to become a distinguished professor of modern languages at Harvard College, left an account of the effect Jefferson's "museum" had on a highly educated and artistically sensitive young visitor from Boston. On entering the hall, Ticknor was struck by what he called the "strange furniture of its walls." He was reminded of a room in the Man of the Hill's house in *Tom Jones*, about which Fielding wrote, "it was adorned with a great number of nicknacks and curiosities which might have engaged the attention of a virtuoso." Among the curiosities Ticknor surely noticed were a reclining marble sculpture of Ariadne in front of the hall fireplace and a model of the pyramid of Cheops over the mantle. Ticknor admired individual specimens, but was critical of the incongruities created by combining, in a single room, a variety of natural curios with paintings and sculpture. In particular, he thought that placing the two leather Indian hangings next to a "fine painting of the Repentence of St.

Peter" was an "odd union." This juxtaposition of primitive drawings on hide with sophisticated European easel painting would not have disturbed Jefferson too much, for he had attended the Salons of Paris, where paintings were jammed onto every available inch of wall space with scant attention to harmony of style or content. He did, however, hang his paintings and prints in tiers, according to subject and size, three tiers in the parlor, two in the dining room. Everything he collected was pressed into some kind of system.

In 1803, a year after Anna Maria Thornton visited Monticello, a list of the artworks at Monticello showed 126 items, including 17 in the entrance hall, 49 in the parlor, 10 in the dining room, and 36 in the tearoom (most of the works in this small room were obviously miniatures). Jefferson was also known to have a large portfolio of unframed prints and drawings. This varied collection of sculpture, paintings, prints, and maps had been acquired the way much of Monticello had been built, by accretion. From his youth, Jefferson had recognized that painting and sculpture, like architecture, music, and literature, were desirable adornments to a gentleman's virtu. When he was making plans for building the first Monticello, he included in his Construction Notebook a wish list of nineteen works of sculpture and painting. His primary interest was sculpture, not surprisingly, for the same classical education that turned him to Rome for architectural inspiration directed him to statuary, the representational art form most directly linked to classical antiquity. At the head of his list were the Medici Venus and the Apollo Belvedere, considered by gentlemen of taste to be the supreme examples of female and male beauty to descend from the ancient world. Copies of these two works were most likely intended for two niches in the parlor of the original house. He never acquired them, but during a lifetime of collecting, he managed to amass a sizeable number of sculptural busts, and enough paintings, prints, and maps to fill the available wall space of the public rooms of Monticello.

Of all these works, only a handful would now be worth serious artistic consideration. Jefferson acquired much of his collection randomly, buying some items in Paris at auction, commissioning copies of others, and receiving some as presentation copies. The one distinguished artist whose work he owned was Jean-Antoine Houdon, whom he became acquainted with in Paris. He brought to Monticello a total of seven busts by Houdon, mostly of American patriots, including the famous Houdon likeness of Jefferson himself. He recalled to a visitor how the great sculptor started the bust by making a life mask. "When I went to him to have my bust taken, he stript me bare down to the shoulders, then his wife, a beautiful little woman, took oil of almonds, and anointed my face and neck while Houdon stood by with his plaster and immediately put it on my face and neck." He owned Houdon busts of Washington, Franklin, John Paul Jones, and Lafayette, all in plaster. These were placed on four brackets in the tearoom, prompting Jefferson to call this his "most honourable suite." There were two other Houdon plaster busts, of Turgot and Voltaire. These stood in the crowded entrance hall along with a larger-than-life marble bust of Jefferson in Roman costume by Ceracchi, and symbolically, directly opposite it, a bust of Alexander Hamilton—"opposed in death as in life," Jefferson was to comment. In the parlor were two other busts, a marble of Napoleon and a plaster of Alexander I of Russia. The English sculptor William Coffee, who had helped Jefferson solve his problem with leaky cisterns, added several small terra-cotta busts of Jefferson and members of his family to the collection. A final addition to Jefferson's gallery of notable American statesmen was a plaster bust of John Adams acquired in 1825, a year before the deaths of the two former Presidents.

Those who accused Jefferson of being antireligious would have been surprised to find that many of the oil paintings he owned were on biblical subjects. A close examination of the titles of these paintings reveals, however, that in purchasing works with religious themes his concern was less with piety than with sentimentality. Among paintings purchased in Paris, for example, were "a flaggelation of the Christ," "Jesus bearing his cross," "Jephtha leading his daughter Leila to be sacrificed," "Sacrifice of Isaac," "A Virgin Mary weeping on the death of Jesus," "St. Peter Weeping for his Offence," "Magdalene Penitent," "The Prodigal Son," and "Herodiade Bearing the Head of St. John on a Platter." (The latter painting, which has been returned to Monticello, was given the place of honor over the parlor fireplace.) All of these paintings invite the same kind of sympathetic pathos found in the literature of sensibility. Their sentimentality rendered them morally uplifting rather than dogmatically spiritual—the kind of religious art an enlightened intellectual like Jefferson could admire. Besides the biblical works, he purchased paintings of subjects from classical antiquity and a number of copies of old masters, including Raphael, Leonardo, and Rubens. (Copies of famous paintings, particularly if done by a competent hand, were considered in good taste in the eighteenth century.)

Jefferson enjoyed showing his religious paintings to visitors at Monticello and relating anecdotes about them. He shocked two clergymen, one of them William Hooper, an Episcopal priest who was to become president of Wake Forest College, when he described to them an anachronistic and irreverent painting he had seen in Europe: "He told us," Hooper recalled, "of a Dutch piece representing the sacrifice of Isaac. 'He, the painter, placed a gun in Abraham's hand, he is taking aim at his son, and an angel is p——s——g in the pan [to prevent the gun from being fired].' This levity on a scripture subject I thought rather indecent before two clergymen, and the use of such a word [pissing] in a man of dignity." Jefferson also told Hooper he thought Gilbert Stuart was the greatest portrait painter in the world. "He not only gave the features," he declared, "but the expression—the mind. But his charges are high."

Jefferson's religious paintings were mostly acquired during his Paris years and even at that time were not intended to be the focus of his collection. Just as he had haunted the booksellers of Paris to add to his library anything having to do with America, he had also decided to decorate the walls of Monticello with geographical and historical scenes of America, and with portraits of its luminaries. He acquired likenesses of such explorers of the Americas as Columbus, Cortez, Magellan, and Vespucci, and of the colonizer of Virginia, Sir Walter Raleigh. To these were added a gallery of paintings or prints of American patriots, including Washington, Adams, Franklin, Lafayette, and Paine. He displayed in the lower tier of works hung in the parlor a set of ten medals of officers who had distinguished themselves during the Revolution. There were also portraits of his private heroes, "the three greatest men the world had ever produced," Bacon, Newton, and Locke. They had contributed to the intellectual foundations of the nation.

Jefferson had encouraged John Trumbull in the artist's plan to paint scenes of the Revolutionary War, and acquired a print of the most famous of these, *The Declaration of Independence*. It was added to a wide collection of Americana, including scenes of Harper's Ferry, Niagara Falls, the Natural Bridge, New Orleans, Mount Vernon, and an elevation of Monticello by Robert Mills.

Like the Indian artifacts and mastodon bones, Jefferson's collection of American art was his private contribution to the creation of a usable past for the new nation. He was acutely conscious of the importance of historical icons in carving out a national identity. This was why, for example, he was so intent on encouraging a public architecture modeled upon traditions of the ancient world. His selection of the Maison Carrée at Nîmes, "the most beautiful and precious morsel of architecture left us by antiquity," as a pattern for the capitol building at Richmond, was intended to do "honor to our country, as presenting to travelers a specimen of taste in our infancy, promising much for our maturity." It was equally important for sculpture to venerate America's *pater patriae* as it had been in Augustan Rome, and the world's greatest living sculptor, Houdon, was brought to America to do a likeness of George Washington. Paintings, drawings, and prints were to satisfy the same purpose—to aggrandize the nation's heroes, commemorate its military and political victories, rejoice in its natural beauties.

But because Jefferson was so intimately involved with the history of the United States, the Americana collection was at once a public record of the nation's glories and of his own private memories. Washington, Franklin, Adams, Madison, and Lafayette were not only national heroes, but close colleagues and friends. He was not merely a character in Trumbull's *Declaration of Independence*, he wrote the document, debated it, and signed it. He was not simply an observer of American history, but a principal player. The collection, therefore, seemingly concerned with objective aesthetic, historical, or patriotic interests, was in fact intensely personal—fitting for a house that was itself the mirror of its architect-builder.

The furniture of Monticello, like the art collection, was acquired from a variety of sources. Much of it came from France, where Jefferson purchased a houseful of tables, chairs, sofas, beds, curtains, and draperies for the Hôtel de Langeac. These were mostly in the Louis XVI style, appropriate for a fashionable residence like Langeac. Chairs and sofas were decorated in gilt and upholstered in blue or crimson damask, velvet, or red morocco. Jefferson was partial to mahogany; a number of the pieces of furniture he acquired in Paris were crafted from this dark, lustrous wood: tables, buffets, consoles, and commodes, some topped with marble or bound in brass. When he returned from France, his furnishings and household goods filled eighty-six packing crates. Their contents showed that during his five years in France he had engaged in an epic shopping binge that included the purchase of fifty-seven chairs, two sofas, six large mirrors, wallpaper, silver, china, linen, clocks, scientific equipment, a cabriolet, and a phaeton. All of this was in addition to his art collection, books, and wine.

Most of Jefferson's Parisian furniture was shipped to Philadelphia, where he kept as stylish a residence as secretary of state as he had kept in France. While in Philadelphia, he bought more chairs, tables, and mirrors, but this was to be the end of his large purchases of furniture. When he returned to Virginia in 1793 at the end of his term as secretary of state, for what he thought would close his public career, he sent most of his furnishings to Monticello. Some pieces were sold, however, because, as his granddaughter Ellen Randolph Coolidge was to write, they were "of a kind not suited to a country house." These were no doubt some of the ornate and expensive Louis Seize pieces. At a time when Jefferson was just beginning to remodel and enlarge Monticello, the sale of his fashionable French furniture hints at the kind of residence the new Monticello was to be. It was to reflect the style and elegance of a Parisian town house on the exterior, but the comfort and convenience of a traditional English country house inside. This split personality led to many of Jefferson's design problems, but it also stamped upon the house his own unique profile.

He could not have anticipated it at the time, but the economic distress he was to suffer when he finally retired from public life at the end of his presidency made his decision to abandon highly ornamental, painted, or upholstered furniture in favor of simpler but well-made mahogany pieces a fortunate one. Although John Hemings and his crew could make and repair mahogany or walnut furniture, they had neither the upholstering skills nor the materials to repair a Louis XVI *fauteuil* or *bergère*. As a result, the upholstering on the furniture quickly deteriorated. Francis Calley Gray, who visited Monticello in 1815 with George Ticknor, reported that on entering the dining room, "the first thing which attracted our attention was the state of the chairs. They had leather bottoms stuffed with hair, but the bottoms were completely worn through and the hair sticking out in all directions."

Jefferson purchased virtually no furniture after he left the presidency. When Monticello's interior was completed, and Dinsmore and Neilson left in 1809, the furniture consisted of a few family pieces originally belonging to his mother or his wife, furnishings brought from Paris and Philadelphia, a handsome Chippendale dining room table believed to have been a gift from George Wythe, side chairs used in the tearoom, which may have been purchased from the Wythe estate, and articles manufactured on the premises by Dinsmore and Hemings.

After Dinsmore's departure, John Hemings continued to supply furniture for Monticello and Poplar Forest until Jefferson's death. The amount of furniture produced by Hemings was considerable. In 1817, for example, Jefferson asked James Oldham to purchase four hundred feet of mahogany to be sent to Monticello "to make up into commodes or chests of drawers." Some of Jefferson's specialized furniture made from his own designs was also manufactured on the premises, such as the architect's table on which he did most of his drawing. Among his surviving furniture designs are drawings or sketches for tables, chests, a ladder-back side chair, and a library ladder. Hemings may also have made some of the small, shelved serving tables, or "dumbwaiters" as Jefferson called them, which were sometimes used at Monticello. One of these tables, three feet high and only eighteen inches square, was placed beside each chair when Jefferson wished to eliminate servants from the dining room for privacy. The various courses of the meal were placed on the three shelves of the table so the diners could serve themselves.

One of the finest pieces crafted by John Hemings met with a sad fate. It was made for Ellen Randolph, perhaps as a wedding present for her marriage to Joseph Coolidge, Jr., in 1825. The vessel carrying Ellen's belongings to Boston, where she was to live with her new husband, sank, and Hemings's gift went down with it. Jefferson reported to her the effect on Hemings of the loss of the lovingly crafted piece of furniture.

He was au desespoir! That beautiful writing desk he had taken so much pains to make for you! Everything else seemed as nothing in his eye, and that loss was everything. Virgil could not have been more afflicted had his Aeneid fallen prey to the flames. I asked him if he could not replace it by making another? No. His eyesight had failed him too much, and his recollection of it was too imperfect.

The anecdote reveals Hemings's pride of craftsmanship. His anguish at the loss of what might have been the finest piece of furniture he ever made was as deeply felt as the loss of a loved one. Any artist could understand his despair, for a part of him perished with the ill-fated ship. Jefferson replaced Hemings's gift with an even more valuable treasure, however; he sent Coolidge the portable desk on which he had written the Declaration of Independence. It had been made from Jefferson's own design by one of Philadelphia's most prestigious cabinetmakers, Benjamin Randolph. One day, he wrote, the desk may be "carried in the procession of our nation's birthday, as the relics of the saints are in those of the church." It was the comment of a man who was well aware of his own place in history.

The rooms of Monticello were not overly furnished by the standard of other large houses of the period. Ellen Randolph Coolidge remarked that "there was but little furniture in [the house] and that of no value," but this was more accurate for the upstairs bedrooms than for the public rooms. A typical bedroom, such as the one the Thorntons slept in during their visit in 1802, would be furnished rather sparsely with a table, a "walnut stand," two "old mahogany chairs," two mirrors, and a candlestick or lamp. The alcove bed would be covered with a counterpane of chintz, calico, or blue and white checks.

The best furniture was in the parlor, dining room, and tearoom. The furniture in the entry hall consisted of two sofas at the entrance, tables for displaying curios, and a number of Windsor chairs, all lined up like regimented troops along the dadoes of the walls. This was the conventional way furniture was arranged in the formal rooms of the great houses of England, and it was a functional grouping for a room that was waiting room, museum, and thoroughfare. The Windsor chairs, which Jefferson called "stick chairs," served a dual purpose; they could be used where they were placed, or could be conveniently carried to the parlor when there were large numbers of visitors, or to the east portico where guests might sit and take the evening air. It was common in the great houses of this period for light furniture to be moved about freely and arranged where it was needed. There was always a large staff of house servants to put things back in order.

The parlor was arranged more in the French style, with tables and chairs placed in conversational groupings before the fireplace or windows. On the rainy February day Francis Gray and George Ticknor visited, the two young men were met by Thomas Mann Randolph and Jefferson in the dining room, where a fire would be kept going all day long. House servants kindled a fire in the parlor for the occasion, and the group retired there for an afternoon's conversation. Several comfortable chairs, a table for the drinks that were served, and a firescreen would be arranged in front of the fireplace for conversations such as this. In the summer, the arrangement could be set in front of one of the windows. Away from the fireplace, the rest of the parlor would have been icy in winter, for its numerous windows would have made heating it with a single fireplace on a cold day nearly impossible.

One other important piece of furniture in the parlor was Martha Randolph's pianoforte, which stood in a corner where musical entertainments were held. Music had been a part of the domestic life of Monticello ever since Jefferson moved into the first house with his wife. His musical tastes were varied; his large library of music included pieces for voice and instrument by such composers as Vivaldi, Corelli, Haydn, and Mozart. But he also had an extensive collection of popular songs, dances, ballad operas—just about every kind of secular music written. He owned a great many books on musical instrumentation and technique as well. He was interested in the technicalities of musical instruments perhaps even more than in the aesthetics of music. He was knowledgeable about the latest advancements in keyboard instruments, and, in ordering them for his daughters or granddaughters, he insisted upon fine craftsmanship and technical innovation. As in the case of everything mechanical that he owned, Jefferson learned the intricacies of his keyboard instruments, tuned and repaired them, and carried on a correspondence with craftsmen and amateurs like himself about such details as the most effective way to quill a harpsichord. Even when his injured wrist made playing the violin impossible, he enjoyed listening to music sung and played by his daughter Martha and his granddaughters.

A formal dining room in a house such as Monticello was an innovation of the late eighteenth century. Previously, meals were served at several small tables, which could be placed in any convenient room and moved away to allow the room to be used for other purposes. In the original Monticello, the dining room was undoubtedly a multipurpose room, for space was scarce. When a large dining table with removable leaves, such as the one Jefferson reportedly acquired from George Wythe, was placed in a room, it was then normally reserved exclusively for dining. In the winter, however, the Monticello dining room served as a lounge and reading room for Jefferson. There was enough room for him to place a comfortable chair and a candlestand before the fireplace and read there after dinner. Francis Gray noted that the dining room mantelpiece was stacked with books. He also observed a harpsichord in a corner of the dining room, suggesting that after-dinner music was performed in the one room that could be kept comfortably warm. The adjoining tearoom and its many drafty windows could be closed off with sliding double glass doors. The tearoom was used for breakfast as well as tea, but its north-facing windows must have made for drafty breakfasting on cold mornings, even with the freestanding stove Jefferson installed in it.

Jefferson did not use tablecloths on the dining room tables; a napkin was placed under each table setting. The tableware was functional rather than elegant. He had brought back a great deal of china from France, but normal attrition in a household of children and guests took a heavy toll. By the time of his death, there was little of his French china left. He also brought back a large amount of silver, including a handsome coffee urn crafted in Paris from his own design. There were candlesticks and candelabra for the dining table, but candles were used sparingly during this period, even in the greatest Virginia houses, and this was undoubtedly also true at Monticello. The young tutor Philip Fithian reported that during a holiday dinner, the dining room at Nomini Hall "looked luminous and splendid; four very large candles burning on the table where we supp'd, three others in different parts of the room." A total of seven candles could not have produced a great amount of light by our standards, but eighteenth-century eyes existed in quite another world of nighttime illumination. A single candle was enough to read by, and four candles could be "luminous and splendid." We would probably find the public rooms of eighteenth-century houses unattractively dark in the evening, with deep shadows and hidden corners, much as Anna Maria Thornton found the dining room of Monticello when she first entered it before any candles had been lit. White or pastel-colored walls and ceilings helped reflect light from a limited source, but by our standards, the spacious rooms of Monticello were dim and cavernous when lit by what Jefferson, his family, and guests would consider adequate illumination.

There were oil lamps at Monticello, but how many and where they were used is not known. While he was in France, Jefferson was enthusiastic about the newly invented Argand "cylinder lamp," named after its hollow, cylindrical wick; he brought two of them to Monticello. He wrote to James Madison that the lamp consumed very little oil and "is thought to give light equal to six or eight candles." (Madison was convinced; he asked Jefferson to send him one.) During his presidency, Jefferson purchased several oil lamps, but it is not clear whether they were for the President's House or Monticello. He used an oil lamp in his private suite, for he made a note in his Farm Book shortly before his death: "May 26, 1826. a gallon of lamp oil, costing D 1.25 has lighted my chamber highly 25. nights, for 6. hours a night which is 5. cents a night & 150. hours." Even during his final illness, a lifetime habit of this kind of observation was impossible to break. Earlier, he had performed one of his typical efficiency experiments on the "comparative expense of candles and lamps":

A common glass lamp with a flat wick $\frac{1}{2}$ an I. wide was placed beside a mould candle of the size called sixes, & allowed both to burn 16$\frac{1}{2}$ hours without being moved. In that time 2$\frac{3}{5}$ candles were consumed, a $\frac{1}{3}$ pint of oil. From the experiment it appears that 1. gallon of oil will burn 402. hours, and that it requires 10$\frac{3}{5}$ lb of candle to burn the same time so that supposing oil to be .75 per gallon, it will be equal to mould candles at 7. cents per lb. which shews the advantage of oil.

Experiments such as this on the efficient management of time and resources were characteristic of Jefferson's compulsive personality, but they were also a guiding principle of his age. The Newtonian universe of the eighteenth century was a mechanistic model based on a clock-work metaphor. There was little doubt that eventually the springs, levers, and gears that powered the machine would be discovered, and this would lead inevitably to universal progress and human happiness. Experimentation, rational analysis, and mathematical rigor were the methodologies that would unlock the secrets of natural law. Enlightenment philosophes accepted these principles as articles of faith.

One reason Jefferson functioned so comfortably in this cultural environment was that the intellectual garments of the age fit so perfectly his personal identity—he was most satisfied and secure when he was saving, measuring, counting, or timing. In order to carry out these enterprises most efficiently, he collected every kind of mechanical aid he could lay his hands on. His most imperative need had been a copying machine to relieve him of the onerous task of hand-copying every piece of correspondence that left his desk. (He was temperamentally incapable of mailing anything without retaining a copy of it.) It was not until 1804, during his first term as President, that he replaced the cumbersome copying press and its often illegible facsimiles with a polygraph manufactured by the artist Charles Willson Peale. The polygraph was based on the mechanical principle of a seventeenth-century invention, the pantograph, a series of rigid rods in the form of a parallelogram with two pens attached. When one pen was used to draw or write, the other pen produced an exact duplicate. The refinement of this device into the polygraph by Peale and John Isaac Hawkins, a Philadelphia inventor, made it possible for Jefferson to produce nearly perfect copies of his vast correspondence. He was infatuated with this machine, owned several versions of it during his lifetime, and collaborated with Peale over a number of years to eliminate the failings of a delicate and fussy instrument with tolerances too fine for the hard labor that Jefferson's writing schedule imposed on it. He kept a polygraph in his private suite at Monticello, and another at Poplar Forest, and it is to these instruments that we owe the historical treasure of thousands of copies of Jefferson's notes and letters, as readable as the day they were written.

For measuring, he had his surveying equipment, pocket sextant, theodolite, thermometer, barometer, pedometer, odometer, and a clever wind vane for recording wind directions at Monticello. He owned two odometers, one purchased in Philadelphia in 1791, and another during his presidency. He enjoyed measuring the distances, with precise accuracy, of the various stops from Washington to Monticello, and of the roundabouts and roads on his plantations. One of the odometers rang a bell every ten miles; "having miles announced by the bell as by milestones on the road" gave him "great satisfaction," he wrote. He had the wind vane installed on an elevated frame on the roof of the east portico of Monticello. The rod of the vane extended through the portico roof to a dial on the ceiling below so the wind direction could be read from the portico or the entry hall.

There were a number of clocks at Monticello; each of the public rooms had a decorative clock on the mantelpiece, and Jefferson kept a clock on a bracket in his bedroom sleeping alcove. This clock, its works supported by two black marble obelisks, was made for him in Paris from his own design. He would rise each morning at daybreak, or, as he was fond of saying, as soon as he could see the hands of this clock on the dial. A conversation piece, in Jefferson's day and still so, was the "Great Clock" over the entrance hall doorway, with a face on the outside portico and another in the hall. This seven-day calendar clock was built from Jefferson's design by Peter Spurck, an apprentice of Philadelphia clockmaker Robert Leslie. Its escapement and ringing mechanism are controlled by weights fashioned from cannonballs, suspended by two cables that run from the clock to pulleys at each corner of the room and then down the walls. The cannonball weights on the south wall tell the day of the week as they pass markers on the wall. There was not enough room for Friday and Saturday, however, so Jefferson cut a hole in the floor, and on Friday afternoon the top weight, which marks the day, passes into the basement and all of the weights remain there until Sunday morning when the clock is rewound with its twenty-two-inch crank. To climb up to the clock, there is an ingenious ladder that can be converted to an unobtrusive pole by folding one side into the other.

The cannonball clock and its ladder were still more of Jefferson's "conveniences"—mechanical novelties that he took delight in designing and showing off. Garry Wills has written that Jefferson would have apologized to David Rittenhouse, a professional clockmaker, for the clock because of its "clumsy mimicking of the clockmaker's real achievement in the eighteenth century." This may have been true, for Jefferson was in awe of the mechanical genius of David Rittenhouse, but he could have argued that the clock was perfectly right for its setting. It may not have been mechanically sophisticated, but it was a conspicuous symbol: cannonballs being put to constructive domestic use—guns beaten into ploughshares, as it were—appropriately, by one intimately associated with the War for Independence. Like the natural history collection and Indian artifacts in the entry hall, the cannonball clock, in striking the hours, sounded a note from America's past, with a reminder of Jefferson's place in it. Cutting a hole in the floor to make the clock work properly was one of the more obvious instances of dozens of similar improvisations that were made in the course of a lifetime of tinkering with the house. It was the kind of solution to a problem that owner-builders have made since houses have been in existence.

Most of the "conveniences" at Monticello were similar attempts to solve the kinds of problems that appear in any domestic establishment. They may not loom large in the great scheme of things, but a daily irritant, unrelieved over a period of time, can interfere more with one's peace of mind than events of national import. It was predictable, for example, that with Jefferson's obsession with organization, he would have devised some system for ordering his clothing. At the foot of his alcove bed he constructed a turntable clothes closet. It was described by Augustus John Foster as "a horse with forty-eight projecting hands on which hung his coats and waistcoats and which he could turn with a long stick, a knick-knack that Jefferson was fond of showing with many other little mechanical inventions." The turntable was one of his favorite mechanical principles. The writing table in his bedroom suite had a revolving top, and the high-backed chair facing it revolved to facilitate getting behind the table. In his final years, when he was afflicted by rheumatic ailments, he added a bench seat to this chair to make a comfortable chaise longue that enabled him to read and write in a semireclining position.

Jefferson's household gadgetry has always presented a problem for his biographers; it did not seem appropriate that the statesman-philosopher-architect-scientist should be expending his time and creative energy on such trivialities. Mrs. Thornton expressed this attitude during her visit to Monticello when she discovered Jefferson "very much engaged and interested in a phaeton which he had constructed after eight years preparation." The carriage had been designed by Jefferson and built at the Monticello joinery shop, and Jefferson, who had very likely done some of the work on it himself, was as excited as a teenager with a new car. "The mind of the p[resident]. of the U.S. ought to have more important occupation[s]," Mrs. Thornton observed tartly.

What has been overlooked about Jefferson's fascination with mechanical contrivances is the element of play involved. How many generations of sons have sat with their fathers to explore the workings of old clocks or broken pieces of machinery in a timeless game of exploration? The purpose of these mechanical excursions is not necessarily to repair clocks or fix machines, but to investigate the world of mechanics—and to share a father-son experience. Jefferson's love of designing, repairing, and tinkering with mechanical devices had something of this boyhood excitement at exploring and mastering the physical world. It was childhood play adapted to an adult world, and may have had its roots in shared experiences with a father who worked with his hands, and whom Jefferson greatly admired. Jefferson made of Monticello a toyshop where the adult "law of convenience"—an arbitrary decision that he did not have to abide by formal rules of architecture or interior design—gave him the liberty to indulge his most boyish enthusiasms. Showing off his ingenious devices to visitors and guests was like the child's twin motivations: pride of accomplishment with an appeal for approval.

Indeed, the entire Monticello building project can be viewed as a form of adult play. "Putting up and pulling down [is] one of my favorite amusements"—the most repeated of Jefferson's comments about Monticello—defines house construction as play. To build a house is serious business; to remodel and reconstruct one for amusement is play. It may seem incongruous for a compulsive personality such as Jefferson to engage in construction as creative play, but it is precisely the obsessive person who requires the spontaneity of play as a counterweight to psychological necessity. Jefferson was full of such seeming contradictions: his outpourings of love and affection for his daughters, his admiration for Ossian and the picturesque garden, his falling in love with Maria Cosway in a backflip of adolescent passion, his sentimentality toward his grandchildren. (It should be noted, however, that these were all controlled releases; only at the death of his wife did he abandon all emotional restraint.) His favorite game was that most intellectual exercise, chess, and his violin playing was mechanical, rather than inspired—"according to the gamut." The "building game" fit these patterns perfectly.

This does not undervalue Jefferson's accomplishments as an architect-builder, or his achievement at Monticello. It merely asserts that, as one writer put it, "because I was once a child, I am always a child." We all retain our capacity for the child's sense of playfulness, no matter how seriously adult we have become—as serious as President of the United States, for example. One of the insights into Thomas Jefferson's career as a builder, then, is that his stately mansion, with its magical mystery tour of architectural legerdemain, was erected in part by a boy.

Afterword

ON JULY 4, 1826, in his familiar alcove bed at Monticello, Thomas Jefferson quietly expired in his eighty-third year. By a coincidence many thought providential, it was on the fiftieth anniversary of the signing of the Declaration of Independence, the document that linked his name forever with such sublime abstractions as liberty, equality, and the pursuit of happiness. The coincidence was compounded by the death, on the same day, of his colleague in rebellion and fellow President of the United States, John Adams. The dying words of Adams were symbolically prophetic: "Thomas Jefferson still survives!" The simultaneous deaths of two of the architects of the American Revolution, men who had laid the cornerstone of a new nation, were rightly seen as the passing of an epoch.

He was buried on July 5 in the graveyard at the foot of Mulberry Row. More than half a century before, he had planned a Gothic memorial for this site, but it remained a simple, unadorned rectangular plot, and he wanted nothing grander for his own burial place. He had designed a stone obelisk, eight feet tall, to bear the inscription: "Here is buried Thomas Jefferson, author of the Declaration of Indepen-

*Jefferson's grave
and tombstone.*

dence, of the Statute of Virginia for Religious Freedom, and Father of
the University of Virginia." The public offices he held—governor of
Virginia, secretary of state, Vice President, and President of the United
States—were not, in his mind, his greatest accomplishments. Even
the purchase of Louisiana, the capstone of his presidency, was not to
be listed among his lasting achievements. The three accomplishments
he chose to be remembered for were, significantly, acts of an architect-
builder: the design of a new nation, the erection of a foundation for
freedom of worship in that nation, and the founding of a great university.

His grave was dug between those of his wife and youngest daughter
by Wormley, the slave who was to recall years later the tumultuous
greeting Jefferson received from the Monticello slaves on his return
from France. In all likelihood, the coffin was lovingly crafted by John
Hemings; in his will, Jefferson had granted Hemings his freedom.

The years following Jefferson's retirement from the presidency in 1809
had been both happy and troubled. The happiness derived from his
return to Monticello, where he settled in as a patriarch of his family
and, increasingly, of his state and nation. Although he officially di-

vested himself of all political attachments when he left the presidency, he had the satisfaction of continuing to exert an indirect influence on national affairs through his close friendship with the successive Presidents Madison and Monroe, to whom he was virtually an Augustan deity. His creative energies were thrown into his "academical village," the University of Virginia; he was its architect and construction superintendent, fundraiser, academic recruiter, library and curriculum consultant, lobbyist, booster—in short, its father. His final years were enriched by the knowledge that he was constructing an institution he hoped would equal in education what his Declaration had created in statecraft.

But his old age was crippled by the specter of ever-increasing insolvency. His presidency, with its generous annual salary of $25,000, should have allowed him to eliminate his debts and even accrue a surplus. Instead, he returned to Virginia after eight years in Washington even more deeply in debt. He hoped to assign the annual income of $2,500 from his Bedford estate, which accounted for half of his land and slaves, to paying off his debts, but steadily declining economic conditions in Virginia, the War of 1812, bad weather, and his own hospitality all conspired to increase these. The sale of his library to the government in 1815 for nearly $24,000 eliminated less than half of this debt, and from that time onward, there was little chance of extracting himself from eventual financial ruin except by massive sales of his only tangible assets, land and slaves. Even this became an impossibility after the economic recession in 1819, when land values tumbled.

The coup de grace came in 1818 when Wilson Carey Nicholas, father-in-law of his grandson, Jefferson Randolph, asked him to endorse notes of $20,000. With misgivings, Jefferson did so, and a year later Nicholas defaulted on the loan. Jefferson was left with an additional large debt, which could be managed only by attempting to meet the interest payments. The final years of his life saw his finances deteriorate rapidly. An attempt to eliminate his debts with a lottery, which offered Monticello and its lands as a prize, but would have allowed him to live in the mansion during his lifetime and retain the Bedford estate and his slaves, was a failure. At his death, he was more than $100,000 in debt.

There is a nagging question about Jefferson's finances: How could a man who recorded every penny he earned or spent, who kept accounts as rigorously as a banker, allow himself to slip so deeply into debt? The explanation by the editors of *Jefferson's Memorandum Books* is as surprising as it is insightful: he rarely ever knew how badly in debt he actually was. Through much of his life in public service, they write, "Jefferson was profoundly ignorant of his own financial condition." In a revealing statement to his former secretary William Short, from whom he had regularly borrowed money over a period of years, he wrote: "I now enclose to you a statement of my account with you. The result of this has astonished me beyond anything which has ever happened in my life, for tho' I kept such exact entries in my daily memorandum book as would enable me, or anybody else, to state the account accurately in a day, yet I had never collected the items, or formed them into an account, till within these few days." When he did balance his accounts, he discovered he was $10,000 further in debt than he thought he was.

In spite of his exacting eye for the details of income and expenditure, he seldom stepped back to observe his economic landscape. Because he notched each financial tree, he thought he knew the forest; until it was too late, he had little idea of his net worth. He was like a man who went through life dutifully recording every check he wrote but blithely failing to balance his checkbook. It should have been apparent to him, for example, that he was living well beyond his income during his eight years in the presidency, and that a day of reckoning must come. It was not until he was leaving office in 1809 and settling his affairs, however, that he discovered he owed yet another $10,000 that he never knew about.

The editors of the *Memorandum Books* observe that it was, ironically, the very act of writing down his daily accounts that contributed to his economic undoing. "The daily ritual of recording pecuniary events," they write, "gave Jefferson an artificial sense of order in his financial world." The very exactness of the accounts, together with an innate optimism "which perpetually overestimated sources of income and underestimated expenditures," prevented him from attempting any real financial planning until it was too late.

Ultimately, his slide into economic ruin demonstrated that, of the vast number of skills he accumulated in the course of a lifetime, financial management ranked very low among them. His personal flaw was perhaps an aristocrat's mentality about money; deep down, he believed it would somehow always be there. He preached to others throughout his life the necessity for keeping out of debt, but he was seldom willing to forgo anything he wanted for himself, his family, or friends, no matter how little he could afford it. Austerity was simply not a part of Jefferson's personal life. It became, however, a part of the life of Monticello.

It was inevitable that his eroding finances would take a toll on Monticello. Because the house was normally crammed with family, relatives, friends, visitors, and passing acquaintances, it was under continued assault by the rub, scrape, and wear of its inhabitants. The elements were also its enemy. In an age when there was little control of humidity, wood was vulnerable to rapid deterioration from dry rot and insects. The only way to keep exterior woodwork sound was by frequent painting. To maintain the exterior properly, the house should have been completely repainted every five or six years. There is no record that this was ever done. The terraces presented the most serious problem, for they were high-maintenance architecture. To prevent the decks and rails from rotting away from exposure to sun, rain, and ice required annual painting, and lumber had to be substituted frequently for splitting and decaying boards and structural members. They never received this kind of care; in fact, after Jefferson's death, the terraces rotted away and collapsed onto the dependency roofs below them.

In short, maintaining a mansion the size of Monticello was constant and costly, and Jefferson did not have the money to spend for adequate maintenance. During his final years, the house could no longer disguise its age and neglect. One visitor in 1824 reported the mansion was "old and going to decay"; the gardens and lawns were "slovenly." The same sad note was echoed by others.

On July 22, 1828, the *Richmond Enquirer* carried a notice signed by "Th. Jefferson Randolph, Exec'r of Thomas Jefferson, dec'd" advertising the sale of "Valuable Lands": "MONTICELLO, in the County of Albemarle, with the Lands of the said estate adjacent thereto, including the Shadwell Mills, will be offered on the premises. . . . The terms will be accommodating, and the prices anticipated low." The previous year, 130 slaves and Monticello's furniture and farm equipment had been sold at auction; now the mansion itself went on the block. In spite of desperate efforts to sell the property, there were no takers. It remained empty and the victim of souvenir-seekers and vandals for another three years before it was sold for $7,500 to an affluent Staunton, Virginia, druggist, James Barclay, who hit upon the dubious scheme of raising silkworms on the estate for the manufacture of silk. The project predictably failed, and within three years, Monticello was once again on the market. The house and 218 acres were sold for $2,500 to Lt. Uriah P. Levy, a U.S. naval officer whose only motivation for acquiring the property appeared to be his admiration for Jefferson. His care, and that of succeeding Levy family members, in restoring and preserving Monticello, saved the mansion from almost certain destruction. Monticello remained in the hands of the Levy family for ninety years, longer than Jefferson had owned it.

The sale of Monticello was particularly distressing for Jefferson's daughter. Martha Randolph had lived in the house for nearly as long as her father. She expressed her emotions at the loss of the property to her daughter Virginia: "There is some prospect of selling Monticello but I do not wish the thing spoken of yet. I thought I had made my mind up upon that subject and I find when it comes to the point, that all my [sorrows] are renewed and that it will be a bitter, bitter heartache to me its going out of the family." After leaving Monticello, and with the death of her husband in 1828, she lived with her daughters in Boston and Washington before moving in with her son, Thomas Jefferson Randolph, at her former home at Edgehill. It was here, a few miles from Monticello, that she spent her remaining years. When her financial need became publicly known, the legislatures of South Carolina and Louisiana each voted her a gift of ten thousand dollars. She died of apoplexy in 1836, at the age of sixty-four, and was buried in the graveyard at Monticello near her parents.

During the Civil War, the Confederate government confiscated Monticello and it was used for a time as a hospital. The greatest damage to the house occurred not during the war, however, but afterward, when the Levy family was involved in a twenty-year suit over ownership of the estate. The house had been turned over to a caretaker, Joseph Wheeler, who augmented his income by renting it out to Charlottesville residents for parties and entertainments. He stabled his

This 1853 engraving by Benson J. Lossing for Harper's New Monthly Magazine *is the earliest known delineation of Jefferson's bedroom. The alcove bed has been removed.*

cattle in the basement during winter, and, as one observer reported, "in the beautiful drawing salon with its handsome parquet floors, Wheeler had a granary where he set up a hand fanning mill and winnowed his grain." Under Wheeler's careless custody, the house steadily deteriorated. A congressman who visited Monticello in 1878 reported, "There is scarcely a whole shingle upon it, except what have been placed there within the last few years. The windows are broken, everything is left to the mercy of the pitiless storm."

After much litigation, the house came into the possession of Jefferson M. Levy, a nephew of the original purchaser of the estate. He improved and restored it, but he also made several changes that altered its profile, the most obvious being the addition of five dormer windows in the roof to replace leaky skylights. By the turn of the century, there was increasing agitation to make Monticello into a national historic monument. After a number of attempts to induce the federal government to acquire the estate failed, a private, nonprofit organization, the Thomas Jefferson Memorial Foundation, succeeded in purchasing the property from Jefferson Levy for $500,000 in 1923—exactly a hundred years after Jefferson completed the house by finishing its porticoes. Over the years, the organization worked patiently to return the mansion to its former condition. In the 1930s, the dependencies were reconstructed, the dormers were removed from the roof, and the skylights were restored. The plinths on the dome, which, like the terraces, had rotted away, were rebuilt. In 1953, the house was given a badly needed structural overhaul. Bricks were repointed, rotting timbers replaced, brick nogging removed, floors reinforced with steel, and a modern heating–air-conditioning system was installed. During the years of careful scientific restoration, many of Jefferson's furnishings and possessions, which had been scattered at his death, found their way back to Monticello through gift and purchase. Nonauthentic pieces of furniture were removed as authentic items were discovered and reintroduced into the mansion. Jefferson's horticultural gardens were replanted by the Garden Club of Virginia, and painstakingly careful archaeological research led to the restoration of his vegetable gardens, orchards, and vineyard.

The number of visitors to Monticello, which helped impoverish Jefferson during his lifetime, never decreased after his death. One reason why the druggist James Barclay sold the mansion was because of the never-ending train of strangers who invaded his privacy by insisting upon viewing the house of the late President. Under the ownership of the Levys, visitors increased to thousands each year. They chipped away at Jefferson's tombstone for souvenirs until only a stump of the obelisk remained. The graveyard eventually had to be enclosed by a fence and a new memorial obelisk installed over the grave. Once the mansion was purchased and restored by the Thomas Jefferson Memorial Foundation, the pilgrims increased to the hundreds of thousands annually, until now a half-million Americans are shown through the mansion each year. What these visitors came to see was time turned back to 1809 when, after forty years of birth pangs, Monticello was finally delivered by its architect-builder. They could view the Monticello that Jefferson knew and loved. Or could they?

"What they have seen," Jefferson biographer Merrill Peterson writes, "is not Monticello as it was in Jefferson's time, overrun with children and slaves (though the visitors were there then too), battered from daily use and showing the ravages of debt; but Monticello expertly restored as an architectural masterpiece, a fascinating museum, a shrine to Jefferson's memory." There is no denying that Monticello has become a Jefferson museum-shrine, but most examples of restored domestic architecture are museums that lift the past out of context and place it on display. An inhabited house, unlike a museum, bears the imprint of its owners: the ashes in the hearth, the fingerprints on the walls, the scuffs, knocks, scrapes, and rubbings of human contact—the detritus of everyday life. All of these vanish beneath the cosmetic touch of the restorer's art.

There is yet another way that historical preservation places distance between the house and its owner. Preserved houses are pieces of material history, and the restorer interprets their physical remains no less than the historian interprets chronological facts. Both impose private mythologies upon the past. The myth created for Monticello by its restorers is that Thomas Jefferson was one of the leading architects of his age, that his architectural practice was shaped by Palladianism, and that his house was completed in 1809 much the way it looks today. All that reinforces this myth has been salvaged and carefully returned to mint condition; all that does not has been allowed noiselessly to disappear. The difficulty with this myth is that this house was not completed in 1809, when Jefferson returned from Washington and dismissed his workmen. It was not until 1823 that the principal architectural features of the exterior, the porticoes, were completed, and by this time the condition of the house, like that of its owner, was in serious decline. Never in Jefferson's lifetime did Monticello appear the way it does today.

An alternate myth is that Jefferson was a housebuilder first, and secondly an architect, that his chief concern at Monticello was comfort, privacy, and serenity for himself and his family—all existing within the shell of a Palladian aesthetic—and that this arcadian ideal was destroyed by mismanagement and debt. This myth would produce two possible Monticellos, the first, the incomplete house of 1809, with its louvered porticles in place and its tulip tree columns supporting the west portico, but its paint fresh—including grass-green floors— and its furnishings and decor pristine. The second myth would create the house of 1823: complete, but everything run-down and unpainted

Monticello, a nineteenth-century view.

save for the newly finished porticoes; its furniture worn, its curtains faded, its orchards and gardens neglected, its terraces in disrepair.

Although both of these alternate mythologies are more "truthful" than the shrine that now sits atop Jefferson's mountain, neither would be acceptable to the American public, nor, it can be argued, should they be. Jefferson's Monticello is irretrievably lost, for the soul of the house perished with its owner-builder. Just as the evolution of Monticello paralleled the patterns of Jefferson's intellectual and emotional life, its disintegration was appropriately parallel to his own. At his death, with the dispersal of his family and the sale of his possessions, Jefferson's Monticello ceased to exist.

It is now America's Monticello, a temple commemorating the apotheosis of Thomas Jefferson, a democratic demigod. As such, it is a much more suitable monument to him than is the Jefferson Memorial in Washington. Although both are shrines, Monticello honors not only Jefferson's divinity, but his humanity as well. It is a reminder to all Americans from the author of the Declaration of Independence that the pursuit of happiness must include the civilized and civilizing comforts of house and home. The rewards of this pursuit are not necessarily to the swift—the task took most of Jefferson's adult life. This may be too long for most of us to invest in building a house, but one of the legacies of Thomas Jefferson—and Monticello—is not only that those who build long build well, but that, to use one of Jefferson's favorite expressions, the habitations they produce are "tasty morsels," to be savored for a lifetime.

A Jefferson Chronology

1743	Born on April 13 (April 2 Old Style) at Shadwell
1752	Enters Latin School conducted by William Douglas
1757	Father, Peter Jefferson, dies August 17
1758–60	Attends school conducted by James Maury
1760–62	Attends William and Mary College
1762–67	Studies law with George Wythe
1769	Begins building Monticello
1772	Marries Martha Wayles Skelton, January 1
	First child, Martha, born September 27
1776	Mother, Jane Randolph Jefferson, dies March 31
	Writes Declaration of Independence in June
1778	Daughter Mary (Maria) born August 1
1779	Elected governor of Virginia in June
1781	Tarleton's raiders arrive at Monticello in June
1782	Wife, Martha Wayles Jefferson, dies September 6
1784	Leaves for France July 5 with daughter Martha and James Hemings
1785	Elected French minister by Congress
	Rents the Hôtel de Langeac
1786	Tours English gardens with John Adams
	Sends model of Maison Carrée for Virginia state capitol
	Meets Maria Cosway; Head and Heart letter

1787   Daughter Maria arrives in Paris with Sally Hemings
        Notes on the State of Virginia published in England
1789   Arrives back in United States in November
1790   Appointed Secretary of State by George Washington
        Martha Jefferson marries Thomas Mann Randolph, February
        23
1794   Leaves government; returns to Monticello
1796   Begins remodeling and construction of second Monticello
        Elected Vice President
1797   Becomes president of the American Philosophical Society
        Maria Jefferson marries John Wayles Eppes, October 13
1800   Tie with Aaron Burr in presidential election
1801   Elected president by the House of Representatives
1802   James Callender alleges liaison with Sally Hemings
1803   Treaty for purchase of Louisiana ratified
1804   Maria Jefferson Eppes dies April 17
        Reelected President
1806   House at Poplar Forest started
        Lewis and Clark expedition returns to St. Louis
1807   Trial of Aaron Burr for treason
        Enactment of the Embargo Act
1809   Ends presidency; returns to Monticello
        Interior of Monticello completed; workmen leave
1812   Renews friendship with John Adams
1815   Sells library to Congress
1817   Creates plan for the University of Virginia
1819   University of Virginia chartered
1823   Monticello completed when porticoes are finished
1826   Lottery to pay debts fails
        Dies at Monticello, July 4

Acknowledgments

WRITING about Thomas Jefferson's housebuilding venture at Monticello, like the enterprise itself, has taken much longer than anticipated. Jefferson's voluminous unpublished papers proved to be a boon, but also an obstruction; they gave up numerous historical gems, but digging through them was painfully slow. This was not because of tedium—just the opposite. It is impossible to track through Jefferson's papers without being lured into fascinating byways of his mind, corners of interest that have nothing to do with the scent you are following. Yet, a number of the insights in this work derive directly from such digressionary explorations.

I am indebted to Clemson University for the year's sabbatical that gave me time to read the unpublished papers, and to James A. Bear, Jr., curator emeritus of Monticello, who urged me to do so. He not only encouraged my early work on this project, but his own Jefferson files at Monticello were invaluable resources. The staff of the Cooper Library at Clemson, particularly Marion Withington, patiently located miles of microfilm and other research materials, and the librarians at the Manuscript Division of the Alderman Library of the University of Virginia were professionally accommodating, particularly Curator of Manuscripts Edmund Berkeley, Jr., and Gregory Johnson. Director Louis L. Tucker, and Ross Urquhart, of the Massachusetts Historical Society, aided me in procuring Jefferson's architectural drawings and other important documents in the society's collection.

Acknowledgments

The book would have been greatly diminished without the assistance of the staff at Monticello. Director Daniel Jordan was hospitable and always helpful; historian William Beiswanger and archaeologist William Kelso kindly offered suggestions or responded to queries. I owe a particular debt of gratitude to Director of Research Lucia C. Stanton, who read most of the manuscript and whose very fine net caught many of my errors. She also made available to me before publication the Bear-Stanton edition of *Jefferson's Memorandum Books*, and was a source of much information and advice.

A number of scholars read portions of the manuscript and offered substantive suggestions, which found their way into the book. John Blassingame of Yale and James Oakes of Northwestern offered useful counsel on Jefferson's slaves and the subject of slavery, and Merrill Peterson of the University of Virginia shared his broad experience in Jefferson studies. Catherine Clinton of Harvard and Mary Beth Norton of Cornell gave me the benefit of their extensive knowledge of colonial American women. Thad W. Tate, director of Colonial Williamsburg, offered advice on colonial construction. Garry Wills of Northwestern, a close student of Jefferson, provided valuable insights. Douglas Wilson of Knox College, editor of the forthcoming edition of Jefferson's Commonplace Books, shared his perceptions of these important documents with me. To all of these readers I offer my sincere thanks for their generosity and encouragement.

My gratitude for particular aid goes to James Britenburg, M.D., Rob Roy McGregor, Carl Lounsbury, Drew Smith, and Sandra Piazza. Robert A. Waller and William G. Koon provided release from academic responsibilities for research and writing, and a Clemson University Provost's Research Grant offered financial support, as did a stipend from the Southern Regional Education Board. Marian Wood of Henry Holt and Company deserves a special mention for her strong support of the book, her superb editing, and her insistence that it be as fine as I was capable of making it.

Finally, and most importantly, my wife Joan was adviser, editor, proofreader, a companion in research, and my patient consultant in writing. To her, this book is lovingly dedicated.

Notes

Thomas Jefferson's papers are the primary resource for all Jefferson studies; they are to be published in their entirety by Princeton University Press. Currently, only twenty-three volumes have been published, to 1792, the beginning of Jefferson's career in national office. Earlier partial editions are edited by Paul Leicester Ford, considered to be the more accurate, and A. A. Lipscomb and A. E. Bergh, the more extensive.

The unpublished papers are available on microfilm from the three major repositories for them, the Library of Congress, which has most of Jefferson's public papers, the Massachusetts Historical Society, which holds architectural drawings and most of his private letters, and the University of Virginia, particularly strong in documents relating to the construction of that university. Other Jefferson papers are scattered among dozens of libraries, and a number are still held by private individuals.

Many of the letters and documents used for this personal biography are contained in two important works by Edwin M. Betts, *Thomas Jefferson's Garden Book*, and *Thomas Jefferson's Farm Book*, both of which contain much material on Jefferson's building projects. *Family Letters*, edited by E. M. Betts and James Bear, Jr., is also a valuable collection. *Jefferson's Memorandum Books*, edited by James A. Bear, Jr., and Lucia C. Stanton, containing his daily accounts kept for a lifetime, is currently in press at Princeton University Press. These memoranda provide a record of Jefferson's building activities at Monticello for half a century. Fiske Kimball's *Thomas Jefferson Architect*, which established Jefferson's reputation as one of America's greatest architects when it was published in 1916, is essential for any study of Monticello.

Among Jefferson's many biographers, Dumas Malone's six-volume *Jefferson and His Time* is definitive. Of the early biographies, Henry Randall's three-volume, *The Life of Thomas Jefferson*, is the most important because of reminiscences by many who knew Jefferson.

All of these sources, and several others, are in the following list of short titles and abbreviations used for frequent references. Full citations to all works consulted are given in the notes; these are related to the text by a page number and a key word or phrase. Quotations from the unpublished Jefferson papers are listed by their repository; if a partial quotation has been previously published, its source is also noted. The place of publication is New York unless otherwise identified.

DLC Manuscript Division, Library of Congress, Washington, D.C. (Library location symbols are those used in the National Union Catalogue in the Library of Congress.)

Domestic Life Sarah N. Randolph. *The Domestic Life of Thomas Jefferson*. 1871. Reprints: Frederick Unger Publishing Co., 1958; Charlottesville: University Press of Virginia, 1978.

Family Letters E. M. Betts and James Bear, Jr. *Letters of Thomas Jefferson*. Columbia: University of Missouri Press, 1966.

Farm Book Edwin M. Betts, ed. *Thomas Jefferson's Farm Book, with Commentary and Relevant Extracts from Other Writings*. Princeton, N.J.: Princeton University Press for the American Philosophical Society, 1953.

Ford Paul Leicester Ford, ed. *The Writings of Thomas Jefferson*. 10 vols. G. P. Putnam's Sons, 1892–1899.

Garden Book Edwin M. Betts, ed. *Thomas Jefferson's Garden Book, 1766–1824, With Relevant Extracts from His Other Writings*. Philadelphia: American Philosophical Society, 1944.

Jefferson at Monticello James A. Bear, Jr., ed. *Jefferson at Monticello*. "Memoirs of a Monticello Slave," as dictated to Charles Campbell by Isaac, and "Jefferson at Monticello: The Private Life of Thomas Jefferson," by Rev. Hamilton W. Pierson. Charlottesville: University Press of Virginia, 1967.

Notes

Kimball Fiske Kimball. *Thomas Jefferson Architect*. Boston, 1916. Reprint with new introduction by Frederick D. Nichols. DaCapo Press, 1968.

L & B A. A. Lipscomb and A. E. Bergh, eds. *The Writings of Thomas Jefferson*. 20 vols. Washington, D.C.: Thomas Jefferson Memorial Foundation, 1903–1905.

Malone Dumas Malone. *Jefferson and His Time*. 6 vols. Boston: Little, Brown, 1948–1981.

MB James A. Bear, Jr., and Lucia C. Stanton, eds. *Jefferson's Memorandum Books, Accounts, with Legal Records and Miscellany 1767–1826*. 2 vols. Princeton, N.J.: Princeton University Press, forthcoming. (This work was consulted in manuscript; therefore, references are by date of entry rather than by page number.)

MHi Massachusetts Historical Society.

Nichols Frederick D. Nichols. *Thomas Jefferson's Architectural Drawings, Completed and with Commentary and a Check List*. Boston: Mass. Historical Society, and Charlottesville: Thomas Jefferson Memorial Foundation and University Press of Virginia, 1961.

Notes William Peden, ed. *Notes on the State of Virginia*. Chapel Hill: University of North Carolina Press for the Institute of Early American History and Culture at Williamsburg, 1955.

Papers Julian P. Boyd et al. eds. *The Papers of Thomas Jefferson*. Princeton, N.J.: Princeton University Press, 1950– .

Randall Henry S. Randall. *The Life of Thomas Jefferson*. 3 vols. 1858. Reprint. Freeport, N.Y.: Books for Libraries Press, 1970.

Thornton Diary "Journal of Anna Maria Brodeau, wife of Dr. William Thornton of Washington, D.C." Manuscript Division, Library of Congress, Washington, D.C.

TJ Thomas Jefferson.

ViU Manuscript Division, Alderman Library, University of Virginia.

CHAPTER 1

Page

2   "we all went to the scales": *Thornton Diary*, May 18, 1800.

2   Gilbert Stuart's portrait: *Thornton Diary*, June 24, 1804: "Sat for the last time to Mr. Stuart. I beg him to draw a plant." Aug. 25, 1804: "We rode to Mr. Stuart's — He dined with us. Dr. T. paid him the balance . . . in all 200$ for our portraits."

3   "fatigued us much": *Thornton Diary*, Sat., Sep. 18, 1802.

4   "be here by half after three": to William Thornton, Sep. 10, 1802. MHi.

4   Foster description: Richard Beale Davis, ed., *Jeffersonian America: Notes on the United States of America Collected in the Years 1805–6–7 and 11–12 by Sir Augustus John Foster, Bart.* (San Marino, Calif.: Huntington Library, 1954), 10.

6   stairs "expensive": to John Brown, Apr. 5, 1797, in Malone, 3:227.

9   sun had not caught him in bed: *Domestic Life*, 338.

9   Monticello breakfast described: Margaret Bayard Smith, *The First Forty Years of Washington Society, Portrayed by the Family Letters of Mrs. Samuel Harrison Smith*, Gaillard Hunt, ed. (Charles Scribner's Sons, 1906), 69. See also Daniel Webster's comment in Randall, 3:505.

10   pancake recipe: Marie Kimball, *Thomas Jefferson's Cookbook* (Charlottesville: University Press of Virginia, 1976), 103.

10   Thornton as inventor: For Thornton's biography see the *Dictionary of American Biography*, 20 vols. (Charles Scribner's Sons, 1928–1937).

10   "making a musical instrument": from William Thornton, June 27, 1814, MHi.

11   "Filtering Machine": from William Thornton, Apr. 3, 1802, DLC.

11   "placed it in the Congressional Library": from William Thornton, Feb. 19, 1817, DLC.

11   William Thornton description: William Dunlap, *History of the Rise and Progress of Design in the United States*, 2 vols. (Boston: C. E. Goodspeed & Co., 1918), 2:8.

11   Thornton a Quaker: His Quakerism did not prevent him from purchasing "a negro named Sam" for $300, and a "Negro man (Daniel) his Wife & child—for 500 Dollars." *Thornton Diary*, Feb. 27, 1796, Feb. 14, 1800.

12   *amateur* definition: Abraham Rees, ed., *The Cyclopaedia; or, Universal Dictionary of Arts, Sciences, and Literature* (Philadelphia: S. F. Bradford, n.d. [1810–1826?]).

12   *mechanic arts* defined: Carl Bridenbaugh, *The Colonial Craftsman* (New York University Press, 1964, c. 1950), 155.

12 Peter Jefferson's strength: Randall, 1:13.

13 Whitman quote: "Crossing Brooklyn Ferry," II, 19–20.

14 "little variety in our life": *Thornton Diary*, Mar. 1, 1800.

14 "tea drinking is very stupid": *Thornton Diary*, July 20, 1800; "it was intolerably stupid": Aug. 9, 1800; "to hear a madman preach": May 13, 1804.

14 "handsome and convenient": *Thornton Diary*, Sept. 19, 1802.

15 "state of commencement and decay": Edward Thornton, quoted in Malone, 4:167.

15 "during a war of 8 years": to Count Constantin François de Volney, Apr. 10, 1796, in *Garden Book*, 248.

20 "constantly locked": *Thornton Diary*, Sept. 10, 1802.

21 "While residing in Paris": to Samuel Harrison Smith, Sept. 21, 1814, in William Dawson Johnston, *History of the Library of Congress*, vol. I, 1800–1864 (Washington, D.C.: Government Printing Office, 1904; reprint, Kraus, 1961), 70.

22 counting peas: *Garden Book*, 4.

23 "I cannot live without books": to John Adams, June 10, 1815; Lester J. Cappon, ed., *The Adams–Jefferson Letters*, 2 vols. (Chapel Hill, N.C.: University of North Carolina Press), 2:443.

24 a series of individual book boxes: see Johnston, 99.

24 "mahogany book case with glass doors": *MB*, Aug. 4, 1773, "My Library." These bookcases are in a list showing the location of the 1,256 books in his library. The entire list is in Charles B. Sanford, *Thomas Jefferson and His Library* (Hamden, Conn.: Archon Books, 1977), 38.

25 TJ's architectural books: See William Howard Adams, ed., *The Eye of Thomas Jefferson* (Washington, D.C.: National Gallery of Art, 1976), 98–99.

25 "Stepping into the boat": *Thornton Diary*, June 14, 1805.

26 "too many clothes": *Thornton Diary*, Note, 1806. See also 1805.

26 gambling in Virginia: *Domestic Life*, 29; Jane Carson, *Colonial Virginians at Play* (Williamsburg, Va.: Colonial Williamsburg, 1965), 73.

26 chess in France: Harry Golombek, *Chess, A History* (Putnam, 1976), 120.

26 "Philidor on chess": to Thomas Mann Randolph, Dec. 4, 1801, DLC.

26 "played with Dr. Franklin": John French, c. 1825, in "Descriptions of Thomas Jefferson and the Grounds Surrounding Monticello, Visitors' Descriptions of, 1780–1966," Monticello Archives.

26 TJ's purchase of chessmen: to Francis Eppes, Apr. 22, 1786, *Papers*, 9:395.

27 "Took a walk of half a mile": *Thornton Diary*, Sept. 22, 1802.

27   Thornton watercolor: This picture, signed "A.M.T. 1802," is puzzling. The south pavilion (on the right) seems to be drawn out of perspective, but this is not the case. Quite possibly working later at her home, Mrs. Thornton attempted to render the south pavilion with the same light source and shadow pattern that she painted on the house and north pavilion. She botched it, however, by placing a shadow on half of the facing wall, and, because she was working in watercolor, could not correct it.

29   living quarters for the house slaves: Extensive archaeological excavations have revealed a great deal about the living conditions, work habits, and diet of slaves housed on Mulberry Row. See William M. Kelso, "The Archaeology of Slave Life at Thomas Jefferson's Monticello: 'A Wolf by the Ears,' " *Journal of New World Archaeology*, vol. 6, no. 4 (June 1986), 5–20.

30   "Rained all the day": *Thornton Diary*, Sept. 23, 1802.

31   "amazingly improved": *Thornton Diary*, c. 1806; Malone, 4:168.

CHAPTER 2

Page

35   "And our own dear Monticello": to Maria Cosway, Oct. 12, 1786, *Papers*, 10:447.

35   "emotions arising from the sublime": *Notes*, 25.

35   building "upon an eminence": Andrea Palladio, *Four Books of Architecture*, trans. Giacomo Leoni, bk. 2, chap. 12 (1742).

37   earliest years: The most authoritative sources for TJ's early years are Malone, 1, and Marie Kimball, *Jefferson: The Road to Glory, 1743 to 1776* (Coward-McCann, 1943).

37   "my great good fortune": *Autobiography*, Ford, 1:5–6.

39   "covering a house": Peter Jefferson's building accounts and a history of archaeological excavations at the Shadwell site are in Fiske Kimball, "In Search of Jefferson's Birthplace," *The Virginia Magazine of History and Biography*, vol. 51, no. 4 (Oct. 1943), 381–406.

40   "rarely constructed of stone or brick": *Notes*, 153.

41   "rude, mis-shapen piles": *Notes*, 153.

42   "our most Skillful Architect": quoted in Marcus Whiffen, *The Public Buildings of Williamsburg* (Williamsburg, Va.: Colonial Williamsburg, 1958), 141. Richard Taliaferro's architectural career is also discussed in Thomas T. Waterman, *The Mansions of Virginia, 1706–1776* (Chapel Hill: University of North Carolina Press, 1945); and Claude Lanciano,

Our Most Skillful Architect (Gloucester, Va.: Lands End Books, 1981).

43 Fauquier "the ornament and delight of Virginia": John Burk, *History of Virginia* (1805), 3:333.

43 "heard more good sense": to L. H. Girardin, Jan. 15, 1815, in L & B, 14:231.

44 "tear himself away": John Page's comparison of his studies with TJ's in Marie Kimball, 45.

44 "hard student": to Dr. Vine Utley, March 21, 1819, *Domestic Life*, 371.

45 "canine appetite for reading": to John Adams, May 17, 1818, in Lester J. Cappon, ed., *The Complete Correspondence Between Thomas Jefferson and John and Abigail Adams* (Chapel Hill: University of North Carolina Press for Institute of Early American History and Culture at Williamsburg, 1959), 2:524.

45 Fauquier-Gibbs relationship: described in Bryal Little, "Francis Fauquier and an English Architect," *William and Mary Quarterly*, 3rd series, no. 12 (July 1955), 475–76.

46 letter recounting the Shadwell fire: to John Page, Feb. 21, 1770, *Papers*, 1:34.

46 "daughter of Isham Randolph": Ford, 1:4, Merrill D. Peterson, ed., *Thomas Jefferson, Writings* (Library of America, 1984), 3.

47 "the death of my mother": to William Randolph, June 1776, *Papers*, 1:409.

47 no expression of emotion or loss: It should be noted, however, that the Virginia gentry of the eighteenth century as a class found it difficult to express grief, in their correspondence and diaries, over the loss of family members. "These men and women believed that to discuss death was to invite stupor; to contemplate it, to succumb." Jan Lewis, *The Pursuit of Happiness, Family and Values in Jefferson's Virginia* (Cambridge University Press, 1983), 70.

47 new piece of evidence: by Douglas L. Wilson, "Thomas Jefferson's Early Notebooks," *William and Mary Quarterly*, 3rd series, no. 42 (Oct. 1985), 433–52.

48 "O! why did God": Gilbert Chinard, *The Literary Bible of Thomas Jefferson, His Commonplace Book of Philosophers and Poets* (Baltimore: Johns Hopkins Press, 1928), 139. For other quotations from this source see: Otway, 158, 159; Euripides, 100, 104; Virgil, 116; Milton, 138, 167, 168; Shakespeare, 147, 148; Rowe, 161; Mallet, 164.

49 "The strain of misogyny": Wilson, 441.

51 "I think to build": to John Page, July 15, 1763, *Papers*, 1:11. Several of the earliest house plans among Jefferson's architectural drawings,

not in his own hand (Kimball, K-1, K-2, K-3), could be related to a desire to build a house in Williamsburg.

54 "Palladio is the Bible": Isaac Coles to John Hartwell Cocke, Feb. 23, 1816, in Kimball, introduction, vii. Coles recounted a conversation he had with Jefferson.

55 English Palladianism: For a history of English Palladianism, see John Summerson, *Architecture in Britain 1530–1830*, 6th rev. ed. (Penguin, 1977). The influence of Wren on colonial architecture is traced in Waterman, 12–17.

56 "proposed for a single Gentleman": Robert Morris, *Select Architecture*, 2nd ed. (1757; reprint, Da Capo Press, 1973), 1.

56 tracing of Morris plan: Kimball, K-119.

57 Robert Carter House: Its cost is in Marcus Whiffen, *The Eighteenth Century Houses of Williamsburg* (Williamsburg, Va.: Colonial Williamsburg, 1960), 215.

58 architectural drawings: For a discussion of TJ's drawing techniques see Kimball, 105–106.

60 "The Capitol is a light and airy structure": *Notes*, 152.

60 the way all owner-builders think: Observations on Jefferson as an owner-builder are drawn from my own experience in building a house, and from research on the owner-builder movement in America. See Jack McLaughlin, *The Housebuilding Experience* (Van Nostrand Reinhold, 1981).

61 octagons admit light and air: TJ was himself aware of this; in his comments to Isaac Coles (see Coles-Cocke letter cited above) he stated that octagons "were charming. They give you a semi-circle of air and light."

62 "Life begins well": Gaston Bachelard, *The Poetics of Space*, trans. Maria Jolas (Orion Press, 1964), 7.

62 "deep nostalgia": Erik Erikson, *Dimensions of a New Identity, Jefferson Lectures in the Humanities, 1973* (W. W. Norton, 1974), 56–57.

64 "nature to advantage dressed": Pope, "Essay on Criticism," II, 297–298.

CHAPTER 3

Page

65 William Stewart correspondence: from George Jefferson, June 17, 1801, Nov. 16, 1801; to George Jefferson, Dec. 3, 1801, *Farm Book*, 425.

66 "for the hire of the woman": to James Walker, Mar. 1, 1807, MHi.

66 Bacon's comment on Stewart: *Jefferson at Monticello*, 69–70.

66 "but give no liquor": to Archibald Stuart, April 5, 1796, *Farm Book*, 457–58.

67 liquor for Dinsmore: Dinsmore and Richardson's drinking habits came under Jefferson's close analytical scrutiny. In *MB* Aug. 30, 1799, he wrote: "Recd. from Higgenbotham's a canteen of whiskey delivd. to Dinsmore." On Sept. 30, he recorded: "The whiskey of Aug. 30. is out, so 3½ galls. have lasted Dinsmore & Richardson 31. days which is 1.8 of a gill, or near half a pint a day each, costing at present 6d."

67 "full of want": summer 1781, *Papers*, 6:129.

67 Watson and Orr hired: *MB*, Apr. 3, 1781: "David Watson a British deserter, housejoiner by trade, to work at Monticello @ 3000 lb. tobo. a year or its worth in paper." Jan. 8, 1782: "Wm Orr the smith begins to work at £3 the month."

67 "both smoked pipes, and both drinkers": *Jefferson at Monticello*, 20.

67 liquor for slaves "injurious and demoralizing": to J. Holmes Freeman, Dec. 21, 1805, *Farm Book*, 417.

68 Anderson account book: Colonial Williamsburg Archives.

68 Francis Bishop blacksmith contract: *MB*, Sept. 1, 1774; *Farm Book*, 422.

69 little stone quarried in Virginia: Late in Jefferson's life, when he was pressing to complete work on the pavilions of the University of Virginia, marble was quarried locally for that project, but Jefferson reported that it was of poor color and not able to "bear the chisel for delicate work." From a letter to Arthur S. Brokenbrough, June 29, 1819, in William B. O'Neal, "The Workmen at the University of Virginia, 1817–1826, with Notes and Documents," *Magazine of Albemarle County History*, vol. 17 (1959), 35.

69 William Rice, an indentured servant: In Philadelphia, Jefferson recorded (*MB*, Dec. 15, 1775), "pd for William Rice (a servant) £17-10." He also purchased trowels and "necessaries" for Rice, and paid for his expenses to Virginia. Rice was one of the few skilled workmen who either brought a wife with him to Monticello or married there: *MB*, Nov. 13, 1778, "Pd. Peggy Rice for 13 chickens 13/."

69 "that he shall make 3 stone columns": *MB*, Feb. 7, 1778; *Garden Book*, 80. Jefferson had noted in his Memorandum Book on Dec. 24, 1776, "charge Rice a month's absence he worked for others while I was in Wmsbgh. to be made up at the end of his time." Rice had borrowed Jupiter to work on "Shelby's tombstone," a moonlighting job Rice had apparently picked up. *MB*, Aug. 25, 1778: "Note he [Rice] still owes me for 18. days work of Jupiter, to be pd. by Rice's

working 9 days." (This indicates that Jefferson valued the services of his indentured servant as twice the hire of a slave workman.)

70 compares stone and bricks: *Farm Book*, pl. 103.

70 "not four stone masons in the whole county": Duke de la Rochefoucauld-Liancourt, *Travels through the United States of North America, in the Years 1795, 1796, 1797*, in *Garden Book*, 145.

71 "a little fire kindled in the room": *Notes*, 154.

71 "tabula rasa": *Notes*, 154.

73 six hogsheads of water to make 2,000 bricks: *Garden Book*, 14.

74 "90,000 workeable bricks": *MB*, Feb. 7, 1778; *Garden Book*, 80. Of the 103,000 bricks in the kiln, 13,000 were "soft outside bricks unfit for use."

74 making and firing brick: James S. Wamsley, *The Crafts of Williamsburg* (Williamsburg, Va.: The Colonial Williamsburg Foundation, 1982), 60–61.

74 Rosewell brick size: *MB*, 1767, architectural section.

74 did not produce a modular wall: Because of the irregular size of the bricks, Jefferson's masons were unable to maintain regular mortar joints. By actual measurement of a section of wall on the east front of the house, four courses measured 12½ inches, eight courses 25½ inches.

77 gray-green glaze: For a description of glazed brick and Flemish bond brickwork at Colonial Williamsburg, see A. Lawrence Kocher and Howard Dearstyne, *Colonial Williamsburg, Its Buildings and Gardens* (Williamsburg, Va.: The Colonial Williamsburg Foundation, 1976), 16–17.

77 "lime-burner's wig": *Oxford English Dictionary*, at "lime-burner."

77 bought a limestone quarry: In his *Farm Book* (pl. 32), Jefferson notes on his land roll of 1794 four acres of "Limestone purchased by T. Jefferson from Robert Sharpe." On the 1810 land roll the four acres are listed as "Limestone quarry on Plumbtree branch" (pl. 127).

77 oystershell lime: For its use at Williamsburg see Marcus Whiffen, *The Eighteenth Century Houses of Williamsburg* (Williamsburg, Va.: Colonial Williamsburg, 1960), 8.

78 "powers of conversation were great": Randall, 3:673.

78 "I am never satiated": to Lafayette, Apr. 11, 1787, *Domestic Life*, 112–13.

79 "those who labour": *Notes*, 164–65.

79 "It is such men as that": Randall, 3:673.

80 "honor the materials": John Lobell, *Between Silence and Light: Spirit in the Architecture of Louis I. Kahn* (Boulder, Colo.: Shambhala, 1979), 40.

80 one hundred tons of nogging: William C. Thatcher, *The Structural Preservation of Monticello* (Charlottesville, Va.: Jarman Printing Co.,

1973). Other details on the preservation of Monticello are from this useful pamphlet.

82 "1.8991666 &c.": Kimball, K-24.
83 "great pains taken": to Archibald Stuart, Apr. 5, 1796, *Farm Book*, 457.
83 "in measuring, this time out": Kimball, K-24.
83 Excerpts from Humphrey Harwood's account book are in Whiffen, 197–99.
83 "a present": Thomas T. Waterman, *The Mansions of Virginia, 1706–1776* (Chapel Hill, N.C.: University of North Carolina Press, 1945), 183.
84 "my Wife *Elizabeth* has eloped": Joseph Royle's *Virginia Gazette*, Feb. 12, 1762, in Whiffen, 26.
84 "without that resource": to Richard Morris, Aug. 29, 1803, *Farm Book*, 339.
85 "stupid slavish work of sawing": Hugh Jones, *The Present State of Virginia*, R. L. Morton, ed. (Chapel Hill, N.C.: University of North Carolina Press, 1956), 142.
85 "considerable quantity of timber": Kimball, K-136; "used at times as a carpenter's shop": K-136.
85 "Joynery is an Art": Joseph Moxon, *Mechanic Exercises* (London, 1683).
86 For a history of the Carpenters' Company see Roger W. Moss, Jr., "The Origins of the Carpenters' Company of Philadelphia," in Charles E. Peterson, ed., *Building Early America* (Radnor, Pa.: Chilton Book Co., 1976).
86 Dinsmore, "faithful, sober, discrete, honest": to Thomas Munro, Mar. 4, 1815, *Farm Book*, 460.
87 "house joiners of the first order": *Farm Book*, 460.
87 Edmund Dickeson inventory: Colonial Williamsburg Archives.
88 "turning wheel": Kimball, K-16.
88 "He shall not absent himself": a typical indenture agreement can be found in Whiffen, 18.
88 "to build a common Clapboard House": Whiffen, 19.
89 75 indentured laborers: Edward Miles Riley, ed., *The Journal of John Harrower* (Williamsburg, Va.: Colonial Williamsburg, 1963), 166–68. Harrower's journal is an account of the plight of unemployed workers in Britain and Scotland who were driven to emigrate as indentured laborers.
89 Buckland to assume "entire direction": Carl Bridenbaugh, *The Colonial Craftsman* (New York University Press, 1964, c. 1950), 12.
90 3 and 4 shillings a day: Wages in the North were much higher. Work-

men at Clivedon, a stone Palladian mansion in Germantown, Pennsylvania, outside Philadelphia, received nearly twice as much as Jefferson's workers. An unskilled worker was paid 3 shillings, 9 pence a day, a master mason made 6 shillings, 6 pence. These wages, however, did not include "finding"—food or lodging. Margaret B. Tinkcom, "Clivedon: The Building of a Philadelphia Countryseat, 1763–1767," *The Pennsylvania Magazine of History and Biography*, vol. 88, no. 1 (Jan. 1964), 26.

91   a shilling would buy: Most of the prices come from Jefferson's Memorandum Books. Odd pence are rounded off.

92   "Agreed with B. Kindred": *MB*, Oct. 25, 1782.

92   "At present he is employed": Duke de la Rochefoucauld-Liancourt, *Travels through the United States of North America, in the Years 1795, 1796, 1797*, in Randall, 2:307; *Garden Book*, 244.

93   "today my workmen assemble": to Count Constantin François de Volney, Apr. 9, 1797, *Garden Book*, 255.

CHAPTER 4

Page

95   "Just think, Anya": *The Cherry Orchard*, Act 2, ed. and trans. Eugene K. Bristow, *Anton Checkov's Plays* (W. W. Norton, 1977), 189–90.

96   "man must be a prodigy": *Notes*, 162.

96   "feed and clothe them well": to Edward Coles, Aug. 25, 1814, *Farm Book*, 37–38.

96   "severely flogged": to Reuben Perry, April 16, 1812, *Farm Book*, 35.

97   "You will excuse the liberty": anonymous, undated [1801–1809], DLC. The note was apparently not sent through the mail because it was not endorsed by Jefferson. Library of Congress archivists conjectured that the note was dated from Jefferson's first term as president because it seemed to be connected with the campaign of vilification directed at him by the Federalists during the Sally Hemings scandal.

97   "the whole commerce between master and slave": *Notes*, 162.

97   "my name annexed in the public papers": to Bowling Clarke, Sept. 21, 1792, *Farm Book*, 13.

97   "stocking farms with men": to John W. Eppes, June 20, 1820, *Farm Book*, 45–46.

98   "Willis' people left off working": *MB*, July 14, 1778.

103   "little enough for his trade": to John Jordan, Dec. 21, 1805, *Farm Book*, 21.

Notes

103 slave competition with free whites: The city was Charleston, South
     Carolina. Carl Bridenbaugh, *The Colonial Craftsman* (New York Uni-
     versity Press, 1964, c. 1950), 140–41.
103 52 "proper slaves": *Farm Book*, pl. 5.
103 erecting a slave house "in 6 days": *Farm Book*, pl. 67.
103 twenty-two tradesmen: *Farm Book*, pl. 128.
103 "an exorbitant price": to Archibald Thweatt, May 29, 1810, DLC.
     Jefferson recalled the purchase of Ursula late in his life in volunteering
     information about debts owed to the estate of John Fleming, who had
     previously owned Ursula.
104 George "steady and industrious": from Thomas Mann Randolph, Apr.
     22, 1798, *Farm Book*, 152.
104 George "pushes your interest": from Thomas Mann Randolph, Apr.
     2, 1798, *Farm Book*, 436.
104 "When the British came in": *Jefferson at Monticello*, 8.
105 "no other way of drawing a line": to Thomas Mann Randolph, June
     14, 1798, *Farm Book*, 16.
105 "ash cake": *Slave Narratives*, vol. 16, *Ohio, Virginia and Tennessee Nar-
     ratives* (Works Projects Administration Writers Program, 1937; St. Clair
     Shores, Mich.: Scholarly Press, republished 1976). See Ohio narrative,
     Ben Brown, 11; James Campbell, 18; and Virginia narrative, Aunt
     Susan's Story, 44.
105 "digging up their small Lots": Hunter Dickinson Farish, ed., *Journal
     and Letters of Philip Vickers Fithian, 1773–1774* (Charlottesville, Va.:
     University Press of Virginia, Dominion Books, 1968), 96.
105 slave hierarchy: see John W. Blassingame, "Status and Social Structure
     in the Slave Community: Evidence from New Sources," in Harry P.
     Owens, ed., *Perspectives and Irony in American Slavery* (Jackson, Miss.:
     University Press of Mississippi, 1976), 137–51. Concerning the am-
     biguous status in the slave community of house servants such as the
     Hemingses, who were in a position to be of material aid to their fellow
     slaves, Blassingame writes: "When house servants were able to walk
     the thin line between maintaining the *appearance* of loyalty to masters
     with the *reality* of serving their fellow blacks they ranked high as
     individuals in the black hierarchy." It is possible that Hemings family
     members may have made this kind of accommodation. I am indebted
     to Professor Blassingame for calling my attention to the two distinct
     slave hierarchies.
107 clothing for the house servants: Martha Jefferson Randolph took par-
     ticular care in dressing her maids. Jefferson wrote her from Philadelphia

in 1791 that he had "just put on board Capt. Stratton a box with the following articles for your three house-maids:

> 36 yds callimanco [calamanco: "a woolen stuff of Flanders, glossy on the surface, and woven with a satin twill and chequered in the warp, so that the checks are seen on one side only" (*Oxford English Dictionary*)]
> 13½ yds calico of different patterns
> 25. yds linen
> 9. yds muslin
> 9. pr cotton stockings
> thread"

to Martha Randolph, Dec. 4, 1791, *Family Letters*, 91.

107   "A boy had been ordered": *Domestic Life*, 321.

108   "I am sorry for him": to Thomas Mann Randolph, Feb. 4, 1800, *Farm Book*, 17.

108   "leaves a void": to Maria Jefferson Eppes, Feb. 12, 1800, *Garden Book*, 269.

108   "conceived himself poisoned": Jupiter's placing his life in the hands of a black conjurer demonstrates the respectability of African medicine in the slave quarters. Many slaves preferred their own tribal medicine to the white man's. See *Family Letters*, 182–83. The identity of the black doctor who treated Jupiter, Ursula, and the two Georges is suggested by an entry in the Memorandum Book: *MB*, Oct. 25, 1798, "Gave Perkins's Sam order on Isaac Miller for 10.D. in full for attendance on smith George." On the role of conjurers in slave society, see Albert J. Raboteau, *Slave Religion: The "Invisible Institution" in the Antebellum South* (Oxford University Press, 1979), 80–86, 275–88; Lawrence W. Levine, *Black Culture and Black Consciousness* (Oxford University Press, 1977), 67–74.

109   "make him a thief": to Dr. Edward Bancroft, Jan. 26, 1788, *Farm Book*, 10.

109   "try the fidelity of Martin": *MB*, Mar. 14, 1774; *Farm Book*, 9.

109   slaves received no pay: John Hemings and Burwell, Jefferson's personal servant, were exceptions. Beginning in 1811, Jefferson paid Hemings $15 annually, "to wit the wages of one month in the year, which I allow him as an encouragement" (*MB*, Apr. 11, 1811). This was increased the next year to $20, and continued until the end of Jefferson's life. Burwell was also granted an annual "gratuity" of $10 (*MB*, May 13, 1812; Dec. 12, 1812) which was increased to $20 and continued until Jefferson's death.

110 "From 10 to 16": *Farm Book*, pl. 77.
110 profit of $1,000: *MB*, note to Jan. 4, 1794.
111 "then he flirts the end": *Farm Book*, 427.
111 "illness of my foreman": May 14, 1799, *Farm Book*, 440.
112 "would destroy their value": to Thomas Mann Randolph, Jan. 23, 1801, *Farm Book*, 442.
112 "2 p.c. on 2127.33": "The Nailery," 1794–1797, ViU.
112 "a pound of meat a week": *Jefferson at Monticello*, 23.
112 "Every article is made on his farm": Duke de la Rochefoucauld-Liancourt, *Travels through the United States of North America, in the Years 1795, 1796, 1797*, in Randall, 2:307; *Garden Book*, 245.
113 "a most barbarous revenge": from Thomas Mann Randolph, May 30, 1803, ViU; "as if put out of the way by death": to Thomas Mann Randolph, June 8, 1803, DLC.
113 "The Barbarity that he maid use of": from James Oldham, Nov. 26, 1804, MHi.
114 "living at bent Crick": from James Oldham, July 16, 1805, MHi.
114 "I can readily excuse the follies": to James Oldham, July 20, 1805, MHi.
114 "I am sorry to inform you": from James Oldham, July 23, 1805, MHi.
114 "gave James Hem.": *MB*, Oct. 12, 1815.
115 Jamey Hubbard: The genealogy of Jamey Hubbard and the Hubbard family is difficult to trace in Jefferson's slave rolls because he owned several Jameys, including two Jamey Hubbards, father and son. (Slaves did not normally append "junior" or "senior" to their names, although Jefferson used the terms occasionally in his slave rolls.) James Hemings, born on April 23, 1787 (*Farm Book*, pl. 30), has been misidentified as Jamey Hubbard. He ran away in April 1804 (causing a confusion with Jamey Hubbard who ran away in 1805). His name is on the same slave roll with Jamey Hubbard in 1798–99, however (pl. 57). Jamey Hubbard was born in 1782 or 1783 (pl. 31), but by 1794, at the age of eleven or twelve, he had been moved from his family at Bedford County to the nailery (pl. 30). He was sold to Reuben Perry in 1812 and his name is crossed off the slave roll of 1810 (pl. 128).
115 "an idiot": *Farm Book*, pl. 57.
115 "He was very much surprised": *Jefferson at Monticello*, 97–98
116 "never again serve any man as a slave": to Reuben Perry, Apr. 16, 1812, *Farm Book*, 34. Hubbard was deeded to Perry, Sept. 3, 1812, *Farm Book*, 35.
116 "he is too ungovernable": to Joel Yancey, Jan. 11, 1818; Feb. 18, 1818, MHi.

116   "a battle ensued": from Joel Yancey, Oct. 20, 1819, MHi; in *Farm Book*, 44–45.

117   Moses' Billy jailed: *MB*, Oct. 29, 1819, "Jonathan Bishop . . . 5.D. in addn. to 5.D. he recieved from Joel Yancey for bringing Moses' Billy from Bedford."

117   "doing great mischief": from Joel Yancey, Oct. 26, 1819, MHi. See also letter from Joel Yancey, Feb. 27, 1819; May 22, 1820; May 31, 1821, MHi.

117   "found guilty of stabbing": from William Radford, Dec. 26, 1822, MHi.

117   "ought to be hung": from Joel Yancey, July 1, 1819, MHi; *Farm Book*, 44.

117   "four prime young men": to Bernard Peyton, Jan. 5, 1824; Aug. 28, 1824, MHi.

118   Two slaves died: Malone 6:449.

119   most slave rebellions are passive: See James Oakes, *The Ruling Race: A History of American Slaveholders* (Alfred A. Knopf, 1982), 179*ff.*

119   "without the least word of difference": to Joseph Dougherty, July 31, 1806, *Farm Book*, 22.

119   ran away to visit Edy: This was the Edy who has been misidentified as one of Sally Hemings's children (Fawn Brodie, *Thomas Jefferson, An Intimate History* [W. W. Norton, 1974], 277). She was listed next to Sally Hemings's name in Jefferson's "Bread List for 1796" (*Farm Book*, 50) and "Ration list for 1796" (51), leading Professor Brodie to assume she was Sally's child. At the time, Sally Hemings was nursing her infant daughter Harriet, born Oct. 5, 1795. Edy, then a nine-year-old, moved in with Hemings to help her with the baby, which may have been ill from birth. Edy was then listed with Hemings on the bread list, in keeping with Jefferson's practice of listing slaves on his rolls, not alphabetically, but by family, or extended family living together. By closely following Jefferson's annual slave rolls, ration, and clothing lists, it is possible to determine the shift of slaves from one living place to another as they appear in different slave cabins with different "families." When Edy moved in with Hemings, for example, she was taken off the family bread list of her mother Isabel; she was returned to Isabel's list when her sister Aggey moved in with Hemings. Aggey, two years younger than Edy, took over the job of Hemings's helper ("Bread list, May 1797," *Farm Book*, 52) until the death of Harriet at the age of two in December 1797. Having a private baby-sitter would have allowed Hemings to continue working in the Monticello house,

Notes

where she was reportedly Jefferson's chambermaid. This is one of the few examples of Jefferson's giving her preferential treatment.

119   "carried off": to William Gordon, July 16, 1788, *Farm Book*, 505.

119   "fled to the enemy": *Farm Book*, pl. 29.

120   "bring their written instructions": to Thomas Mann Randolph, Feb. 15, 1798, DLC.

120   "read print": Interview with former Jefferson slave, Israel Jefferson in the *Pike County Republican*, Dec. 25, 1873, in John Blassingame, ed., *Slave Testimony* (Baton Rouge, La.: Louisiana State University Press, 1977), 486.

120   "teach me the letters": Madison Hemings memoir, *Pike County Republican*, March 13, 1873, in Blassingame, *Slave Testimony*, 478.

120   Hannah's letter: Nov. 15, 1818, *Farm Book*, 41–42. Punctuation added.

121   James Hemings inventory: Feb. 20, 1796, DLC.

122   Betty Hemings is Wayles's "concubine": Madison Hemings, in Blassingame, *Slave Testimony*, 475.

122   "old Mr. Wayles's children": *Jefferson at Monticello*, 3.

122   "first-rate workman": *Jefferson at Monticello*, 101–02.

122   haunted the carpenter shop: This and other anecdotal material on John Hemings is in James A. Bear, Jr., *The Hemings Family of Monticello* (Ivy, Va., 1980), 15–18.

123   John Hemings letter: in Blassingame, *Slave Testimony*, 16–17. Photostat in Bear, *The Hemings Family of Monticello*, opposite p. 10.

123   Hemings's signature: Hemings spelled his name with two m's, although Jefferson normally used one. In keeping with the arbitrary spelling of eighteenth-century writers, the name was apparently spelled either way.

124   Aunt Priscilla: See Elizabeth Langhorne, *Monticello, A Family Story* (Chapel Hill, N.C.: Algonquin Books of Chapel Hill, 1987), 257. This also contains new material on Sally Hemings's life after Jefferson's death.

124   "Bringhouse was a short . . .": *Jefferson at Monticello*, 14.

125   "rather tall, of strong frame": *Jefferson at Monticello*, 23.

125   "treated him mighty well": *Jefferson at Monticello*, 16.

125   Isaac gets his father's tools: to Thomas Mann Randolph, Jan. 25, 1798, DLC.

126   "I count on their setting up for delivery": to Mr. Colclaser, Aug. 8, 1817, MHi; see also letter to Edmund Bacon, Nov. 18, 1817, MHi.

126   Jefferson paid him for eighteen barrels: *MB*, Dec. 21, 1816, "Gave Barnaby . . . for the price of 18. Barrels to wit 1. in every 31 . . . Note

he has delivered . . . 563. barrels frm Oct. 9. to this day inclusive."

126 "lost the avails of my cooper's shop": to Bernard Peyton, Aug. 28, 1824, MHi.

126 "Run away from the subscriber": *Papers*, 1:33.

127 "abject, degraded and unprincipled race": to William Wirt, Aug. 5, 1815, Ford, 11:412 (Federal ed.).

128 "punishing her, as he supposes": Jan. 6, 1815, *Garden Book*, 540.

128 "concluded to sell Dinah": to Thomas Mann Randolph, Oct. 12, 1792, *Farm Book*, 14.

128 "nobody feels more strongly": to Randolph Lewis, Apr. 23, 1807, *Farm Book*, 26.

141 "We have been unfortunate": from Joel Yancey, Dec. 22, 1821, MHi.

141 "at a fair valuation": to Joel Yancey, Jan. 2, 1821, MHi.

141 "headmen": The term "driver" was used in the cotton states of the deep South, but it is not a term Jefferson would have used. Eugene D. Genovese, in *Roll, Jordan, Roll: The World the Slaves Made* (Random House, Pantheon, 1974), 365–68, discusses the role of black drivers.

141 "a larger for a foreman": *Farm Book*, pl. 46.

141 "Nace, the former headman": memorandum to Jeremiah A. Goodman, Dec. 1811, *Garden Book*, 466. Ten years after Jefferson wrote this memorandum, Nace was accused by John Hemings of taking produce from the vegetable garden at Poplar Forest during Jefferson's absence and selling it for his own profit. "Such conduct as his is . . . wrongfully and unjustly committed," Hemings wrote angrily. He was particularly incensed because the slaves did not have even "common greens" for themselves (letter from John Hemings, Nov. 29, 1821, MHi).

142 "If a physician": memorandum to Jeremiah A. Goodman, Dec. 1811, *Garden Book*, 467.

143 "5 little ones in four years": to Joel Yancey, Jan. 17, 1819, *Farm Book*, 42.

143 "a constant puking": from Martha Jefferson Randolph, Jan. 30, 1800, *Family Letters*, 183.

143 "the state of Ursula is remarkable": to Thomas Mann Randolph, Mar. 31, 1800, *Farm Book*, 17.

143 slave cottage drawings: Kimball, K-16.

144 "cheaper and better way": Kimball, K-56, K-57.

144 outbuildings on Jefferson's mountaintop: Archaeologist William Kelso's recent excavations of the slave quarters on Mulberry Row have revealed some fascinating details about how Jefferson's preferred servants were housed. Slave housing varied greatly; some houses were only twelve-

by-fourteen-foot log cabins with wood-clay chimneys and dirt floors, but there was also a thirty-four-by-seventeen-foot stone house with a stone and brick fireplace and wooden floor that was occupied at times by slaves. The earth-floor cabins had root cellars for storing food, and one cabin seems to have had a stone fireplace and an attic loft. See William M. Kelso, "The Archaeology of Slave Life at Thomas Jefferson's Monticello: 'A Wolf by the Ears,' " *Journal of New World Archaeology*, vol. 6, no. 4 (June 1986), 15–20.

144   "of wood, with a wooden chimney": 1796 fire insurance drawing, *Farm Book*, 6.

144   slaves ate and drank from porcelain: Kelso, 6–7.

145   slaves ate and slept in buildings they worked in: Kelso, 11.

CHAPTER 5

Page

146   "new Rowanty": to Robert Skipwith, Aug. 3, 1771, *Papers*, 1:78. The editors of the *Papers* note that "TJ evidently associates Monticello with 'The mountain of the world' or Rowandiz, the Accadian Olympos . . . believed to be the pivot on which the heaven rested" (81n).

147   "his great industry": *Autobiography*, Ford 1:8.

147   slave trade: John Wayles's involvement in the slave trade is documented in the correspondence between Wayles and his London agents Farell & Jones, *Papers* 15:649–55. Wayles had received at least one other consignment of slaves, from the ship *Amelia*, and there is a suggestion that he received others in the past. Of four hundred slaves who reportedly embarked from the African Coast aboard *The Prince of Wales*, only 280 arrived in Virginia alive.

147   "spinster": Bond for Marriage License [December 23, 1771], *Papers*, 1:87–87n.

148   "I was prepared to say a great deal": to John Page, Oct. 7, 1763, *Papers*, 1:11.

148   "determined to be married": to William Fleming, Mar. 10, 1764, *Papers*, 1:16.

149   prostitution is a candidate: On the history of white and slave prostitution in the antebellum South see Eugene D. Genovese, *Roll, Jordan, Roll: The World the Slaves Made* (Random House, Pantheon, 1974), 460–61.

150   "offered love to a handsome lady": to Robert Smith, July 1, 1805, in Malone 1:448.

151   ten years of "unchequered happiness": *Autobiography*, Ford, 1:80.

151 "an advocate for the passion": to John Page, Feb. 2, 1770, *Papers*, 1:71.
151 "worthy the acceptance of a lady": to Thomas Adams, June 1, 1771, *Papers*, 1:71.
151 "fine clear voice": *Jefferson at Monticello*, 13.
151 trip to nearby Shirley: *MB*, Jan. 11, 1772, "Pd ferriage at Shirley 2/6."
152 whether Jefferson had a hand in Shirley design: Thomas T. Waterman, *The Mansions of Virginia* (Chapel Hill, N.C.: University of North Carolina Press, 1945), 342–50.
152 "one of the finest of its period": Waterman, 353.
152 paid John 50 shillings: *MB*, Jan. 12, 1772: "Pd John at Shirley for mendg. Phaeton 50/." Individual tips to members of the Hemings family are also listed here.
153 "horrible dreariness of such a house": Martha Randolph's reminiscence in Randall, 1:64.
153 "song, merriment, and laughter": Randall, 1:65.
153 expensive double bed: *MB*, Dec. 16, 1771, "Pd. Richd. Scott in part for a bed £3-16-3. The remaing £4. I am to pay to Rob. Baine."
154 "plank kiln": Survey and Plat of Monticello, Aug. 3, 1806, ViU.
154 "in the wane of the moon": Andrea Palladio, *The Four Books of Architecture*, trans. Isaac Ware (reprint, Dover, 1965), bk. 1, ch. 2.
154 sawyers sawed chestnut boards: *MB*, Dec. 24, 1767.
154 a level made: *MB*, Mar. 23, 1768.
154 "level 250 f. square on top of the mountain": *MB*, May 15, 1768; *Garden Book*, 12–13.
155 "a middling hand": *MB*, [Dec.] 1770; *Garden Book*, 16.
155 "a man digs & carries": *Farm Book*, pl. 66.
155 "fills the two-wheeled barrow": *MB*, July 23, 1772; *Farm Book*, pl. 66; *Garden Book*, July 31, 1772, 33.
156 Beck worked on the well forty-six days: *MB*, Oct. 2, 1769.
156 history of the well: *Garden Book*, 629.
157 "if this conflagration": to John Page, Feb. 21, 1770, *Papers*, 1:35.
157 "this winter is employed": to Stephen Willis, Nov. 12, 1792, *Garden Book*, 173.
158 310,000 bricks: This estimate is derived primarily from two sources: TJ's building notes, *MB*, 1767, architectural section, give estimates of bricks needed for the south pavilion and wings; his demolition notes of Jan. 1, 1796 (Kimball, K-142) give accurate figures for the number of bricks actually in the middle building. Numbers have been rounded off.

158 batch of bricks made by George Dudley: TJ recorded, *MB*, July 16, 1769: "George Dudley began on Friday 14th. inst. about my bricks. I am to give him 3/ pr. 1000 for mouldg. and burning, and 4/ a week diet." Dudley was paid £11-15-1½ in cash and commodities.

158 hired a slave, Phil: *MB*, Oct. 2, 1769. The Memorandum Books for 1769 and 1770 detail the sums paid to workmen for various jobs.

158 lawsuit against Willis: *MB*, Fee Book, Aug. 25, 1768: "Edward Lee (Albermarle) and John Moore v. Stephen Willis (Hanover) To bring a suit for bricklayer's work . . . amounting to £12-11-11."

158 framing and carpentry as well: Jefferson did not appear to have a skilled carpenter or housejoiner working for him when the south pavilion was completed. Willis may have been quite capable of supervising the complete construction of a building as small as this. Some of his slaves may have been skilled carpenters.

158 1,600 bricks a day: "Chisholm & 2 apprentices (one of them a new beginner) lay 1600 bricks a day." *Farm Book*, pl. 102.

159 three to five perch a day: "a man lays generally 3. perch a day. & even 5. in very thick wall." *Farm Book*, pl. 103.

159 number of workers on the mountaintop: There were men on the building site that summer whose trades cannot be clearly identified. Richard Sorrels was a laborer who was commissioned to cut and shape fence palings to enclose Jefferson's garden, and he also helped in digging the cellars. Bartlet Ford, whose slave Phil was hired by Jefferson, was possibly a utility worker who also helped with farming. James Defoe burned lime, but he may also have laid stone for the cellars. Julius Shard was a brickmason and general laborer.

159 "dovetail-hinges for doors": *Papers*, 1:37.

159 "for hinges &c.": *MB*, Nov. 5, 1770.

159 the house he moved into: the south pavilion was not exactly the way it looks today. It was remodeled in 1809 to match the newly built north pavilion. Two windows, one on each side of the fireplace, were added at that time.

160 "more elbow room this summer": to James Ogilvie, Feb. 10, 1771, *Papers*, 1:63.

160 account for John Skelton: Malone, 1:56–57.

160 "procure me an architect": *Papers*, 1:72.

161 Stephen Willis was on the site: Willis was paid nearly £45 for three months' work, a large amount.

161 working floor plan of the dining room: This floor plan, Kimball, K-15, was drawn from an early plan of the house, K-18. The rectangular

shape of the chimney firebox is identical on both plans; this compares with the angled firebox on Jefferson's later working floor plan, K-24. It is interesting to note that the two dumbwaiters that are in the dining room today are shown added to the early floor plan, K-18, but are not in K-24.

162 As work progressed on the rest of the house: It is possible to deduce from Jefferson's working floor plan (Kimball, K-24) the order of construction of various parts of the house. A note on the plan indicates that dimensions are for walls above the water table. Wherever these dimensions are given in Jefferson's precise figures ("18f. 6.87l."), it is certain that these were measurements taken of rooms already under construction. Those rooms with no dimensions (the bedroom) or with regular ones (the dressing room) were not yet built. Using these criteria, the dining room, north bowroom, parlor, and "anti-chamber" were built first, possibly in that order. The main staircase (the stairs are not yet indicated), the dressing room, and the bedroom (south bowroom) were to be built later. There is a logic to this order: the north bowroom, which in the remodeled house became the tea room, gave the Jeffersons more entertaining space by extending the already completed dining room. The parlor and study above it were the most important rooms in the house and were contiguous with the dining room; they would normally be constructed next. The staircase in the "anti-chamber" would give access to the second-floor study during construction. (It should be noted, however, that the main stairwell and the east front of the building would have to be finished before the entire middle building could be roofed over.) Because the Jeffersons had their bedroom already established in the south pavilion, the dressing room and its attached bowroom were not immediately needed.

162 a drawing dated August 4, 1772: Kimball, K-34. This date is on a note; the plan may have been drawn earlier.

163 "high as desk & bookcase": *MB*, Dec. 3, 1773.

163 Jefferson sent a detailed letter: to Archibald Cary and Benjamin Harrison, Dec. 9, 1774, *Papers*, 1:154.

164 crown glass: On the technology of crown glass see Kenneth M. Wilson, "Window Glass in America," in Charles E. Peterson, ed., *Building Early America* (Radnor, Pa.: Chilton Book Co., 1976).

164 "double flint" glass: Kimball, K-78.

164 mirror image of the east portico: Kimball, K-18, shows his original intention.

165 a total of thirty-seven feet above the water table: See Kimball, K-42.

The figures for the "anti-chamber" are: to the water table 4½ feet, the lower story 19 feet, the upper story 18 feet. The measurements for the middle building would be the same as these. K-146 describes changing the dimensions to make the dining room a cube.

165 Doric column larger than specified: see Kimball, K-68, K-69, K-70. The column diameter was "20.11766" inches instead of 19 inches.

166 railings in the Chinese style: see Kimball, K-83.

166 William Pond was hired to make bricks: *MB*, June 2, 1774; *Garden Book*, 57.

166 two wagons brought two loads of stone: *MB*, Fee Book, Feb. 8, 1775; *Garden Book*, 68.

166 Randolph Johnson, bricklayer, hired: *MB*, Sept. 13, 1776; *Farm Book*, 80.

166 "ninety thousand workable bricks made": *MB*, Feb. 7, 1778; *Garden Book*, 80.

166 "fine flooring plank": *MB*, Feb. 13, 1777; *Garden Book*, 72.

167 "on the top of the house": *Garden Book*, 80.

167 Humphrey Gaines sent to Marlboro Iron Works: to Isaac Zane, Feb. 26, 1778, *Papers*, 2:175n.

167 wrote to his friend John Harvie: from John Harvie, Sept. 15, 1778, *Papers*, 2:212.

167 Isaac's description of Neilson: *Jefferson at Monticello*, 3.

167 Joseph Neilson still working in 1779: Jefferson recorded, *MB*, Aug. 3, 1779, "Nelson begins to work at £3 a day." On Neilson, see James Bear, Jr., *The Hemings Family of Monticello* (Ivy, Va., 1980).

168 Jouett's ride: see Virginius Dabney, "Jack Jouett's Ride," *American Heritage*, XIII (Dec. 1961), 56–59; John Cook Wylie, "Writings About Jack Jouett and Tarleton's Raid on Charlottesville, in 1781," *The Magazine of Albemarle County History*, vol. 17 (1958–1959), 49–56.

168 under the floor boards of the east portico: This indicates that the floors of the porticoes were wood. They probably remained so, even after the house was remodeled, until 1823 when Jefferson finished them in slate.

168 "Fire away, then": Randall 1:538–39. Caesar was a farm laborer whom Jefferson was later to characterize as "being notorious for his rogueries."

169 "The house, of which Mr. Jefferson was the architect": Marquis de Chastellux, *Travels in North America in the Years 1780, 1781 and 1782*, trans. Howard C. Rice, Jr. (Chapel Hill, N.C.: University of North Carolina Press, 1963), 2:391.

170 historians have been uncomfortable: Randall, for example, stated that

"the remark is to be taken with some qualifications." Randall, 1:377.

170   "for amusement he would work": *Jefferson at Monticello*, 18.

170   "had acquired much practical skill": George Tucker, *The Life of Thomas Jefferson* (London, 1837), 2:341. What lends credibility to Tucker's remark is that his is a political biography and this is one of the few detailed comments on Jefferson's personal habits in the two volumes. He mentions visiting Monticello on at least two occasions, 2:40n, and 2:544.

170   architectural models: Randall, 1:376.

170   "bill of scantling": Bill of Scantling delivd mr Frazer, June 1783, ViU; Nichols, N-506.

171   "6 rooms Doric and Ionic": the six rooms cannot be positively identified, but they are possibly four rooms in the middle building, and two in the north wing.

173   Davy Watson was still working: to John Key, Mar. 2, 1784: "Watson may be discharged when stairs done, or before, if necessary. . . ." *Papers*, 7:3.

174   "The unprofitable condition": to Mary Jefferson Eppes, Jan. 7, 1798, *Domestic Life*, 247.

174   "I made it a point": to Nicholas Lewis, July 11, 1788, *Papers*, 13:342.

175   "a spark of electricity": de Chastellux, 2:392.

CHAPTER 6

Page

178   one in every ten bore twelve or more: Catherine Clinton, *The Plantation Mistress* (Pantheon, 1982), appendix B, table 7, p. 242. This work is a rich source of information on eighteenth-century plantation wives.

178   "Mrs Carter reads more than the Parson": Hunter Dickinson Farish, ed., *Journal and Letters of Philip Vickers Fithian, 1773–1774* (Charlottesville, Va.: The University Press of Virginia, Dominion Books, 1968), 66.

178   "Stagnate the Blood": Christian Barnes to Elizabeth Smith, Nov. 24, 1770, The Letterbooks of Christian Barnes, 1768–1783, DLC, quoted in Mary Beth Norton, *Liberty's Daughters* (Boston: Little, Brown, 1980), 39.

179   two dependency wings: see Kimball, K-31.

180   "small beer": Martha Jefferson Account Book, Feb. 27, 1772 (Account Book with Record of Cases Tried in Virginia Courts, 1768–69), DLC. Subsequent references by date are to this Account Book.

180 "bought 7 lb hops": Oct. 24, 1774.
181 "Montichello": *Papers*, 5:431–32n; "monnttesello" and "mountey-selley" spellings: Account of Mr. Wanscher from Aug. 15, 1801 to Apr. 29, 1802, MHi. There is also in his papers an address: "Colo Jefferson, Montochollo." Undated, MHi.
181 making soft soap: see Alice Morse Earle, *Home Life in Colonial Days* (New York: Macmillan Co., 1917), 253–55.
182 "borrowed 10 lb sugar": Jan. 21, 1774.
183 "all Virginians are fond of Music": from Jacob Rubsamen, *Papers*, 4:174; Malone, 1:296.
183 leather-bound notebook: Thomas Jefferson Memorial Foundation Deposit, Box 4, 5385ab, ViU.
184 "On my way here": *Papers*, 6:161.
185 economical way to measure and brew coffee: Nov. 25, 1772.
186 purchase of Ursula: *MB*, Jan. 21, 1773, "Bot. Ursula, and her sons George and Bagwell of Fleming's estate for £210. 12. month's credit."
186 "a good breast of milk": to Thomas Mann Randolph, Oct. 19, 1792, DLC.
186 "Mrs. Jefferson would come out there": *Jefferson at Monticello*, 3.
187 "slightly but exquisitely formed": the physical descriptions of Martha Jefferson are from family tradition, in Randall, 1:63.
187 "tall like her father": *Jefferson at Monticello*, 5.
187 "not yet lost a tooth by age": to Doctor Vine Utley, Mar. 21, 1819, Randall, 3:450. In *MB*, Nov. 30, 1808, however, Jefferson recorded: ". . . pd Dr. Bruff extractg. a tooth 5.D."
187 a Williamsburg dentist: in *MB*, Apr. 14, 1772, Jefferson recorded, "Pd. Baker the dentist 30/," and on May 3, "Pd. Baker the dentist 20/."
187 "she is not handsome": *Thornton Diary*, Sept. 19, 1802.
188 "more qualified than common": *Papers*, 11:251.
188 "The plan of reading": *Papers*, 6:374.
191 "nothing but her needle for employment": *Papers*, 11:251.
191 "she can learn nothing here": to Elizabeth Wayles Eppes, July 28, 1787, *Papers*, 11:634.
191 "how many hours you sew": to Mary [Maria] Jefferson, Apr. 11, 1790, *Domestic Life*, 181. Maria was, as a child, called Mary.
191 "Your last two letters": to Martha Jefferson Randolph, Feb. 9, 1791, *Domestic Life*, 192.
192 "The tender breasts of ladies": to Angelica Schuyler Church, Sept. 21, 1788, *Papers*, 11:623.

192 inferior to her older and brighter sister: see Ellen Randolph Coolidge's letter to Henry Randall in Randall, 3:101–3.

192 "the happiness of your life": to Martha Jefferson Randolph, Apr. 4, 1790, *Domestic Life*, 180.

193 "Would to god": to Mary Jefferson, June 26, 1791, *Papers*, 20:571.

193 "I value the enjoyments": to Martha Jefferson Randolph, Mar. 27, 1797, *Domestic Life*, 243.

193 "Nothing can preserve affections": to Mary Jefferson Eppes, Jan. 7, 1798, *Domestic Life*, 246–47.

194 "become solvenly": to Mary Jefferson Eppes, Jan. 7, 1798, *Domestic Life*, 247.

194 buy the latest fashion accessories: *MB*, July 4, 1776, "Pd. for 7 pr. women's gloves, 27/"; Aug. 27, "Pd. Mrs. Nelson for sundries bot. for Mrs. Jefferson £18-13-3½"; Aug. 28, "Pd. Simpson 6 pr. women's shoes £4." There was something for the children: May 27, "Pd. for toys 1/7."; May 28, "Pd. for a Doll 2/."

194 "clean, whole, and properly put on": to Martha Jefferson, Dec. 22, 1783, *Papers*, 6:417.

195 associate women's sexuality with filth: It was Norman O. Brown who described the equating of sex with dirt as the "excremental vision," now recognized as a common anal-retentive profile. He cited Jonathan Swift as the archetypical model for it. Throughout Swift's works, women's sexuality is seen as filthy and repugnant, in part because the organs of generation, Brown argues, are the same as those of elimination. Norman O. Brown, *Life Against Death* (Middleton, Conn.: Wesleyan University Press, 1959), 179–201.

195 indoor privies: It was thought until recently that waste fell into a cart in the underground airshaft tunnel and was removed with a rope pulley. This was not the case; slaves shoveled it from what Jefferson termed the "sewers" and were paid a small fee for doing it.

196 "certain small contrivances": Kenneth Roberts and Anna M. Roberts, *Moreau de St. Mery's American Journey* (Garden City, N.Y.: Doubleday, 1947), 177–78. Condoms were being advertised and sold in London in 1776. See Lawrence Stone, *The Family, Sex and Marriage in England 1500–1800* (London: Weidenfeld and Nicolson, 1977), 422–23.

196 syringes: *MB*, Aug. 24, 1786, "Pd. for a syringe 6 f 12"; Mar. 25, 1800, "Pd. for syringe 5.D."

196 contraceptive effect of lactation: Norton, 232–34.

197 "for my sake, come": to Richard Henry Lee, July 29, 1776, *Papers*, 1:477.

197 getting her pregnant: Jefferson was at Monticello from Sept. 9 to Sept. 27. See chronology in Ford, 1:xvii.

197 "continues very dangerously ill": to James Monroe, May 20, 1782, *Papers*, 6:192.

197 "Nothing could so completely divest us": to James Monroe, May 20, 1782, *Papers*, 6:186.

197 "when not at her bed": Randall, 1:196.

198 *Tristram Shandy*: *Papers*, 6:196.

199 "when Mrs. Jefferson died": *Jefferson at Monticello*, 99–100. Bacon erred in the number of children the Jeffersons had at Martha's death. There were only three. Jefferson's slave Israel also recalled that "it was a general statement among the older servants at Monticello, that Mr. Jefferson promised his wife, on her death bed, that he would not again marry" ("Reminiscences of Israel Jefferson," in John Blassingame, ed., *Slave Testimony* [Baton Rouge: Louisiana State University Press, 1977], 486).

199 Martha was herself a stepchild: see the Wayles family genealogy in Malone, 1:432–33.

200 "A moment before the closing scene": Randall, 1:382; *Papers*, 6:199–200n.

200 "domestic happiness in the first class": *Papers*, 6:199n.

200 "too burdensome to be borne": *Papers*, 6:198.

201 familiar mourning pattern: See Elisabeth Kübler-Ross, *On Death and Dying* (Macmillan, 1969).

201 "gentle and amiable wife": Marquis de Chastellux, *Travels in North America, 1780, 1781 and 1782*, trans. Howard C. Rice, Jr. (Chapel Hill, N.C.: University of North Carolina Press, 1963), 2:391.

203 "even lost the small estimation": to James Monroe, May 20, 1782, *Papers*, 6:185

203 recorded in the family bible: Main Series 3, 1732–1790, ViU.

203 "bilious fever": On the death and burial of Dabney Carr, see Malone, 1:160–61.

203 "2 hands grubbed": *Garden Book*, 40.

203 "Nay, if even in the house of Hades": Homer, *The Iliad*, trans. A. T. Murray (Cambridge, Mass.: Harvard University Press, 1925), book 22, l.389–90, p. 483.

203 "W. Hornsby's method for preserving birds": *Garden Book*, 95.

204 "could the objects of my affection have been immortal: to Elizabeth Blair, *Papers*, 11:57.

205   "to that unfortunate accident": from John Wayles Eppes, July 14, 1802, ViU.

205   "rising in her breast": from John Wayles Eppes, Mar. 23, 1804, ViU.

205   "I find it often hard to bear up": Maria Jefferson Eppes to John Wayles Eppes, Feb. 6, 1804, Eppes Family Papers, ViU.

206   "the dismal doom": Thomas Mann Randolph to C. A. Rodney, Apr. 16, 1804, Historical Society of Missouri (John H. Gundlach collection).

206   controlled emotion typical of his generation: Jan Lewis, *The Pursuit of Happiness, Family and Values in Jefferson's Virginia* (Cambridge University Press, 1983), 36, 70–71.

206   "took their ultimate form": to James Madison, Apr. 21, 1804, DLC.

206   "slender thread of a single life": to John Page, June 25, 1804, L & B, 11:31.

207   old list of various kinds of lumber: Bill of Scantling delivd mr Frazer, June 1783, ViU.; Nichols, N-506.

208   rough sketch of the floor plan: Nichols, N-46 verso, ViU. Nichols dates the recto sketch of the east elevation 1769–70, but the verso floor plan may be much later.

CHAPTER 7

Page

209   "violently smitten": to Madame de Tessé, Mar. 20, 1787, *Papers*, 11:226.

210   "two tiers of them": to John Brown, Apr. 5, 1797, DLC; Malone, 3:227.

210   "Hôtel de Salm: a description of the Hôtel de Salm is in William Howard Adams, ed., *The Eye of Thomas Jefferson* (Washington, D.C.: National Gallery of Art, 1976), pp. 125, 171.

211   ladies "I did not know": from William Short, Mar. 26, Apr. 4, Apr. 6, 1787, *Papers*, 11:239, 269, 275. See also Howard C. Rice, Jr., *Thomas Jefferson's Paris* (Princeton, N.J.: Princeton University Press, 1976), 104–5. This is the definitive work on the Paris Jefferson knew.

211   "family soupes": to Maria Cosway, Oct. 12, 1786, *Papers*, 10:453.

212   Hôtel de Langeac: Floor plans of the Hôtel de Langeac are in Howard C. Rice, Jr., *L'Hôtel de Langeac, Jefferson's Paris Residence* (Charlottesville, Va.: Thomas Jefferson Memorial Foundation, 1947). See also *Papers*, 8:xxxiii, 247.

212   housed the private quarters: Jefferson's instructions to Short for packing

his belongings suggest the use of the various rooms; to William Short, Mar. 12, 1790, *Papers*, 16:229.

213   overcharging him: TJ compared a year's worth of dinners by both Marc and Petit and found that Petit's dinners were more than three livres cheaper. *MB*, Dec. 14, 1786.

213   quickly grew fond: While Short was on a trip to Rome, he heard a rumor that Jefferson had moved from the Hôtel de Langeac. "I hope still sincerely it is not [so]," he wrote, "because I know how much you were attached to that habitation"; from William Short, Jan. 14, 1788, *Papers*, 14:452.

213   infatuated the moment he set eyes on her: For a detailed account of the Cosway romance, see Helen D. Bullock, *My Head and My Heart: A Little Chronicle of Thomas Jefferson and Maria Cosway* (Putnam's, 1945).

214   dislocated his wrist: Exactly how this happened is not known but new information on it is revealed in a letter to Jefferson from a European bookseller. William Goldsmith, from whom Jefferson purchased books while he was in Paris, wrote from Amsterdam during Jefferson's presidency and reminded him that ". . . when your Excellency had the misfortune to hurt his Arm by a fall from his horse, while living at Challiot the writer was honored to write dictated by your Excellency himself" (from W. Goldsmith, Apr. 20, 1807, DLC). This sentence adds the information that Jefferson was on horseback instead of on foot when the fall occurred, and that Goldsmith acted as his amenuensis when he was unable to write with his injured hand. "Challiot" refers to the Grille de Chaillot where the Hôtel de Langeac was located. See *Papers*, 10:432n.

214   one of the notable love letters in the English language: by Julian P. Boyd, ed., *Papers*, 10:453n.

214   Head-Heart letter: to Maria Cosway, Oct. 12, 1786, *Papers*, 10:443–54.

216   identity theme: The term *identity theme* is from the work of Norman Holland. See *The I* (New Haven: Yale University Press, 1985), 23–50.

217   "Our own dear Monticello": to Maria Cosway, Oct. 12, 1786, *Papers*, 10:447.

218   "I could think of nothing at Strasbourg but the promontory of noses": to Maria Cosway, Apr. 24, 1788, *Papers* 13:104. "Slawkenburgius's Tale" in Laurence Sterne's *Tristram Shandy* is at the beginning of Vol. IV. See also Vol. III, chaps. 31–42. Sterne's bawdiness was certainly partly responsible for Jefferson's admiration for *Tristram Shandy*. The

Latin sexual and scatological puns and the arcane ribaldry were the kinds of learned wit that would have appealed to Jefferson.

218 "Many things to say": from Maria Cosway, Apr. 29, 1788, *Papers*, 13:115.

219 "Think of it then": to Angelica Schuyler Church, Aug. 17, 1788, *Papers*, 13:521.

219 Halle aux Bleds: for a description see Rice, *Thomas Jefferson's Paris*, 18–21.

219 "like a lover at his mistress": to Madame de Tessé, Mar. 20, 1787, *Papers*, 11:226.

220 "How is taste in this beautiful art": to James Madison, Sept. 20, 1785, *Papers*, 8:534–35.

220 "Fix yourself in some family": to Thomas Mann Randolph, Jr., July 6, 1787, *Papers*, 11:456.

220 apprentice James Hemings to a chef: "I propose for a particular purpose to carry my servant James with me"; to William Short, May 7, 1784, *Papers*, 7:229.

221 "has forgot how to speak English": to Antonio Giannini, Feb. 5, 1786, *Papers*, 9:254.

221 "*Sotisses Les plus durs*": from Perrault, Jan. 9, 1789, *Papers*, 14:426n.

221 apprenticed to several cooks and a *pâtissier*: MB, Dec. 4, 1784, "Pd the Traiteur 150 f. being the half of what I am to pay him for teaching James. the other half to be paid when he is taken away." Feb. 2, 1786, "Combeaux, balance James's apprentices 150-0#." Jan 10, 1787, "pd James's apprenticeship with Patisier 72#." See also from Philip Mazzei, Apr. 17, 1787, *Papers*, 11:297.

221 put on the payroll: According to MB, Nov. 1, 1787, James started receiving 24 f. a month. On Jan. 1, 1788, both he and Sally Hemings received 24 f., plus the usual New Year's gift, or *étrennes*, of 12 f. Hemings continued to be paid when he served as cook in Philadelphia during Jefferson's tenure as secretary of state.

221 "the laws of France give him freedom": to Paul Bentalou, Aug. 25, 1786, *Papers*, 10:296. There was some self-interest in this advice. If Bentalou had asked for a "dispensation from the law," it might well have called attention to Jefferson's ownership of Hemings.

222 a promise of future freedom: Both the promise to emancipate, Sept. 15, 1793, and the emancipation indenture, Feb. 5, 1796, are in *Farm Book*, 15. The promise of freedom is a strange and highly unusual document. If slaveholders made any promises of freedom to slaves, they were usually verbal. A written promise such as Jefferson's would

have been legally worthless to Hemings, because slaves could not sue in court, nor could they testify. Hemings obviously wanted the agreement on paper, however, and Jefferson complied. It is one of many instances of the preferential treatment given members of the Hemings family.

Sally Hemings's return from France, where she too could have remained as a free person, was also induced by promises of "extraordinary privileges," according to her son, Madison. Jefferson "made a solemn pledge that her children should be freed at the age of twenty-one years," he reported. "In consequence of his promises, on which she implicitly relied, she returned with him to Virginia." Madison Hemings interview, *Pike County* (Ohio) *Republican*, Mar. 13, 1873, in John W. Blassingame, ed., *Slave Testimony* (Baton Rouge: Louisiana State University Press, 1977), 476.

222 "James is returned to this place": in James A. Bear, Jr., *The Hemings Family of Monticello* (Ivy, Va., 1980), 12.

222 paid him $30 wages: *MB*, Sept. 19, 1801, "Pd. James Hemings a month & a half's wages 30. D."

222 "The report respecting James Hemings": from William Evans, Nov. 5, 1801, Bear, *The Hemings Family of Monticello*, 12.

228 Anything could be made palatable: Barbara Ketcham Wheaton, *Savoring the Past* (Philadelphia: University of Pennsylvania Press, 1983), 209.

228 Rousseau in *Émile*: Wheaton, 225.

228 *cuisine à la bourgeoise*: Wheaton, 232.

228 "with good taste they unite temperance": to Charles Bellini, Sept. 30, 1785, *Papers*, 8:569.

228 *La Cuisinière Bourgeoise* sent to Martha: to Martha Jefferson Randolph, Dec. 4, 1791, MHi; *Family Letters*, 91.

229 list of menus and recipes: MHi undated. The menus in translation are in Marie Kimball, *Thomas Jefferson's Cook Book* (Charlottesville, Va.: University of Virginia Press, 1976), 30–35. This history of Jefferson's dining habits includes a collection of modernized recipes taken from the Monticello cookbook copied by generations of Jefferson grandchildren and great-grandchildren.

229 macaroni, the macaroni machine, and Short's criticism of the Naples product: from William Short, Feb. 11, 1789, *Papers*, 14:540–41; Jefferson's notes on macaroni manufacture: *Papers*, 14:544.

230 collecting recipes a habit: see Randall 1:47–48.

230 necessary accompaniments: MHi, undated.

230 James Hemings's kitchen inventory: Feb. 20, 1796, DLC. The complete inventory:

19 Copper Stewpans—19 Covers
6 Small Saucepans
3 Copper Baking Moulds
2 Small preserving pans
2 Large Ditto
2 Copper Fish kettles
2 Copper Brazing pans
2 Round Large Ditto
2 Iron Stewpans
2 Large Boiling kettles tin'd inside
1 Large Brass Ditto
12 pewter water Dishes
12 _____ _____ plates
3 Tin Coffiepots
8 Tin Dish Covers
2 frying pans of Iron & one of Copper
4 Round Baking Copper sheets tin'd
4 Square Copper Ditto untin'd
1 Copper Boiler
1 Copper tea kettle 1 Iron Ditto
1 Turkish Bonnet Baking mould
3 Waffle Irons
2 Grid Irons
2 Spits—1 Jack—3 cleavers—2 holdfasts
3 Copper laidles—4 Copper spoons—1 Basing [basting] spoon
3 Copper skimmers—2 Cast Iron Bakers
2 pair Tongs—2 shovels—1 poker—1 Bake shovel
2 Large Iron pots—2 Dutch ovens
1 Iron Chaffing Dish—21 small Copper Baking moulds
2 Jelly moulds—2 Freising [freezing] moulds
1 Butter Tinkettle—2 Culinders—1 tin 1 of pewter
1 Brass Culinder 2 Graters—1 old Copper fish kettle
9 wooden spoons—2 past cuting [pastry cutting] moulds
1 Brass pistle & morter—1 marble Ditto
2 wooden paste Rolers—2 Chopping Knives
6 Iron Crevets—3 tin tart moulds—5 Kitchen approns
1 old Brass Kettle—1 Iron Candlestick
2 Brass Chaffing Dishes

Notes

For a list of kitchen and dining articles shipped from France see *Papers*, 18:33–39n.

231   "stewholes": to Henry J. Foxall, Mar. 24, 1809; from Henry J. Foxall, Apr. 11, 1809, MHi; *Garden Book*, 84–85.

231   eighteenth-century cooking utensils: See Alice Morse Earle, *Home Life in Colonial Days* (New York: Macmillan Co., 1917), chs. 3, 4; Audrey Noel Hume, *Food*, Colonial Williamsburg Archaeological Series No. 9 (Williamsburg, Va.: Colonial Williamsburg Foundation, 1978), 51–58.

232   "You prove the proper heat": undated, DLC.

232   Martha Randolph recipes: Account Book with Record of Cases Tried in Virginia Courts, 1768–69, DLC. Interestingly, in the recipe for fish, Martha Randolph spells pint, "point," which suggests how she may have pronounced it.

232   "famous sunday pudding": ViU, Martha Randolph 5385aa. A modernized variation of this recipe and another for bread pudding are in Marie Kimball, *Thomas Jefferson's Cook Book*, 85–86.

233   dinner parties as "campaigns": Malone 4:370.

233   entertainment lists: after Nov. 30, 1804, MHi.

233   "fatigues of the table": to Martha Randolph, Oct. 7, 1804, MHi; Malone, 4:370.

233   "French servants in livery": from Adams papers, MHi, quoted in Malone 4:374.

234   fruit and vegetable chart: This table (pictured on p. 226), more than any of Jefferson's detailed lists, indexes, and accounts, has convinced scholars that Jefferson's compulsive data collecting was wasteful of his energies, and intellectually trivial. It implies that he haunted the markets watching for the arrival of a tray of carrots or a basket of melons. Jefferson was not only thorough in the collection of detailed facts, however; he was also efficient. The lists of fruits and vegetables could have been kept current quite simply by instructing his maître d'hôtel always to purchase any item the first time it appeared at the market, and to continue buying it periodically until it disappeared. He would then simply have to notice the date it showed up and vanished from his dinner table. This does not mean he did not occasionally accompany his maître d'hôtel to the market; as an avid gardener, it was a pleasure he would not deny himself.

234   cost of groceries and wine: *MB*, Mar. 8, 1802, "Analysis of expenditures from Mar. 4. 1801. to Mar. 4. 1802"; Randall, 3:21.

234   "I always trust you for quality": to Parent, Jan. 27, 1789, *Papers* 14:480 *(Je me fie à vous toujours pour la qualité, et que le prix soit ce qu'il doit être, toujours pourtant regardant la qualité plus que le prix.)* Translated in

Samuel Maggio, "Parent: Jefferson's Burgundy 'Wine Man,' " in R. de Treville Lawrence, St., ed., *Jefferson and Wine* (The Plains, Va.: Vinifera Wine Growers Association, 1896), 54.

235   "a hamper of Champagne": *MB*, Dec. 20, 1802; "Wine Stocks at the White House," de Treville Lawrence, 168.

235   "The consumption then has been 207 bottles": *MB*, Mar. 20, 1804.

235   "silky": to Victor Adolphus Sasserno, May 26, 1819, "Jefferson's Tasting Vocabulary," de Treville Lawrence, 63–64.

235   three glasses of wine daily: to Dr. Vine Utley, Mar. 21, 1818, *Domestic Life*, 371.

235   "till the cloth is removed": *Thornton Diary*, Sep. 19, 1802, DLC. Daniel Webster made virtually the same comment after visiting Monticello twenty-two years later in 1824: "No wine is put on the table till the cloth is removed"; in Rice, *Thomas Jefferson's Paris*, 125.

235   "the poison of whiskey": to M. de Neuville, Dec. 13, 1818, L & B 15:177; "Appendix A," de Treville Lawrence, 185.

236   "species of gambling": to William Drayton, July 30, 1787, *Papers* 11:646–47; *Garden Book*, 126.

237   "it will take centuries to adapt to our soil": to John Adlum, Oct. 7, 1809, *Garden Book*, 415; de Treville Lawrence, 124.

238   "The passage of the Patowmac": *Notes*, 19.

238   "All my wishes end": to George Gilmer, Aug. 12, 1787, *Papers*, 12:26.

CHAPTER 8

Page

240   "The shouting": Randall, 1:552–53. See also Wormley's recollections made to Randall.

241   Randolph–Martha Jefferson meeting: See William H. Gaines, Jr., *Thomas Mann Randolph, Jefferson's Son-in-Law* (Baton Rouge: Louisiana State University Press, 1966), 24

241   rushed marriage: Hasty courtships and brief engagements were common during this period. Premarital pregnancies were also not unusual: an estimate in one Virginia parish places the number of women who were pregnant on the day of their first marriage at one-quarter to one-third. See Daniel Blake Smith, *Inside the Great House: Planter Family Life in Eighteenth Century Chesapeake Society* (Ithaca, N.Y.: Cornell University Press, 1980), 132, 139.

242   "rather homely": Margaret Bayard Smith, *The First Forty Years of Washington Society, Portrayed by the Family Letters of Mrs. Samuel Har-*

rison Smith, Gaillard Hunt, ed. (Charles Scribner's Sons, 1906), 34.

242   Randolph was tall, lean, and swarthy: Randall, 1:558–59.

242   "Genealogy of Pocahontas": undated, DLC.

242   not the "blockhead" Jefferson feared: to François Barbe-Barbois, Dec. 5, 1775, *Papers*, 16:373–74.

243   "took fire": Gaines, 33.

243   "manufacturing mill": See *Farm Book*, 341–43.

244   "I had digested a plan": to Thomas Mann Randolph, Feb. 3, 1792, MHi; *Farm Book*, 347.

245   "Having long ago fixed": to Stephen Willis, Nov. 12, 1792, MHi; *Garden Book*, 173.

246   "of logs, covered with clapboard": memorandum for Nicholas Lewis, c. Nov. 7, 1790, *Papers*, 18:29.

246   fire insurance policy: reproduced in *Garden Book*, 6.

246   "of chestnut logs, hewed on two sides": memorandum to Samuel Clarkson, Sept. 23, 1792, ViU. For archaeological findings on these buildings see William M. Kelso, "The Archaeology of Slave Life at Thomas Jefferson's Monticello: 'A Wolf by the Ears,' " *Journal of New World Archaeology*, vol. 6, no. 4 (June 1986), 5–20.

247   "took it into his head to make charcoal of them": from Thomas Mann Randolph, Feb. 7, 1793, MHi.

247   "the men having been so much deceived": from Thomas Mann Randolph, Aug. 14, 1793, MHi.

247   Jupiter hired out to a brickmason: See Nicholas Lewis Account, June 1792, ViU. Jupiter was hired to Thomas Whitlough, who built an oven in the kitchen of the south pavilion for Jefferson.

247   quarry one thousand bushels of limestone: memorandum to Samuel Clarkson, Sept. 23, 1792, ViU.

247   "Jupiter from what I can learn": from Thomas Mann Randolph, Jan. 19, 1793, MHi.

247   quarry below the fourth roundabout: In the memorandum to Clarkson, Jefferson wrote, "150 perch of stone are to be raised at the bottom of the park & brought up here by the oxcart." The north fence of this park was at the fourth roundabout; see *Garden Book*, pl. XIII. After his return from France, Jefferson converted the deer park into cropland. The name was then changed to Parkfield. See *Farm Book*, "Jefferson's survey of the Monticello fields," pl. at 336–337. Adjoining the park was a plot known as "Slatefield," and it is here that Jefferson may have quarried slate for the floors of the all-weather passages and porticoes.

247   "much more time than I had any idea of": from Thomas Mann Randolph, June 19, 1793, MHi.

247   "Davy can use the wheelwright's tools": from Thomas Mann Randolph, June 19, 1793, MHi.

248   made arrangements for a mason: memorandum of Dec. 5, 1792, "Fraquair, stonecutter, corner of 10th & Market Streets Phila now writes to his friend in Edinburgh to send me a person capable of laying & cutting stone @ £30 sterl. a year—to be engaged 4 years" (MHi). Fraquair was the same stone mason with whom Jefferson's workman Richard Richardson served an apprenticeship.

248   "engage Nanny Brewer": to Thomas Pleasants, June 7, 1794, DLC. Jefferson paid her various small amounts while she was at Monticello, including "for knitting 24/" (MB, July 8, 1778).

250   symmetrical floor plan: Jefferson's geometrically balanced designs may have been influenced by his switch, while in France, to the use of engraved coordinate paper and pencil for his architectural drawings. He had learned from Clérisseau that this is the medium of the professional architect rather than the pen and ink he had previously used. Coordinate paper encouraged the mathematically regular design that Jefferson had always favored. Pencil, on the other hand, with its ability to be erased, allowed for experimentation and greater freedom. Fiske Kimball believed that the freedom of the pencil was "more than overbalanced" by the constrictions imposed by the regular grid of coordinate paper (Kimball, 46).

250   "My essay in architecture": to Benjamin Latrobe, Oct. 10, 1809, DLC; Malone, 6:8.

250   "his local and domestic arrangements": Smith, 386–87.

251   "In my middle room": to William Coffee, July 10, 1822, MHi; Kimball, 72n.

251   "That house only ought to be called convenient": Andrea Palladio, The Four Books of Architecture, trans. Isaac Ware (Dover, 1965), bk. 2, ch. 1. For a provocative essay on the evolution of convenience and comfort in domestic architecture see Witold Rybczynski, Home, A Short History of an Idea (Viking, 1986), particularly chs. 4 and 5.

252   dome room for a billiard room: Domestic Life, 332. No law prohibiting billiard tables has been found, but there was obviously strong sentiment in the Virginia General Assembly against billiards. In 1781, a law was passed taxing billiard tables annually at fifty pounds each. It was reduced the following year to fifteen pounds, still a prohibitory amount (a horse was taxed at two shillings, a slave at ten shillings, and a carriage

at one pound). In designing his dome room as a billiard room, Jefferson may have been unaware of this tax, and may not have learned of it, as his granddaughter suggested, until after the dome was started. William W. Hening, *The Statutes at Large: being a collection of the Laws of Virginia, from the first session of the legislature, in the year 1619* (R. & W. & G. Bartow, 1819–1823), vol. 10, May 1781, 504; vol. 11, Nov. 1782, 93, 113, 418.

253 the balcony a virtue of necessity: Jefferson had a precedent from Palladio for placing a balcony in the hall. The house of Paolo Almerico (Palladio, *The Four Books of Architecture*, bk. 2, pl. 13) illustrates a balcony over the great circular hall in the center of the house, "a place to walk round the hall, fifteen foot and a half wide." Jefferson must have read the description of the house with great interest, for it closely resembles his own building site: "The site is as pleasant and as delightful as can be found; because it is upon a small hill, of very easy access, and is watered on one side by the *Bacchglione*, a navigable river; and on the other it is encompassed with most pleasant risings, which look like a great theatre, and are all cultivated, and abound with most excellent fruits, and most exquisite vines: and therefore, as it enjoys from every part most beautiful views, some of which are limited, some more extended, and others which terminate with the horizon . . ." (Dover ed., 41).

254 Fowler, his spiritual descendant: see Orson S. Fowler, *The Octagon House: A Home for All* (1853; reprint, Dover, 1973). Fowler also argued that the octagon shape saves in building costs.

254 eliminates dark corners: most houses today invariably have a lamp placed in the corners of rooms.

256 retired to a hermitage: see Howard C. Rice, Jr., *Thomas Jefferson's Paris* (Princeton, N.J.: Princeton University Press, 1976), 105–06.

257 "a place to retire and write in": to Thomas Leiper, Dec. 16, 1792, Kimball, 152.

257 "The walls are so solid": to Thomas Mann Randolph, Apr. 11, 1796, *Garden Book*, 249.

258 salvaged 29,000 whole bricks: Kimball K-142.

258 "we are now living in a brick-kiln": to George Wythe, DLC; *Garden Book*, 224.

258 contracts made with two sawyers: *MB*, Oct. 5, 1795, "Agreed with David Barnet and Robinson to come & saw for me at 4/ a hundred, where the hewing is done, & 4/6 where he hews, & find them provisions." Hewing refers to shaping the rounded parts of a tree into flat boards.

258   "We cannot proceed . . . till the columns are taken away": to Thomas Mann Randolph, Feb. 7, 1796, MHi.

258   wood eaten with rot: to Martha Jefferson Randolph, Feb. 14, 1796, *Family Letters*, 136.

258   "The tumbling of brick bats": to Thomas Mann Randolph, Apr. 11, 1796, DLC; *Garden Book*, 249.

258   "a tumble thro' the floor": to Thomas Mann Randolph, Jan. 27, 1797, DLC; she fell out of a door: Malone, 3:240.

258   workman's death: *MB*, Jan. 22, 1801, "J. Holmes (my workman) died on the 14th inst." "Sober genteel young man," from Daniel Trump, Aug. 4. 1800, MHi.

259   "the eye of a brick-kiln to poke you into": to William Giles, Mar. 19, 1796, Ford 8:229; *Garden Book*, 248.

259   "mild, easy and obliging temper": Duke de la Rochefoucauld-Liancourt, *Travels through the United States of North America, in the years 1795, 1796, 1797* (London, 1799); in Randall, 2:302–07.

259   "the noise, confusion and discomfort": to Count Constantin François de Volney, Apr. 10, 1796, DLC.

260   bricks made by Henry Duke: A "mr Adams" also made bricks; a notation in *MB*, Aug. 29, 1796, reads, "Adams (brickmaker) begins @ 5. a month." Dec. 1, 1796: "settled with Adams brickmaker." Bricks were possibly made by slaves as well; the skill was not that difficult to learn, and Jefferson's slaves had ample experience as helpers.

260   "send mr Duke a brick": to Thomas Mann Randolph, Apr. 19, 1798, DLC.

260   "as cheap as we can": to Archibald Stuart, Apr. 6, 1796, MHi.

260   "perpetual rains": to Thomas Mann Randolph, Aug. 19, 1796, DLC.

260   Willis at Monticello two weeks after this: *MB*, Aug. 31, 1796: "Furnished Stephen Willis a pr. shoes 12/6 . . ."

260   rehired Davy Watson: Watson worked at Monticello for nearly two and a half years, from 1795 until April 1797.

261   broken window sashes: See Kimball, K-149. This page of Jefferson's Construction Notebook contains a list of the number and sizes of sashes needed for the various rooms.

261   "the winds make a very stout quality of glass necessary": to Joseph Donath, Dec. 4, 1796, MHi.

261   "My works are arrested": to Thomas Mann Randolph, Nov. 28, 1796, DLC; *Garden Book*, 252.

261   "eight days more": to James Madison, Dec. 17, 1796, DLC; *Garden Book*, 252

262   paid off the workers: See *MB*, 1796–97, for various payments. Among his workers were John H. Buck, a carpenter who was put to work producing flooring for the new sections of the house; Hugh Chisholm, a brickmaker-bricklayer who was to do a considerable amount of work for Jefferson over the years; Adams, a brickmaker-bricklayer; Will Beck, who burnt limestone; and Felty Millar, Joseph Moran, and Richard Richardson, stonemasons. Stephen Willis, who undoubtedly acted as the supervisor of brickmasonry for Jefferson, was the highest paid of all of the workmen. For three months' work he received £95, which included £15 for his bricklayer Shell and for the hire of his slave bricklayer Ned. Jefferson had also hired a dozen slaves to work at Monticello, including two slave sawyers for whom he paid a premium price, £40 a year. *MB*, Feb. 16, 1797, "Mrs. Carter £40-10 for hire of her two sawyers last year.

262   "must suspend their work": to Count Constantin François de Volney, Apr. 3, 1797, DLC. Brickwork continued during his absence, however. His daughter Maria wrote him in June that his workmen "today began to raise the walls of the hall, the other rooms are done" (from Maria Jefferson, June 12, 1797, *Family Letters*, 147–48).

262   "reserve from the harvest season": to Thomas Mann Randolph, June 17, 1797, DLC.

262   "it will probably be a month": to Count Constantin François de Volney, Aug. 5, 1797, DLC.

263   "I know no such useless bauble": to Elizabeth Eppes, Oct. 31, 1790, *Papers*, 17:658. Jefferson's hand in Eppes's education is summarized in *Papers*, 20:152n.

263   "She could not have been more to my wishes": to Martha Jefferson Randolph, June 8, 1797, *Family Letters*, 146.

263   "possesses every quality": to Maria Jefferson, June 14, 1797, *Family Letters*, 148.

264   "pritty lady jist like her mother": *Jefferson at Monticello*, 5.

264   "sunny" and "warm": Randall, 2:360–61.

264   "Dearest and adored Father": from Martha Jefferson Randolph, July 1, 1798, *Family Letters*, 166.

265   "I begin to feel with great anxiety": to Thomas Mann Randolph, Feb. 15, 1798, DLC.

265   balustrade installed much later: "We have nearly got the balustrade finished . . ."; from James Dinsmore, Dec. 1, 1808, MHi. The balusters were turned on a lathe by the slave carpenter Lewis, who was John Hemings's helper: "I was in hopes that Abram could have hewed

locust as fast as Lewis could turn it, but if he cannot let mr Perry supply it as I would wish Lewis to be constantly engaged in getting ready those ballusters . . ." (to James Dinsmore, Dec. 15, 1807, MHi).

265   roofed the house with tin: "John Heming and his two aids have been engaged in covering this house with tin which is not yet finished"; to Francis Wayles Eppes, Apr. 1825, *Family Letters*, 453.

265   covered with sheet iron in 1808: from John Perry, Dec. 11, 1807, MHi. Jefferson's final word on sheet iron, which was cast iron pressed into thin sheets, was that it was inferior to pitch-covered wood, particularly for use in rain gutters, because it rusted. While supervising construction of the University of Virginia, he advised that "sheet iron unquestionably endangers leaking and will rust out . . ." (to Arthur Brockenborough, Sep. 1, 1819, DLC). His experience with sheet iron was extensive: not only did he replace shakes with an iron roof on the dependencies and use it for gutters, he also placed it on the level top of the Monticello roof (to Samuel Mifflin, Apr. 11, 1806, MHi; Kimball, K-143). When they were first constructed, Jefferson had considered covering the dependency roofs with tin, a more durable, but more expensive metal. He wrote to Dinsmore, "I am very disposed to cover the terras at once with tin. I find that it may be done of the thickest tin for 18 Dollars a square; and it will be proof against fire" (to James Dinsmore, Dec. 1, 1802, ViU). The terrace roofs initially were covered with shakes, however, possibly because shakes were readily available and neither iron nor tin was at hand when the roofs were ready to go up.

266   "the whole house would have gone": *Jefferson at Monticello*, 3–4.

266   books moved to south pavilion: by Feb. 15, 1798, the books were still there. He asked Randolph for some writing paper and mentioned his walnut book presses in the study-library (to Thomas Mann Randolph, Feb. 15, 1798, DLC).

266   a "strong force sawing": to Thomas Mann Randolph, Feb. 15, 1798, DLC.

266   "enable us to close": memorandum to mr Arnold, Apr. 12, 1798, DLC. See also: to Thomas Mann Randolph, Apr. 12, 1798, DLC.

267   "O welcome hour whenever!": to Thomas Mann Randolph, May 3, 1798, DLC.

267   "Davenport has done nothing": from Thomas Mann Randolph, Apr. 29, 1798, MHi.

267   work underway on architraves of the doorways: Late in August, Jefferson asked Randolph for the return of a plane for making ogee moldings. Randolph had borrowed it to make windows at the Edgehill house; to Thomas Mann Randolph, Aug. 29, 1798, DLC.

267   hired McGehee: *MB*, Dec. 17, 1798, "Pd. Mr Megee on account £15-7-5."

268   "scarcely a stroke has been done": to Maria Jefferson Eppes, Mar. 8, 1799, *Family Letters*, 177.

268   Thomas Buck quits: ". . . Buck's leaving us, without laying any more floors has prevented our getting the use of any other room" (to Maria Jefferson Eppes, Dec. 8, 1798, *Family Letters*, 169). Building floors was particularly slow work because Jefferson inserted brick nogging—partially burned and broken bricks, chinked with straw and clay—under the floor boards for insulation and fire protection.

268   "cannot proceed an hour without me": to Maria Jefferson Eppes, July 13, 1798, *Family Letters*, 167.

269   "I never had the pleasure": from Martha Jefferson Randolph, Jan. 31, 1801, *Family Letters*, 192–93.

269   "The manner and usages of our country": to Martha Jefferson Randolph, Feb. 5, 1801, *Family Letters*, 195–96. Jefferson failed to admit his own responsibility for turning his house into an inn; virtually every letter to one of his scientific or philosophic friends or his close associates in government ended with an invitation to visit Monticello. And all too often, they accepted.

270   the floors of Monticello: see "The Preservation and Restoration of Monticello, 1936–1960: Field Notes and Drawings by Milton Grigg," floor detail, G 80, Monticello Archives.

270   Monticello floor lumber: Much of the floor lumber was sawed by John Fagg, who demanded more than the standard rate for sawing flooring plank. The dispute was placed in arbitration and Fagg was awarded "£6 per M for all pine plank laid in the floors & 1 d. a foot for the rest . . ." *MB*, Sept. 1, 1800.

270   bedroom to be plastered: to Richard Richardson, Mar. 31, 1800, ViU.

270   a skill he had studied in Philadelphia: On May 17, 1798, Jefferson wrote to Martha that Richardson was leaving Philadelphia for Virginia and that he would be "with you ready to work" on building the Randolph house at Edgehill. Jefferson reported that "he is much improved" from what he had seen and done in Philadelphia. *Family Letters*, 162.

270   plastering by Hugh Chisholm: *MB*, Aug. 23, 1801, "Paid Chisholm for plaistering &c. in full £4-10."

270   "The plaistering at Monticello goes on": from Martha Jefferson Randolph, *Family Letters*, 213.

271   "A very coarse & uninformed carpenter": William Howard Adams, *Jefferson's Monticello* (Abbeville Press, 1983), 98.

271 framing trusses of dome: see Grigg, "The Preservation and Restoration of Monticello," for a section of the dome roof.

272 "during the sickly season": to Maria Jefferson Eppes, Apr. 11, 1801, *Family Letters*, 201.

272 the chief danger was malaria: see Todd L. Savitt, *Medicine and Slavery* (Urbana: University of Illinois Press, 1978), 18ff.

CHAPTER 9

Page

287 were found to be "not perpendicular": from Thomas Mann Randolph, Jan. 3, 1801, ViU.

287 "dressing and gal[l]anting": from Thomas Mann Randolph, Apr. 25, 1800, ViU.

287 "never experience[d] so troublesome a job": from Richard Richardson, Dec. 22, 1800, MHi.

287 columns not in place for two more years: Richardson left Monticello in the spring of 1801 (*MB*, Apr. 24, 1801, "Settled with Richardson . . .") with the columns still not completed. Jefferson recorded, *MB*, Sept. 22, 1803, "Paid Robert Hope for setting up columns 20. D."

288 Oldham started working: *MB*, Mar. 24, 1801.

288 "started from the citey Washington": Account of Mr. Wanscher from Aug. 15, 1801 to Apr. 29, 1802, MHi.

288 Dinsmore acted as a guide: Jefferson sent him instructions, for example, to show Monticello to "Prince Ruspoli, a Roman Noble," who was passing through. He also asked Thomas Mann Randolph to be present, however, because the Roman would "have his enquiries more satisfactorily answered" by Randolph than by Dinsmore. To Thomas Mann Randolph, Feb. 3, 1802, DLC.

288 Dinsmore's salary was $480 annually: *MB*, Mar. 8, 1802, "Analysis of expenditures from Mar. 4, 1801, Mar. 4, 1802."

289 abandoning pilasters: The only place Jefferson used pilasters was at the entrance doors to the dome room, which was seldom used.

289 *Parallèle de l'Architecture* survived the Library of Congress fire: Frederick D. Nichols and James A. Bear, Jr., *Monticello: A Guidebook* (Monticello: Thomas Jefferson Memorial Foundation, 1982), 23. Among Jefferson's surviving architectural papers are a number of full-scale drawings he made from this book and others. See Kimball, 162, 166–67.

289 "The internal of the house contains specimens": *Niles Weekly Register*,

vol. 2, supplement to no. 19 (Jan. 4, 1817), 318. This is a description of Monticello by John Edward Caldwell. (See "Descriptions of Jefferson and the Grounds Surrounding Monticello, Visitors' Descriptions of, 1780–1966," Monticello Archives.)

290 *Édifices Antiques de Rome*: Desgodets's book not only offered superbly engraved plates showing the finest detail, but also precise measurements for each entablature.

290 cornice ornaments reproduced by Andrews: Jefferson specified the particular ornaments needed for a Corinthian cornice in a letter to Oldham, Jan. 19, 1805, DLC.

290 mounted by Dinsmore: The sculptor William Coffee, who executed the Poplar Forest ornaments for Jefferson, sent instructions for how John Hemings was to install them: "The Human Masks and the Ox skull ornaments should be put up with white lead as stiff as bookbinder's Paste, and to One of those small holes that is in Every One a small screw should be put. . . ." Small "enrichments" were to be glued in place, and joints between the ornaments were to be filled with "dry white lead whiting and good drying oil to make a paste." This was undoubtedly the same method used by Dinsmore at Monticello. From William J. Coffee, Jan. 3, 1923, ViU.

290 "I observe you are fitting up a Corinthian room": to James Oldham, Jan. 19, 1805, DLC. Oldham also built an icehouse for Gallego; see letter from James Oldham, Jan. 11, 1805, DLC.

291 "done in the Juish stile": from James Oldham, Mar. 19, 1805, DLC. It is unclear what Oldham meant by this term.

291 "far handsomer than those of the Parlour": to James Oldham, May 2, 1805, DLC.

291 "As they warp a little in drying": to James Oldham, July 10, 1805, MHi.

291 "steady and uniform" business of the presidency: to Thomas Mann Randolph, Nov. 16, 1801, DLC.

291 report his progress: In 1804, Jefferson wrote Dinsmore, "I will thank you to keep me informed of your progress, of mr Wanscher's and of J Perry's as I am anxious to have the information" (to James Dinsmore, May 24, 1804, ViU). Jefferson gave instructions to Hemings to write once a week (to John Hemings, Dec. 2, 1819, MHi).

292 "tongue & groove giving way": from James Dinsmore, Jan. 1, 1802, ViU.

292 forced to give his workmen autonomy: In the construction of Poplar Forest, workmen made even more basic decisions. The mason Hugh

Chisholm, who did the brick work on the house, reported to Jefferson that he had made a kiln of bricks, including specially molded bricks for the "Basis and caps & all the colloms as I thought it would make a better Job than to have them of wood" (from Hugh Chisholm, July 22, 1808, MHi). The housejoiner John Perry was allowed to make the decision on how the floors were to be constructed. Jefferson simply suggested, "perhaps it may be easier done in herring bone, as the hall floor at Monticello was" (to John Perry, Mar. 29, 1808, MHi). Chisholm and Perry functioned much more as traditional building contractors working from a nonresident architect's plans than did any of the craftsmen working at Monticello.

292 "I leave this to yourself to decide": to James Dinsmore, Dec. 1, 1802, ViU.

293 "a 7 I[nch]. architrave having been put [up] by mistake": Kimball, 167.

293 Dinsmore replacing ornaments: from James Dinsmore, Feb. 12, 1802, ViU.

293 did not fit "any of the new [window] frames": from James Dinsmore, Jan. 23, 1802, ViU.

293 lead was three to four times as expensive: to James Dinsmore, Oct. 18, 1807, TJ noted that one thousand pounds of lead would cost $167; iron only $50. MHi.

293 some cutting and fitting could be done: from James Dinsmore, Oct. 24, 1807, MHi.

294 "will probably render them useless": to James Dinsmore, Nov. 1, 1807, MHi.

294 "it will answer much better": from James Dinsmore, Nov. 9, 1807, MHi.

294 "transcended all the bounds of moderation": to John B. Magruder, Sept. 23, 1804, MHi.

294 "good men of our mutual choice": to John B. Magruder, Nov. 14, 1805, MHi. Although arbitration in this case favored Magruder, workers were wary of it because they believed abitrators favored the gentry. Jefferson's millwright, James Walker, expressed this fear in a disagreement with him over wages. Walker wrote that he was currently involved in a dispute with one of Jefferson's neighbors: "Mr. Scott is willing to refer to arbitration but that their shall be no workmen appointed as arbitrators, but men who probably never done a days work nor perhaps never had a days work of this kind done, and perhaps men who are interested in reducing prices of work as low as possible" (from James Walker, Oct. 10, 1805, MHi; *Farm Book*, 358).

Notes

294   cut the timber and return it to Magruder: to John Perry, Jan. 20, 1810, MHi.

294   "that I may at length be done with it": to John Perry, Feb. 16, 1812, MHi. A footnote to the dispute is that Magruder, after Jefferson's death, purchased, with a partner in 1829, Jefferson's Shadwell mill (*Farm Book*, 343).

295   "Mr. Hudson . . . must therefore be declined": to Thomas Mann Randolph, May 5, 1803, DLC.

295   Lilly directed digging the north wing: to James Dinsmore, Mar. 19, 1802, ". . . I suppose mr Lilly is digging the North West Offices & Ice House . . ." DLC; *Garden Book*, 278.

295   Joseph Moran quit unexpectedly: from James Dinsmore, Dec. 12, 1801, "Mr Moran has quit some time ago." ViU.

296   instructions for building his icehouse: to James Dinsmore, Mar. 19, 1802, DLC; June 22, 1802, ViU.

296   "It would be a real calamity": to Edmund Bacon, Jan. 3, 1809, *Garden Book*, 400.

301   "a pump maker at Charlottesville": to Edmund Bacon, Nov. 10, 1806, DLC.

301   "Nail a bit of stiff leather": to James Dinsmore, Dec. 10, 1802, Betts Papers, Long Island Historical Society; Monticello Archives.

301   "make Joe draw off the water": to James Dinsmore, May 24, 1804, ViU.

301   ice lasted until September or October: See "Diary of the state of the ice or snow in the ice house," Weather Record 1776–1818, undated, DLC. The latest date that ice lasted was in 1815, when it gave out on Oct. 5.

302   the icehouse at Monticello was filled with snow: *Garden Book*, 497: "Dec. 24. [1813] filled the ice house with snow." *Garden Book*, 565: "Jan. 20. [1817] filled the Ice house at the river with ice." "Mar. 13. [1817] filled the Snow house here [Monticello] with snow."

302   used directly in drinks or ices: Margaret Bayard Smith recorded that during her stay at the Madison house, Montpelier, a servant awakened her in the morning, and "brought me ice and water (this is universal here, even in taverns)." Margaret Bayard Smith, *The First Forty Years of Washington Society, Portrayed by the Family Letters of Mrs. Samuel Harrison Smith* (Charles Scribner's Sons, 1906), 83.

302   "my ice house here": *Garden Book*, 281.

302   "at a moment's warning": to Edmund Bacon, Nov. 10, 1806, DLC. On Jan. 12, 1809, Bacon informed Jefferson that the icehouse was

filled in two days "with 6 wagons the first day and 8 the second." ViU.

302   "Ice of 1¾ I. thick": Weather Record 1776–1818, 1808, p. 55, undated, DLC.

302   Diderot and d'Alembert's *Encyclopédie*: see the article under *glacière*. The *Encyclopédie* makes a distinction between the Italian habit of preserving pure snow, which was placed in wine and drinks, and the French method of storing blocks of ice taken from rivers or lakes, used only for refrigeration. In his Notebook for remodeling Monticello, Jefferson also made notes on "Mr. Zane's Icehouse." He had apparently written these after inspecting the icehouse of Isaac Zane, who conducted the Marlboro Iron Works in the Shenandoah Valley, and who was a creative experimenter like Jefferson (Kimball, 161).

302   north pavilion fire: *MB*, Apr. 11, 1819, "On the 9th inst. the N. Pavilion was burnt." To an unknown addressee, May 5, 1819, "Our snow house enabled us . . . [to] cover with snow the adjacent terras which connected it with the main building as to prevent its affecting that. . . . The injury I received by a fall during the conflagration was slight." MHi.

302   "so that we may hereafter lead the water": to James Dinsmore, Nov. 7, 1808, MHi.

303   furnish him with six hundred gallons of water a day: see "The Cisterns of Monticello," *Garden Book*, 630; to William Thornton, Feb. 9, 1815, MHi; *Garden Book*, 541

303   William Thornton offered two solutions: from William Thornton, Apr. 2, 1815, DLC.

303   "My only reward": from William Coffee, Nov. 7, 1818, DLC.

303   "instructed a bricklayer, a black man": to Dr. John Brockenbrough, June 4, 1823, DLC.

303   an inch of rainfall raised the water nine inches: "Cistern No 3," undated [1822–1824], DLC.

304   "troubled him greatly": Kimball, 127.

304   "shafts to be no higher than the balustrading": Kimball, 127.

305   "smoke ceases to be interesting": John Ruskin, *The Poetry of Architecture* (London, 1893; reprint, St. Clair Shores, Mich.: Scholarly Press, 1972), 63.

305   Count Rumford biography: The Rumford biographical material is from Sanborn C. Brown, *Benjamin Thompson, Count Rumford* (Cambridge, Mass.: MIT Press, 1979).

306   Rumford's method of altering a standard fireplace: Sanborn C. Brown, ed., *Collected Works of Count Rumford* (Cambridge, Mass.: MIT Press, 1968–1970 [5 vols.]), vol. II, 222–307.

306 "Rumfordize": the word entered the language as a method "to improve a chimney on Count Rumford's system" (*Oxford English Dictionary*).

307 essentially what is now found: the sides of a Rumford fireplace were more severely angled than are those of a modern fireplace.

307 converted two of his fireplaces: "Count Rumford's fire places in the square rooms . . ." Kimball, 162. Rumford did not publish an American edition of his essays until 1798, so Jefferson, who owned a copy of this edition, did not learn of the Rumford fireplace until after he had constructed Monticello's fireplaces.

307 "I am obliged to give them up": to Benjamin Latrobe, Jan. 16, 1805, DLC.

307 select three "of the handsomest stoves": to Benjamin Latrobe, Nov. 4, 1804, DLC; *Farm Book*, 84.

307 "as an artist he has exhibited": *Notes*, 64.

307 Rittenhouse improved the Franklin stove: Brooke Hindle, *David Rittenhouse* (Princeton, N.J.: Princeton University Press, 1964), 247.

308 "it is pretty clear from careful reading": Brown, *Benjamin Thompson, Count Rumford*, 169. Rittenhouse, unlike Franklin, did not publish the details of his stove, so Rumford very likely did not know about it.

308 Benjamin Franklin, *Observations on the Cause and Cure of Smoky Chimneys* (London, 1787).

308 Rumford received permission from John Adams: Brown, *Benjamin Thompson, Count Rumford*, 210.

308 whether a welcome would have been offered to Rumford: It should be noted, however, that Jefferson hung a portrait of Count Rumford in the parlor of Monticello: but he also had busts of Hamilton and Napoleon, neither of whom was a favorite of his.

308 asking for black lead: to Thomas Mann Randolph, Feb. 19, 1795, DLC; *Farm Book*, 83.

308 "10. plate stove in my room": Oct. 14, *Farm Book*, 85.

308 A ten-plate stove is a rectangular box: See Josephine H. Pierce, *Fire on the Hearth* (Springfield, Mass.: Pond-Ekberg, 1951), 94, for an illustration of a ten-plate stove.

309 a freestanding stove: The term *stove* was used for both the fireplace insert and a freestanding model. The fireplace stove was termed by Jefferson an "open stove."

309 "I have set it up": See letter from Henry J. Foxall, Apr. 11, 1809, MHi; *Farm Book*, 85; to Henry J. Foxall, Mar. 16, 1812, MHi. The cost of the stove was "55.46½ D."

309 "Niche in the Tearoom": Cornelia's floor plan of Monticello, ViU

#5385ac. This floor plan is printed in *Domestic Life*, 334, but the stove reference is omitted.

309   freestanding stoves at Barboursville: See Nichols, N-5; pl. 22.

309   freestanding stoves for the University of Virginia: see William Howard Adams, ed., *The Eye of Thomas Jefferson* (Washington, D.C.: National Gallery of Art, 1976), 289–94; also Nichols, N-321, N-357.

309   *Apotheosis of Homer*: this plaque is illustrated in Fiske Kimball, *Domestic Architecture of the American Colonies and of the Early Republic* (Charles Scribner's Sons, 1922; reprint, Dover, 1966), 256. The original plaques were removed by Confederate soldiers encamped in the house during the war, but were replaced by Jefferson Levy when he restored Monticello after the war.

310   marble fireplace fascias: See letter from Thomas Appleton, July 28, 1824 ("cost of all 8 [marble fascias] $180"), May 8, 1825, June 22, 1825, MHi; to Thomas Appleton, May 18, 1824, MHi.

310   "with one of the three larger ones": to Thomas Appleton, May 18, 1824, MHi.

310   "no pains were spared": from Thomas Appleton, June 22, 1825, MHi.

310   "from a new quarry lately discover'd": from Thomas Appleton, July 28, 1824, MHi.

310   "Venato Nuvotato": from Thomas Appleton, May 8, 1825, MHi.

310   chain-and-pulley mechanism: this is illustrated in Nichols and Bear, *Monticello: A Guidebook*.

311   "able workman in housejoinery": to Colonel Harvie, Sept. 27, 1804, MHi; *Farm Book*, 458.

311   a number of doors and window sashes: from James Oldham, Apr. 7, 1806, MHi. This letter lists the doors and sashes shipped to Monticello.

311   "money to pay for the Lumber": from James Oldham, Oct. 25, 1804, MHi. Jefferson had promised to keep Oldham on his payroll, as he "had no intention that you should have been out of business on such short notice; and therefore shall consider your wages going on till you have a reasonable time to get into employ" (to James Oldham, Oct. 11, 1804, MHi).

311   "all the sawmills in the cuntery": from James Oldham, Nov. 26, 1804, MHi. It is possible that Oldham had in fact procured more lucrative work than Jefferson's and used the green lumber as an excuse to delay his job. Building craftsmen are still known to use variations of this ploy.

311   "do all their housejoinery with green stuff": to James Oldham, Nov. 30, 1804, DLC.

311 "there is no such thing as a Kiln": from James Oldham, Dec. 17, 1804, MHi.

312 "very nice plank for the purpose": from James Oldham, Mar. 5, 1805, DLC.

312 "Unfortunately for me": from James Oldham, Mar. 19, 1805, DLC.

312 "just finished drying plank for your worke": from James Oldham, May 5, 1805, MHi.

312 "Your doors are now in hand": from James Oldham, June 4, 1805, MHi.

312 "I took these measures with great accuracy": to James Oldham, June 14, 1805, MHi.

312 "my calculating the quantity two scant": from James Oldham, June 30, 1805, MHi.

312 supply Oldham with two dozen door hinges: to Gibson & Jefferson, Aug. 4, 1805, MHi; from George Jefferson, Aug. 13, 1805, MHi.

312 "your dores and sashes are not all in redyness": from James Oldham, Oct. 25, 1805, MHi.

312 "It is now become very material": to James Oldham, Feb. 23, 1805, MHi.

313 "The largest portion of the work": from James Oldham, Apr. 7, 1806, MHi.

314 goodwill, benefits, and emoluments: Jefferson's relationship with Oldham continued for a number of years after the housejoiner finished the doors and sashes. Oldham, who later became a captain in the militia (to Capt. James Oldham, Sept. 27, 1814, MHi), obtained mahogany plank for four tables for Jefferson (to James Oldham, Oct. 12, 1807; from James Oldham, Dec. 24, 1807, MHi), and searched for window glass for him (to Capt. James Oldham, Sept. 27, 1814; from James Oldham, Oct. 11, 1814, Dec. 14, 1814, MHi). Jefferson in return gave Oldham advice on whether to purchase Albemarle land the housejoiner was interested in (from James Oldham, May 24, 1808; to James Oldham, June 15, 1808, MHi).

314 "His temper is unhappy": to J. C. Cabell, Feb. 4, 1823, ViU; William B. O'Neal, "The Workmen at the University of Virginia 1817–1826, with Notes and Documents," *Magazine of Albemarle County History*, vol. 17 (1959), 40.

314 "one of the moost vilest reches on earth": from James Oldham, Nov. 26, 1804, MHi.

314 Lilly and Perry plotted murder: from James Oldham, Dec. 17, 1804, MHi.

315   "It is my rule never to take a side": to James Oldham, Nov. 30, 1804, DLC.

315   Oldham shot a neighbor's son: O'Neal, 16.

315   "misfortune that has happn'd at Monticello": Maria Jefferson Eppes to John Eppes, Jan. 21, 1804, Eppes-Randolph Family Correspondence, 7109, ViU.

315   "the floor of the hall": from Anne Cary Randolph, Jan. 21, 1804, *Family Letters*, 254

315   fireproof kiln: to James Dinsmore, Jan. 28, 1804, Sotheby Auction Catalogue, Jan. 26, 1923, Item 87, Monticello Archives.

315   1806 survey of the property: Survey and Plat of Monticello, Aug. 3, 1806, ViU.

315   laid by John Hemings: Randall, 3:337n.

316   "The floor of this room": *Domestic Life*, 335.

316   drawings of several parquet floor patterns: Kimball, K-160n–K-160p.

316   Stuart's enthusiasm for green floors: to James Dinsmore, June 8, 1805, MHi.

316   "covered with a glossy oil cloth": William Hooper, describing a visit to Monticello Sept. 20, 1823, "Descriptions of Monticello 1780–1826," Monticello Archives.

317   Barry hired at $30 a month: Richard Barry to Mr. Lenox, Dec. 2, 1804, MHi; *Farm Book*, 339.

318   "the Plarstring is all finished": from Hugh Chisholm, Dec. 4, 1807, MHi. The sentence is ambiguous: it could mean that Chisholm achieved a rough surface by coating the columns with a sandy mortar slip, which was painted by Barry after it hardened. Or Chisholm's letter could read that he was smoothing the columns with sandpaper in preparation for painting. Traditionally, painters "sanded" a surface by sprinkling sand on wet paint. The process of "sanding" and other early nineteenth-century painting techniques are discussed in Alvah H. Sabin, *The Industrial and Artistic Technology of Paint and Varnish* (John Wiley & Sons, 1905).

318   four coats of paint: At Clivedon in Philadelphia, only three coats of paint were used; this was probably the norm. Margaret B. Tinkcom, "Clivedon: The Building of a Philadelphia Countryseat, 1763–1767," *The Pennsylvania Magazine of History and Biography*, vol. 87, no. 1 (Jan. 1964), 23. The four coats at Monticello lasted more than ten years before Jefferson decided the house required repainting. ("I shall certainly want a very great quantity [of paint] in the course of the present year, as I have to renew the whole outer painting of this house and

the terrasses" [to David Higgenbotham, Mar. 16, 1817, MHi]. Even with four coats, however, in ten years the paint would have been in poor condition, particularly the terraces. Only one coat of paint, plus "cement," was used on the shake roof of the house. Exactly what Barry meant by "cement" is conjectural; "fish oil" or tar were commonly used on wooden roofs. For an example of the kinds of paints used in Virginia during this period see "Agreement Relating to the Painting of the St. George Tucker House," in Marcus Whiffen, *The Eighteenth Century Houses of Williamsburg* (Williamsburg, Va.: Colonial Williamsburg, 1960), 201–2.

318   Barry's estimate of paint needed to cover the house: Richard Barry to mr Lennox, undated, MHi; *Farm Book*, 340. When Barry arrived at Monticello, Jefferson ordered additional pigments and supplies. This is the palette which, when mixed with white paint, produced the colors of Monticello (to George Jefferson, Apr. 6, 1805 MHi):

> 7 lb red lead
> 7 lb stone ochre
> 2 lb umber
> 2 lb Terradisiana [terra di siena, or sienna, a reddish-brown pigment]
> 6 lb litharge [a drying agent]
> 2 lb rose-pink
> 4 oz white vitriol [zinc sulfate, for clearing linseed oil]
> 6 books of gold leaf
> 25 lb whiting [a filler for putty]
> 5 oz Vermillion
> 6 small sash brushes

Seven months later he ordered more linseed oil and white lead, plus the following pigments and varnishes (to John Taggert, Nov. 9, 1805, MHi):

> 20 lb stone ocre
> 3 lb Turkey umber
> 6 lb Terra di Siena
> 3 gallons Copral varnish

The following year, 1806, more linseed oil and white lead were ordered, along with "100 lb Spanish brown" (to John Taggert, Oct. 13, 1806, MHi).

318   whitewash frequently applied to walls: A. Lawrence Kocher and How-

ard Dearstyne, *Colonial Williamsburg, Its Buildings and Gardens* (Williamsburg, Va.: The Colonial Williamsburg Foundation, 1976), 31.

318   "I think the hall": from Ellen Wayles Randolph, Apr. 14, 1808, *Family Letters*, 341. It is quite possible that the colors of Monticello were brighter than those applied by restorers. At Mount Vernon, bright colors have replaced the subdued pastel colors previously found on the interior because scientific analysis of the original paint determined that eighteenth-century colors were much brighter than originally supposed. Matthew J. Mosca, a New York architectural conservator and paint historian, found that colors popularized by the restoration of Colonial Williamsburg in the 1920s and 1930s were supposed at the time to be historically accurate. "But they did not take into account the aging process," Mosca stated. "What were thought to be Williamsburg colors appeared darker, muddier and far less brilliant than 18th-century colors actually were when they were applied. Williamsburg colors are merely the faded originals, drastically different than the original shades." "Renovation Brightens Mt. Vernon," *New York Times*, Feb. 11, 1982, p. C-8.

318   fresco paintings: see the correspondence with Henry Ramsden, and TJ's notes, *Farm Book*, 500–503.

319   145 rolls of wallpaper: *Papers*, 18:34, 37, 494. See also Nichols and Bear, *Monticello: A Guidebook*, 39.

319   "as the most important thing you have to do here": to Richard Barry, Apr. 18, 1807, MHi.

319   "I have had four applications": from Richard Barry, May 4, 1807, MHi.

319   "on winding up my affairs": to Richard Barry, Nov. 30, 1809, MHi.

320   "if it was one hundred times the sum": from Richard Barry, Dec. 5, 1809, MHi.

320   "I shall ever be ready to render": to Richard Barry, Dec. 16, 1809, MHi.

320   "As I now intend to build myself a House": from Richard Barry, Jan. 29, 1811, MHi.

320   promised to send him money in April: to Richard Barry, Mar. 18, 1811, Apr. 3, 1811, MHi.

320   Barry had still not received the balance due him: from Richard Barry, Dec. 11, 1811, Jan. 16, 1812; to Richard Barry, Jan. 27, 1812, MHi.

320   did not include a glazier's diamond worth $8.80: from Richard Barry, Mar. 27, 1812, MHi.

320   "remarkably good one": from Richard Barry, Aug. 11, 1808, MHi.

321 "oranges, Mimosa Farnesiana": to William Hamilton, Mar. 1, 1808, DLC; *Garden Book*, 366.

321 "are to have Venetian blinds of a particular construction": to James Oldham, June 14, 1805, MHi.

321 Louvered blinds introduced into Virginia: Frameless, cloth-connected venetian blinds were being sold as early as 1770 by a Williamsburg joiner, Joshua Kendall, who advertised in the *Virginia Gazette* that he made the "newest invented *Venetian* SUN BLINDS for windows, that move to any position so as to give different lights, they screen from the scorching rays of the sun, draw up as a curtain, prevent being overlooked, give a cool refreshing air in hot weather, and are the greatest preservatives of furniture of anything of the kind ever invented" (Kocher and Dearstyne, 27).

321 The windows he wanted them in: to James Dinsmore, Oct. 4, 1807, MHi.

322 "The only windows in the house where they could be used": from James Dinsmore, Oct. 16, 1807, MHi.

322 six pairs of blinds for the first house: to William Brown, Apr. 18, 1790, *Papers*, 16:350. In his Remodeling Notebook (Kimball, K-149b, 15, "Venetian Blinds on hand") TJ lists 5 "treble" sash blinds, "4 for parlour" and "1. for Dining room." These appear to be for the first house.

322 "fixed laths, folding together": from Peter Lenox, May 26, 1804, MHi. The list of shutters TJ ordered are added to this letter.

322 "I know that the method proposed": to Benjamin Latrobe, Sept. 8, 1805, DLC.

322 louvered blinds for the porticoes: Kimball, K-149b, 15; K-149s shows a sketch of the columns and shutters.

323 calculations for portico shutters: Kimball, K-149ff.

323 "read for half an hour": Randall, 3:675.

323 "sitting in the shade of his porticoes": Randall, 3:331.

323 "porticles": This seems to be a word of Jefferson's coinage; it is not in the *Oxford English Dictionary*. It is apparently derived from the Latin *porticula*, a small portico.

323 "we have finished the shutters & sashes": from James Dinsmore, Jan. 30, 1808, MHi.

323 "I do not propose any Chinese railing": to James Dinsmore, Feb. 6, 1808, MHi.

323 Hemings constructed porticles: John Hemings became quite expert in building louvered shutters. Jefferson noted in his *Farm Book* that "Johnny

Notes

Hemings & Lewis make a set of Venetian blinds with fixed slats, i. e. 2. pair 3 f. 3 I. square in 6. days, splitting out the slats from common plank with the handsaw. Say a window a week." *Farm Book*, pl. 114.

324 "You enquire whether I have a hot house": to Bernard McMahon, Apr. 8, 1811, DLC; *Farm Book*, 455. Jefferson wrote similarly to his granddaughter, Ann Randolph Bankhead, "In fact, the Mimosa Nilotica and Orange are the only things I have ever proposed to have in my Green house" (to Ann Randolph Bankhead, Dec. 8, 1808, *Family Letters*, 369). He also kept his workbench and tools in the greenhouse. In a drawing for the first house, Jefferson planned a working greenhouse, to be placed on Mulberry Row (Kimball, K-56, K-57).

324 "the folding mahogany sash": to James Dinsmore, Dec. 30, 1808, MHi. The fact that this window sash "closed" his bed alcove indicates that it was inserted into a wooden panel that covered the entire cabinet side of the alcove. The sash was approximately 3½ by 7 feet. (In a list of "sashes to be procured" with panes "18 I. by 12 I.," the alcove sash was listed: "Alcove. Chamber. 1. [sash] of 6 × 2 [panes] = 12 [panes]" [Kimball, K-149].) The position of this sash in the alcove can only be guessed at. Jefferson indicated that it opened "horizontally" rather than vertically, as would the new pair of screens, so it apparently folded upward on hinges, perhaps with a rope and pulley to lift it. The most likely placement of the window would be to have the bottom of the sash at bed level to provide ventilation when it was raised. This position would also satisfy another function of both the sash and the screen, to allow the servants "to get at the bed to make it up." A sash of this size would have been difficult to lift—and dangerous. Jefferson called it "heavy and troublesome." The glass sash offered no privacy, as the new opaque screens would, unless it was covered by a curtain. Randall, on information from contemporary sources, reported that "in the winter, the library side was closed by cloth hangings" (Randall, 3:337).

Although it is commonly stated that Jefferson's alcove bed allowed him to get out of bed in the morning into either his bedroom or his library, he apparently never had his alcove open on both sides, as it is today. The list on which the alcove sash appears was written before Oct. 20, 1795, at the beginning of his remodeling, when the alcove was first created. With a fireplace directly opposite the alcove on the bedroom side—one without a flue damper—and an unheated room on the cabinet side—one with most of the walls of glass—Jefferson would have had a cold draft blowing across his bed the first winter after the alcove was constructed. This would have been motivation enough to close off one side of it.

325 Dinsmore did not understand how to make the screen: from James Dinsmore, Jan. 19, 1809, MHi.

325 "to be merely a light frame": to James Dinsmore, Jan. 30, 1809, MHi. The paper used to cover the screen was wallpaper, apparently "2. rolls" left over from the 145 rolls of wallpaper brought back from Paris.

325 constructed as an aviary by John Hemings: Kimball, K-1491, "reserved for J. Hemings . . . the aviary." See Fiske and Marie Kimball, "Jefferson's Curtains at Monticello," *The Magazine Antique*, no. 52 (Oct. 1947), 68. A floor plan by architect Milton Grigg shows the Kimballs' placement of the aviary in the east porticle.

325 urged Martha to become acquainted with the mockingbird: to Martha Jefferson, May 21, 1787, *Papers*, 11:370; mockingbird at the President's House: Margaret Bayard Smith, 385; "my birds arrived": to Stephen Lemaire, Apr. 28, 1809, MHi.

326 porticles removed by Jefferson M. Levy: The photograph on page 298, taken about 1890, shows the porticles; in subsequent photographs they are missing.

328 A Tuscan order planned for the pavilions: Kimball, K-81. Kimball, K-166 and K-167 are drawings for the two floors of the north pavilion.

328 "I presume mr Perry": to James Dinsmore, Mar. 20, 1808, MHi.

328 Chisholm is "very good-humoured": to James Madison, Sept. 9, 1808, in Conover Hunt-Jones, *Dolley and the 'great little Madison'* (Washington: American Institute of Architects Foundation, 1977), 66–67.

328 "24,000 bricks of our usual size": to Hugh Chisholm, Dec. 15, 1807, MHi.

328 "every possible care not to injure the floor": to Hugh Chisholm, Feb. 23, 1808, MHi.

329 "have it done before you move your Books": from James Dinsmore, Apr. 21, 1808, MHi.

329 "a new coat of shingling": to James Dinsmore, Apr. 26, 1808, MHi.

329 eight trunks of books: "I am just now sending off to Richmond 8 trunks of books . . ."; to Edmund Bacon, Nov. 9, 1807, *Jefferson at Monticello*, 67.

329 "Mr Perry has got the roof on": from James Dinsmore, Apr. 21, 1808, MHi.

330 accordionlike roof: Jefferson described the details of this roof in a letter to F. R. Hassler, Dec. 3, 1825, MHi: "In the house in which I live, and it's offices, I have flat roofs. . . . They consist of rooflets 30

I. wide with gutters between them. There are 2 strata of joists, the one about 9 I. higher than the other. . . . A single length of shingles reaches from the top of the upper joists to halfway down the gutter which is made in the lower joists, overlapping just enough to deliver the water safely into the gutter. These gutter joists, as well as those constituting the ridges of the rooflet have a descent of 6 I. from their middle point to each end, which overjets the wall so as to deliver its water clearly over it. A floor is laid over the whole to walk on, the water first falling on that & passing thro' it's cracks drops into the gutters. I have had upwards of 20 years experience of these roofs in this house, also on one I built at another residence [Poplar Forest], and more than half our buildings at the university are flat and so covered. They never have leaked, cost less than a rafter roof, as needing no rafters and admit repairs more easily than any other."

Jefferson's enthusiasm for this roof may have shaded his memory. The flat roof at Poplar Forest leaked badly for a time because the gutters sagged in the middle, allowing water to collect in them (see letter from John Hemings, Sept. 26, 1819, MHi). The flat roofs at the University of Virginia also eventually leaked and had to be replaced by pitched roofs of slate. (Frederick D. Nichols, *Thomas Jefferson's Architectural Drawings*, 4th rev. ed. [Boston: Massachusetts Historical Society, 1978], 9.) Shortly after Jefferson's death, the sheet-iron flat roof over the dependencies also failed and had to be replaced by a gabled roof. This remained in place until modern restoration. (James A. Bear, Jr., *Old Pictures of Monticello* [Charlottesville, Va.: University Press of Virginia, 1957], 1.)

330   "It would suit me much better": from John Perry, Dec. 11, 1807, MHi.

330   "while you are about the residue": to John Perry, Dec. 15, 1807, MHi.

330   "we are engaged at the Chinese railing": to James Dinsmore, July 1, 1808, MHi.

331   chinoiserie: See John Summerson, *Architecture in Britain 1530–1830*, 6th rev. ed. (Penguin, 1979), 412. William Halfpenny also published a book of Chinese designs.

331   Chinese railings for the terrace questionable: Dinsmore appeared to make a distinction in describing a simple railing and the Chinese railing, which was an unusual design for him. On Jan. 30, 1808, he wrote, "I do not expect we will be able to get the railing round the teras done as the stuff is only now got into the kiln" (MHi). He did not call this terrace railing "Chinese." An account in the *Niles Weekly Register* (vol.

2, Supplement to no. 19 [Jan. 4, 1817], p. 318) by John Edward Caldwell mentions, however, that the roofs of the offices form "an agreeable walk" with "a Chinese railing." It is possible the Chinese railing was completed on only one side of the terrace walk, the side with an eight-foot drop.

331 contemporary paintings: The watercolor by Anna Maria Thornton is on page 274. The watercolor by Jane Bradick, executed in 1825, is reproduced in Adams, *The Eye of Thomas Jefferson*, 329. Both watercolors show simple vertical-rail fences on the terraces. The Remodeling Notebook sketches, notes, and lumber list are in Kimball, K-149bb recto and verso.

331 egg-and-dart cornice: from James Dinsmore, Feb. 24, 1809, MHi.

332 "narrow flight of wooden steps": Hooper, Monticello Archives.

332 "the stems of four tulip trees": Richard Beale Davis, ed., *Jeffersonian America: Notes on the United States of America Collected in the Years 1805–6–7 and 11–12 by Sir Augustus Foster, Bart.* (San Marino, Calif.: Huntington Library, 1954), 144.

332 columns from the original house: If the tulip tree columns were indeed in place on the original house, they were shaped to equal size. Jefferson recorded in his Construction Notebook on Apr. 11, 1796, that the two middle columns were "semi-diam. 11.49 I." Kimball, K-144.

332 "of well burnt brick": to Benjamin Latrobe, Feb. 28, 1804, DLC.

333 "I have been questioning Francis Gilmer": from Elizabeth Trist, July 29, 1814, MHi.

333 "sober, skillful and industrious": to Arthur Brockenbrough, July 29, 1819, ViU; O'Neal, 35. Gorman also polished and laid marble for hearths at Poplar Forest.

333 "two additional hands": to John Gorman, Feb. 8, 1822, DLC; *Farm Book*, 46. Thrimston got into some kind of trouble for which Jefferson had given him a "proper reprimand." He advised Gorman to punish him if he "should misconduct himself again."

333 "a tolerable good stone cutter": from John Gorman, Aug. 30, 1823, MHi. This letter, endorsed by Jefferson, "Gorman John acct for the columns," includes Gorman's bill for quarrying, cutting, and setting in place the stone for the bases and capitals:

27 Days quarrying a [@] $1.50	40.50
6 Days seting Bases a 1.50	9.00
7 do [ditto] do Caps a 1.50	10.50
5 do do by James Campbell	7.50

hauling caps & Bases from the quarry	10.00
2 days cuting old sub plinths	3.00
4 Bases 21.3 Ft Superficial [square]	
Measurement in each a 75c p.ft	63.76
6 Caps a 20.4 Sup: in each 75c p.ft	91.50
4 New Sub-plinths 14.ft 9 I in each a 25c p.ft	14.72
2 Cavettos & fillets a 5.10 each a 75c	8.75
	$259.23

Taking thirteen days for placing the bases and capitals implies that Gorman also built the brick shafts and included them in these items. The fact that he "laid stone" in the portico floor suggests that he was capable of laying up the column bricks.

This account indicates that Jefferson already had some parts of the columns on hand. Gorman recut two "old sub plinths," the square blocks of stone on which the column bases sit, and he made only four bases instead of six. These may have been cut by the indentured servant William Rice when he made the columns for the east portico forty-five years earlier. The account also shows why Gorman was hired; he worked for $1.50 a day, a modest wage for a skilled worker. (The stonecutting was done on a piece work basis, however.) Gorman's insistence that he receive board as well as wages for laying the stone floors and steps suggests that he may have been aware that he was working too cheaply. See also "Observns on mr Gorman's account" (undated, DLC), which gives a breakdown of Gorman's bill to a cost of $3.75 a day.

333   list of bricks for the columns: "Estimate of bricks for 6. shafts of Dor. column," May 13, 1822, ViU. Jefferson added to this list, "wrote to J. Perry to provide them." Notes on an envelope, "1822. Aug. 30. col. bricks," (ViU) show that two slaves, Jerry and Isaac, hauled 3,000 column bricks in two days.

334   "half of every Saturday": TJ's notes on bottom of letter from John Gorman, June 12, 1823, MHi.

334   "Dinsmore and Neilson are set out": to James Madison, Apr. 19, 1809, DLC; Robert A. Rutland et al., eds., *The Papers of James Madison*, Presidential Series, vol. 1 (Charlottesville: University Press of Virginia, 1984), 124. Subsequently referred to as *Madison Papers*.

334   Dinsmore an Irishman: *Jefferson at Monticello*, 32.

334   Dinsmore visited his family in Philadelphia: from Thomas Jefferson Randolph, Oct. 30, 1803, "Mr Dinsmore . . . was to set out for Phil-

adelphia today," ViU. Dinsmore also sent $400 to "Andrew Dinsmore near Wilmington, Delaware," apparently his father. *MB*, June 15, 1801.

335 Dinsmore worked at night: from James Dinsmore, Feb. 12, 1802, ViU.

335 may have moved to Milton: In his effort to induce the fresco painter Schneider to come to Monticello, Jefferson had described Milton as "the cheapest part of America for subsistence, beef being 2 cents per lb. wheat half a dollar the bushel" (to Henry Ramsden, Jr., Nov. 25, 1792, DLC; *Farm Book*, 502).

335 Chisholm also worked at Montpelier: *Madison Papers*, 127n.

335 "done the whole of the joiner's work": to Benjamin Latrobe, May 11, 1815, DLC. TJ sent a similar letter of recommendation to Thomas Munro, Mar. 4, 1815, *Farm Book*, 460.

335 "promote his interest": from Benjamin Latrobe, July 12, 1815, DLC.

335 TJ offered Dinsmore and Neilson work at University of Virginia: to James Dinsmore, Apr. 13, 1817, ViU.; O'Neal, 17.

336 settled his debt to Dinsmore in 1813: *MB*, Aug. 2, 1813.

336 renegotiated note with Neilson for $843: *MB*, May 31, 1820.

336 gives no compound interest: to John Neilson, Nov. 8, 1818, MHi.

336 workers "find themselves": In a memorandum to the overseer Edmund Bacon, TJ instructed him, "Mr Dinsmore is to be furnished with bread grain from the mill. . . . He provides his own provisions and for Mr. Nelson and Barry" (*Jefferson at Monticello*, 55). The typical diet of Monticello's workmen is indicated by purchases made by Dinsmore from one of Jefferson's tenant farmers, John Craven. Dinsmore's account for a year included butter, beef, veal, pork, potatoes, cabbages, and salt (John H. Craven account, Jan. 1, 1808, MHi).

336 John Perry purchased a slave with wages: *MB*, Apr. 20, 1804.

336 Wanscher instructed his friends in Germany: to John Barnes, June 28, 1818, MHi.

337 Richardson family correspondence: to Richard Richardson, Aug. 15, 1804; from Richard Richardson, Aug. 24, 1804; to Dudley Richardson, Nov. 2, 1809; from Dudley Richardson, Mar. 4, 1811; to George Richardson, Jan. 16, 1810, July 15, 1823; from George Richardson, June 16, 1823, MHi. The history of Richardson's Jamaican legacy, with passport, an identification document, and a letter of instructions, is in W. J. Holland, "Thomas Jefferson, Housekeeper," *New York Times*, Apr. 15, 1923, sec. 4, 1–5.

337 Oldham traveled to St. Louis: from James Oldham, June 15, 1818, MHi.

337 "much disappointed in my engagements": from James Oldham, Dec. 26, 1818, MHi.
337 Dinsmore inquired whether he should buy land: from James Dinsmore, Dec. 1, 1808, MHi.
337 advice on Orleans land: to James Dinsmore, Dec. 11, 1808, MHi.

CHAPTER 10

Page

340 gardens of James River plantations: James D. Kornwolf ("The Picturesque in the American Garden and Landscape before 1800," in Robert P. Maccubbin and Peter Martin, *British and American Gardens in the Eighteenth Century* [Williamsburg: The Colonial Williamsburg Foundation, 1984], 93–103) questions whether all of these houses had formal, symmetrical gardens. There is little historical or archaeological evidence, however, to support the existence of a picturesque English garden such as Jefferson wished to design.

340 "all nature is a garden": Morris R. Brownell, *Alexander Pope & the Arts of Georgian England* (Oxford University Press, 1978), 171.

341 "some unfrequented vale": *Garden Book*, 25–27. Rowe's original lines are in Gilbert Chinard, *The Literary Bible of Thomas Jefferson, His Commonplace Book of Philosophers and Poets* (Baltimore: Johns Hopkins Press, 1928), 188. Significantly, in copying Rowe's lines, "Who had long since, like me by love undone / Sought that sad place out, to despair and die in," Jefferson omitted "like me by love undone." This was written in 1771, when he was courting, and perhaps already betrothed to, Martha Wayles Skelton.

341 *puellarum optima*: The verse

Jane Jefferson
Ah! Joanna, Puellarum optima!
Ah! aevi virentis flore praerpte!
Sit tibi terra laevis!
Longe, longeque valeto!

appears to be derived from "On an Ornamented Urn," by William Shenstone, one of Jefferson's favorite poets:

Ah Maria
Puellarum elegantissima,
Ah flore venustasis abrepta,

Vale!
Heu quanto minus est
Cum reliquis versari,
Quam tui
Meminisse!

(*The Poetical Works of William Shenstone* [D. Appleton, 1854; reprint, Westport, Conn.: Greenwood Press, 1968], 279.) Jefferson owned a copy of Shenstone's works; he was to visit Shenstone's garden, the Leasowes, during his tour with John Adams of the gardens of England.

342 "Build up the sides": *Garden Book*, 26–27.

342 *nympha loci*: The pseudoclassical verses

Huius Nympha loci, sacri custodia fontis
Dormio, dum blandae sentio murmur aquae.
Parce meum, quisquis tangis cava marmora, somnum
Rumpere, seu bibas, sive lavere, tace.

were common in gardens throughout England from the fifteenth century on. They were usually placed near a statue of a reclining nymph. See Otto Kurz, "Huius nympha loci," *Journal of the Warburg and Courtauld Institutes*, vol. 16 (1952), 177; Maynard Mack, *The Garden and the City* (Toronto: University of Toronto Press, 1969), 77–79.

342 "nymph of the grot": John Butt, ed., *The Poems of Alexander Pope*, Twickenham edition (New Haven: Yale University Press, 1961–1969), 6:248.

343 "inscriptions in various places": *Garden Book*, 27.

343 "*elegance* is the peculiar excellence of a garden": Thomas Whately, *Observations on Modern Gardening* (London, 1770; reprint, Garland Publishing, 1982), 157.

344 "so justly characterized": *Papers*, 9:369.

344 "said to have cost 7000.£": *Papers*, 9:370.

344 "It is said he died of heartaches": *Papers*, 9:371.

344 early park: In *MB*, Sept. 20, 1769, Jefferson recorded, "my park on North side of mountain is in circumfrence 1850. yds." See *Farm Book*, 336ff., for surveys showing the location of the park on the south side of the mountain.

344 "two or three miles round": *Jefferson at Monticello*, 21.

344 "he amuses himself": Marquis de Chastellux, *Travels in North America in the Years 1780, 1781, 1782*, Howard C. Rice, Jr., trans. (Chapel Hill, N.C.: University of North Carolina Press, 1963), 2:394.

345 "clever garden": to Abigail Adams, Sept. 4, 1785, *Papers*, 8:473.

345 working sketches of Langeac garden: see page 349, and Frederick D. Nichols and Ralph E. Griswold, *Thomas Jefferson, Landscape Architect* (Charlottesville, Va.: University Press of Virginia, 1978), 121.

345 *"tout en arbres"*: to de Langeac, Feb. 22, 1787, *Papers*, 11:175–76.

345 credit for work done on the house: from William Short, Dec. 23, 1790, *Papers*, 18:358.

345 "earliest surviving plan": Kornwolf, 100.

346 "Purple hyacinth begins to bloom": *Garden Book*, 1.

346 "No occupation is so delightful to me": to Charles Willson Peale, Aug. 20, 1811, L & B, 13:78–79; *Garden Book*, 461.

346 "By applying the principle of natural soil stratigraphy": William M. Kelso, "Landscape Archaeology: A Key to Virginia's Cultivated Past," in Maccubbin and Martin, 159–60.

347 "so much of what had been constructed": Kelso, 165.

347 "in making a stone wall": *Garden Book*, 54. This wall was apparently located below the stable at the eastern end of Mulberry Row. Jefferson wrote, in his "General ideas for the improvement of Monticello" (Kimball, K-161) that some of the stone for the new retaining wall would come from "the old stone fence below the stable."

347 "We had to blow out the rock": *Jefferson at Monticello*, 47.

347 "Were we to go on reducing the whole": to Edmund Bacon, Feb. 23, 1808, *Garden Book*, 364.

348 "as not to let even a young hare in": to Mr. Watkins, Sep. 27, 1808, MHi; *Garden Book*, 377. Jefferson sent the carpenter Watkins explicit instructions on how the fence was to be constructed. Locust fence posts were inserted into 2½-foot holes nine feet apart; these were connected with three pine rails. The chestnut fence palings, five to seven inches wide, and five feet three inches long, were joined in an ingenious way to make the ten-foot height. One end of each paling was "dubbed"—feathered with an adze—and the ends were then overlapped "like clapboards" at the center rail and joined to it with a single nail—one of many examples of Jefferson's designing with maximum economy of materials in mind. See also Nichols and Griswold, 108.

348 vegetable garden restored: A Historic Plant Center has been established at Monticello to serve as a research facility and clearinghouse for information on the restoration and cultivation of historic plants.

348 a small, brick pavilion constructed: for an account of other garden structures planned by Jefferson see William L. Beiswanger, "The

Temple in the Garden: Thomas Jefferson's Vision of the Monticello Landscape," in Maccubbin and Martin, 170–188.

353 "General ideas for the improvement of Monticello": Kimball, K-161; *Garden Book*, pl. XX.

354 "Swarms of impertinent gazers": Randall, 3:337.

354 "takes away from me the first beauty in gardening": to William Hamilton, July 1806, DLC; *Garden Book*, 322–24.

355 "I find that the limited number of our flower beds": to Ann Randolph, June 7, 1807, MHi; *Garden Book*, 349, pl. XXIV, XXV.

356 "the surprisingly beautiful creations": Randall, 3:346–7.

357 "useful and ornamental collection": John Edward Caldwell, *Niles Weekly Register*, vol. 11, 1816/1817 (Jan. 4, 1816), 318.

357 called the Indian Hall: to Merriweather Lewis, Oct. 20, 1806, "I am in fact preparing a kind of Indian hall." DLC.

357 "belt and shot pouch of the famous Tecumseh": Adam Hodgson, *Letters from North America* (London, 1834), 314ff.

357 "sculptured by savages": Harold E. Dickson, " 'TH.J.' Art Collector," in William Howard Adams, ed., *Jefferson and the Arts: An Extended View* (Washington, D.C.: National Gallery of Art, 1976), 124.

357 brief history of American Indian tribes: *Notes*, Query XI.

358 "for a special kind of Cabinet": to Dr. Casper Wistar, Dec. 19, 1807, in Howard Rice, Jr., "Jefferson's Gift of Fossils to the Museum of Natural History in Paris," *Proceedings of the American Philosophical Society*, vol. 95, no. 6 (Dec. 1951), 605.

358 "that nature is less active": *Notes*, 47. Earlier, Jefferson had sent to Buffon in Paris, at considerable expense, the head, skeleton, and skin of a moose, and horns of a caribou, elk, and deer to prove the superior size of North American animals.

359 "I think therefore still": to Francis A. Van der Kemp, Feb. 9, 1818, DLC. Jefferson seems to have harbored the hope that a live mastodon might one day be found. He wrote to Ezra Stiles, "I understand from four different quarters that the Indians beleive this animal still existing" (*Papers*, 7:305), and to John Rutledge, Jr., "The Indians of America say it still exists very far North in our continent" (*Papers*, 13:594). I thank Garry Wills for pointing this out to me.

359 "petrifications, chrystalizations, minerals, shells": [Caldwell], *Niles Register*, 318.

359 "strange furniture of its walls": George Ticknor, *Life, Letters, and Journals* (Boston, 1876), 1:34; also in Francis Coleman Rosenberger, ed., *Jefferson Reader* (E. P. Dutton, 1953), 81. Ticknor's memory was some-

what faulty; he elevated the character from the Man of the Hill to the Man of the Mountain. On the other hand, his memory had retrieved what was only a one-sentence description in a very long novel. See *Tom Jones*, book 8, ch. 10.

360   paintings were jammed into every available inch of wall space: see "Salons 1785, 1787, 1789," in William Howard Adams, ed., *The Eye of Thomas Jefferson* (Washington, D.C.: National Gallery of Art, 1976), 152–54.

360   126 items of artwork at Monticello: Dickson, 122–23. I am indebted to Dickson's article for material on Jefferson's art collection and how it was hung.

360   a wish list of nineteen works of sculpture and painting: Dickson, 109.

361   "he stript me bare": William Hooper, visit to Monticello, Sept. 20, 1823, Monticello Archives.

361   "opposed in death as in life": Randall, 3:336.

361   paintings acquired in Paris: a list of the paintings Jefferson acquired in Paris is in Marie Kimball, *Jefferson: The Scene of Europe, 1784–1789* (Coward-McCann, 1950), 323–27n.

362   "a Dutch piece representing the sacrifice of Isaac": William Hooper, visit to Monticello, Sept. 20, 1823, Monticello Archives.

362   "the three greatest men": *Domestic Life*, 351.

363   "the most beautiful and precious morsel": to James Madison, Sept. 20, 1785, *Papers*, 8:535.

363   mostly in the Louis XVI style: Marie Kimball, 111.

364   eighty-six packing crates: for a complete list of items brought back from France see *Papers*, 18:34–39n.

364   "of a kind not suited to a country house": Ellen Randolph Coolidge Correspondence 1826–1830, Essay on Thomas Jefferson: 1826, #9090, ViU.

365   "the first thing which attracted our attention": Rosenberger, 78.

365   "to make up into commodes": to Capt. James Oldham, May 1, 1817, MHi.

365   "dumbwaiters": See Adams, 312.

366   "He was au desespoir": to Ellen Randolph Coolidge, Nov. 14, 1825, *Family Letters*, 461; "carried in the procession," 462.

366   "there was but little furniture": Ellen Randolph Coolidge, ViU.

366   "a walnut stand": James A. Bear, Jr., "The Furniture and Furnishings of Monticello," *Antiques*, no. 102 (July 1972), 121.

366   the conventional way of arranging furniture: Edward Lucie-Smith, *Furniture: a Concise History* (Oxford University Press, 1979), 93–94.

367   common for furniture to be moved about freely: Lucie-Smith, 95.

367   parlor furniture arrangement: a sketch of the placement of artworks and furniture at Monticello by Cornelia Randolph is in Dickson, 123; *Domestic Life*, 334.

367   Gray-Ticknor visit: Rosenberger, 78.

367   music part of the domestic life of Monticello: See Helen Cripe, *Thomas Jefferson and Music* (Charlottesville, Va.: University Press of Virginia, 1974), on Jefferson's interest in music and musical instruments.

368   formal dining room an innovation of the eighteenth century: Lucie-Smith, 96.

368   "luminous and splendid": Hunter Dickinson Farish, ed., *Journal and Letters of Philip Vickers Fithian, 1773–1774* (Charlottesville, Va.: University Press of Virginia, 1968), 34.

369   "light equal to six or eight candles": to James Madison, Nov. 11, 1784, *Papers*, 7:505. *MB*, Mar. 27, 1789, "Pd. for a plated reading lamp 316."

369   "a gallon of lamp oil," "A common glass lamp": *Farm Book*, pl. 71.

370   replaced the copying press with the polygraph: Silvio A. Bedini, *Thomas Jefferson and His Copying Machine* (Charlottesville, Va.: University Press of Virginia, 1984), 31. This is a well-researched history of the copying press, polygraph, and Jefferson's use of them.

371   "having miles announced by the bell": Edwin T. Martin, *Thomas Jefferson: Scientist* (Henry Schuman, 1952), 93.

371   "Great Clock": *MB*, Apr. 27, 1793, "Pd. R. Leslie for Great clock 113.80."

372   "clumsy mimicking of the clockmaker's real achievement": Garry Wills, *Inventing America: Jefferson's Declaration of Independence* (Garden City, N.Y.: Doubleday, 1978), 108.

372   cannonball clock: The weights for the "Great Clock" were once thought to be Revolutionary War cannonballs, but Jefferson's Memorandum Book shows that he purchased them in 1804 from the Foxall Iron Foundry in Washington, from which he also purchased cast-iron stoves. Foxall supplied the government with ordnance, so the weights were probably newly manufactured cannonballs, modified to Jefferson's specifications. *MB*, July 9, 1804: "Sent by Jos. Dougherty to Mr. Foxall for clock weights 20.24." I thank Lucia C. Stanton at Monticello for calling this to my attention.

372   "a horse with forty-eight projecting hands": Richard Beale Davis, ed., *Notes on the United States of America Collected in the Years 1805–6–7 and 11–12 by Sir Augustus Fohn Foster, Bart.* (San Marino, Calif.: Huntington Library, 1954), 144.

373   "very much engaged and interested in a phaeton": *Thornton Diary*, Wed., Sept. 22, 1802.

Notes

373   "Putting up and pulling down": B. L. Rayner, *Sketches of the Life, Writings, and Opinions of Thomas Jefferson* (1832), 524.

374   "according to the gamut": Malone, 1:48.

374   "because I was once a child": Madeleine L'Engle, *A Circle of Quiet* (Minneapolis: Seabury Press, 1972), 199.

AFTERWORD

Page

375   Jefferson quietly expired: His death was apparently caused by complications from an enlarged prostate, which constricted the urethra. This was treated by catheterization; he was given laudanum for pain. He also suffered from severe diarrhea, which contributed to his physical weakness. (Malone, 6:447–48, 496.)

375   "Thomas Jefferson still survives": Malone, 6:498.

375   "Here is buried": Randall, 3:563.

376   John Hemings freed: Also freed in Jefferson's will were the house servant Burwell; Joe Fosset, Monticello's blacksmith; and Sally Hemings's sons, Madison and Eston, on becoming twenty-one. (Malone, 6:488.)

377   Nicholas loan default: Malone, 6:302–5, 309–14, and appendix II, "Jefferson's Financial Affairs," 505–12.

378   "profoundly ignorant of his own financial condition": *MB*, introduction. "The daily ritual of recording" is also from the Bear-Stanton introduction.

378   "I now enclose to you": to William Short, Apr. 13, 1800, *MB*, introduction.

379   terraces rotted away: James A. Bear, Jr., *Old Pictures of Monticello* (Charlottesville, Va.: University of Virginia Press, 1957), 1.

379   "old and going to decay": Samuel Whitcomb, "Interview with Thomas Jefferson," May 31, 1824, ViU.

379   "Valuable Lands": William Howard Adams, *Jefferson's Monticello* (Abbeville Press, 1983), 237. This is a recent account of the history of Monticello after Jefferson's death.

380   Monticello sold to Barclay and Levy: Merrill Peterson, *The Jefferson Image in the American Mind* (Oxford University Press, 1960), 380.

380   "a bitter, bitter heartache": Martha Jefferson Randolph to Virginia Randolph Trist, July 5, 1831, Trist Papers, University of North Carolina; Monticello Archives.

381   "in the beautiful drawing salon": Thomas L. Rhodes, as told to Frank

B. Lord, *The Story of Monticello* (Washington, D.C.: American Publishing Company, 1928), 91.

381 "There is scarcely a whole shingle upon it": Rep. A. A. Hardenbergh of New Jersey, quoted in Charles B. Hosmer, Jr., "The Levys and the Restoration of Monticello," *American Jewish Historical Quarterly*, vol. 53, no. 3 (May 1964), 224–25.

381 Thomas Jefferson Memorial Foundation purchase of the property: Peterson traces the history of the struggle to wrest Monticello from Jefferson Levy, 381–84. Hosmer also gives a detailed account of Jefferson Levy's ownership of the property.

382 "What they have seen": Peterson, 388.

Picture Credits

Photographs are by courtesy and permission of the following:

The American Philosophical Society: David Rittenhouse, by Charles Willson Peale, p. 134; Jefferson bust by Houdon, p. 133.

Bayly Art Museum at the University of Virginia: Natural Bridge, by Frederick Edwin Church, p. 31.

Bibliotheque Nationale: Maria Cosway, p. 131; elevation and floor plan, Hôtel de Langeac, p. 223; Halle aux Bleds, p. 223.

The Colonial Williamsburg Foundation: George Wythe House, p. 136; John Blair House, p. 136; second Virginia capitol building, p. 136.

The Huntington Library, San Marino, California: garden sketches of the Hôtel de Langeac, p. 349.

Independence National Historical Park Collection: Jefferson, by Charles Willson Peale, 1791, p. 129.

Thomas Jefferson Memorial Foundation, Inc., Charlottesville, Virginia: chess set, p. 19; conjectural elevation of first Monticello, p. 137; floor plan of second house, p. 276; kitchen (James T. Tkatch), p. 277; library (James T. Tkatch), p. 279; Jefferson's bedroom, p. 279; entrance hall (James T. Tkatch), p. 277, 278; parlor (James T. Tkatch), p. 278; dining room (James T. Tkatch), p. 280; tea room (James T. Tkatch), p. 281; Martha Jefferson Randolph, by Thomas Sully, p. 75; pivot window, p. 275; dome room, p. 282; staircase, p. 275; south square room, p. 282; dining room and tea room, p. 281.

Library of Congress: Jefferson, by Rembrandt Peale, p. 17; Jefferson, by Thomas Sully, p. 352; letter from William Thornton, Apr. 3, 1815, filtering machine, p. 19; undated, macaroni extrusion machine, p. 226; ice cream etc. recipes, p. 225; anonymous note, p. 100; letter to Dinsmore, Mar. 19, 1802, about icehouse, p. 296; James Hemings, Feb. 20, 1796, kitchen inventory, p. 100; Memorandum Book, Sept. 6, 1782, wife died, p. 190; Memorandum Book, Jan. 4, 1782, whiskey purchased, p. 190; vegetable market, 1801–1808, p. 226; letter to James Oldham, Jan. 19, 1805, chaste architecture, p. 292; Martha Jefferson's household Account Book, p. 189.

Maryland Historical Society, Baltimore: Jefferson, by Henry Latrobe (?), p. 135.

Massachusetts Historical Society: dining room floor plan (K-15), p. 162; sketch of slave house (K-16), p. 101; elevation of first Monticello (K-23), p. 137; floor plan of first Monticello (K-24), p. 138; floor plan and dependencies of first Monticello (K-31), p. 139; landscape plan of first Monticello (K-34), p. 140; arches and jambs of porticle (K-149p), p. 299; venetian blinds in porticoes (K-149s), p. 299.

Massachusetts Historical Society, Thomas Jefferson Papers: Nov. 30, 1804, entertainment list, p. 227; June 1807, sketch of west lawn and serpentine walk, p. 349; Dec. 30, 1808, sketch of alcove screen, p. 297; Apr. 15, 1809, Dinsmore's memo of carpenter's tools, p. 300; Sept. 26, 1819, letter from John Hemings, p. 99; Nov. 15, 1818, letter from Hannah, p. 99; undated, first Monticello library, p. 140.

Joseph and Margaret Muscarelle Museum of Art, College of William and Mary in Virginia: William Short, by Rembrandt Peale, p. 134.

Musée Carnavalet, musées de la Ville de Paris (copyright by SPADEM 1987): Construction of the Hôtel de Salm, p. 210.

Museum of Early Southern Decorative Arts, Winston-Salem, North Carolina: Monticello, by Anna Maria Thornton, p. 274.

National Gallery of Art, Washington, D.C., Andrew W. Mellon Collection: William Thornton, Anna Maria Thornton, by Gilbert Stuart, p. 18.

U.S. Department of State, Diplomatic Reception Rooms: Martha Jefferson miniature, p. 132.

University of Virginia Library, Manuscripts Department: Monticello photo, 1890, p. 298.

University of Virginia, Tracy W. McGregor Library: Isaac Jefferson daguerreotype by John Plumbe, Jr., ca. 1845, p. 134.

University of Virginia, Thomas Jefferson Papers: Monticello, first house floor plan addition (N-46 verso), p. 189; University of Virginia pavilion VI, elevation and floor plan (N-324), p. 298; Poplar Forest floor plan by Cornelia Jefferson Randolph (N-350), p. 350; Poplar Forest elevation by Cornelia Jefferson Randolph (N-351), p. 350; June 1783 bill of scantling Mr. Frazer (FC-2384), p. 172; Aug. 6–29, 1822, table of slave labor (FC-3012), p. 101; May 13–Aug. 31, 1822, estimate of bricks (TB-1397), p. 300.

University of Virginia, Rare Book Department, Alderman Library: title page, *Notes on the State of Virginia*, p. 227.

University of Virginia, University Archives: rotunda, south facade, p. 351.

The Virginia State Library: model of Virginia State capitol, capitol building, p. 224.

Yale University Art Gallery: The Declaration of Independence (copyright Yale University Art Gallery), by John Trumbull, p. 130.

Index

Abram (slave), 103
Adams, John, 308, 343, 354, 361–63, 375, 451
Adams, Thomas, 160, 429
Adams, William Short, 418
Aeschylus, 74
Aggey (slave), 406
Alcove beds, 8–9, 20, 251, 252, 366, 372, 444–45
Alembert, Jean Le Rond d', 79, 302
Alexander I, tsar of Russia, 361
Almerico, Paolo, 427
Alps, 35
Ambler, Jacquelin, 148
Amelia (ship), 409
American Institute of Architects Foundation, 12
American Philosophical Society, 155, 196, 358
Amsterdam, booksellers in, 21
Anderson, John, 68
Andrews, George, 290, 291, 433
"Anecdote of the Jar" (Stevens), 339
Annapolis (Md.), 56, 86, 89, 207

Antiquités de la France (Clérisseau), 25
Apollo Belvedere, 360
Apotheosis of Homer, 309
Appleton, Thomas, 310
Apprenticeship system, 88–89, 304
   slaves in, 102, 103, 109, 110, 120, 124–25, 333
Architectural drawings, 57–64, 162–66, 173, 179, 397–98, 412, 426, 432, 444
Argand "cylinder lamp," 369
Ariss, John, 89
Aristotle, 53
Arnold, Benedict, 202
Art collection, 359–63
Artisans
   slaves as, 23, 102–3, 108–9, 120, 124–26, 158, 166, 246, 266, 333, 334, 338
   See also specific crafts
Attica, Parthenon of, 286
Attic order, 290
Augers, 88
Augustus Caesar, 53
Aviary, 324, 325, 445

Burgoyne, Gen. John, 183
Burk, John, 43
Burke, Edmund, 34, 341
Burlington, Lord, 55, 56
Burlington, Richard Boyle, Earl of, 340
Burr, Aaron, 271
Burwell (slave), 118, 317, 404, 456
Burwell, Carter, 83, 89
Burwell, Rebecca, 49, 51, 148, 151
Butter making, 181
Byrd, William II, 42

Caesar (slave), 168, 169, 413
Caldwell, John Edward, 433, 447
Candles
  lighting with, 368–69
  making, 182
Canon (Polyclitus), 53
Capitol building (Washington), 10, 12, 322, 332, 335
Carpenter, Davy, 102, 103, 120, 247, 266
Carpenters, 67, 84–90, 167, 271, 329, 411, 429
  slaves as, 96, 103, 120, 122, 246, 247, 266
Carpenters' Company, 86
Carr, Dabney, 44, 151, 203, 204, 207
Carr, Martha Jefferson, 198, 207
Carrée, Maison, 25, 219, 363
Carter, Charles, 151
Carter, Col. Edward, 153, 168
Carter, Robert "King," 56, 83, 105, 120, 178
Carter's Grove, 42, 83, 89, 340, 346
Cary (slave), 112
Cellars, excavation of, 154–55, 158
Cement, hydraulic, 303–4
Central College. *See* Virginia, University of
Ceracchi (artist), 361
Chambers, William, 331
Champagne, 235
Charleston (S.C.), 86
Charlottesville (Va.), 157, 168, 258

Chastellux, Marquis de, 169–70, 175–76, 183, 201, 344
Chekhov, Anton, 94
Cherokee tribe, 357
Cherry Orchard, The (Chekhov), 95
Chess, 26
Chevalier d'Anmours, Charles-François, 184–85
Childbearing, 177–78, 186–88, 196–97
Chimneys, 304–5, 329
Chinese ornamentation, 166, 265, 330–31, 446–47
Chippendale furniture, 365
Chisels, 88
Chisholm, Hugh, 313, 315, 336, 429, 433–34
  Madison and, 335
  plastering by, 270, 318, 331, 440
  at Poplar Forest, 332
  south pavilion remodeled by, 328–29
Chiswick House, 55
Church, Angelica, 218–19
Cisterns, 11, 157, 302–4
Civil War, 42, 380, 438
Clark, William, 358
Clarkson, Samuel, 425
Classical Revival style, 220
Clérisseau, Charles-Louis, 25, 219–20, 426
Clinton, Catherine, 414
Clivedon (mansion), 402, 440
Clocks, 371–72, 455
Closets, 8, 20
  turntable, 372
Clothing
  of house servants, 106–7, 185, 403–4
  inventories of, 181, 185
  of plantation wives, 178, 194–95
  of workers, 91
Coffee, William, 251, 303, 361, 433
Coles, Isaac, 398
Colle house, 236
Colonial Williamsburg, 40, 59–60, 77, 400, 442

Index

Mont Calvaire, 256
Monticello
aesthetic vs. practical considerations
in design of, 35–36
Anna Maria Thornton on, 3–16, 20,
21, 24–32
architectural drawings for, 57–64, 161,
163–66, 173, 179
art collection at, 359–63
bedrooms of, 7–9, 20, 252–53, 255–
56, 366, 412
blacksmiths at, 65–69
brick construction of, 69–74, 77–84
Chastellux's visit to, 169–70, 175–76
chimneys of, 304–5
cisterns at, 157, 302–4
deer park at, 344–45, 425
demolition of original house, 257–60,
263
dependencies of. See Dependencies
described in Head-Heart letter, 217
dining room of, 3–4, 161, 256, 289–
90, 309, 366, 368, 411–12
dome of, 36, 219, 249, 250, 252, 265,
266, 271, 290, 426–27
financing of, 174–75, 379
fireplaces of, 305–10, 437
floors of, 166, 270–71, 295, 315–17,
413, 425, 431
furniture of, 361–68
graveyard at, 203, 241, 375, 380
ice house at, 296, 301–2
industrial activities at, 30
and Jefferson's marriage, 146–47, 152–
53, 160–61
Jefferson's private quarters at, 20, 40,
257, 324–27
kitchen of, 27–29, 230–32, 422
landscaping of, 339–48, 353–56
library at, 20–25, 162–63, 395, 430
lighting of, 368–70
louvered blinds used in, 321–23, 327
Martha Jefferson as mistress of, 179–
82, 185–86, 201–2
meals at, 9–10

mechanical contrivances at, 370–73
natural history collection at, 356–59
octagon rooms of, 12, 60–62, 74, 77,
179, 253–54, 398, 427
overseers at, 127–28
painting of, 316–21
parlor of, 310–11, 315–16, 366–68,
412
perfectionism and, 92–93
plastering of, 270, 301
play and building of, 373–74
porticles of, 323–28, 445
porticoes of. See Porticoes
redesign of, 208, 210, 248–57
restoration and preservation of, 381–
83, 401
Jefferson's return from France to, 238–
41
during Revolutionary War, 166–69
roof of, 262, 265–68, 270, 329–30,
430, 445–46
sales of, 379–82
shell of new house constructed, 260–
63
as shrine to Jefferson, 383–85
site of, 33–36, 52
slaves at, 94–98, 102–28, 141–45
south pavilion of, 153–60, 328–39,
396, 411
staircases of, 5–7, 163–64, 252, 255,
256, 412
tearoom of, 3–4, 254, 309, 366, 368,
412
viticulture at, 236–37
water supply of, 156–57, 302–4
weddings at, 263–64
windows of, 163–64, 252, 254–55, 261,
293, 320–21, 329
woodwork of, 84–88, 170–71, 173,
266, 289–93
Montlezun, Baron de, 357
Montpelier (Madison house), 2, 9, 334,
335, 435
Moore, John, 154
Moral sense philosophies, 341

Index

Shadwell (cont'd)
  construction of, 39–40, 396
  garden at, 346
  mill at, 243, 435
  overseers at, 127
Shakespeare, William, 49–50, 54
Shard, Julius, 155, 411
Shell (bricklayer), 429
Shenstone, William, 344, 450–51
Shirley (Carter mansion), 151–52, 166, 340
Shoemaker, Phill, 102, 126
Shoemakers, 125, 126
Short, William, 10, 38, 211, 220, 229, 378, 418–19
Sizes (woodworking tools), 87–88
Skelton, Bathurst, 147
Skelton, John, 160
Skelton, Martha Wayles, 29. See Jefferson, Martha Wayles
Skylights, 213, 253
Slatefield, 425
Slate floors, 413, 425
Slaves, 36, 94–98, 102–28, 141–45, 175
  apprenticeship of, 102, 103, 109, 110, 120, 124–25, 333
  artisan, 23, 102–3, 108–9, 120, 124–26, 158, 166, 246, 266, 333, 334, 338
  as blacksmiths, 66, 68
  brickmaking by, 73, 428
  construction work by, 39, 57, 429
  construction work paid for with, 336
  excavation of cellars by, 154–55, 158
  field hands, 127–28
  fire and, 27
  food provided for, 105
  freeing of, 104, 114–15, 118, 222, 420–21, 456
  gathering around deathbeds of owners by, 198–99
  health of, 142–43
  hierarchy of, 105–9, 127, 403
  hospitality and, 269–70
  housing for, 28–30, 143–45, 159, 246–47, 330, 396, 408–9

  industrial activities of, 30
  and Jefferson's return from France, 239–40
  liquor provided to, 67
  literacy among, 120–21
  marriages of, 128
  Martha Jefferson and, 185–86
  in mill construction projects, 244
  mortar mixing by, 77
  nail making by, 109–13, 115, 116, 118
  names of, 102
  owned by Thornton, 394
  rolls of, 78, 405, 406
  runaway, 113–19, 126, 405
  sales of, 377
  as sawyers, 84
  at Shadwell, 40
  soap making by, 182
  wages paid to, 404
  Wayles and, 147, 409
Small, William, 37–38, 41–43, 45, 56
Smallpox, 142
Smith, Adam, 97
Smith, Daniel Blake, 424
Smith, Margaret Bayard, 9, 250–51, 325, 435
Smith, Samuel Harrison, 21
Smith George (slave), 111–12, 125, 143, 186
Soap making, 181–82
Society of Friends. See Quakers
Sorrels, Richard, 411
South pavilion, 28–29, 153–60, 328–29, 396, 411
Spectator, The, 341
Spurck, Peter, 371
Stables, 30, 159, 246
Staircases, 5–7, 163–64, 252, 255, 256, 412
  at Langeac, 213
Stanton, Lucia C., 378, 391
Statute of Virginia for Religious Freedom, 376
Steptoe, Dr., 142
Sterne, Lawrence, 198, 218–19, 419–20

[478]

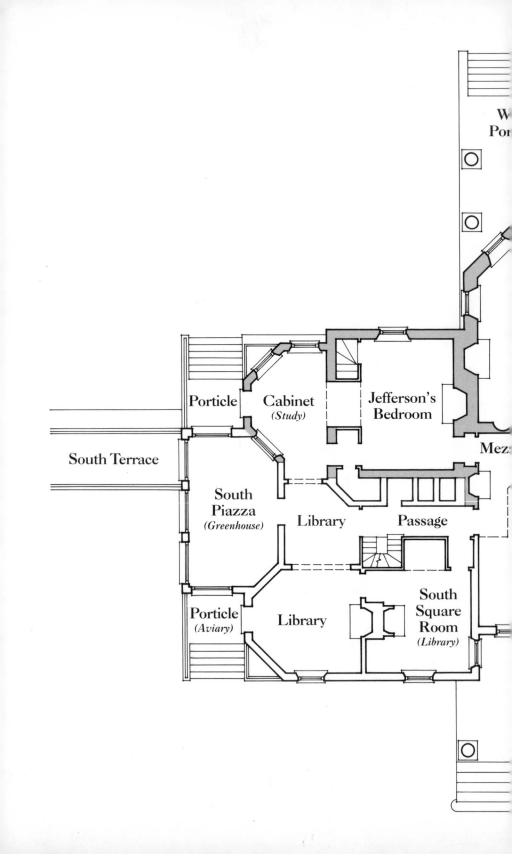

W
Por

Porticle

Cabinet
(Study)

Jefferson's
Bedroom

Mez

South Terrace

South
Piazza
(Greenhouse)

Library

Passage

Porticle
(Aviary)

Library

South
Square
Room
(Library)